Brief Contents

Contents

Graphic Design History
A Critical Guide
Second Edition

Graphic Design History
A Critical Guide

Second Edition

Johanna Drucker
University of California, Los Angeles

Emily McVarish
California College of the Arts

Boston Columbus Indianapolis New York San Francisco Upper Saddle River
Amsterdam Cape Town Dubai London Madrid Milan Munich Paris Montréal Toronto
Delhi Mexico City São Paulo Sydney Hong Kong Seoul Singapore Taipei Tokyo

Editor-in-Chief: Sarah Touborg
Editorial Assistant: Carla Worner
Editorial Director: Craig Campanella
Director of Marketing: Brandy Dawson
Executive Marketing Manager: Kate Mitchell
Managing Editor: Melissa Feimer
Production Liaison: Joe Scordato
Full-Service Management: Laurence King Publishing/Kara Hattersley-Smith
Production Editor: Laurence King Publishing/Melissa Danny
Production Manager: Laurence King Publishing/Simon Walsh
Photo Research and Permissions: Laurence King Publishing/Ida Riveros
Manufacturing and Operations Manager: Mary Fischer
Senior Operations Specialist: Brian Mackey
Cover Photos: **top**: Scribe's tools, twelfth century (detail). Staatsbibliothek Bamberg.
Photo: Gerald Raab; **second from top**: Nicholaus Copernicus, *On the Revolutions of
the Heavenly Spheres*, 1543 (detail). University of Glasgow Library, Dept. of Special
Collections; **third from top**: Elena Semenova, poster, 1920s (detail). Merrill C. Berman
Collection. Photo: Jim Frank; **bottom**: Laszlo Moholy-Nagy, *Staatliches Bauhaus in Weimar
1919–1923*, catalog announcement, 1923 (detail). Merrill C. Berman Collection. Photo:
Jim Frank. © Hattula Moholy-Nagy/DACS 2011
Interior and Cover Design: Emily McVarish and Johanna Drucker
Creative Director (Cover): Pat Smythe
Senior Digital Media Editor: David Alick
Digital Media Project Manager: Rich Barnes
Composition: Laurence King Publishing Ltd
Printer/Binder: The Courier Companies
Cover Printer: Lehigh-Phoenix Color Corp

Credits and acknowledgments borrowed from other sources and reproduced,
with permission, in this textbook appear on appropriate page within text
(or on pages 375–379).

Library of Congress Cataloging-in-Publication Data

Drucker, Johanna
  Graphic design history : a critical guide / Johanna Drucker,
  Emily McVarish. -- 2nd ed.
    p. cm.
Includes bibliographical references and index.
ISBN-13: 978-0-205-21946-9 (pbk. : alk. paper)
ISBN-10: 0-205-21946-2 (pbk. : alk. paper)
1. Graphic arts--History. 2. Art and society--History. I. McVarish,
  Emily. II. Title.
NC998.D78 2012
741.609--dc23
                                    2011037952

10 9 8 7 6 5 4 3 2 1

ISBN 10: 0-205-21946-2
ISBN 13: 978-0-205-21946-9

Preface This book evolved from our practice as artists and teachers. We both make use of theory and research in our creative work, and we are regularly struck by the realization that many of the models we follow and forms we use have long histories. Insight into the role of history in daily practice can be thrilling, just as critical concepts can be powerful tools for thinking about a design process or product. Our sheer enthusiasm for these ideas and a desire to share them led to this project. We didn't want to tell the story of graphic design, as if it were something that happened in the past, but to expose the many principles of current composition and communication that are grounded in historical precedent.

The span and shape of our book were inspired by graphic design educators' frequently expressed desire for a book that would begin with prehistory and trace the impulses of mark-making and early symbolic expression forward to present currents of thought. Early chapters have enormous temporal sweep. Later chapters are focused on shorter periods and changes in the profession. The culture of graphic design has changed as much as the technology through which it realizes its tasks, but basic principles from the earliest circumstances of human communication and exchange are still operative. Our approach has attempted to keep historical perspectives in view while demonstrating profound continuities in the practice of graphic arts, visual expression, and design.

In this endeavor, we have drawn on many sources. All who work in this field are indebted to Philip Meggs, whose groundbreaking *A History of Graphic Design* is a major reference work that has provided a descriptive historical foundation for the field. We were inspired by insights into the cultural contexts of design practice contained in the admirably succinct *Graphic Design: A Concise History* by Richard Hollis. Our methodological approach was sympathetically informed by Paul Jobling and David Crowley's *Graphic Design: Reproduction and Representation since 1800*. But a greater influence on our critical approach came from the social historian Max Gallo's *The Poster in History*. The demonstration of the links in that book between graphic works and the social forces and conditions of their production sparked epiphanies. Other classic works and writings by our peers, too numerous to mention here, are listed in the bibliography. These texts are of real value and use to a field that has only begun to formulate itself: the critical history of graphic design.

New to this second edition In response to readers' requests, numerous improvements have been made throughout the text. In particular:
• Wherever possible, images have been enlarged to make details and points in captions more legible.
• Twenty new images have been added, including contemporary Iranian (16.6a and b), Chinese (16.7a and b), and South African (16.8a) designs.

There are two new chapters:

1. From Prehistory to Early Writing condenses material formerly occupying two chapters and highlights the emergence of elemental graphic forms and concepts.

16. Graphic Design and Globalization asks how graphic design participates in creating our concept of a global world, and how the interconnected flows of information, money, influence, and communication alter the conditions in which graphic designers work.

Digital Resources for *Graphic Design History*

PowerPoints: Instructors who adopt *Graphic Design History* get access to an expanded set of PowerPoints containing nearly every image in the book at high resolution for optimal projection and easy download. Contact your Pearson representative or visit pearsonhighered.com/art for details.

MySearchLab with eText: MySearchLab provides a fully illustrated eText version of *Graphic Design History*, along with access to writing and research tools and a variety of academic journals and news feeds. To order this text with MySearchLab with eText at no additional cost, use this ISBN: 0205867715.

CourseSmart Textbooks Online: Students can also subscribe online to the same content of this text and save up to 60% off the suggested list price of the print version. Visit www.coursesmart.com for more information.

Acknowledgments

The authors would like to thank Sarah Touborg for her constant confidence and commitment to this book; Black Dot Group for their masterful coordination of the first edition's editorial process; the equally deft team at Laurence King Publishers for their work on this edition; the picture researchers who persisted in a sometimes difficult task; and, above all, the designers who generously granted us permission to reproduce their work. We are grateful to the many careful, sometimes anonymous, readers of our work who provided constructive suggestions and spotted factual and conceptual errors both in early drafts and in published form. Specifically, for their help with this edition, we thank John Luttropp, Montclair State University; Peter Hall, University of Texas at Austin; Martha Scotford, North Carolina State University; Janet O'Neil, Fairleigh Dickinson University; Grace Fowler, Palomar College; Gary Rozanc, Columbia College Chicago. Finally, we thank our colleagues and students from whom we continue to learn.

Johanna: Thanks to Gino Lee, as always, for wise counsel and friendship. A fond memory for Boris Drucker whose enthusiasm for this project never flagged, and Jane Drucker who continues to support my work. Mostly, thanks to Emily. I know few collaborators could have shown such constant goodwill and humor in combination with intellectual rigor.

Emily: Thanks to Johanna for all her formative interventions, for every mind-rousing conversation, and for the immense gift of this collaboration. And thanks to my partner, Becky Bond, without whose support and big-picture faith I might have remained lost in troublesome details on a hundred occasions.

Reading *Graphic Design History* This book is organized to provide basic insights and ideas, detailed discussion, historical contrast, and technical context. Chapters and the sections within them are meant to be complementary, offering different lenses onto the multifaceted development of graphic design.

Chapter framework Chapters are framed by critical issues and historical themes, rather than neat chronological divisions, so the dates defining one chapter's period in relation to the next may overlap. These overlaps dispel the pretense of a strictly linear or unified progression in favor of a layered understanding of history's structure.

Captions and body text Captions are integral to the text of *Graphic Design History*. In addition to critical principles and terms, they carry specific analyses and facts that demonstrate concepts presented more broadly in a chapter's body text.

Timelines These lists situate graphic events in relation to other cultural and political markers. Like all timelines, they are selective and, by their juxtapositions, inevitably suggestive of interpretations. In early chapters, many dates are approximate. Highlighted items have specific relevance for graphic design.

Tools of the trade These lists contain items that might be used by a graphic artist or designer for original production in the period corresponding to the chapter dates. They also contain technologies that would be used for reproduction in the period, even if not directly by a designer. (A graphic artist or designer would need to be aware of available methods of reproduction in order to fashion images or text suitable to those methods.) Media, tools, material supports, and technologies of production and reproduction are thus included.

These inventories are by no means exhaustive but are meant to be suggestive. The timeframe within which an item appears does not necessarily correspond to the moment of its invention but may rather indicate the point at which it was commonly adopted. And carryover from one period to another is, for the most part, implicit.

Graphic design is never *just there*.

Graphic artifacts always serve a purpose and contain an agenda, no matter how neutral or natural they appear to be.

Someone is addressing someone else, for some reason,

through every object of designed communication.

The graphic forms of design

are expressions of the forces that shape our lives.

We need a critical history of graphic design:

To provide ways of thinking about graphic form Interest in the historical inventory of graphic design is high. Practitioners plunder the vast archive of visual forms for inspiration. Students look for precedents. The industries of mass multimedia consume ideas at a terrifying pace. Rapidly expanding online and in-print graphic resources are accessible and ubiquitous. Designers seek striking models to make their work stand out in the fields of advertising, packaging, identity, publication, and information design.

But the history of *ideas about form* is difficult to recover. We need a vocabulary to grasp the way graphic design communicates. Beyond the catalog of style samples, historical insight offers an understanding of how design takes shape within cultural systems. How are we to understand the relations between style and technology? Between cultural moments and forms of expression? Between the persuasive tactics of graphic design and the messages they embody?

When these questions are correlated with the history of graphic developments, critical dimensions come into stark relief. Ideas about form offer their own possibilities for increasing our understanding of the way graphic design works to reflect or create values in our time.

To gain insight into design as a cultural practice As a cultural phenomenon, graphic design is embedded in institutions. Design studios, advertising agencies, publishing houses, print shops, and media companies, as well as the schools and programs that provide professional training, are all shaped by cultural and historical forces.

As a profession, graphic design operates within a network of constraints. Legal and economic issues, business and trade conventions, social and cultural mores, and attitudes toward imagery, language, composition, and representation are invisible—but potent—influences on the individual designer and the field as a whole. Graphic designers were once artisans of the manuscript page and painted sign. Then they were tradesmen in print shops, working at type cases and imposing tables. Then they became professionals with specialized skills. More recently, they have come to be thought of as artists—or even celebrities. As workers in the industries of consumer culture, how much choice do they have about the interests their work serves?

A critical approach to graphic design and its history is useful to anyone engaged in reading the cultural landscape of contemporary life. For designers, such an approach provides conceptual skills (ways of thinking) that extend their production capabilities (ways of making). Recognizing the historical dimension of the field sheds light on the choices that individual practitioners make on a daily basis—as well as the cultural dynamics within which they operate.

The shape of a critical history of graphic design Rather than tell the "story" of graphic design, we will outline some basic principles for thinking about the way historical origins inform contemporary practice. At issue is not just a history of designs but a history of ideas and assumptions about forms of communication.

Why does this page look the way it does? Why does it have margins and page numbers? Why are the lines this length? But even more, what assumptions about reading, about texts and information, and about imagined readers or actual audiences are encoded in its format? These questions can be answered, in part, by a purely formal analysis (with attention to proportion, balance, choice of typeface, size, and style). Skills for reading these visual properties are crucial tools.

But what historical aspects of graphic forms are *invisible?* A critical approach to graphic design exposes the rhetorical workings expressed in formal structures. (The shape of text blocks and use of page numbers express expectations about how this book will be read. These forms are the legacy of shifts in reading practices in the late Middle Ages, not just pleasing arrangements grounded in "universal" ideals of legibility.)

Graphic forms carry their history encoded as conventions, charged with cultural values—and loaded with social implications. The authority of any particular text is often linked to the codes of its presentation. (Does it look like a bible, an official document, or a tabloid newspaper?) In choosing a particular form of communication—whether it is a grid, type style, decorative element, or illustration—we perpetuate ways of thinking. Any system of formal organization expresses an attitude toward knowledge and its representation. Critically informed historical knowledge shows us how the structure of information becomes part of its meaning as form.

The critical approach to graphic design history is not a series of descriptions of artifacts but a set of theoretical frameworks for seeing the forces and conditions within which those objects came into being. The history of style is a history of culture. Analysis of form is a way to see that history reworked in the objects of contemporary life.

What, then, should we look at—and just as important, how?

The definition of the field

Identity of the graphic designer

Activities, trades, skills, and capabilities that mark the designer's changing identity

Professional institutions

Guilds, shops, studios, agencies, schools, professional associations, industry and government support programs

Internal discourse

Venues and means by which the field acquires legitimacy: trade publications, competitions that foster critical attention and recognition

Graphic design profession Graphic designers are defined by the tasks they perform, and our idea of a designer's identity at any given historical moment is a product of circumstances, not independent of those circumstances. The once anonymous practitioner may now aspire to "star" status. But graphic designers' work frequently ends up circulating without attribution, unmarked, as a free ion in the communications infosphere. Many graphic objects are made by committee or through a complicated chain of decisions in dialogue with a client. Design choices may be unwittingly constrained by cultural conventions about what is and is not allowed to be said or shown. Thus, a graphic artifact is as much a product of a complicated cultural system as it is the work of an individual designer. The designer's vision is often overwhelmed by professional exigencies. Meanwhile, the identity of the field as a whole changes in any given era. Critical reflection on graphic design developed mainly in the twentieth century, although harbingers of such internal discourse existed in the work of earlier practitioners—many of whom would not have known the term *graphic designer* or identified with the profession. Professional organizations have altered the landscape of graphic design, codifying a hierarchy of status and prestige within the field. But even as accomplished designers are now recognized with awards and prizes for their work, the majority of the public remain surprisingly ignorant of the names and contributions of those whose designs they make use of every day. Try subtracting everything set in typefaces designed by John Baskerville or Matthew Carter or Zuzana Licko from the visual landscape. The image of that gap-toothed universe makes a dramatic point.

The making of an artifact

General technology

> Inventions and innovations that
> are widespread in their effects
> but without which specific design
> technologies could not emerge

Design production and reproduction
processes and technology

> Methods of making and reproducing
> a design through all stages of its
> creation and circulation

Technology Style choices in design are not entirely under the control of designers but are related to the ways technology develops in a broader cultural sphere. Mass production required power sources and high-speed machines, which, in turn, were developed through industrial processes. But technology does not determine social or formal change; it operates within changing cultural circumstances. (Electrification did not *create* digital media; it simply contributed a necessary element to its development.) Possibilities for production are called into being by particular cultural needs or eclipsed by shifting desires. The capabilities of production always constitute affordances, within which design practices can be conceived as well as realized. Many technologies of graphic design have long aesthetic traditions associated with them. The development of new tools and materials often leaps ahead of the conception of a graphic style suited to them. The history of design is as filled with peculiar attempts to reconcile inherited formal models and new technologies as it is with the spontaneous invention of appropriate styles. Images look radically different when the main method of production shifts from pen and ink to metal, or from hand-drawn lithographic pictures to photographs. But the aesthetic of a particular medium develops in relation to ideas, not just as an automatic or immediate effect of a new material or tool. (Visual approaches, like the photographic close-up or montage, embody ideas about images as materials that can be manipulated and recombined rather than simply received as realistic documents.)

**Elements of form and format,
from individual mark
to overall convention**

Text design

    Lettering, micro- and macro-
    typography, format

Imagery and iconography

    Pictorial elements, their history
    and meaning

Decorative elements

    Motifs, ornaments, borders

Marks of production

    Visual syntax at the elementary
    level of dots, lines, tone

Graphic logic and rhetoric

    Composition as organization
    and argument

Aesthetic sensibility

    Cultural history of attitudes
    toward form

Style Style can be studied at macro and micro levels. The method by which marks are made produces a "syntax"—formal graphic language—of images, letterforms, and decorative elements. Likewise, every material aspect (such as the slickness or softness of paper) participates in the graphic production of meaning. The conventions for picturing the world, or forms of address in a text, can appear perfectly natural, a simple statement of the way things are. But these appearances conceal the exclusionary tactics of their rhetoric. Many familiar conventions contain biases that carry cultural implications (for example, the north–south orientation of maps, the rationalization of space by perspective, or the representation of a person of a particular gender or class). Decorative elements and ornaments produce cultural identity in ways that are often rendered invisible by their use as mere motifs. (Where do we get our ideas of what looks "Japanese" in a style like "Japonisme"?) Even our basic understanding of letterforms changes. Renaissance type designer Geoffrey Tory saw letters as symbols of cosmological principles, whereas the twentieth-century designer Ed Fella sees in them vivid expressions of vernacular poetics. The very shapes and proportions of alphabetical forms are products of cultural influences. Such notions change constantly. Every graphic artifact expresses a point of view, implicitly or explicitly, that participates in power structures, asserting subtle and not-so-subtle control over ways of thinking and acting.

Social relations, practices, and processes that have a major impact on graphic design and communication

Institutions

Publishing: Readerships, sites of use, distribution, circulation

Collections: Public and private repositories, libraries, archives

Educational institutions: Sites of formalized study

Transportation and communication

Structure and infrastructure for distribution and dissemination

Economic systems

Patterns of trade, markets, policy

Legal and political issues

Intellectual property, censorship, licensing

Entertainment and media industry

Forms of consumption in changing venues, formats, and audiences

Events and trends

Political, cultural, and environmental developments

Cultural conditions and attitudes Social institutions and cultural attitudes situate designed artifacts within specific networks of use and circulation. In turn, these institutions themselves are constantly being modified by cultural changes in technology, work settings and labor configurations, economic viability, and political factors. Printing and publishing contributed to the spread of literacy and creation of communities of knowledge. As means of reproducing and disseminating knowledge evolve, the notion of the public sphere as a realm of shared information and common assumptions changes. Patterns of commerce and trade—such as the way we have come to recognize branding as a feature of our cultural landscape—have economic and social implications that far outstrip the formal properties of the objects in question. For example, the graphic language of brand design is not just about creating a concise, recognizable visual identity but about generating image-value within competitive markets. The economics of graphic design are also bound up with political battles over the shape and ownership of discourse, intellectual property, and censorship mechanisms. Every graphic artifact mediates social relations. Design shapes communication, and communication systems exert an enormous force in constructing the world we believe in. Showing *how they do so* is a challenging task.

Specific concrete examples

Public discourse

> Civic or commercial notices, posters, flyers, signage, billboards, point-of-purchase displays, pop-up ads

Mass-circulation publications

> Magazines, newspapers, journals, and other print media supported by advertising

Graphic commodities

> Books and publications for entertainment, instruction, or reference, such as comics, novels, encyclopedias, bibles, cookbooks, and manuals

Information graphics

> Menus, maps, timetables, charts, graphs, and other displays of quantitative or qualitative data

Useful ephemera

> Tickets, money, stamps, receipts, and other graphic items designed to transact or record an exchange or to perform another function

Identity and branding systems

> Logos, letterhead, packaging, and signage for corporate and public entities

Milestones

> Individuals, works, or campaigns of note

Graphic artifacts Discussion of any particular bit of imagery leads immediately into rich cultural inquiry. Whether images present bodies or objects, worlds for study or fantasy consumption, they can be readily taken apart—although the longer history of their forms may be obscure. Less evident is the way in which the structure of information as a system and a rhetoric establishes an argument and persuades a reader of the authority of its presentation. Underlying such systems are aesthetic principles, often founded on belief systems and attitudes toward form that have their roots in classicism, romanticism, and rationalism. Even fundamental values like clarity and legibility, or harmony and proportion, are fraught with cultural baggage.

Critical principles When we realize that graphic design shapes our conceptual horizons as well as our visible world, we have to come to terms with the way our view of what is possible—or not possible—within human experience, action, and understanding is embodied in communication media. If all artifacts serve a purpose, as we have said, then so do histories. A critical history tries to unmask the ideological bases that are concealed by a conventional history. By definition, any seamless linear story is false, concealing the multiple layers of disjunction and tension at work in a culture. The critical approach offered here brings particular themes and issues to the fore. Cutting across historical periods with thematic categories, this approach implies that many of the issues that come into focus in any one historical moment might be useful in examining another. To promote this investigation, we have compiled a basic list of critical principles.

- **No graphic object is discrete or isolated.**
  All cultural expressions participate in systems of production.
  (How was it made? When? Where? Read the traces of production to recover
  the object as an expression of social relations.)

- **All designed communications serve vested interests.**
  In most cases, these interests are concealed
  by the apparent message of the work.
  (Who paid for it? What do they hope to gain? Follow the money.)

- **Ease of consumption is expensive to produce.**
  (An inverse relation exists between production values and effortlessness of
  consumption, such that many social, environmental, or human costs are
  hidden in the seamless look of a final product.)

- **The more "natural" something appears,**
  the more culturally indicative it is.
  (Images do not show us the "way things are"—they construct a world-as-image
  and then pass it off as "natural.")

- **Anything that claims to be universal is highly suspicious.**
  (Every object expresses a point of view with particular cultural biases.
  Why is this bias being imposed? Who benefits? Whose values are excluded?)

- **Every graphic artifact constitutes an exchange**
  among individuals, groups, or entities.
  (Graphic objects are part of a network of communication.)

- **Meaning is made not transmitted.**
  (Every act of reading and viewing is a creative act of interpretation.)

- **Communication is a dynamic system.**
  (A work creates a viewer as much as a viewer creates a work.)

- **Technology is not determinant.**
  (Cultural receptivity shapes the use of any new medium or invention.
  Something will not catch on without a collective desire for its development.)

- **Style is an agent of culture.**
  (Graphic forms are instrumental in transforming meanings, values, and beliefs.)

Graphic Design History
A Critical Guide

Second Edition

1. From Prehistory to Early Writing 35,000–500 BCE

- From its beginnings, **graphic** communication has depended not only on workable tools and production processes but also on **visual** principles and the design of **symbolic forms** (**signs** and images) that can be recognized according to the conventions and beliefs of a community.

- The design of **proto-writing** systems introduced the first stable codes for graphic **representation** of things and quantities by signs and tokens.

- The meaningful organization of graphic signs depended on compositional principles, such as juxtaposition, sequence, **hierarchy**, and direction, that followed systematic rules.

- The impulse to design symbolic forms suggests that humans do not simply use signs to record their needs and activities but place great value on the representation of *ideas*.

- Literate culture developed when a social group agreed on conventions for the representation of **language** by a **visual code**. The effects of writing as a form of social control and power spring from this consensus.

1.1 Stenciled hand, Pech Merle, France, 23,000–18,000 BCE. The urge to make marks is a fundamental human impulse. Creating external symbols gives back an image of the self while leaving a sign in the world. The stenciled hand shown here is thousands of years old, but similar signs can be found throughout history. Graphic design arises from the relation between that basic impulse and the system of communication that connects individuals within a culture. The impulse toward personal expression and compliance with convention are the twin engines of all graphic design.

Cro-Magnon culture in Europe laid the foundations for graphic **communication** in cave paintings and other designs around 35,000 BCE. Prehistoric artists shared a visual vocabulary, indicating that they worked within a system of socially recognized **conventions**. They organized their surfaces to support **figure** and **ground** distinctions and used forms consistently for their **symbolic value** as signs. This systematic use of signs is the basis of communication. On these foundations, proto-writing took shape in tokens and seals after about 10,000 BCE. By 3000 BCE, more specialized tools for carving, inscribing, and marking were developed and used on material supports of varying durability, such as clay, stone, papyrus, skin, bone, wax, metal, and wood. But the design of writing as a stable **code** to represent language depended on more than tools and media. It required the conceptual linkage of visual signs to a linguistic system. The shapes of the first **glyphs**, **letters**, and signs are related to present-day **alphabetic** and **character**-based **scripts**. Our writing still uses versions of some of the earliest written **symbols** ever invented. Writing changed the power of language by aligning it with the administration of culture through economic, political, religious, and other social activities. Writing conveyed laws and constraints that could be enforced by symbolic rather than physical force. The uses and effects of written language distinguish **literate** from **oral** cultures. Oral communication is ephemeral and takes place in real-time circumstances that rely on presence. **Inscriptions** and textual records can reach contexts that are remote in time and space from their author or moment of origin (Fig. **1.1**).

1.2 Painted stones, Mas-d'Azil, France, 10,000 BCE. These are some of the earliest remains of systematic mark-making. The careful graphic execution and regular repetition of marks indicate deliberate intention. Though too few in number to represent a language, they may have been conventionalized representations of things. The stick-figure form is referred to as the "hallelujah man" because it appears to be a person with arms raised in jubilation. This sign, like the other simple forms on these rocks, is common to many so-called "primitive" systems of marks. Even when they develop independently, human scripts often share formal characteristics. This does not suggest that a **"universal"** code underlies all writing but rather, pragmatically, that simple lines and shapes can be combined in a certain number of fairly predictable ways.

1.3 Carved spear thrower, Mas-d'Azil, France, 16,000–9000 BCE. Carved tools and other decorated artifacts have been found among human settlements dating back to the Upper Paleolithic period (the last phase of the Old Stone Age), about 40,000–10,000 BCE, although humans first made crude tools as early as 2.6 million years ago. Design clearly mattered in the crafting of these objects. Considerable effort went into shaping and decorating them. The care taken suggests that the object's symbolic purpose was as important as its effectiveness in propelling a spear. The ability to create meaningful patterns and attach symbolic value to forms is a distinctly human characteristic. Other animals may produce exquisitely shaped or highly organized nests, dances, or songs, but no other animal makes recognizable **effigies** or adds decoration to its tools or environment.

Mark-making Mark-making is the most basic form of graphic expression and design. Drawing a line in the sand or making a handprint on a wall is a direct sign of individual identity. Such imprints have a curious existence: a mark that is a sign of the self is also always *other* than the self. Once made, **marks** exist independently of their makers. A line makes a division, whether in physical space as a boundary or in an intellectual zone to define a category. Differentiating between marked and unmarked things is a conceptual act of enormous significance. We might even suggest that the idea of **difference** forms the basis of human knowledge, and that the making of a mark is the primary way of inscribing such difference. On this simple principle of differentiation, we can structure the complicated oppositions of I/you, this/that, self/other, and subject/object, which form our understanding of the world. Marks are not only different from each other but also distinct from the ground on which they are made and from the **intervals** that separate them. We take these notions for granted and rarely pause to consider the conceptual leap required for their development (Fig. **1.2**).

Prehistory The terms Paleolithic, Mesolithic, and Neolithic describe states of cultural complexity, not chronological periods, and occur at different moments in different parts of the world. In Western Europe, by about 35,000 BCE, Paleolithic (Stone Age) sculptures and cave paintings exhibit the high level of craft that characterizes Cro-Magnon art. **Artifacts** of this period can be considered the origin of graphic design insofar as they present clear evidence of conscious decisions about form. They often feature decorative images and marks. Their striking shapes, styles, and

1.4 Cave painting, Altamira, Spain, 16,000–9000 BCE. When the cave paintings at Altamira, Spain, were discovered in the late 1870s, they created a sensation. Far from being primitive expressions by unskilled artists, these paintings were sophisticated at every level of conception and execution. Because they were recognized as finely made, they challenged concepts of progress in art. The figures are clear and distinct, and the ground on which they appear is a well-prepared and organized surface. These paintings are not only powerful **aesthetic** expressions, they also document a long history. Successive waves of climate change, for example, were recorded in cave art. Images of reindeer, painted on earlier layers, were replaced by those of ibexes and other animals as the ice sheets receded in later millennia. Although drawn from memory, the images are naturalistic. What is remarkable, however, is how much similarity exists among cave paintings. This striking fact shows that a distinct set of visual conventions had been established for producing artworks. Although it would be a stretch to call the world of prehistoric cave painters a **design community**, rules governing what was formally possible and acceptable were followed by these artists. The artists did not simply invent visual solutions at random in response to circumstances or impulses. They produced highly organized works of art, designed according to formal and cultural conventions. This social basis for form arguably marks the beginning of graphic communication.

imagery carry information about social and ritual practices and have thus been the focus of **anthropological** study. These artifacts have much to tell us about the **technological** and cultural conditions that produced them. They show us that human beings could imagine a shape and purpose for an object independent of their embodiment in a specific thing. These people had ideas about form-giving and an abstract model in mind to guide tool-making (Fig. **1.3**).

Prehistoric graphic signs embody values and express beliefs.

Cro-Magnon painters approached their subjects realistically. Dating from 15,000–10,000 BCE, renderings of bison, deer, and other game in the cave art of Altamira, Spain, and Lascaux, France are still recognizable. But the graphic qualities of these images go beyond **likeness**. The **composition**, elegance of line, care in production, and considerations of scale, color, and pattern in these paintings display a considerable investment in the quality of their visual design. These artists did not simply use raw materials lifted from the campfire but mixed their **pigments** deliberately. Evidence of advanced material preparation implies a pause between conception and execution that allows for critical reflection upon the act of making. This gap between thinking and making is crucial to all forms of design. As for the meaning of cave art, it has traditionally been interpreted as a form of sympathetic hunting magic. More recent theories suggest that these graphic forms are the symbolic expression of a worldview rather than simply an attempt to gain power over the uncertain forces of nature. The realization that prehistoric graphic signs embody values and express beliefs places them on a continuum that includes contemporary design (Fig. **1.4**).

1.5 Clay tokens, Susa, Iran, fourth millennium BCE. These regularly shaped objects served as a form of notation for business transactions. Their shapes each corresponded to a different category of agricultural product. The marks on their surfaces were highly schematic and used for detailed accounting. When these tokens were pressed into wet clay, their imprints were part of a graphic system in which relative size, shape, orientation, and groupings were all significant. These tokens demonstrate the emergence of a set of sophisticated graphic principles. The spatial organization of the surface and the elaboration of rules governing the use of visual signs are evidence of graphic refinement. This notation system is still not considered "writing" because that term designates the representation of language, and these tokens are basically accounting receipts or tallies.

1.6a Chinese writing, second millennium BCE to the present. The transformation of Chinese characters from their pictorial origins to schematic signs happened with relative rapidity. Chinese characters most frequently represent either words or sounds, or some combination of the two. No writing system that required a sign for every word would be practical. The adaptation of characters for Japanese, Korean, and other languages demonstrates the versatility of Chinese script.

Proto-writing

The Mesolithic period (or Middle Stone Age)—about 10,000–7000 BCE—is characterized by the development of agriculture, leading to the rise of cities and civic organization in the ancient Middle East. It is also marked by a huge leap in graphic communication: the appearance of proto-writing. This development is linked to changes in the social organization of human settlements, such as the appearance of city structures within clearly defined boundaries (the walls in the ancient city of Jericho were 13 feet high by 8000 BCE). The invention of proto-writing coincides with the successful cultivation of hard grains (capable of being stored without rotting) at the beginning of the Neolithic period (or New Stone Age)—about 8000–4000 BCE—in the ancient Mesopotamian region. When more of this grain could be grown in a season than was needed for immediate or local use, accounting systems became necessary to help monitor its ownership, distribution, and storage. For the first time, these systems relied on symbols designed to signify numerical values and specific objects in the world. After about 8000 BCE, the numeric and **pictographic** signs of this proto-writing were used on tokens and clay tablets to mark ownership and quantities of goods. Proto-writing systems made use of fundamental **graphic principles** to order the shape, size, placement, and sequence of signs. Accounting tokens were designed to make impressions in clay. These impressions were precursors to the wedge-shaped signs of **cuneiform**, probably the oldest system of actual writing (Fig. **1.5**).

Early writing

Graphic **media** entered a new era when writing proper evolved in ancient Mesopotamia around 3200 BCE, in the so-called Fertile Crescent that lies between the Tigris and Euphrates rivers. Fully developed writing has the capacity to represent language in a stable system of signs, and cuneiform is the first known example of such a system. Egyptian writing may have been a simultaneous development, or it may have evolved, in part, as an imitation of cuneiform scripts. In China, writing emerged

1.6b Dresden codex, Yucatan, 1200–1250 CE *(right)*. Mesoamerican writing, both Mayan and Aztec, appears to have been an independent invention and has a uniquely graphic feature: it uses spatial organization in a meaningful way, arranging different elements of language such as prefixes and suffixes so that they are legible according to their placement around a central glyph. Mayan glyphs take advantage of visual structure in a manner very different from that of alphabetic sequence or cuneiform and **hieroglyphic** organizations. These glyphs can be very elaborate, with additional graphic elements known as **attributes** spreading over a large area. Although the earliest existing artifacts of Mayan writing date to only about 200–300 CE, some scholars believe that the system evolved from earlier practices. In the sixteenth century, European conquerors destroyed the majority of Mayan and Aztec codices and written documents, making recovery of this history almost impossible.

Fully developed writing has the capacity to represent language.

1.7 Clay tablet with cuneiform, Iraq, 3000 BCE *(above)*. The signs on this clay tablet are considered an early form of cuneiform writing. Made with many small strokes, the signs seem to be drawings of particular things. The pictorial origins of cuneiform can be traced in these and other artifacts. These signs are considered writing because they can be related to the sounds in the Sumerian language. The visual structure of cuneiform tablets is well ordered. The surface is usually divided into columns and/or rows, either by visible or implied lines. The size and spacing of the marks are regular, and their rhythm has a momentum that carries the eye forward. The marks are grouped according to a system which, visually, is as elaborate a code for language as speech is verbally. Graphic organization aids the signs' production of meaning.

after 1500 BCE, apparently independently, although some debate suggests cultural influences from Europe to Asia. Glyphic writing originated in Mesoamerican cultures around 900 BCE, in advance of contact with Europeans, and has its own graphic rules (Figs. **1.6a** and **1.6b**).

Cuneiform was first used to represent ancient Sumerian, one of a handful of languages that have never been deciphered. The number of cuneiform signs suggests that they represented words in a **logographic** script. Signs recovered from sites like the city of Uruk in ancient Sumeria indicate pictographic origins, but these Sumerian **pictograms** soon became schematized so that they could be drawn in a few quick strokes of the stylus on a soft tablet. Writing and sign-making were directly related to administrative tasks and the social structures that enable civil societies. For instance, by 3000 BCE, the state bureaucracy of Uruk had ten different numerical systems in use, each associated with a specialized sphere of activity. Writing codified law, and its enforcement came to supplement (and sometimes replace) violence as an instrument of power (Fig. **1.7**).

Cuneiform script spread through the ancient Near East and was used extensively across various cultures and languages for diplomatic purposes

PICTOGRAMS			'CLASSICAL' SUMERIAN		OLD-AKKADIAN	OLD-ASSYRIAN	OLD-BABYLONIAN	NEO-ASSYRIAN	NEO-BABYLONIAN	Picture	Meaning
URUK UPRIGHT c.3100 B.C.	c.3100 B.C. TURNED 90° TO LEFT	JEMDET NASR c.2800 B.C.	LINEAR	c.2400 B.C. CUNEIFORM	c.2200 B.C.	c.1900 B.C.	c.1700 B.C.	c.700 B.C.	c.600 B.C.		
										NECK + HEAD	HEAD FRONT
										NECK+HEAD + BEARD or TEETH	MOUTH NOSE TOOTH VOICE SPEAK WORD
										SHROUDED BODY (?)	MAN
										SITTING BIRD	BIRD
										BULL'S HEAD	OX
										STAR	SKY HEAVEN-GOD GOD
										STREAM of WATER	WATER SEED FATHER SON
										LAND-PLOT + TREES	ORCHARD GREENERY TO GROW TO WRITE

1.8 Development of cuneiform, 3100–600 BCE. The need for efficiency in writing systems propelled simplification from pictorial to schematic signs. A stylus in wet clay made some marks more easily than others, and the orientation as well as the shape and combination of these marks changed as writing became stabilized. Sumerian **linear** and cuneiform marks from about 2400 BCE were adopted by successive peoples in the same geographic regions: Akkadians, Babylonians, and Assyrians each used cuneiform for their own distinct language. Not only was cuneiform graphically efficient, but also it represented an enormous conceptual advancement: it was a fully developed, adaptable written code for language.

in the third and second millennia BCE. The popularity of cuneiform reached its peak in about 1400 BCE, when its diplomatic use extended throughout a region that included present-day Iraq, Turkey, Syria, Egypt, Palestine, Lebanon, and Israel. Cuneiform signs were used by language groups from Indo-European, Afro-Asiatic, and other families. The adoption of a **writing system** developed for one language by another is a pattern that is repeated many times in the history of scripts (Fig. **1.8**).

The spread of writing as idea and script
The *idea* of writing that developed with cuneiform may have been as influential as the actual script. Both spread to other areas in the ancient Near East. A host of scripts developed throughout the ancient Near and Middle East in the second millennium BCE, varying in form from hybrids of cuneiform and pictographic scripts to advanced **schematic** sign systems. But only a few sustained widespread use. The oldest artifacts containing Egyptian hieroglyphics—from the Greek words *hiero* ("sacred") and *glyph* ("carving")—show them almost fully developed. Many of their standard shapes were already set by the time they were adopted in 3200–3100 BCE. Little **archeological** evidence exists for dating Egyptian hieroglyphs any earlier (Fig. **1.9**).

From Prehistory to Early Writing

1.9 Hieroglyphics, lintel from the reign of Sesostris III, Egypt, 1887–1850 BCE. An underlying grid organizes these signs into quadrants according to a principle of graphic efficiency rather than grammar. Hieroglyphics were meaningful as representations of words and syllables, but their direction and groupings were also significant. Signs in proximity were read as a unit. Note that a graphic system constrains the size of these signs. Objects that are very unlike in scale are allotted the same unitary area in conformance with a distinct design principle. Although figurative in their appearance, hieroglyphics could represent words (**logograms**), sounds (**phonograms**), or categories (**determinatives**). Determinatives, or classifiers, were used to clarify the meaning of sign combinations. For instance, one combination of signs means "to be stable," unless it is accompanied by the image of a sparrow, the sign for evil, in which case it is read as "to be bad."

1.10 Hieratic and demotic scripts, 2900–100 BCE. The evolution of a **hieratic** script from hieroglyphic forms provided a far more efficient system that could be written quickly with a brush and ink. **Demotic** script represented an even more schematic, informal writing form used for daily occasions. The more elaborate pictorial forms of hieroglyphics were used for formal, official purposes. After the Greek conquest of Egypt around 332 BCE, by Alexander the Great, hieroglyphics took on their arcane and esoteric associations. The priestly caste introduced a deliberate obscurity into the use of hieroglyphics as a way of resisting Greek influence.

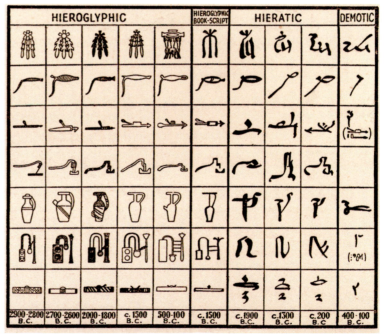

Connections between the Egyptian writing system and those of the ancient Near East are debated. Some evidence of cultural influence can be found along the trade routes that passed through Syria. In any case, hieroglyphics did not spread. Both hieroglyphics and cuneiform fell out of use, although for different reasons. Hieroglyphics were banned when Christianity became the state religion in Egypt in the fourth century CE, while cuneiform was displaced by the more efficient alphabetic system beginning in the second millennium BCE (Fig. **1.10**).

1.11 Development of alphabetic letterforms, ninth to first century BCE. Many different scripts developed in the ancient Near East. All of these scripts are directly related to the earliest formation of the alphabet. This chart shows some of the stages through which the alphabet passed. New developments did not always replace earlier ones. Some changes occurred as the alphabet spread through various geographical and cultural locations. Others occurred over time, or in response to cultural influences and technical constraints imposed by the availability of materials.

Letter name	Phonetic value	Moab. IX.C., B.C.	Nineveh IX.C., B.C.	Siloam VIII.C., B.C.	Nineveh VII.C., B.C.	Sidon VI.C., B.C.	Samaritan	Jerusalem I.C., B.C.	Modern Hebrew	Modern Arabic
Aleph	'a									
Beth	b									
Gimel	g									
Daleth	d									
He	h									
Vau	v									
Zayin	z									
Cheth	ch									
Teth	t									
Yod	y									
Kaph	k									
Lamed	l									
Mem	m									
Nun	n									
Samekh	s									
'Ayin	'a									
Pe	p									
Tsade	ts									
Q'oph	q									
Resh	r									
Shin	sh									
Tau	t									
		I	II	III	IV	V	VI	VII	VIII	IX

The alphabet The letters used in the type on this page first appeared in a limited, schematic system in the cosmopolitan Canaanite culture that flourished in the Sinai region 4,000 years ago. This system consisted of about twenty signs and combined the simplified forms of the Egyptian hieratic script with principles of sound representation that were the basis of cuneiform **syllabaries**. The efficiency and flexibility of the early alphabet represented an advance over both of these precedents. The order of the letters seems to have been fixed almost from the outset. Archaeological remains reveal that this sequence was used as a guide for assembling architectural elements in the building of temples (Fig. **1.11**).

The alphabet was a remarkable invention. The letters were assigned names as an aid to memory and use. A word beginning with a given letter was often used as that letter's name. According to this **acrophonic** principle, the early *a* was called *aleph* (from the Hebrew word for "ox"), and *b* was *beth* (from the Hebrew word for "house"). The letters' shapes were not necessarily derived from an ox and a house, but their schematic forms

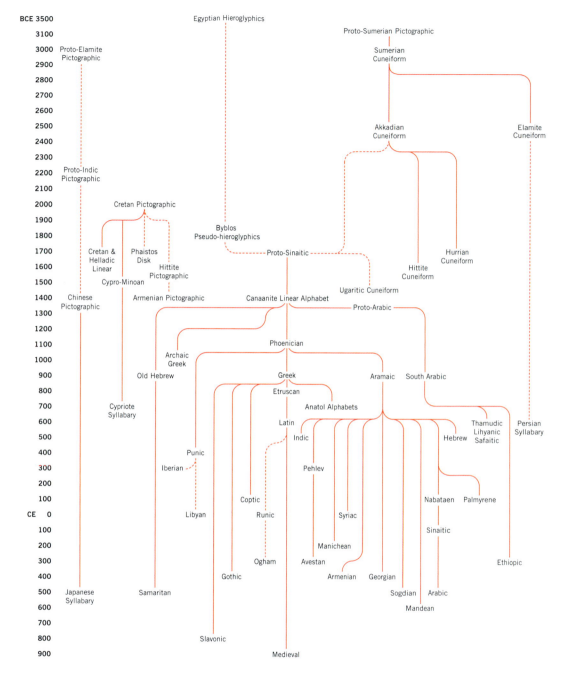

1.12a Origins and development of alphabetic scripts, 3500 BCE–900 CE. The incredible variety of forms into which alphabets have evolved creates the illusion of a proliferation of different scripts. In fact, most of the alphabets of the world are derived from a single source whose sequence and basic forms provided a foundation for scripts in Africa, the Near East, Asia, Europe, and the Americas. Chinese characters are the other successful script form and, like the alphabet, were adopted and modified for use across a remarkable number of languages.

resembled these objects enough to make taking their names work as a memory device. No myth is more persistent than that of the pictorial origin of the alphabet. Actually, the schematic and arbitrary nature of alphabetic signs was partly responsible for their efficiency and rapid spread. Easily drawn, alphabetic letters could be combined to represent the sounds of many languages. When disseminated by Phoenician traders who sailed throughout the Mediterranean region, the alphabet gained a foothold among Etruscan and Greek people who spoke quite different tongues. The alphabet also spread into northern Africa, throughout the Middle East, into India, and beyond (Figs. **1.12a** and **1.12b**).

1.12b Funerary stele, Greece, 459 BCE.
The regular, simplified shapes of Greek
lettering on this funerary stele fill space
in a stable and ordered way that seems
to indicate the influence of geometry on
design. But the most important Greek
contribution to the alphabet was the
addition of signs to represent vowels
around 700 BCE. The new letters can be
seen throughout this inscription. In early
alphabetic scripts, vowel sounds were
indicated by small dots or points (later
known by the term *matres lectionis*—or
"aids for reading"). The Greeks' Indo-
European language depended more
heavily on vowels to clarify the meaning
of words than did the Semitic language
spoken by the alphabet's inventors,
hence their addition.

**1.13 Hammurabi's code, Iraq,
eighteenth century BCE.** This stele is
inscribed with a detailed code of law,
governing behavior in daily Babylonian life.
Hammurabi's code is the oldest existing
written document of laws. It consists of
several hundred laws, concerning all
aspects of life: conspiracy, marriage, rape,
slavery, property, damages for negligence,
and so on. The code provides a great deal
of information about gender roles. It shows
that women were in business in Babylonia
and had certain rights with respect to
adultery and childbearing. The image
depicts Hammurabi receiving the gift of
law from Shamash, the god of justice.

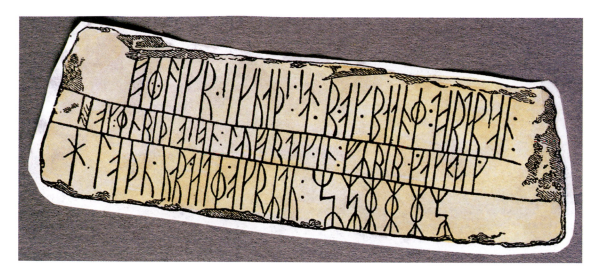

1.14 Runes, ca. 600 CE. Runes were a version of the alphabet invented by Germanic and Scandinavian people in the early centuries of the Common Era. The *futhark* alphabet is one of the earliest of such rune writing systems and consists of only twenty-four characters. Although runes are frequently associated with mysterious cults and ritual practices, they are really just another modification of the alphabet whose forms were determined largely by the tools and materials of wood and stone inscription. Runes are somewhat different in form than Latin letters, and each has a distinctive name. The significance attributed to these names fostered the use of runes as signs with magical properties, not just as a practical means for expressing language.

The alphabet's development, spread, and longevity are proof of its viability as a system of writing. Some variations of the **alphabetic script**, such as those found in Arabic and Indonesian writing, look so different from our letters that it is difficult to see their connection. Yet the order, number, and even names of the letters indicate the common origin of these scripts. Myths and misconceptions continue to surround the history of writing. Many scholars place the beginnings of **literacy** at the time of the Greek alphabet's consolidation of vowel **notation**. Yet the list of cultural accomplishments and written texts that predate the advent of the Greek alphabet is a long one. On this list are the ancient Near Eastern tale of Gilgamesh with its legend of the flood; the Babylonian law code of Hammurabi; the developed philosophical systems of India and Asia; successes of astronomy, navigation, cartography; civic structures and administration; and advanced arts of poetry (Fig. **1.13**).

Conclusion The cultural impact of writing was so far-reaching that it was considered by many societies to have been a divine gift. Its invention seemed beyond the skills of any mere mortal. The creation of writing was attributed to the tracks of birds, the constellations in the heavens, the Indian god Ganesh, the Egyptian deity Thoth, and the tablets Moses brought down from Mount Sinai. The Greeks attributed responsibility to Prometheus, who, according to legend, stole writing from the gods along with fire, thereby incurring eternal punishment. Theoretical distinctions between oral and literate cultures stress the power of written documents to **codify** law, produce historical records, **objectify** experience, and facilitate rational, logical processes. Oral cultures, by contrast, rely on reinforcing memory by means of repetition or rhythmic pattern and tend to see language as a form of action (naming, telling, performing) associated with events in the present. In literate cultures, a record has its own existence, independent of its original context. The authority of the written word derives, in part, from this ability to circulate independently. The permanence of a written record lends its autonomy a power that is almost mythic (Fig. **1.14**).

From Prehistory to Early Writing 35,000–500 BCE

2 billion years ago	Protozoan life forms
300 million years ago	Life on land, amphibians and reptiles
65–55 million years ago	**Paleocene epoch: warm, tropical, proto-primates like lemurs**
40 million years ago	Proto-monkeys
25–5 million years ago	**Miocene epoch: beginning of human evolution as distinctive branch**
4 million years ago	Australopithecus, early hominid
2–1.5 million years ago	Advanced australopithecus and proto-human use of tools
1.8 million–10,000 years ago	**Pleistocene epoch: Homo erectus**
700,000 years ago	Erectines (upright hominids) throughout Africa and Asia
220,000–30,000 years ago	Neanderthals, a separate species, coexist with modern humans
150,000 years ago	Homo sapiens sapiens develops and begins displacing Neanderthals
	Evidence of language through tools and social organization
100,000 years ago	Migration of Homo sapiens into Middle East, then India, East Asia, Australia
40,000 years ago	Migration to Europe (Stone Age people, Cro-Magnon culture)
34,000 years ago	First cave art
19,000 years ago	Warming trends: migration to North America over Bering Strait
12,000–6,000 years ago	**Mesolithic period**
12,000 years ago	End of glaciation, earliest settlements in Americas
9000–8500 BCE	Major cities developing in Levant, including Jericho
8000 BCE	Limited navigation of Mediterranean
8000–6000 BCE	Fired clay pottery and clay tokens for agricultural economy
6000–3500 BCE	**Neolithic period in Middle East**
6000–5000 BCE	Cultivation of hard grains, irrigation, early civic bureaucracy in Sumer
5000 BCE	Saharan region dry, population migrates toward Nile valley
4000–2000 BCE	**Neolithic culture in Europe**
4000s BCE	Ancient Egyptian culture begins
3700–2700 BCE	Clay tokens enclosed in envelopes
3200 BCE	Primitive sailboats in Egypt
3100 BCE	Cuneiform script used as a syllabary by Sumerians
	Hieroglyphics make their first appearance in Egypt
3000 BCE	Yams, coffee, watermelon, gourds cultivated in West Africa
	Narmer Palette; coherent sentences and stable hieroglyphics in Egypt
2800 BCE	Egyptian lunar calendar established with twenty-eight-day cycle
2800 BCE	Rice cultivated in China
2800–1500 BCE	Stonehenge built in stages
2650–2000 BCE	*Legend of Gilgamesh* composed (with flood narrative)
2600–1800 BCE	Indus Valley script and culture flourish and disappear
2575–2465 BCE	Great pyramids and Sphinx constructed at Giza
2500–2300 BCE	Biblical flood
2300–1400 BCE	Minoan civilization in Crete
2000–1500 BCE	Age of patriarchs Abraham, Isaac, and Jacob
1800 BCE	Early Bronze Age in China
1750 BCE	Signs of zodiac invented in Babylonia
1700 BCE	Canaanites and proto-alphabet
1700–1400 BCE	Palace at Knossos built
1600 BCE	Hittites adopt cuneiform for Indo-European language
	Volcano erupts on island of Santorini (legendary Atlantis)
1500 BCE	Iron perfected by Hittites
	Earliest remaining Egyptian *Book of the Dead*
	Earliest Olmec culture in Mesoamerica
	Hindu religion brought by nomads to India
1447 BCE	Exodus of Jews from Egypt begins

1400 BCE Cuneiform peaks as diplomatic script in Near East

1325 BCE Death of King Tutankhamun

1300 BCE Shang dynasty in China, earliest oracle writing

1100 BCE Phoenicians adopt, modify, and spread Canaanite alphabet

1100–1000 BCE Etruscans settle in southern Italy

1000 BCE Mayan culture begins in Mesoamerica

900s BCE Phoenician traders from Syrian coast go as far as Spain

900 BCE *I Ching*, oldest Chinese classical text composed

650 BCE Phoenicians circumnavigate Africa

Assurbanipal's library contains 22,000 tablets

600 BCE Hanging gardens of Babylon built by Nebuchadnezzar II

582–500 BCE Life of Pythagoras, Greek mathematician

580–500 BCE Life of Lao Tzu, founder of Taoism

531 BCE Enlightenment of Siddhartha (Buddha)

Tools of the Trade

Pigments (animal, vegetable, mineral)

Ash and charcoal

Water

Spittle (medium)

Hands

Mouth (spray)

Flint burins

Bone tools

Metal blades for knives and chisels

Primitive stencils

Frayed twigs and notched sticks

Animal skin and leather

Knotted cords

Surfaces of stone, marble, clay, wood, papyrus, wax

Animal fat, candles, oil lamps

Ink from soot, water, gum arabic

Reed, wood, and bone styluses

Hair and reed brushes

Limestone flakes as surface

Cloth

Carved seals

Lead

Gold

Glass (after 2500 BCE)

Candles

Oil lamps (nut and olive oils, fats)

2. Classical Literacy 700 BCE–400 CE

- In the Classical period, graphic design became a component of literacy. Design literacy suggests the existence of a common cultural understanding of the meaning of the visual forms, as well as the materials and contexts, of graphic information.

- In Classical culture, the functions of written language were encoded in distinct graphic forms:

  Informal communication between individuals was expressed in the ephemeral form of handwritten script, often on impermanent materials.

  Conventional communication regarding professional, personal, or public business relied on standard codes and consistent, legible letterforms written on **papyrus**, **parchment**, or wax.

  Commemorative writing used permanent materials, such as stone or clay, to inscribe acts of official memory or tribute in formal scripts and highly visible public spaces that signified importance.

  Performative discourse—containing statements that enacted events, laws, or decrees—was marked by ritual or ceremonial warrants, seals, official signs, and sites that conferred authority.

- The distinction between spoken and written language became more elaborate, as writing came to be considered not merely a transcription of speech but a communication system with its own formal properties.

- The design of letters was defined in two very different ways: as a sequence of expressive gestures and as a set of ideal shapes or constructed models to be copied.

- Access to writing did not map precisely onto class or gender divisions, but the shift from oral to literate culture introduced new means of representing and administering power.

2.1 Inscription from a Dipylon vase, 730–720 BCE. This early Greek inscription almost seems to have been scratched into the neck of the vase as an afterthought. It says, "Who now of all dancers most delicately performs, may he accept this." Expressive in character, the line feels spontaneously emotional, as if a celebratory mood had moved its author to this act of writing. The letters are crudely made but regular enough to be readable. Their sticklike forms have sharp angles and few curves. The writing reads from right to left, as in Phoenician texts, and the letters lie on their sides—another feature of the older or "parent" alphabet that gave rise to both Greek and Latin scripts.

In the Classical period, literacy took on new graphic and cultural dimensions. When the alphabet arrived in ancient Greece and Italy around 700 BCE, earlier writing systems had fallen out of use, but their legacy had established the value of written communication in many areas of public and private life. Within the city-states of Greece and the extensive, multicultural empire of Rome, reading entailed more than the recognition of letters and words. A text's physical and social setting were taken into account, and its graphic and material codes were interpreted. Classical Greek and Roman cultures used writing for individual expression, communication, commemorative acts of public record, and decrees or commands. These functions were distinguished graphically by letterforms and styles, and physically by the contexts in which messages were located. Formal properties signaled to a reader important information about the relative authority of their source and the intended effect of their message

2.2a Gortyna inscription, 638 BCE, and 2.2b Site of the inscription. This inscription is nearly 8 feet high and twelve columns wide and was found in the wall of a public theater in Crete. The text follows the early **boustrophedon** format: each line changes direction, winding first right to left, then left to right. The orientation of the letters switches as well, so that the letters in alternate lines are reversed. Like many early **monumental** texts, this inscription defines the state's ability to regulate the affairs of its citizens. As a permanent display of statutes, it presents a clear example of civic communication that encodes state power in a public image. The laws concern domestic issues: "the status of slaves, the rights of widows, heirs at law, children born after divorce, the adoption of children, property rights, and many other laws relating to domestic and family relations." The text was unearthed in 1881 near the ancient city of Gortyna. Known in antiquity as the "well-walled" city, Gortyna was associated with the legendary King Minos and his labyrinth. Although the inscription's letters exhibit the developed shape of Classical Greek, it contains only one (upsilon) of the five vowels that Greek incorporated.

even before texts were read. Urban and cosmopolitan, Classical societies were attuned to such graphic nuances. Degrees of literacy marked social distinctions and shaped networks of political power. In this cultural context, two very different approaches to the design of letters were established: one based on gestures and expressive forms and the other based on ideal **models** and **constructed forms**. These two approaches would continue to diverge in subsequent centuries. Basic principles of visual literacy in the production and reception of graphic forms were encoded in the Classical period in enduring and thus familiar ways (Fig. **2.1**).

Variations of literacy and the alphabet
Variants of the alphabet were used in Greece and southern Italy in the Classical period. With the exception of early indigenous writing in Crete, all were derived from scripts in the ancient Near East and dispersed by Phoenicians along their trade routes throughout the Mediterranean. By the eighth century BCE, this alphabet had taken hold among the Greeks, as well as the Etruscans (who populated southern Italy before the Romans). In Greece, the new writing system was linked to democracy insofar as literacy was a requirement for citizenship and its rights. But whether the unique properties of Greek writing *caused* the advent of this form of government or merely participated in its institutions is an open question (Figs. **2.2a** and **2.2b**).

Classical Literacy

2.3 Decree on a marble stele describing procedures for tribute, 426 BCE. This formal inscription outlines procedures to be followed in case of a dispute over the payment of tribute money to the city of Athens. As a prescription of behavior, it communicates the power of one city-state over the populace of another. The letters are carefully arranged with both vertical and horizontal columns maintained in a style known as **stoichedon** ("files"). The military procession evoked by this term and the strict graphic organization it describes seem well suited to the imposition of rule among warring city-states. The letters are written from left to right, a practice that became standard in Western scripts. For right-handed writers, this direction allows the text to be visible as it is written, not obscured by the writing hand. In wet media, it prevents smearing.

Rules for reading direction and word spacing were not yet fixed.

The oldest Greek inscriptions used letters that were very close in shape to their Phoenician sources. These scripts had only **majuscules** (uppercase letters). Lowercase versions of the letters (**minuscules**) came later. The format of early Classical inscriptions was varied, as was the orientation of writing. Conventions for basic elements of graphic presentation, such as reading direction and word spacing, were not yet fixed. The distinctive style of arrangement known as *boustrophedon* (literally, "as the ox ploughs") had precedents in Egyptian hieroglyphics. By the sixth and fifth centuries BCE, a clean, **monoline** script with little variation in weight became typical of Greek Classical letterform design. This writing was very evenly spaced and aligned, and the letters were regular in size and proportion (Fig. **2.3**).

Greek and early Latin alphabets were soon modified. Like dialects of a spoken language, scripts developed local variations. Many of these variants are referred to by their geographical location. Thus, Eastern, Western, and Chalcidian scripts derive their names from parts of Greece. Other forms of the alphabet, such as the Etruscan and Roman, came from Italy. In spite of their differences, remarkable consistency united these alphabets, and many innovations were shared among them—a sign of close communication

ΒΑΣΙΛΕΟΣΕΛΘΟΝΤΟΣΕΣΕΛΕΦΑΝΤΙΝΑΝΨΑΜΑΤΙΧΟ
ΝΑΥΤΑΕΓΡΑΥΑΝΤΟΙΣΥΝΨΑΜΜΑΤΙΧΟΙΤΟΙΘΕΟΚΛΟΣ
ΕΓΛΕΟΝΒΛΘΘΟΝΔΕΚΕΡΚΙΟΣΚΑΤΥΓΕΔΘΕΥΙΣΟΠΟΤΑΜΟΣ
ΑΝΙΒΑΛΟΓΛΟΣΟΣΘΥΕΠΟΤΑΣΙΜΤΟΑΙΓΥΠΤΙΟΣΔΕΡΜΑΣΙΣ
ΕΓΡΑΦΕΔΑΜΕΑΡΧΟΝΑΜΟΙΒΙΥΟΚΑΙΠΕΛΕΩΟΣΟΥΔΑΜΟ

2.4a Ionic inscription, late fifth century BCE, and 2.4b Abu Simbel, site of the inscription. This commemorative Ionic Greek inscription was carved into one of the monumental statues of Ramses II at the temple of Abu Simbel on the west bank of the Nile in Egypt. The Egyptian monument had been built about 1000 BCE, and this Greek text records the travels of a certain King Psamatichos to its site. The inscription's two authors are identified as Archon and Pelegnos, Greek mercenary soldiers traveling with the king. They describe their journey up the Nile and include the name of their Egyptian guide. One of the oldest Greek inscriptions, this graffiti was scraped into a knee of the giant limestone figure, which was half-buried in desert sand. Contrast this script with that of the Temple of Minerva at Priene (Fig. 2.7).

among peoples of the region. Their variations were a cultural equivalent to individual handwriting. The alphabet was the same in sequence and number of letters, but each local graphic version had different shapes and proportions. The Ionic script became the official Greek alphabet in 403 BCE, but such decrees had as much to do with the consolidation of political power as they did with the value of one design over another. Military conquests took the Roman alphabet into new territories as an instrument of imperial administration and cultural domination (Figs. **2.4a** and **2.4b**).

The most significant modification made by the Greeks to the alphabet was the addition of five letters to denote vowels. These were derived from Phoenician signs for consonants. Vowels provided considerable flexibility in adapting the script to a wide range of tongues. Because of its efficiency, the Greek alphabet may have been easier to learn than its precedents in the Near East. But the increase in literacy in Greece and Rome was also related to changes in educational patterns and assumptions about the place of writing in politics and the business of everyday life. Precise details about literacy rates among Classical populations are difficult to determine, but certainly reading and writing were no longer limited to a small class of **scribes**. Literacy among men was higher than among women, and many more people could read than write, but a large portion of the population could compose a personal message or conduct daily affairs in writing. In fourth century Athens, schools were established, including the famous gymnasium (school) where Plato taught in a park called Akademeia. **Rhetorical** skills essential to Greek politics were taught in these schools and so were the values on which the social networks of power rested. Literacy training inculcated pupils with cultural norms and social codes even as it passed on the poetry of Homer and the heroic tradition (Fig. **2.5**).

In their graphic evolution, Greek and Latin alphabets followed independent paths, and the distinctions that emerged in the seventh and sixth centuries BCE remain characteristic of them today. Both, however, adopted the convention of writing from left to right, with letters consistently oriented in that direction. Roman letterforms were marked by a blocklike geometrical regularity. The tilting diagonals and angular points of earlier scripts were regulated and codified as even curves and upright lines that expressed stasis and solidity rather than movement. Regimentation and administrative organization were basic features of Roman society, too. Extrapolating from the graphic qualities of a script to characterize a culture can be a risky proposition, but it is safe to say that the graphic stability of Roman letterforms conveyed an image of solid state power and authority (Fig. **2.6**).

Classical Literacy

2.5 Boy writing, fifth century BCE. The boy in this elegant painting is posed with a stylus and tablet on his lap. Along with papyrus and parchment, these were the most common writing materials. The tablet could be warmed and smoothed over for repeated use. Writing was a higher-order skill than reading, but literacy in Classical Greece was not limited to a single social group. By the fourth century, state-funded public education existed in Athens and other Greek city-states. Although full citizenship, which required literacy, was restricted to free, native-born, property-owning men, enough slaves and women were literate to allow reading and writing to be an integral part of daily life. No evidence exists of girls going to school, and most likely they were taught at home, but they were not prohibited by their gender from learning to read and write. Outstanding figures, such as the poet Sappho (sixth century BCE) and the philosopher/playwright Hipparchia (300 BCE), provide evidence of women's participation in the intellectual life of Classical Greece.

2.6 Chart of Greek and Roman letters. Variations in the number and forms of letters that constitute each script are vividly apparent here. These representations have been simplified, but they show the evolution of reading direction and the basic shapes and orientation of letters in the independent developments of Greek and Italian alphabets. Direction became standardized—not only from letter to letter but also within the component parts of letters. Crossbars and "arms" became horizontal and vertical. Diagonal strokes and curves were regularized. The distinctive features of each letter within its alphabet became graphically marked and aesthetically considered. The regularity of monumental carving in the Classical period came to conform to concepts of order and harmony. Efficiency and effectiveness were not the only governing principles in the design of letters or texts. After all, the early Latin script would have sufficed in practical terms.

Phoenician	Phonetic value	Greek Alphabets			Phonetic value	Italian Alphabets			
		Eastern	Western	Chalcidian		Pelasgian	Etruscan	Early Latin	Roman
𐤀	a	A	A	A A A	a	A A	A N A	A A A	A
𐤁	b	B	B B	B	b	B		B B	B
𐤂	g,c	Γ	<	Λ C	g,c	< C	) C G	< C G	C G
𐤃	d	Δ	D	Δ D	d	D		D D	D
𐤄	e	E	E	E E E	e	E E	3 3 3 E 3	E E II	E
𐤅	f,v,u		F	F	w,f	F		F F I'	F
𐤆	z	I	I	I	z	I I			
𐤇	ē,h	H	H	B H	h	B	B B	H	H
𐤈	th.	⊗	⊕	⊕ ⊙	th	⊕ ⊙	⊗ ⊙ ◇		
𐤉	i	I	I	I	i	I	I	I	I
𐤊	k	K	K	K	k	K	K	K K	K
𐤋	l	Λ	L	L	l	L	L	L L	L
𐤌	m	M	M	M M	m	M	M M M	M M M	M
𐤍	n	N	N	N N	n	N	M M N	N N	N
𐤎	x	Ξ	+	+	x	⊞			
𐤏	o	O Ω	O	O ◇	o	⊙		◇ O	O
𐤐	p	Γ	Γ	Γ Π	p	P Γ	⋀ ⋀	Γ P P	P
𐤑	ts				s	M M	M M		
𐤒	q	Φ	Q	Q	q	Q Q		Q Q Q	Q
𐤓	r	P	R	P R R	r	P	D D P	R R R	R
𐤔	s	Σ	S	S S	s	E E	S S	S S	S
𐤕	t	T	T	T	t	T T	T T	T	T
	u	Y V	Y V	Y V	u,v	Y	Y V V	V V	V
					ch	+ X		X	X
	ph	Φ		Φ Φ	ph	Q	Φ Φ		
	ps			↓	ch	Y	↓		
					f		8 8		

The function of graphic codes

Writing had served many purposes in Egyptian, Babylonian, and Canaanite cultures of the ancient Near East. Legal and literary texts, business records and accounts, official decrees and documents, maps, ritual prayers, and expressive graffiti had all been developed. Long before the alphabet was imported to Greece and Italy, writing included a range of social *functions* and a set of visual *forms*. The relations between specialized functions and particular forms were embodied in the design of letters, their material production, and physical contexts. Chisels, broad brushes, pens, and styluses each had characteristic formal effects. Surfaces were also varied, and marble, papyrus, wax, and pottery each posed specific challenges. But material conditions alone did not determine the style of scripts. The forms and material contexts

of writing reflected the occasions and functions for which inscriptions were made. Scale, placement, visibility, and attention to workmanship all contributed to the way a visual communication was received. Formal inscriptions had appeared on temples and monuments throughout the ancient Near East, but in Classical culture, the types and locations of inscriptions multiplied. Tombs, commemorative plaques, milestones, and markers assume literacy, and from their remains we can deduce that it was widespread.

Tablets and **scrolls** remained the basic portable media, while stone carving indicated site-specific, official text. The invention of the bound book, enabled by the flexibility of parchment, was an economical and convenient innovation that appeared in the second to fourth centuries CE. But for hundreds of years, the scroll remained the preferred format for literary texts, whereas bound books were more likely to be used for notes. Booksellers employed copyists and effectively published texts. Literary and historical works, although copied by hand, circulated widely among the Classical Greek and Roman populations (Fig. **2.7**).

We can artificially distinguish between the way writing looks and what it says, but specific lettering styles and materials have their own rhetorical force. Stylistic inflection often reinforces unstated assumptions about the

Graphic and material codes distinguished broad categories

function of a text—who it is for and what it is meant to do. Graphic and material codes distinguished broad categories of written language from each other in the Classical period. When writing functioned as a form of personal expression in a letter or graffiti, it usually took the form of a **cursive** script that was **gestural** and informal. Such letters were made with a pen or brush on papyrus, or scratched into a wall, wax tablet, or other readily available material support. **Ostraca**—bits of discarded pottery— often served as scratch paper. These materials may have simply been convenient, whereas others carried explicit symbolic value. *Defixiones* were magic spells written on small sheets of lead that were rolled up and buried to preserve their power. Inscriptions on publicly circulated coins carried the authority of their stated value, backed by their weight in a given metal (Fig. **2.8**).

Acts of communication in the Classical period ran the gamut from informal correspondences to more structured and elaborate lists of rules, laws, or contracts. Agreements between city-states or admonitions to citizens were carved with care into walls or tablets and meant to have a permanent presence and carry authority. When an inscription voiced the

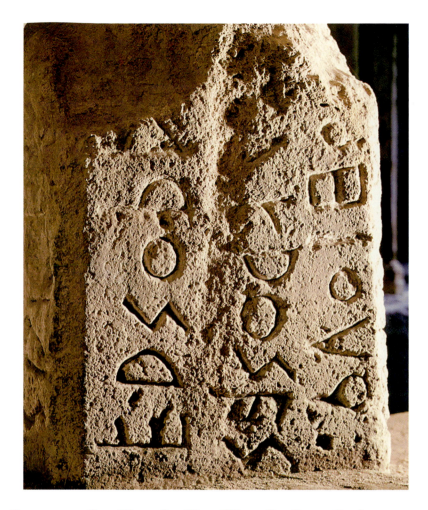

2.9 Lapis Niger, mid-sixth century BCE.
One of the oldest Latin inscriptions found in Rome is carved into a milestone. The text describes the correct way to observe rites at the altar next to which it was found. But curiously, the writing is on four sides and cannot be read in any systematic way or all at once from any angle. The text seems ceremonial, as if its significance depended more on its presence than on its ability to communicate. The inscription is a set of instructions relevant to the site, not a set of laws or general principles being communicated to a broad public by a ruler or conqueror. After the Romans conquered the Etruscans at Cumae in 281 BCE, vestiges of the earlier culture remained. Of their script's twenty-six letters, the Romans took twenty-one into their original alphabet and then added some of their own.

of written language from each other in the Classical period.

omnipotence of the state or ruler, a script's measured character reinforced the sense that its text was law. A text that was closely tied to an official site could aspire to enduring significance but might also draw meaning from its geographical or architectural position. Milestones are an interesting instance of writing that defines and derives value from its place in the landscape. These markers also provide evidence of the spread of political power and cultural influence along roads used for commercial and military purposes. A traveler did not need to read Latin to feel the symbolic impact of Roman authority embodied in such stones (Fig **2.9**).

Commemorative statements on funeral steles, tributes celebrating victory, and inscriptions marking other civic occasions took on considerable gravity when carved in the most elegant of majuscules. A variety of writing styles existed in Greek and Roman cultures, ranging from highly ordered Greek letters aligned with the regularity of soldiers in formation to Roman majuscules arranged in unbroken lines on a marble surface and carved large enough to be visible from across an open forum. Language at this scale claims public space, naming and marking it with a reference that places citizens in relation to the authority of the state. Scale

2.10 Rustic brushwork, before 79 CE. This **rustic** brushwork was found on a wall at Pompeii, an ancient Italian city that was buried in ash when Vesuvius erupted. This vigorous style of majuscule was used to advertise gladiatorial events, wares for sale, and upcoming elections. A combination of tabloid, billboard, and flyer, this sort of inscription communicates with great efficacy. Its messages are timely and ephemeral, and the swift execution of the script signals the freshness of the information. Latin rustic script provided models for writing on papyrus and inscriptions in marble, which preserved the energetic character of brush forms.

inscribes social hierarchy as well, distinguishing the relative importance of events and persons within a shared environment. More ephemeral forms of communication rarely formalized their script to so fine a degree (Fig. **2.10**).

Writing in the Classical period could have the power of a command or decree. Such acts of writing remained a feature of civic life throughout the Middle Ages and into the **Renaissance**. Read aloud, a posted notice by a ruling official could enact a law or prohibition. Vestiges of these acts remain today. Performative documents can prescribe behavior or set limits and terms of responsibility in contractual matters. Performative uses of writing depend upon an assumption of explicit authority. Someone is "speaking" to someone else according to a power vested in their person or office. Performativity can be materially enacted, as in the case of wax seals on vellum or parchment documents. The seal is a sign of security that performs a protective and evidential function. If it is broken, trust has been violated, even if the text inside remains unaltered. The ability to

As the social character of written language came to be inscribed

2.11 Rustic letters, 194 CE. Rustic letters carved in marble inscribe a military tribute to the Roman Emperor Septimius Severus. Such praise constitutes a performative use of language because it enacts the celebration of the emperor rather than simply describing it. This inscription demonstrates that models of letterforms, rather than just material constraints, govern graphic expression. Carving letters in stone with a chisel is a multiple-stage process and involves conceptual forethought and design decisions. Here, the first line is in formal majuscules and contains an address to the "Imperial Caesar." Next, the writing switches to the message. The decision to use one form of lettering to show respect and another to compress the substance of the tribute indicates that these choices carry meaning. Rustic majuscules and formal capitals are both brush-based in their design, and nothing about their shape is natural to the medium of stone carving. Rather, the *idea* of a letterform—a rustic majuscule—was at work in the series of decisions that led to execution of this carving.

show or record change is one of the ways in which the material context of a graphic text participates in its signification. Monumental claims for permanence are perhaps the most basic form of the material inscription of authority (Fig. **2.11**).

Graphic communication took shape in the Classical period in ways that directly connect to the present day. Basic design decisions about the way something looked as a function of what it communicated were everywhere apparent in the Classical world, and we still use the square majuscules of the Romans for commemorative inscriptions. No explicit manuals or rule books existed that set out the conditions for using one type of script or another, just as no such definitive typographic guide exists now. Rather, these conventions come to be understood and followed by consensus among a cultural community and the designers or scribes who work within its tacit codes. Roman scribes were employed by the state and divided into clearly defined professional classes. In general, their role was to compose or copy a written text or to transcribe speech. They even used shorthand (invented by Tiro, the slave of Cicero, to record his master's speeches in the Roman forum). Literary language and vernacular speech were distinct, and

formal composition was governed by strict rules. But writing tasks were further specialized according to the media they involved. Stone carvers had the task of designing appropriate styles for each inscription, and their work took distance, sight lines, and scale into account. Preliminary designs were often sketched by an **ordinator** who provided the outlines the carver would follow. Such specialization suggests a well-developed professional culture. Urban environments were particularly important sites for the management of communication and the formation of social values (Fig. **2.12**).

As the social character of written language came to be inscribed in its design, conventions were communicated and understood by example. If Classical readers could register the graphic difference between a formal script and an informal script, then the visual distinction could be given a value that was understood as part of its message. Graphic codes operated within a social context as well as a physical one. In the stratified,

in its design, conventions were communicated by example.

hierarchical societies of Greece and Rome, propertied and nonpropertied, patrician and plebian classes were delineated. This social organization found formal expression in the physical structure of urban space and the orders of architecture. Funeral monuments carved in stone marked the graves of persons of status. Literary works circulated in scrolls and tablets before books gained favor. Daily business exchanges depended on ink, on clay scraps or bits of papyrus, and on wax-covered or painted wood tablets. Writing was abundant, but scarce materials, such as precious metals, had intrinsic as well as symbolic value. All of these features of production, placement, and format were legible within a Classical society. The legacy of this design literacy is very much with us. It guides our reading and writing of visual forms, and our perception and use of their material contexts (Fig. **2.13**).

Models of writing: gestural and constructed
The use of models for lettering was essential to the development of a culture of literacy. Without them, shared signs and conventions for their use could not have become stable. Scribes relied upon models they could copy, as

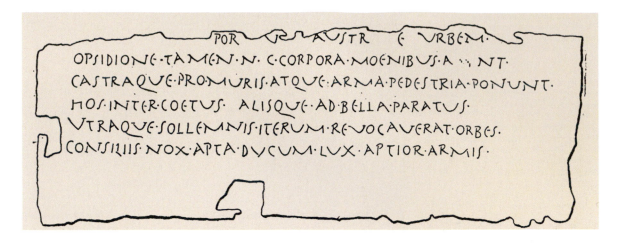

POR ... AVSTR ... E·VRBEM·
OPSIDIONE·TAMEN·N·C·CORPORA·MOENIBVS·A...NT·
CASTRAQVE·PRO·MVRIS·ATQVE·ARMA·PEDESTRIA·PONVNT·
HOS·INTER·COETVS·ALISQVE·AD·BELLA·PARATVS·
VTRAQVE·SOLLEMNIS·ITERVM·REVOCAVERAT·ORBES·
CONSILIIS·NOX·APTA·DVCVM·LVX·APTIOR·ARMIS·

CEPI·PRETIVM·G·ENARIO... G·V·CENTO... ITAVT... S·SEST

2.14 Cursive script, early CE (above). The cursive script on this papyrus from Herculaneum features swash tails and other traits that mimic the expansive lettering of more formal inscriptions. The rhythm of this text has the vitality and immediacy of handwriting, yet it attributes importance to this excerpt of Epicurean philosophy. Thus, the "great words" are given a quasi-monumental treatment, although they are rendered in an ephemeral material.

2.15 Roman cursive, 166 CE (below). By contrast, this cursive indicates far more gestural efficiency. One can almost see the movement of the scribe's hand over the papyrus surface, a swiftly running stream of strokes. Although the scribe obviously holds an "image" of the letters in mind, his practiced hand outstrips the considered construction associated with drawing or carving more elaborate letterforms.

they trained their hands to render shapes. Such knowledge quickly became somatic (bodily), and gestural patterns of production became habitual. Two fundamentally distinct approaches to the design of letters developed in the Classical period, and they may be defined as gestural, cursive forms and intellectually constructed forms (Fig. **2.14**).

Cursives are rapidly produced, handwritten versions of the alphabet that are gestural in nature. Often produced under time constraints or for ephemeral purposes, cursives are written immediately and reflect the mood and skill of their author. Although cursives are based on convention, they are executed in a series of physical movements that are as corporeal as dance steps. Cursive scripts were rarely used for any monumental or official documents, and their design often had the idiosyncratic quality of handwriting. The purpose of cursives was to produce texts that were legible and efficient, rather than to create aesthetic forms (Fig. **2.15**).

Constructed letters followed a more labored sequence of design stages and sought to achieve formal beauty through principles of proportion and harmony. Constructed letters could be made in any material, but, in monumental inscriptions, they had the effect of conferring gravity upon a text. Preparation for such designs involved laying out the inscription or document as a whole and paying careful attention to the form of each letter. Because its production involved multiple steps, a carved letterform might have its origins in the shapes made by a brush used to sketch it on a marble surface, even if the ultimate use of a chisel somewhat modified the design. Constructed letters may have been based on a system of proportion that was calculated as a division of a grid. But as they were carved their makers took liberties, softening the precise forms through the touch of the hand and a corrective eye. The grace and liveliness of the greatest of Classical letterforms belie any strict adherence to a mathematical design. Instead, they show the sophistication of designers who subtly transformed the idealized images of letters that served as their models (Figs. **2.16a** and **2.16b**).

SENATVSPOPVLVSQVER
IMPCAESARIDIVINERVA
TRAIANOAVGGERMDAC
MAXIMOTRIBPOTXVIIIM
ADDECLARANDVMQVANTA
MONSETLOCVSTAN...IBVS

2.16a Trajan's column, detail, 114 CE, and 2.16b Trajan's column. The formal capitals inscribed on the base of Trajan's column have long been considered the pinnacle of Roman letter design. Copied and studied by artists and designers over the centuries, the letters are remarkable for their combination of consistency and variety, as well as for the harmony of their nonmechanical proportions. These letters were not constructed by use of a compass or ruler, and yet their effect on the eye is one of profound order and geometrical regularity. These majuscules were based on designs first made with a flat brush. Their layout was the work of an ordinator, who may or may not have been the same person as the carver. The incised chisel work makes a deep V-shape in the stone's surface. By turning the chisel at the end of the stroke, a serif is appended. The differences between thick and thin strokes in the letters are vestiges of the brush stage of their design: thicker downstrokes and thinner upstrokes characterize calligraphy. These designs have been translated into carved forms with enormous care, and the constructed nature of the script through this multistage process never interferes with the confident reinterpretation of each letter as it is sensitively executed. The text commemorates Trajan's victories over the Dacians, and its monumental significance is strengthened by the treatment and scale of the letters. The power of the emperor and state of Rome become aligned with the grandeur of the script, which, not surprisingly, has served as a model for many nations in circumstances that call for an air of seriousness.

2.17 Inkwell from a tomb in Caere, showing an early Etruscan abecedary, late seventh century BCE. The earliest inscriptions in Latin were actually made by Etruscans, using letters very close to the Phoenician originals. This alphabet was inscribed on an inkwell, no doubt to keep models of the letters before the eyes of a scribe—a device as convenient as the letters on a modern keyboard. This early instance of Latin lettering displays the same gestural (or **ductal**) approach as was common in early Greek lettering. The models offer instructions for making the letters as a series of strokes rather than simply providing forms to copy or modify.

Whether constructed or cursive, letter designs are always based on internalized models and shaped by the training their designers receive. Samples of writing in the Classical age existed in public places, but, in the gymnasium, students were also given examples to copy. Only one visual model existed for each letter: the one we call the majuscule, or capital. The shape of the letterforms was basically the same in cursives and constructed forms, but the production methods and aesthetic goals were different. The development of the first variants of majuscules, known as **uncial** and **half-uncial** scripts, came later—in the third and fourth centuries CE—and were much more common in book formats than in monumental inscriptions. The development of these graphic variations of writing would signal a major cultural change as the Classical period came to an end (Fig. **2.17**).

2.18 Christian inscription, fourth century CE *(above).* The lettering on this inscription from a Christian catacomb has a distinctive aesthetic but lacks the formal control of monumental Roman scripts. A passionate energy is palpable, but this is not the work of a skilled designer or carver. Variation in the length of lines, fit of letters, and shape of individual characters indicates more ad hoc accommodation than forethought. Such qualities characterized the tombstones of Christians who were less educated and tended to exist outside the ruling class of Roman society—a fact that would have been communicated to contemporaries by the very look of this inscription.

2.19 Filocalus, fourth century CE *(above right).* This inscription was created by a known calligrapher, Filocalus, at San Calisto in Rome. He was a Christian whose hand and style were recognized, and these letterforms are attributed to him as his own invention. The overall quality of the script, its robust roundness and delicate, decoratively curled serifs, anticipate book hands. But such elaborate carving would soon diminish, as the Church replaced the Roman Empire as the major force in Western culture. This broad cultural shift was marked by changes not only in the form but also in the location of scripts. Books, not buildings, would provide the main site of writing in the next centuries. The sack of Rome coincided with the rise of the **codex**—the familiar bound form of the book—and thus marked a turning point from Classical to Medieval literacy, with all of the consequences for design that this transition entailed.

Writing at the end of the Classical age The sack of Rome in 410 CE by northern invaders marked the end of the Classical period. By then, the identification of Greek and Latin letterforms with the Eastern and Western branches of the Holy Roman Empire had begun to charge their use with a new political meaning. One form of the *A* was so strongly associated with the Eastern Church that its mere appearance seemed to flaunt a claim for the power of Byzantium. During the first centuries of the Common Era, Classical literacy became increasingly absorbed into Church institutions and practices. Early Christians had been marginal in Roman society, and their inscriptions demonstrated a lower level of literacy than those of the dominant culture. But the Church would soon change this situation dramatically. By the fourth century, monastic orders became the main institutions for the production and preservation of knowledge in Western culture (Fig. **2.18**).

Conclusion In Classical antiquity, writing was conspicuous in public spaces and was used for many personal and commercial purposes. Rome in the early centuries of the Common Era had a lively culture of graphic signage. But sites and contexts were about to change. The development of graphic conventions in the Medieval period had more to do with pages and inked script styles than monumental inscriptions. Direct lines of transmission connected Classical letterforms and visual codes with Medieval and modern usage. But scripts and the instruments of their circulation and use were soon to be altered by the cultural ascendancy of a recently arrived format: the bound book (Fig. **2.19**).

Classical Literacy 700 BCE–400 CE

800–700 BCE Eighteen-letter Phoenician alphabet introduced to Greece and Italy
776 BCE First Olympic Games
753 BCE Rome founded
750 BCE Homer composes *Odyssey*
700 BCE Marsiliana tablet's script with Phoenician roots in Etruscan lands
700–600 BCE Aramean alphabet consolidated in Syria
600 BCE Latin alphabet emerges from Greek root
Praeneste fibula's early Latin inscription, "Manius made me for Numasius"
586 BCE Temple in Jerusalem destroyed
544 BCE First public library founded in Athens
536 BCE Second Temple begun in Jerusalem
522 BCE Confucius edits sacred Chinese books
516 BCE Second Temple in Jerusalem finished
509 BCE Roman republic founded
508 BCE Beginning of Athenian democracy
478 BCE Esther becomes queen of Persia
474 BCE Etruscans conquered at Cumae
442 BCE Parthenon built
440 BCE Democritus proposes existence of the atom
431–404 BCE Peloponnesian War with Sparta
427–347 BCE Life of Plato, Greek philosopher
406 BCE Soldiers in Rome first paid
400 BCE Catapult invented
Mahabharata, Indian legends, composed
Panini's grammar of Sanskrit written
399 BCE Greek philosopher Socrates drinks hemlock
395–330 BCE Life of Praxiteles, Greek realist sculptor
384–322 BCE Life of Aristotle, Greek philospher
356 BCE Birth of Alexander the Great
332 BCE Alexander conquers Egypt; Hellenistic period begins in Greece
Egyptian demotic script used for Greek language (later makes Rosetta stone decipherable)
320–275 BCE Life of Euclid, Greek mathematician
312 BCE Aqua Appia, first Roman aqueduct; Via Appia, 350-mile-long road
300–280 BCE Money first coined in Rome
284 BCE Library at Alexandria founded, eventually contains over 500,000 volumes
273–232 BCE Asoka rules great Mauryan empire in India
270 BCE Mechanical water clocks in Rome
250 BCE Letter *G* made by "bearding" a *C*
Archimedes makes a mechanical globe
221 BCE Great Wall of China begun (eventually 1,200 miles long)
213 BCE Chin Tain Shihuangti, Emperor of China, orders all books destroyed
200 BCE Ox-powered irrigation
196 BCE Rosetta stone inscribed
174 BCE Paved streets in Rome
106 BCE Birth of Cicero, Roman orator
70 BCE Birth of Virgil, Roman poet
63 BCE Tiro, Cicero's slave, invents shorthand
51 BCE Cleopatra becomes Queen of Egypt
50 BCE Glass blowing with metal pipes in Rome
44 BCE Julius Caesar killed
27 BCE–14 CE Augustus Caesar and Golden Age of Rome
20 BCE Vitruvius's *On Architecture*

1 BCE Ovid's *Metamorphosis*

0 World population 25 million

Strabo's *Geography* composed

25 CE Claudius writes *How to Win at Dice*, first gambling theory text

32 CE John the Baptist beheaded

37 CE Christmas celebrated for first time

48 CE Census: 7 million citizens in Rome, more than 20 million in Empire

52–96 CE New Testament written

54–68 CE Nero, tyrannical and decadent emperor, rules Rome

61 CE Roman legions defeat Queen Boadicea in Britain

70 CE Jerusalem destroyed by Roman army, led by Titus

79 CE Eruption of Vesuvius destroys Pompeii

84 CE Britain recognized as an island after Romans circumnavigate

100–600 CE City of Teotihuacan flourishes in Mesoamerica

105 CE Paper originates in China

178 CE Christian missionaries in Britain

200s CE Parchment invented

Silk Route brings trade from China to Rome

300s CE *Codex Augusteus:* early appearance of bound book

First paragraphing and punctuation

320–650 CE Golden Age in India, Gupta Empire

324 CE Emperor Constantine unites Europe, declares himself Christian

387 CE Rome sacked by Gauls

400 CE Saint Jerome edits and translates Gospels

410 CE Rome sacked by Visigoths

Tools of the Trade

Powdered pigments

Ink from soot, gum, oil

Turpentine

Double blade ruling pens

Quill pens from feathers

Bronze pens imitating quills

Metal and bone styluses

Tied hair and frayed reed brushes

Sharpened reeds

Stencils

Pounces for blotting

Rulers

Straightedges

Protractors

Bronze calipers

Proportional dividers

Compasses

Chisels

Cross-bladed scissors (100 CE)

Stone

Lead

Chalk

Wood panels with painted surfaces

Wax tablets

Parchment from animal skins

Paper (China only)

Scrolls

Hinged tablets with leather thongs

Codex books (100–300 CE)

Candles

Oil lamps

Pottery lamps

3. Medieval Letterforms and Book Formats 400–1450

- In the Middle Ages, letterforms emerged that are still in use and whose designs contain information about their history and diffusion.

- The format of the codex book, along with many of its now familiar graphic features, developed as a result of changes in the uses of texts.

- These graphic features combined aesthetic and functional qualities, which served to distinguish different types of documents and to encode their cultural value.

- Illustrations and schematic images, such as maps, charts, and diagrams, began to be used to configure and disseminate certain kinds of knowledge, although power over intellectual life remained centered in the Church.

- Publishing became an industry, serving specialized needs in medicine, law, and theology, and a popular interest in literature, while drawing lines of exclusion and inclusion around literate communities.

3.1a Jean Miélot, monk working, 1456. Much can be gleaned from this image of a monk at work on a large manuscript page. The scene includes a scroll and what appears to be a box of bookmaking tools. The specialized desk, with its shelf for ink and paint pots, implies a highly developed craft. We also get a sense of the design of these books. The double-columned text of the open codex on the far right indicates a religious work, whereas the smaller volume open on the lectern to the left, with its single text block, would seem to be a secular text. The heavy bindings, with their leather fittings and worked designs, show the Medieval codex at a mature stage of development.

In the long period known in Europe as the Middle Ages, critical developments affected the means and scope of graphic design. These included the invention of the codex book's familiar features, the emergence of basic letterforms and styles, an increasing engagement with images as embodiments of knowledge, and the rise of a publishing industry that served a lay public as well as religious institutions. These developments of graphic media were linked to broad historical changes that resulted from the decline of the Roman Empire as a unifying force, the rise of the Catholic Church, and other rearrangements of the political and social landscape. Literacy was rare in the early part of this period, and the production of knowledge was wielded as an instrument of cultural and political power by the institutions that controlled it. Trade routes served as lines of exchange for graphic forms along with other goods and ideas—so did paths of invasion and migration. Increasing political stability fostered centers of business and learning in France, Italy, and, to some extent, Germany, Flanders, and southern England. By the thirteenth century, a **secular** culture, including literate guilds and professions, had emerged and with it, a publishing industry. Publication was done by hand, but works were produced in multiple copies, especially in university towns. The graphic features of these works embodied knowledge, shaping and structuring its communication. By the end of the Middle Ages, the form and function of many varieties of books, handwriting, and images had become conventionalized in intellectual, political, and religious spheres. The **ideology** of textual production became encoded in graphic forms that actively participated in the control and use of knowledge (Fig. **3.1a**).

Medieval culture and graphic communication One thousand years separate the decline of the Roman Empire and the invention of printing

3.1b Scribe's tools, twelfth century.
Hand-copying by Medieval monks played a crucial role in preserving the texts that became the core of Western knowledge. In the early Middle Ages, before the rise of universities and commerce fostered a broader publishing industry, monasteries were practically the sole producers of books. This German image from the early twelfth century shows scribes at work preparing animal skins for vellum, writing, correcting, and illuminating manuscripts.

in Western Europe. Although often referred to by the blanket term *Middle Ages,* this period was far from monolithic or homogeneous. In this respect, the many changes that occurred in graphic communication during these centuries are emblematic. A literate public had existed in the Classical

Medieval lettering was linked to specific geographical locations.

period, but, in the largely decentralized culture of the early Middle Ages, almost all formal education took place within religious orders. Control over **knowledge production** and dissemination was centered in the Church, and, at times, the tensions between science and the charge of heresy brought this power into sharp relief. The codex was developed in the third and fourth centuries and, by 400, had mostly replaced other formats. In the fifth through the eighth centuries, monasteries became the institutions most concerned with producing texts. The era of the codex book (made with vellum from animal skins) succeeded that of wall inscriptions, wood and wax tablets, and papyrus and vellum scrolls. The earlier public face of language took refuge in the contemplative and devotional occupations of the cloister, and literacy remained almost exclusively associated with religious training for several hundred years. When scholarly study joined prayer and contemplation as a use for codex volumes, books acquired chapter headers and other navigational devices. These features of page formatting remain an integral part of graphic templates (Fig. **3.1b**).

Alongside the continuing use of letterforms that had developed in antiquity, new styles and forms emerged. Had printing arrived at the end

Lines showing the alphabet in various medieval book hands, labeled I through IX.

3.2 Contrast of Medieval book hands.
This comparison of major letterforms in the Middle Ages, taken from William Mason's *A History of Writing*, implies an "evolution" of the minuscule. But the process by which scripts were modified was less straightforward. Monastic copying tended to be conservative. Monks worked from the examples they had at hand. Changes in scripts came through slow mutation, accidents, and the varied skill levels of individual copyists. A letterform may be thought of as a shape to be copied, as in the case of the Roman monumental capitals on line I. But it may also be conceived of as a series of more or less continuous hand movements—as in the rustic capitals of line III or the cursive letters of line VI—that swiftly and efficiently produce their forms. The uncial letters (lines IV and V) fall somewhere in between. They required careful attention to a model but were produced as a series of strokes rather than drawn and filled in. Constructed letterforms, such as the capitals of line I, were often based on ideal proportions. Sometimes they were drawn with a compass or straightedge, and, generally, they followed an intellectual scheme as to the shape a letter should take. Cursive letterforms (line VI) arose from the ductal—or stroke-based—gestures of a scribe and a tool's ability to register varying degrees of stress in a line. The familiarity and clarity of the letters in line VIII are all the more remarkable when one considers that they were made more than 1,000 years ago. The letters in line IX show the "breaking" of curved forms into several strokes and the effect of pen angles and stress on stroke weights. These scripts are variants on the same forms, adapted to specific needs in different locations and situations.

of the Classical period, without the graphic developments that took place in the Middle Ages, contemporary written communication would look very different. The letterforms of antiquity were limited to a few cursive styles, formal inscriptions, majuscules, and, later, uncials. These Roman letterforms provided models for new forms of handwriting. Medieval lettering was linked to specific geographical locations and institutional sites, the first of which were monasteries. The inventory of Medieval scripts is extensive, and each variation carries indications of the place and time of its origin. A local script might derive its style from a particular monastery, but it might also share traits with the scripts of monasteries in the vicinity, since monks learned to write from each other. By the eighth century, some local manuscript hands had become regional and were associated with the administration of kingdoms and territories, rather than simply practiced within monastery walls (Fig. **3.2**).

Graphic forms helped forge the complex cultural identities that emerged in the Middle Ages. European populations and settlements were still very much in flux between the fifth and eighth centuries. Germanic and Slavic tribes invaded from the North and East, along coastlines and over land, continually introducing changes and threats to stability. Modern European nations did not exist, although kingdoms and principalities with distinct identities arose from the remains of the Roman Empire. Between periods of relative calm, waves of Scandinavian and Arab invasion continued to change the European and Mediterranean world until the tenth century. The Church was the main cultural institution to survive in Europe throughout this period, and its doctrines set an agenda for scientific inquiry that aligned with religious belief. Between the ninth and eleventh centuries, knowledge of Greek declined in Western Europe, which was sparsely populated by contrast with the great cultural center of Constantinople. Arab scholarship made advances in the natural sciences and served to preserve texts from antiquity. These texts passed into European hands after the Crusades began in the eleventh century. Important works of Greek and Latin scholarship were recovered in Arabic translations, while decorative styles of **calligraphy** and imagery exerted their own influence. Patterns of cultural exchange can be traced in decoration and **illumination**, as well as in the content of texts and images. Illuminated manuscripts created

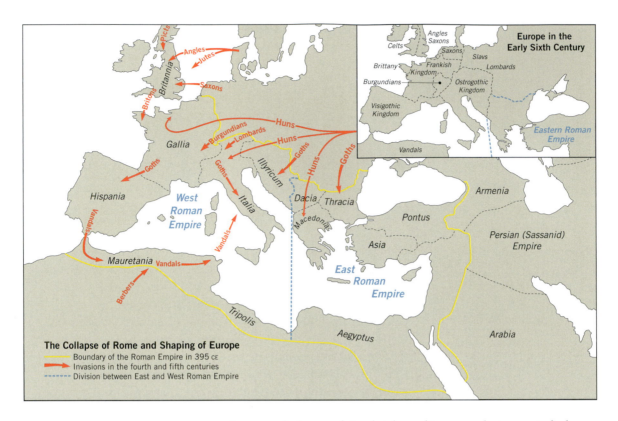

Inset map label: **Europe in the Early Sixth Century**

The Collapse of Rome and Shaping of Europe
— Boundary of the Roman Empire in 395 CE
→ Invasions in the fourth and fifth centuries
----- Division between East and West Roman Empire

3.3 Map of invasions. This map shows some of the invasions that successively changed the cultural composition of Europe. While some invaders came and went, taking and leaving what they pleased, others became part of the blend of peoples that gave rise to modern Europe. Jutes, Picts, Angles, and Saxons invaded the British Isles early in the Common Era. Goths and Visigoths invaded the lands of France, Spain, and Italy in the fifth through eighth centuries. The Slavic invasion of the Balkans in the sixth and seventh centuries contributed to the split between Eastern and Western Europe along linguistic (Greek v. Latin) and religious (Orthodoxy v. Catholicism) lines. Viking Danes invaded the British Isles and the western coasts of Europe in the eighth, ninth, and tenth centuries. Magyars and Turks invaded from Asia Minor. The Arab empire's expansion in the eighth and ninth centuries caused upheaval in Southern Europe. But the Arabs also brought aesthetic influences that can be discerned in the pictorial and decorative sensibilities of the later Middle Ages. Beginning late in the eleventh century, Christian Crusades to repel Islamic culture were another agent of exchange. Routes established by silk and spice traders brought contact with the Far East. The materials and visual forms of European graphic arts in the Middle Ages developed in the context of these cultural interchanges to which they also contributed.

and preserved a legacy of visual styles and **iconography** in a period when copying was a common practice. Illuminations often contained a great deal of incidental information about Medieval life, but images were also used to transmit technical knowledge pertaining to mathematics, astronomy, alchemy, botany, and other sciences whose value was practical as well as theoretical (Fig. **3.3**).

Graphic media and contexts Isolation and self-sufficiency were characteristics of European Medieval communities, particularly in the early centuries following the breakup of the Holy Roman Empire. Thus, the materials that went into Medieval manuscripts had to be produced on site, as did most other goods—such as cheese, wine, grain, and ale—that sustained daily life in the monastery. Parchment, or vellum, was made from animal skins. Ink was made with carbon from lampblack, oak gall, tannin, and gum. Red and blue pigments from animal, mineral, and plant sources were bound in egg tempera. Gold was first used in powder form and then in sheets (gold leaf). Papyrus fell out of favor by the seventh and eighth centuries since it was too brittle for use in the codex form. Parchment had the advantage of flexibility and could be made smooth for writing on both sides. A parchment shortage in the eighth century produced an abundance of **palimpsests**—manuscripts that were reused—with traces of earlier texts often still visible. Paper was a late arrival, produced in a few locations and distributed as the book trade began to increase. Invented in the first or second century in China, paper was in wide use by the ninth century. From China it spread to the Near East, Egypt, and Morocco. Paper technology

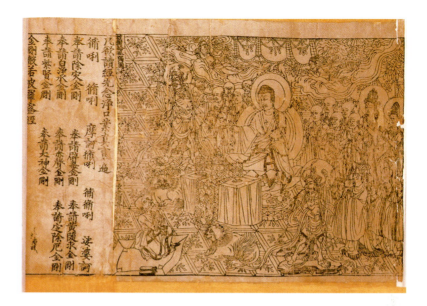

3.4 Diamond Sutra, 868. The Diamond Sutra, printed in China in 868, is considered the oldest extant printed book. The text is a favorite work of Buddhist scripture. The printing and graphic skills that produced it are highly sophisticated. The block is expertly carved, the weight and rhythm of its lines are nearly flawless, and the visual dialogue between text and image is harmonious. The scroll measures about 1 foot in height and about 16 feet in length and is printed entirely from blocks. The technical complexity of this work argues for considerable precedent in Chinese design for print. Although this particular object was not discovered until the twentieth century, Chinese **woodblocks** were carried east into Korea and Japan and west through the Arab world in the late Middle Ages. Charms, money, and playing cards were among the everyday items printed in Asia centuries before **letterpress** developed in Europe.

progressed in late Medieval culture when Arabs replaced the mulberry bark used in China with more readily available linen fiber, making sheets that were more affordable. Papermaking appeared in Spain by about 1150 and in Italy in the late thirteenth century, at Fabriano, a site still renowned for paper manufacture. Because of its association with Islamic culture, paper was shunned by the Church for its documents and sacred texts. Thus, the choice of materials for graphic production became culturally marked. Meanwhile, trade with the East opened European cultures to new commodities (spices, textiles, etc.) and new ideas that advanced science and technology, including printing (Fig. **3.4**).

Chinese woodblocks were carried west through the Arab world.

By the eighth century, the so-called barbarian invasions had mostly subsided, leaving every level of European social organization transformed. This new order had an impact on graphic activity. In the early Medieval period, very few civic monuments of the type that remain from classical and ancient history were erected, and thus public inscriptions diminished. Graphic media had been confined to the cloister and court and limited to manuscripts. Yet visual communication was essential to promoting the values of the Church, and it did take other forms. Beginning in the ninth century, an increase in the demand for churches led to the development of decorative architecture. Stained-glass windows and sculptural motifs began to catch up with the vivid imagery of illuminated manuscripts. Works of graphic art were housed in particular institutions. Scholars visited libraries and monasteries because books did not circulate. But writing and imagery served secular institutions and social purposes, too. In the eighth-century empire of Charlemagne, these graphic expressions contributed to a coherent representation of power, and, in the following centuries, emerging civic and trade organizations, such as courts, banks, and guilds, would depend on written records and documents. Although writing and literacy were

3.5a Bayeux Tapestry, 1066 *(above).*
As major Medieval artifacts, the Bayeux Tapestry and the Magna Carta (Fig. 3.5b) exemplify very different graphic strategies and impacts. The Bayeux Tapestry is a single work of embroidery, depicting the events of the Battle of Hastings and the victory of William the Conqueror over the British armies. Its text and images form a long frieze, parts of which are presumed missing. Narrative and celebratory, the work was made to commemorate a major military and political triumph and to communicate effectively using graphic means that clearly and simply tell a story. With few exceptions, extended examples of two-dimensional narratives had been rudimentary in ancient times. Medieval artists became adept at portraying dramatic action in a sequence of scenes —or within a single frame—to recount mythic and historical tales. Graphic literacy operated independently of texts.

A general, pragmatic literacy developed in the eleventh century.

3.5b Magna Carta, 1215 *(above right).*
The Magna Carta (Great Charter) was a political document that listed concessions made by King John of England to his nobles, many of whom were feeling overburdened by taxes to support the king's military campaigns. It was "published" in multiple manuscript copies that were distributed to bishops, sheriffs, and other officials to be displayed prominently. The symbolic effect of such a display was clearly important, since the detailed points outlined in the charter could not be read very easily. The force of this effect has carried across centuries: the Magna Carta is often cited as a successfully imposed limit on a king's power, whereas, in fact, it was a nuanced and complicated set of legal agreements. Its visual impact required knowledge of its content and significance. Conversely, the tightly written and much corrected text made publicly visible the material evidence of this significance.

restricted to a small, privileged segment of early Medieval society, a general, pragmatic literacy developed after the eleventh century. Written language became increasingly integrated into social and administrative functions in every area of cultural life (Figs. **3.5a** and **3.5b**).

The codex book Perhaps no graphic form was as important, or went through as many critical changes, in the Medieval period as the codex book. Its adoption and development coincide with the Middle Ages. Without it, church life would have been profoundly different, and the cultural legacy of antiquity would not have passed as it did to the present-day world. Medieval learning centered on a fairly stable group of texts. Religious works included gospels, bibles, psalms, liturgical instruments, and writings of the Church fathers. The corpus of classical works studied in the Middle Ages comprised a wide range of texts from history and philosophy to medicine, rhetoric, drama, and poetry. Novels did not exist, although dramatic and poetic works of the Classical age were kept in circulation. Reading in the early Medieval period mostly served contemplative or scholarly purposes. Religious study was central not only to Christian life,

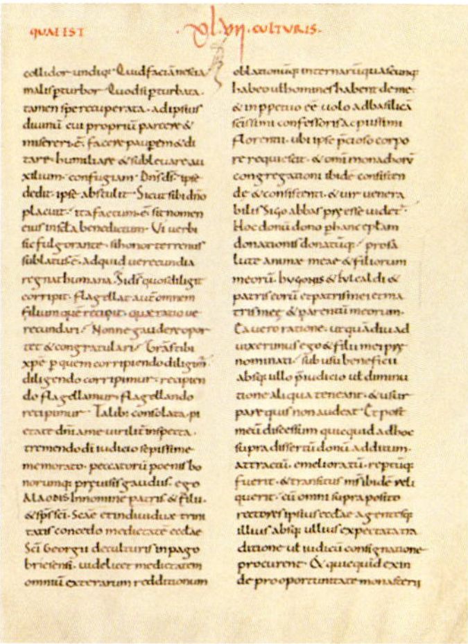

3.6a Book structure, thirteenth century.
Book forms emerged slowly, and, as they did, their features modeled attitudes and ideas about what a text *was*—how it produced meaning and structured use, not merely how it looked. The earliest page designs were simple with single, unbroken text blocks meant to be contemplated. Because reading was a devotional and even ritual act, not an intellectual exercise or a form of entertainment, the text was simply followed in a linear fashion from beginning to end. A double-columned page was generally adopted for larger format books.

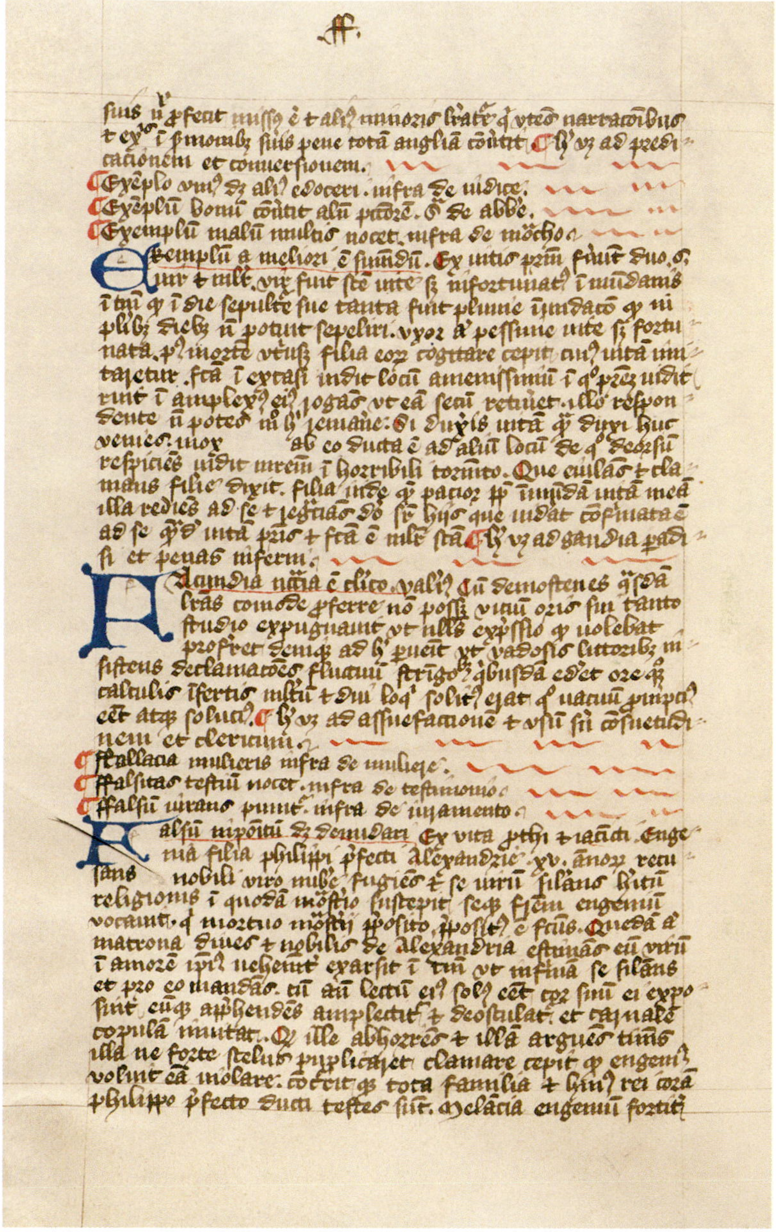

3.6b *Auctoritates*, fifteenth century.
Auctoritates, or collections of excerpts, were a common type of Medieval text. The practice known as **scholasticism** was brought about, in part, by a revival of the classical philosopher Aristotle. Translations of his works became available by way of Arabic scholars in the tenth and eleventh centuries and prompted lively debate and public dialogue that had not been part of monastic study. To be able to search a text for a salient passage and use it to support an argument, a scholar needed navigational aids built into the design of a book. One of the first such devices, seen here, was simply the alphabetic organization of excerpts according to their first word. Primitive as this may seem, it was an enormous advance. Such devices provided a conceptual map of a work, so that its contents could be used more effectively.

but also to Jewish and Islamic cultures. All three Abrahamic religions were text-based. Synagogues and mosques were centers of learning whose graphic conventions influenced book design and decoration in the Medieval period. The basic theological and scholarly practices of reading, interpreting, and commenting were accommodated and standardized in graphic form (Fig. **3.6a**).

As the technology of the codex (individual pages of uniform size, bound in sequence) replaced the scroll, graphic conventions for the layout and organization of books developed. The textual structure of manuscripts laid the formal and functional foundation for the conventions of later print culture. Knowledge was created and preserved as much by the graphic forms of these artifacts as by their texts (Fig. **3.6b**).

3.6c Book structure, late twelfth century.
Text and commentary spaces on this page are distinguished by a clear graphic hierarchy. **Marginalia** and textual **glosses** were often added in interlinear spaces by later scholars who offered their own arguments about the way a text should be read. Graphic distinctions organize our reading. We know in advance what the original and secondary texts are by their graphic qualities and placement. We take these conventions for granted, but when we consider the book as a dynamic instrument, rather than a static form, we realize what a dramatic conceptual leap took place in this period.

3.6d Decretals of Gregory IX, 1241.
Highly legible and clearly structured, this dense page reveals the extent to which books served as sites of communication and exchange. The original text, in the center, is surrounded by a gloss or interpretative commentary. Interwoven in the margins, along the edges, and, in some cases, between lines are other comments. Differences in ink and handwriting show that these were written at different times. The conversation recorded on this page takes place across time but in a single graphic space. Decretals were letters written by the Pope and bishops that stated Church laws. They were taught in Medieval universities, particularly in Bologna and Paris, and the commentary on these pages might have been added during lectures. The idea of a manuscript as a living document is clearly demonstrated here, as are the principles of graphic organization and hierarchy that make relationships between commentary, gloss, and text clear and functional.

Design changes were not brought about by technical innovation alone. New attitudes toward texts played a role. In the tenth and eleventh centuries, devotional reading, which was meditative and continuous, was replaced, in part, by scholastic study. Scholars had new requirements. They needed a way to navigate texts for reference purposes, and they wanted guideposts and an information structure that called effectively to the eye. Many classical texts had been written without word separations. Early bibles and religious volumes had not had chapters or verses but simply long passages of unbroken text. The architecture of the book was a Medieval invention. The introduction of paragraph breaks and chapter titles, running heads, **indices**, and tables of contents established the formats that would be standardized in print (Fig. **3.6c**).

Unlike the scroll, in which information must be accessed serially, the codex functions as a random access device. Page headers, indices, and chapter titles function as navigational aids. Some guiding features had yet

3.7a–k Medieval book hands
3.7a Rustic capitals, Virgil, sixth century.
The text of this sixth-century manuscript of the Latin poet Virgil is rendered in square capitals whose slightly curved strokes have a **rustic** flavor. Although each letter has its idiosyncrasies, the overall texture of the page is very even in tone, combining the best of lively and stable graphic effects. Note, however, that words are not separated, and, with the exception of the initial letter's fanciful pattern, this composition could as easily be a monumental inscription as a page of text. Conventions for page structure had yet to evolve.

to be invented in the Middle Ages. Page numbers did not appear until the printing industry created groupings of sheets that had to be assembled in proper order by binders. Title pages were unheard of, since they would have been a profligate use of precious vellum. Many Medieval manuscripts were not illuminated. Many had just a few opening pages of illumination and decoration, followed by simple, unadorned texts. Often a **colophon** at the end of a book recorded information about its scribe and the circumstances of its production. Our image of the Medieval manuscript has been distorted by magnificent exemplary works, but many Medieval sheets are crisscrossed with errors and commentary, and alongside finely made pages, inelegant and incongruous works fill the archives (Fig. **3.6d**).

Letterforms, manuscript hands, and pattern books

A number of the monasteries established in Europe beginning in the fourth

A script is a model of letterforms. A hand is the actual writing.

century would become renowned for their particular graphic styles. To a Medieval eye, the contrast among the styles of these scripts was as clearly legible as the cut of a costume or a manner of speech. But the significance of some of these distinctions might escape a contemporary viewer. For instance, certain kinds of **chancery**—an elaborately elongated handwriting used for official documents—were deliberately and arduously produced to make such documents less susceptible to forgery. Scripts in the British Isles had similarities that differentiated them from Continental **hands**. As in the Classical period, these formal distinctions resulted from a combination of available tools and attitudes about letterforms and their design. The inventiveness of individual scribes is evident in every manuscript, no matter how strict the desire to adhere to an ideal form. A *script* is a normative model of letterforms, and a *hand* is the actual writing that a scribe produces. Paradoxically, the *model* exists only through specific instantiations, even when these are pattern books meant for imitation. The fact that models of letter shapes persisted and have come down to us is all the more remarkable when one considers that every example is the work of an individual scribe, a *manuscript* (*scripta* ["written"]; *manu* ["by hand"]) (Figs. **3.7a–k**).

3.7i Gothic rotunda, page and detail, fourteenth century. An early fourteenth-century page written in a **rotunda** hand. Rotundas were derived from Carolingian minuscules, which formed the basis of many book scripts. As book hands proliferated, they became more distinct in form and more specialized in purpose. Although their proportions ranged somewhat from one region to another, rotundas tended to be broader and less angular than other scripts. The amount of variation in size, shape, pressure, and rhythm in this writing makes it unlikely that one person could have written it, even at different sittings. The elaborately **historiated** initial (a letter that contains a narrative illustration) sprouts vinelike forms that cover the entire page, weaving the many elements of the text into a whole. Variations in the script seem minor next to these motifs, and the **versals** (decorative initials that appear mainly on the outside edge of the left column) distract the eye from any unevenness in the text. Rotunda scripts were associated with religious texts that were customarily split into two columns. These scripts persisted, even as humanist book hands became popular for use in the longer lines of classical texts. (See Fig. 3.7k.)

3.7j Gothic script, late thirteenth century. The gothic book hand on this late thirteenth-century page is more open and legible than many earlier textura scripts whose pointed shapes echoed architectural forms of the era. The characteristic "breaking" of curves into angular forms required two or more combined strokes. In the early thirteenth century, gothic scripts had been more condensed (vertical) and made extensive use of ligatures or joined letters that were more efficient to write. In the fourteenth century the "hands" and "feet" of the letters, as well as the ascenders and descenders, became shorter, more robust. Used by the Catholic Church, gothic scripts carried a religious connotation that reflected the aspiration to move upward toward spiritual realms. German and English **blackletter** types preserved these forms in the era of printing.

Medieval Letterforms and Book Formats

3.7k Bastarda, fifteenth century. This early fifteenth-century page features an elegant and energetic **bastarda** script. The term *bastarda* means "lowborn" and was used to signal the script's association with scholars, rather than clerics. Used for legal documents and correspondence, these letterforms are closer at their source to Roman cursive hands than to capitals. They show the rhythm of the writer's gestures and can be written at greater speed and with fewer strokes than uncials. Monastic culture was conservative, but in the flourishing towns of the later Middle Ages, schools for writing and counting (the fundamental business skills), secular publishing, and other worldly pursuits fostered the use of scripts like this one. They served a prosperous population and an increasingly money-based, commercial economy that was superceding older feudal and barter-based models. Although such general changes were widespread, each location had its own regional culture of which variations in handwriting were indicative. Differences in the amount of tapering in the descenders and other such divergences are still used to identify the geographical source and period of individual examples.

For the most part, copying techniques relied on immediate examples. The relative isolation of monastic life reinforced the development of distinctive scripts and decorative approaches. In the later Middle Ages, pattern books for decorative letters, scripts, designs, and motifs provided models of exotic animals and intricate devices. Scribes, illuminators, and binders had their own networks for exchanging information, and letterforms followed routes established by trade, pilgrimages, and other travel. Patterns and shapes were copied and circulated as goods in their own right. Local scripts were formed and standardized in seclusion, but they were disseminated and adapted more widely as time went on. Although individual talent and skill were recognized, copying was the central feature of Medieval writing and art work. Originality was not prized as highly as virtuosity. Competent imitation and excellent execution of existing styles were valued. Still, human nature is idiosyncratic, and individual scribes often included self-portraits or traces of their own artistry in the illumination and decoration of manuscripts. The image of the Medieval monk creating elaborately decorated manuscripts as acts of devotion may be accurate, but scribes were human. In the final lines of their copying, monks often commented on the tediousness of their work, on their cramped hands, aching necks, or weary eyes (Figs. **3.8a–d**).

3.8a–d Decorative letters, pattern books.

3.8a Versals, England, ca. 1400. The term *versals* refers to letters that are based on uncial forms but made up of many intricately interwoven strokes. Variations of their decorative approach appear frequently in Medieval manuscripts. Pattern books that carried these designs helped diffuse their basic forms, which were then embellished according to the whim and talent of individual scribes.

3.8b Lindisfarne Gospels, ca. 700. This page from the Lindisfarne Gospels features the interlaced style typical of the decorative scripts of the British Isles. Lindisfarne was a monastery famous for its manuscript illumination, and this book is renowned for its elegant and elaborate opening pages. Word shapes and separations are far less important than the overall decorative effect. It would seem that this was not a page to be read, since legibility has been sacrificed to ornamentation. Every letter is treated individually, and a clear distinction is not always present between border and stroke or positive and negative space. Note the *A* with the forked crossbar. It reveals a Byzantine influence or allegiance with the Eastern branch of the Church. Such differences were often fraught with political implications.

3.8c Manuscript from the scriptorium of the monastery at Corbie, end of eighth century. Distinctive approaches to initial capitals demonstrate local styles. These compass-drawn Merovingian letters, interlaced with birds and fishes, are typical of the French style. The capitals that appear as illuminated letters in Merovingian manuscripts were often made with a compass and thus have a striking geometrical regularity that contrasts with elongated book hands. Merovingian scribes seem to have been particularly aware of the properties of the page as a surface and of design as a flat pattern. They recognized and took advantage of the two-dimensional character of the vellum sheet in their outlining and decorative work and often took liberties with the basic structure of letters. The Medieval concept of **horror vacui** ("fear of the void") was a design principle that carried theological connotations regarding the physical laws of the universe. In relation to page decoration, *horror vacui* describes the impulse to cover an entire surface, to fill graphic space.

3.8d Alphabet pattern book, twelfth century. This is a page from the earliest known example of an alphabet pattern book, produced in Tuscany in the mid-twelfth century. The dialogue between imitation and invention was crucial to design in this period. As designers might in any era, scribes constantly confronted the question of where to go for sources of inspiration or models for work. Pattern books were an early response to the need for a point of departure. Whether copied faithfully or modified, these patterns served to establish conventions in graphic forms. Motifs and treatments became standardized, as did imagery and approaches to decoration. Such was the influence of visual models on scribal culture.

3.9a Geometry text, 1266–1277. This exquisitely organized page presents graphic information about Euclidean geometry. Angles, shapes, and the length of sides and relative size of elements within a form are all visual qualities. The inclusion of sketched guidelines for the creation of geometrical figures demonstrates that they were not copied as shapes but created through a series of steps following mathematical principles. Such information is integral to the image and part of the knowledge that it communicates.

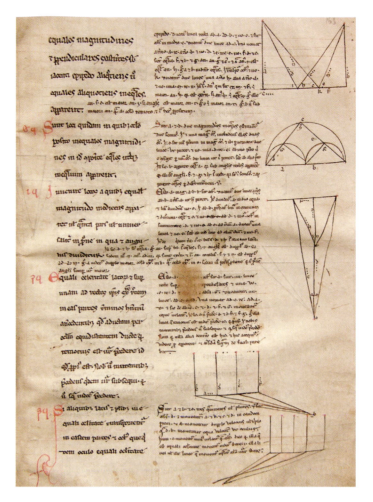

Graphic forms of knowledge

In addition to religious texts, many secular works were copied within monastery walls. European science did not advance much beyond the Classical legacy of the third and fourth centuries until the Renaissance. Most classical treatises were strictly textual, but some included images. Copying images required a different set of skills than the basic knowledge of the alphabet and book hands needed for text reproduction. Medieval scholars relied on graphic forms to depict the order of a world structured by divine plan. The concept of the heavens as a set of fixed spheres, for instance, derived from the work of the second-century Greek astronomer and mathematician Ptolemy. Cosmological systems were convincingly rendered by perfect geometrical forms. These images helped structure thought but were so powerful as models that they also limited advances in later centuries. The perfection of Ptolemy's system mapped neatly onto a Medieval mind-set in which the universe, including the earth-centered solar system, must embody symmetry and regularity. Astronomers who tried to reconcile observations of the heavens with such models faced serious obstacles, since their increasingly sophisticated calculations did not match these perfect diagrams. While graphic forms communicate information, they also provide intellectual parameters, according to which knowledge is shaped (Fig. **3.9a**).

3.9b Herbal, 1431. Herbals, used by monks for the selection and processing of plants as remedies, were among the most common illustrated books in the Middle Ages. The need to accurately identify plants pushed botanical illustration further than zoological imagery of the period. Although some animals, particularly familiar breeds, were well observed, bestiaries often contained fantastic creatures based on textual descriptions. Plants, such as those depicted here, were more easily drawn from observation of collected specimens. Note that the text is written in a humanist book hand. Such hands were associated with scholar scribes, who derived their forms from the Carolingian minuscule.

Knowledge was not only transmitted but also shaped graphically.

Medieval botany, astronomy, and geometry relied on knowledge that took visual as well as verbal form. Geometry depended heavily on diagrams for its proofs and its successful application to architecture and engineering. **Bestiaries** were useless without images, but their depictions of animals were sometimes fanciful inventions based on texts. As it had for thousands of years—and would for hundreds more—knowledge of plants and their uses formed the basis of medical practice. Being able to recognize plants and knowing how to prepare them in order to extract beneficial properties required visual recognition as well as verbal instruction. Astronomy and astrology were tightly linked fields in the Middle Ages, and the signs of the zodiac were recognizable graphic elements that carried powerful connotations wherever they appeared. These signs were a shorthand for a worldview in which Mercury, Mars, Venus, and other images stood for elements or forces within the universe. Knowledge production—the creation and consensual standardization of human thought—was facilitated in the Medieval period by graphic aids to specific areas of study (Fig. **3.9b**).

Illuminated manuscripts sometimes captured rich details of the habits and customs of the times. **Books of hours** recorded facts about agricultural

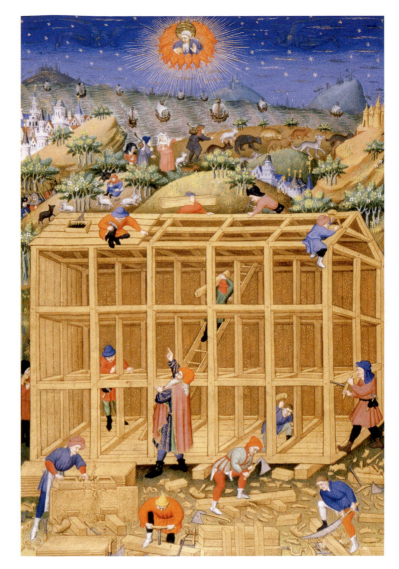

3.9c Book of hours, 1423. Illuminated books, including books of hours and calendars, continued to be produced well after the invention of printing. The imagery of these books was rich and detailed, and many were made for collectors. Here, we see the construction of Medieval architecture in various phases and can glean specific information about tools and building practices. Cutting, planing, drilling, shaving, and assembly are all shown in detail. Many books of hours included calendars and details of seasonal activities for each month of the year. These images have become informative documents of Medieval life.

life and methods as "incidental" graphic information. Works of geometry, astronomy, cartography, and botany contained knowledge that was graphic in a primary sense: Their images were essential to conveying information that would have been too vague in a verbal description. Advances in pharmacology, astronomy, medicine, and other fields came by way of Arab scholars who had preserved many classical texts in translation. Enlightened Muslim rulers in the eighth and ninth centuries promoted progress in the natural sciences, and Islamic libraries flourished. Maps, anatomical drawings, star charts, and botanical illustrations were essential to these fields, although copying often introduced distortions into visual information. Images and texts had distinct roles in the transmission of information, and together they formed the corpus of Medieval texts. Manuscript images were always hand drawn, and irregularities caused by artists of varying skill were an impediment to scientific knowledge that only the standardization brought by print technology in the fifteenth century could overcome (Fig. **3.9c**).

3.10a Hippocrates, thirteenth century.
This late thirteenth-century translation of an ancient Greek medical textbook is illustrated and annotated. Notations in various hands in the margins and between the lines indicate many users. This is an elaborate edition. Its detailed versals, illumination, and decoration would not have been typical of the more rapidly produced texts used by students. Like the work of another Greek, Galen, this text was copied and preserved in manuscript many times. Western science was hampered by a perceived conflict between the truth of logical reasoning and the truth of divine revelation, but Islamic scholars made advances based on observation that would contribute to the revival of science in the Renaissance.

3.10b *Lancelot*, page and detail, ca. 1300. This manuscript version of the legend of Lancelot dates to about 1300 and contains an illustration of the knight kissing Guinevere. The text is in French, and the writing is even and regular, suggesting that it is a book meant to be read. Works in the **vernacular** languages were popularized by repeated copying. This diffusion, in turn, lent credibility to French, English, German, and Italian as literary languages. Works like this romance often drew on long traditions of song or verse, and the legends they contained were much older than their publication, although publication certainly increased such legends' renown.

Publishing communities and graphic arts

The first universities were established in the late twelfth and thirteenth centuries. With them came a demand for copies of important works. Faculties were divided into four major areas: arts (divided into two categories inherited from antiquity: the **trivium** of grammar, rhetoric, and logic, and the **quadrivium** of arithmetic, geometry, music, and astronomy); law; medicine; and theology; and all of them depended on books. In addition to direct copying, scribes worked from dictation to produce multiple copies simultaneously, introducing spelling variations (and textual errors) that were copied in turn. Texts used by students in the universities were copied as efficiently (and inexpensively) as possible, spawning a veritable publishing industry. Unlike masterpieces of illumination that were created as devotional works, these books were made to be used by scholars interested in practical applications of the knowledge that they acquired. By the beginning of the thirteenth century, production by professional scribes had eclipsed the work of monks, and, in general, the beauty and quality of books had declined considerably. Paris was a major center of university publishing, but literacy rates were rising in many towns and cities among a nascent middle class supported by increased business and trade. Reading for entertainment also had a place in Medieval culture (Figs. **3.10a** and **3.10b**).

3.11 Ars Moriendi, after 1450. *Ars Moriendi (The Art of Dying)* is the title of this popular graphic book of religious instruction. Printed from woodblocks, it was issued in as many as twelve different editions. The book was a manual for dying well, with lessons on ways to resist temptation by demons in the final struggles of mortal life. Like the *Biblia Pauperum*, or paupers' Bible, this work communicated its moral and religious lessons so graphically that the accompanying text was almost redundant. Lives of saints, tales of the Apocalypse, and other works, whose striking pictorial qualities anticipate graphic novels of our times, were produced mainly in the Netherlands and Germany in the early fifteenth century. Related books continued to be produced well into the eighteenth century.

A readership interested in contemporary vernacular (English, Italian, French, and German) literature emerged in the twelfth and thirteenth centuries. The audience for books was growing more rapidly than production. Popular writers included Petrarch, who wrote love sonnets, and the masterful storyteller Boccaccio, whose *Decameron* is a cycle of stories told among a group distracting themselves while in exile from the perils of a plague. The "Hell," "Purgatory," and "Paradise" cantos of Dante's *Divine Comedy* articulated the Medieval worldview in a highly structured, hierarchical description that lent itself to illustration and reinterpretation for generations. Legendary works, such as *Beowulf*, the *Song of Roland*, and the Arthurian legends in Old English and Old French were widely circulated and frequently illuminated. The idea of courtly love became wildly popular in the late Medieval period. Together with other political and literary forms, its expression produced texts that were sometimes quite profane, witty, or irreverent. Alongside such literary developments, writing continued to serve many of the public functions that had become specialized in antiquity. In the daily life of the growing merchant class and burgeoning towns, commercial, official, useful, and recreational communications (as well as popular graphics) increased. Two languages were in use—one that served an expanding literate population and one that engaged nonliterate readers through visual imagery; each created a community of users (Fig. **3.11**).

3.12 Playing cards, 1470. Playing cards were among the earliest printed artifacts. Also known as sheet dice, they came from China and became so pervasive that they were outlawed among working people in a number of European towns in the fourteenth century. Playing cards invariably seemed to trigger the vice of gambling, and to the pious clerics and monarchs of the period their use flew in the face of religious teachings. The popularity of playing cards continued to grow despite injunctions. The suits and basic designs of the numbered and face cards have remained intact from the earliest times. Such objects broadened the base of visual literacy and created an audience and market for printed graphic works before the invention of **movable type**.

In the Medieval period, we can speak of knowledge production as an industry for the first time. Its participants were involved in organized networks of publication and dissemination. Some interests in these networks were merely financial. Other stakes were larger: Power and influence were established through the circulation of texts just as

Graphic forms were established that would be extended in print.

consequentially as by political or military victories. Communities formed around a shared intellectual reference-base were increasingly widespread. Dedicated to nourishing and preserving culture, Medieval scribes had a clear sense of the importance of their task. Odd as it may seem now, early Medieval monks and Jewish and Muslim scholars were already antiquarians. That is, they were aware that the classical heritage had to be kept alive through careful study and perpetuation. But a lay culture of scholarship developed as well. Interest in the analysis of texts broadened, and a desire for applied knowledge gained ground. Thus began a pursuit of the intellectual questions that would drive the Renaissance. Scribes knew that they were guardians of a future legacy and instruments of the cultural diffusion of knowledge. *We* are the beneficiaries of their labor. Through the combined energies of monks and scholars, sacred and secular works stretching back to antiquity have been transmitted to us. The graphic codes of these works are as vital a legacy as the texts that they embody. **Visual culture** was expanded by the unprecedented number of copied images that circulated in the late Middle Ages. Printing was on the horizon, and printing would start with images (Fig. **3.12**).

3.13 Saint Christopher woodblock, 1423. Printing first arrived in Europe from Asia in the form of reproduced images. This block print of Saint Christopher, dated 1423, is the earliest printed artifact we can date with certainty in Europe. The patterning of its landscape reveals an Asian influence. The treatment of the water, in particular, suggests a Chinese source, with its rhythmic lines, its boldly stylized waves, and its fish motif. The technology of woodblock printing had come from the Far East, so it is not surprising that treatments would as well. But the specific cultural origins of stylistic elements were often forgotten, as graphic designs absorbed decorative motifs in the broad mix of late Medieval visual forms. Woodblock printing most likely developed in Europe in the fourteenth century, although no early artifacts remain. The color wash on this print was added by hand at a later date.

Conclusion What is the legacy of the Medieval period to contemporary design? Its most important and enduring influence lies in the forms of letters—particularly text **faces**—and the contextual information about origins, historical change, and cultural exchange that they embody. These products of Medieval monasteries and courts laid the foundation for secular and commercial practices in private and public life. As scholarship increased, the form of the book developed. A radical design change occurred, as the serial (linear) access mode of the scroll shifted to the random access mode of the codex with its graphic navigational systems. Format features still integral to book design were invented, and visual knowledge was generated and sustained. The great legacy of classical and theological literature was preserved and studied, and conventions for illustration and graphic forms of information were established. The secularization of knowledge amid changing cultural conditions was marked by the emergence of publishing practices that were poised to flourish with the arrival of printing. The major contributions of Medieval design and learning would be extended through the technologies of the Renaissance. Texts and images would reach a broader public than ever in a standardized form that was an essential feature of their production (Fig. **3.13**).

Medieval Letterforms and Book Formats 400–1450

300s–700s **Early Middle Ages: Barbarian invasions and monastic culture established**

315–397 Life of Martin of Tours, founder of first monasteries in France

354–430 Life of Saint Augustine, author of *The City of God*

395 Roman Empire split into eastern and western halves

400s Patrick, a Romano-Briton, first taken to Ireland

400s–700s Gothic and Visigothic invasions of Europe

410 Rome sacked by Alaric I, king of Visigoths

460 Indian empire of Gupta defeats invading Huns

480–547 Life of Benedict, founder of Benedictine order in Italy

490 Saint Brigid founds Celldara monastery in Ireland

537 Hagia Sophia basilica completed in Constantinople

Purported death of legendary King Arthur

550s Silkworms smuggled out of China to Europe

570–632 Life of Mohammed, founding prophet of Islam

600 Pope Gregory codifies chant forms for church music

600s Koran written (always produced in calligraphy)

Islam spreads throughout Africa, southern Europe, Asia Minor

700s Irish monks bring their script forms to Europe

Beowulf probably composed

Shortage of vellum, end of papyrus production

711 Moors invade Iberian Peninsula in Spain

715 Lindisfarne Gospels produced in northern Britain

732 Charles Martel halts Arab invasion at Battle of Tours

768 Charlemagne crowned King of Franks

790–850 Vikings invade British Isles and France

800s–900s **High Middle Ages: Consolidation of national identities**

800 Book of Kells produced, probably at Iona monastery in Ireland

Charlemagne becomes Emperor of Holy Roman Empire

800s Paper money used in China

843 Carolingian Empire divided

846 Arabs sack Saint Peter's in Rome

850 Polyphonic musical forms introduced in Western Church

868 Diamond Sutra, first dated woodblock book, printed in China

878 King Alfred frees England from Danish attacks

900 Mayan Classical period ends

900–1130 Golden age of Anasazi pueblo culture in American Southwest

900s Paper made in Egypt

V and *U* become distinct letters

910–920 Rhazes, Persian doctor, identifies smallpox

982 Eric the Red travels from Iceland to Greenland

1000s–1300s **Late Middle Ages: Rise of cities and vernacular literature**

1000 Leif Ericson finds North America, calls it Vinland

Magnetic compass invented in China

1000s Troubadours' art of the love song flourishes in France

1040–1105 Rashi (Rabbi Solomon Ben Isaac) writes his Talmudic commentary

1050 Crossbow produced in France

1054 Eastern and Western Churches permanently split

1064 Pisa cathedral begun

1066 French prince William the Conqueror leads Norman invasion of England

1087 Domesday Book, a factual record of English life, is produced

1088 Bologna University founded

1095 Pope Urban II launches First Crusade to free Holy Land from Muslim rule

1100	Paper made in Morocco
1100s	*The Song of Roland* composed
	Translations of classical Greek works into Latin
	Classical philosophy discovered by way of Arab sources
1150	Paper made in Spain
1153	Notre Dame Cathedral begun
1180s	Horizontal axle windmills invented in northwestern Europe
1200s	Saint Francis inspires Franciscan order
	Guns invented in China
1202	Fibonacci introduces Arabic numerals to West
1204	Cambridge University founded
1211	Ghengis Khan and Mongols enter China
1215	Magna Carta guarantees fundamental civil liberties to English people
1221	Saint Dominic dies; Dominican order arises
1225–1274	Life of Thomas Aquinas, author of *Summa Theologica*
1231	Pope Gregory IX begins Papal Inquisition
1250–1350s	Mongols invade Russia, Hungary, Poland, Germany
1257	Sorbonne University founded in Paris
1260–94	Kublai Khan conquers China
1263	Balliol College founded in Oxford
1267	Roger Bacon's formula for gunpowder
1270	Paper made at Fabriano in Italy
1270s	Crusades diminish
1271–1292	Venetian explorer Marco Polo in China
1282	Early watermarks on paper
1284	Eyeglasses produced in Florence
1295	Modern glassmaking in Europe
1300	Magnetic compass in Europe and rudimentary cannons in Europe
1300s	Mapping, navigational tools, and ship design improve; explorations expand
	Hourglass invented
	Pilgrimage routes and destinations increase
1304–1374	Life of Petrarch, author of lyric love poetry
1308–1321	Dante writes *The Divine Comedy*
1312–1337	Mali Empire in Africa flourishes
1325	Aztecs establish Tenochtitlan on site of modern Mexico City
1328	Sawmills used in Europe
1343–1400	Life of Chaucer, author of *The Canterbury Tales*
1347	Bubonic plague brought by ship from China to Italy, kills 20 million
1348–1353	Boccaccio writes *The Decameron* (tales of diversion from plague)
1368	Charles V establishes National Library of France
	Mongol Empire falls; trade routes to East from Europe closed
1380s–1390s	Card playing outlawed in Nuremberg and Paris
1400s	*J* and *I* become distinct letters
1408	First modern bank in Genoa, Italy
1423	Saint Christopher woodblock, earliest surviving European print
1431	Joan of Arc martyred
1438	Inca Empire begins expansion
1450s	Portuguese explorers reach Cape Verde
	Machu Picchu constructed
1453	Constantinople falls to Turks

Tools of the Trade

Powdered pigments

Ink from iron salt, tannin, oak galls, gum

Egg tempera medium

Gold leaf and powder

Glue from protein, starch, sugar, gum

Garlic juice for priming glass or wood

Starch sizing

Quill pens

Horn ink containers

Brushes

Styluses

Gouges

Compass

Wood rulers

Stencils

Knife

Pen knife

Sharpening stones

Prickers for tracing

Vellum from calfskin

Paper (earlier in China)

Linen thread

Leather

Stained glass

Woodblock (earlier in China)

Pattern books

Camera obscura without lens (1000)

Magnifying glass (after 1250)

Candles

Oil lamps

Genesis

Incipit liber bresith quē nos genesim
dicim9. In principio creauit deus celū
et terram. Terra autem erat inanis et
vacua: et tenebre erāt sup facie abissi.
et sps dni ferebaf sup aquas. Dixitqz
deus. Fiat lux. Et facta e lux. Et vidit
deus lucem cp esset bona: z diuisit lucē
a tenebris. appellauitqz lucem diem z
tenebras nocte. Factūqz est vespe et
mane dies vnus. Dixit qz deus. Fiat
firmamentū in medio aquas: z diui
dat aquas ab aquis. Et fecit deus fir
mamentū: diuisitqz aquas que erāt
sub firmamento ab hys q erant sup
firmamentū. et factū e ita. Vocauitqz
deus firmamentū celū: z factū e vespe
et mane dies secud9. Dixit vero deus.
Congregēt aque que sub celo sūt in
locū vnū z appareat arida. Et factū e
ita. Et vocauit deus aridam terram:
congregacionesqz aquaz appellauit
maria. Et vidit deus cp esset bonū. et
ait. Germinet terra herbā virentem et
facientē semen: z lignū pomifez faciēs
fructū iuxta genus suū. cui9 semen in
semetipo sit sup terrā. Et factū e ita. Et
protulit terra herbā virente z faciente
semē iuxta genus suū: lignūqz faciēs
fructū z habes vnūqdqz sementē scdm
specie suā. Et vidit deus cp esset bonū:
et factū est vespe et mane dies tercius.
Dixitqz autē deus. Fiant luminaria
in firmameto celi: z diuidāt diem ac
nocte: z sint in signa z tpa et dies z
annos. ut luceāt in firmameto celi et
illuminēt terrā. Et factū e ita. Fecitqz
deus duo lumiaria magna: lumiare
maius ut pesset diei et lumiare min9
ut pesset nocti z stellas. z posuit eas in
firmameto celi ut lucerent sup terrā: et

pessent diei ac nocti. z diuiderent luce
ac tenebras. Et vidit de9 cp esset bonū:
et factū e vespe z mane dies quartus.
Dixit eciā de9. Producāt aque reptile
aīe viuentis z volatile super terrā.
sub firmameto celi. Creauitqz deus cete
grandia. et omnē aīam viuentē atqz
motabilē quā pduxerāt aque ī species
suas. z omne volatile scdm gen9 suū.
Et vidit deus cp esset bonū. benedixitqz
eis dicens. Crescite z mltiplicamini. z
replete aquas maris. auesqz mltipli
cent sup terrā. Et factū e vespe z mane
dies quitus. Dixit quoqz deus. Pro
ducat terra aīam viuente in genē suo.
iumenta z reptilia. z bestias terre scdm
species suas. Factūqz e ita. Et fecit de9
bestias terre iuxta species suas. iumen
ta z omne reptile terre ī genere suo. Et
vidit deus cp esset bonū. et ait. Facia
mus hoiem ad ymagine z similitudinē
nostrā. z presit piscibz maris. et vola
tilibz celi z bestijs vniuersqz terre. omiqz
reptili qd mouetur ī terra. Et creauit
deus hoiem ad ymaginē z similitudinē
suā. ad ymaginē dei creauit illū. ma
sculū z feminā creauit eos. Benedixit
qz illis deus. z ait. Crescite z mltiplica
mini z replete terrā. et sbicite eā. et dna
mini piscibz maris. et volatilibz celi.
et vniuersis animātibz que mouent
sup terrā. Dixitqz de9. Ecce dedi vobis
omne herbā afferentē semen sup terrā.
et vniūsa ligna que hūt in semetipis
sementē genis sui. ut sint vobis ī escā
z cunctis aīantibz terre. oniqz voluci
celi z vniuersis q mouetur in terra. z ī
quibz est anima viuēs. ut habeāt ad
vescendū. Et factū est ita. Viditqz deus
cuncta que fecerat. z erāt valde bona.

4. Renaissance Design: Standardization and Modularization in Print
1450–1660

- Graphic design in the Renaissance was formally and technically bound to the development of letterpress printing.

- Late Medieval letterforms, page formats, and layout conventions were standardized as they migrated to printed forms, and print had a similar effect on other disciplines, establishing norms of written composition, rhetoric, and visual representation.

- With the increasingly visible and powerful impact of print on all cultural areas came an equally expanded role for graphic design in shaping and circulating knowledge.

- The creation of multiple copies of printed texts and images produced a shared knowledge-base that supported a revival of classical learning and **humanistic** inquiry and fostered the development of science and exploration.

- The modularity of print technology exemplified modern production methods, bringing segmentation and specialization to processes that had been organically integrated in traditional crafts.

4.1 Gutenberg Bible, 1455. The famous forty-two-line Bible of 1455 is considered the first book printed with movable type. Attributed to Johannes Gutenberg, the book is a major achievement of Renaissance design and technology. The double-column format is a holdover from the manuscript tradition of religious texts. The letterforms also betray their debt to manuscript models. The emphatic initial strokes of the majuscules enhance legibility, giving the eye an easy way to find the beginning of sentences. Illuminated decorations were added by hand to the page. The printed edition is estimated to have been about 180 copies, an enormous number compared to the output of manuscript copyists.

The invention of the printing press and **movable type** had an enormous cultural impact. Print technology brought major changes to publishing and knowledge production in **Renaissance** Europe, including standardized letterforms, new writing styles and page designs, and a broad distribution of reproduced texts. The **humanistic** sensibility that characterized the Renaissance was intimately connected to the revival of classical learning and art. Print promoted this revival and stimulated inquiry through the diffusion of texts and images. As letterpress technology spread throughout Europe, it transformed design and production both conceptually and graphically. Printing techniques were based on modularization: the breakdown of complex processes into smaller units. This **modular** approach to production was critically distinct from traditional handicrafts and made letterpress a **prototype** for industrialization. For the first time, texts could be assembled and mass-produced, and images could be reproduced alongside them. To paraphrase William Ivins, historian of graphic art, the possibility of exactly repeated statements was a crucial breakthrough for any field that depended on visual information. These technological innovations placed graphic design squarely within political, religious, and economic life. The political climate was defined by powerful monarchs whose reigns extended to the control of what was in print. Protestants challenged the Catholic Church, using the medium of print as a tool of reform. Economic conditions were bolstered by trade, and geographical exploration benefited from improved maps. With the growth of global empires came the trade in African slaves; European wealth was built on often brutal exploitation of human and natural resources abroad. At the same time, major

Indulgences of the kind printed by Johannes Gutenberg were sold by representatives of the Catholic Church as remissions of sin. Gutenberg's design combined two sizes of metal type and somewhat more crudely cut **versals** in a composition that bore the hallmarks of commercial work: headlines, hierarchy, and visual variety. Note the name of Paulinus Chappe in the first line. He was an emissary of the king of Cyprus, sanctioned by the Pope to sell indulgences to generate funds to fight the Turks. He went to Mainz to have them printed, no doubt for the quantitative advantage that printing held over scribal production. The Protestant reformer Martin Luther objected to such practices, which he considered decadent and dishonest. He made the indulgences a target of his first attack against what he saw as a corrupt church.

methodological advances affected every scientific discipline, and religious institutions no longer had a monolithic grip on education or research. The cultural legacy of antiquity migrated from manuscripts to printed editions and provoked an era of unparalleled intellectual vibrancy. Patterns of readership changed dramatically. Exchanges of information had never been so rapid or so widespread, and graphic design played a major role in shaping ideas in the form of printed and circulated texts and images (Fig. **4.1**).

Early print design In the first fifty years after the development of printing in the 1450s, Renaissance printers adopted and transformed Medieval graphic conventions. But as print culture flourished, the variety and uses of printed materials opened possibilities for graphic design that had been inconceivable in the restricted economy of the Middle Ages. Renaissance Europeans referred to their culture as "modern," and many of the changes that this term implied were tied to printing and its capacities to produce and disseminate knowledge. The foundations of letterpress technology were well in place by the mid-fifteenth century. Wood presses for wine and oil had been used for centuries. Goldsmiths had designed **punches** for stamping letters. Gutenberg was not the only person who tried to develop a method of **typecasting**, but his name is associated with the first successful achievements in the field. The desire for books and the demand for more copies made the investment of energy and capital needed to advance the technology worthwhile (Fig. **4.2**).

Renaissance Design: Standardization and Modularization in Print

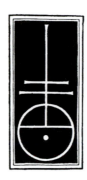

4.3a–c Printers' marks
4.3a Aldus Manutius, ca. 1500 *(left)*,
4.3b Nicolas Jenson, 1481 *(middle)*,
and 4.3c William Caxton, after 1477
(right). Printers' marks were a form of
branding. They expressed pride in graphic
work and staked a claim on a share of
the printing market. These marks were
used on title pages and in **colophons** to
identify a book's producer. As the industry
became more competitive in the decades
immediately following the invention of
printing, such marks served as a subtle
form of advertising. Some were allegorical:
Aldus Manutius's dolphin and anchor
combined the properties of swiftness and
security stated in his motto *Festina Lente*
("Make haste slowly"). Others had ancient
roots: The widely used orb and cross sign
derived from Egyptian iconography of the
heavens and the earth. Interlaced initials
or monograms were another popular
form of printers' marks, such as that of
English printer William Caxton. No matter
what their form, they demonstrate that
individual designer-printers had something
to gain from making their work identifiable
to current and prospective clients by easily
recognizable graphic signs.

Medieval letterforms and layout conventions served as the first models
for Renaissance typography and book design. From the 1450s until about
1500, type designs were adapted directly from existing manuscript hands.
Humanistic round hands, gothic letterforms, and tightly wrought scripts
that had been perfected by scribes were replicated in metal in the first
types. Similarly, the proportions of manuscript pages were carried over
as the foundation of harmonious compositions for print. These were the
only models available. It took time before the unique properties of print
fostered an aesthetic that took advantage of metal casting to express its
precision in fine lines, compact **fit**, and so on. But although the look of
type suggested continuity with manuscripts, a profound transformation,
nonetheless, accompanied the shift to print culture. Letterpress technology
was founded on principles of mechanical standardization that allowed
for interchangeable parts. Type production involved many steps: carving
punches, making **matrices**, and casting and cleaning letters. These were
arduous stages, but once the first two were set in place, the second two
could be repeated to produce a stream of metal characters that belonged to

It took time before the properties of print fostered an aesthetic.

a modular system. Unlike traditional craft production, in which an object
is made entirely by a single person from start to finish, this approach was
based on discrete tasks. This segmentation promoted specialization, and,
by the sixteenth century, each step of the production process depended
on different skills. These changes in production methods had far-reaching
effects on the way techniques and knowledge were envisioned and
transmitted. In the workshops of Renaissance printers, design involved a
conception of the rhetorical power of graphic form that was closer to our
own ideas about formal meaning than it was to the scribal practices of a
century earlier. Graphic design became an integral part of the printing
industry and a self-conscious art (Figs. **4.3a–c**).

In the latter half of the fifteenth century, European print technology
centered on two innovations: the invention of movable type (or, more
properly, the means of casting it) and the development of reliable methods
for reproducing images in substantial editions. (Obstacles to making exact
copies of visual works had been insurmountable prior to the invention of
print.) These new processes helped shape Renaissance culture. Printing
technology and artifacts were quickly and widely disseminated. The fifty

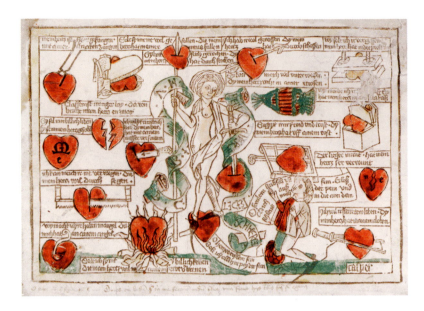

4.4 Casper of Regensburg, *My Heart Doth Smart*, 1485. Although only a small portion of what is referred to as *graphic incunabula*—that is, illustrated works printed before 1500—were not religious, these works were often richly satirical and humorous. This image shows a lover complaining to his lady about the plight of his suit. His tormented heart is depicted being sawn, hooked, roasted, pierced, stuck in a vise, and wounded in various ways—all of which are also glossed in poetic couplets. This is a comic piece, but other popular graphic works took a higher moral tone. Many conformed to religious attitudes and illustrated sacred themes. Yet the imaginative uses of print technology could not be confined to any particular purpose, and the entertainment value of graphic art gained an eager audience in Renaissance Europe.

years between the appearance of the first page printed from metal type in 1450 and the end of the century is known as the **incunabula** (infancy) period. In that period, 27,000–30,000 different editions were produced, totaling about 15–20 million books. In addition to the book business, printers found lucrative work in the production of popular prints. By the early sixteenth century, illustrated **broadsides** could be bought in Germany for the price of a dozen eggs or a couple of sausages. By virtue of this affordability, printed artifacts not only became widespread, but also they became the basis of new and persuasive modes of communication. Beyond the clergy and aristocracy, a general readership arose in the Renaissance

Print technology could not be confined to any particular use,

with interests in popular, historical, and travel literature, erotic and fantastic images, as well as religious and scientific texts. Any suggestion that the printing press was the sole or main cause of cultural transformation, or that technology directly determines paths of change, would be too simplistic, but print technology did participate in cultural transformations that were systemic and widespread in Europe during the Renaissance (Fig. **4.4**).

This new cultural sensibility favored a humanistic approach to artistic and intellectual endeavors—that is, one that placed human beings, rather than their gods, at the center of knowledge and understanding. Humanism emerged within the stratified societies of Renaissance Europe, as rural feudalism began to shift to principalities that sustained a new urban culture. Renaissance social hierarchy granted greater privileges to men than women. Unless they belonged to a religious order or were born into a family that gave them access to education, women were still largely excluded from intellectual activities; however, the values of rational thought, scientific inquiry, and secular culture were on the rise. With them came a desire for works in the vernacular on all kinds of topics. Religious institutions and theological politics were still central to European life in the fifteenth

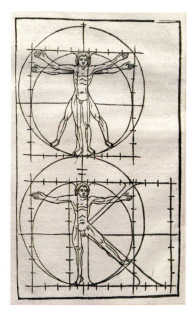

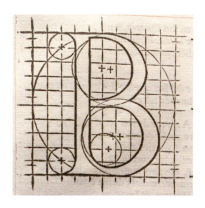

4.5a Geofroy Tory, *Champfleury*, 1529. Geofroy Tory's use of human proportions as a basis for letter design embodies the essence of Renaissance humanistic principles. In 1529, Tory published a graphic design thesis entitled *Champfleury*. The book combined mythical and rational approaches to the letters, as these examples indicate. In his system, the straight and curved forms of *I* and *O* were the essential formal products of a straightedge and compass, but they also carried masculine and feminine connotations. Among other things, Tory's three-volume work was a passionate defense of the French tongue, with instructions for spelling and pronunciation. Print was a great stabilizing force for language.

and sixteenth centuries. The Protestant Reformation that split the Roman Catholic Church was initiated by the distribution of a printed version of Martin Luther's protest of church practices first aired in Wittenberg, Germany, in 1517. But the Renaissance was also an era of secular pursuits that were cultivated to a high degree of sophistication. Religious and nonreligious works of Renaissance art remain unsurpassed in beauty and intelligence. Nowhere are the aesthetic achievements of the Renaissance more remarkable than in the realm of graphic design. Graphic artists brought many kinds of texts and images into being in the form of books,

and the entertainment value of graphic art gained an audience.

4.5b Geofroy Tory, *Champfleury*, initial letter, 1529. Tory's design for a constructed initial was based on the application of geometrical principles to the creation of ideal letterforms. Such approaches were not applied strictly mechanically in the Renaissance any more than they had been in antiquity. Adjustments that took the eye and hand into account belonged to the period's aesthetic. Although Tory's work was far from mechanistic, it did have a rational basis in principles of order and measure that could be extrapolated as rules for graphic design.

broadsides, public monuments, and maps. Figures from classical mythology and poetry appeared in paintings based on live models and studies of anatomy. Illustrated works of natural science substituted rational inquiry and observation for revelation as an intellectual method. Tensions between Church-sanctioned beliefs and scientific approaches continued to have extreme and often tragic consequences throughout the Renaissance, and, ultimately, the circulation of knowledge enabled by print made it impossible for the Catholic Church (or any government) to exercise complete control. By the end of the Renaissance period, European and **New World** thinkers would be poised for the era of Enlightenment, when reason became the central term and guiding concept (Figs. **4.5a** and **4.5b**).

Graphic communication in Renaissance culture By the
beginning of the fifteenth century, feudalism and other Medieval social structures were being displaced by a thriving market economy in Europe. Diplomacy, banking, and administrative systems developed rapidly. These conditions and institutions depended on graphic artifacts to record transactions and keep accounts. They also created new markets for printed

4.6 Herodotus, *Historia*, Johannes and Gregorius de Gregoriis, Venice, 1494.
The works of many Greek and Roman writers were revived in the Renaissance. The study of languages broadened, and scholarship of the past was enriched by new editions of ancient works. The illustrational motifs and decorative borders on this page feature satyrs and singers, urns, skulls, and garlands, but this frame might have been reused for any number of printing projects (a versatility made possible by the modularity of print). Herodotus is being crowned in the illustration that opens the book, and the initial *H* is clearly meant to be added: A lowercase place holder has been printed in the space left for its illumination. The type is a Venetian roman face, well spaced and carefully printed. The design of the page is exemplary of the humanistic approach to graphic arts in the Renaissance with its array of classical forms and mythological references.

Working parts in all sorts of machines became more precise.

books. Medieval guild structures were largely adopted by the new printing trade. Strict rules governed apprenticeship (five to ten years), which was followed by a similar period as a **journeyman**. These terms kept the printing trade exclusive. The price of entry was not only skill—demonstrated by production of a masterwork—but also the capital to set up shop. Many printers had rich patrons, but entrepreneurial spirit abounded. Publisher-printers (the two roles were largely combined in the period) were always eager to produce editions that could sell. At the same time, a striking characteristic of early printers was their outstanding erudition and commitment to the transmission of a cultural heritage. Classical works of art, architecture, and literature had been discovered among archaeological remains and inspired contemporary artists and poets. Preserving, re-editing, and publishing the legacy of antiquity was the task of printers who were often also scholars and designers (Fig. **4.6**).

Printed works spread applied knowledge in many fields. In engineering, for instance, the development of mechanical devices fostered the printing of diagrams. Improvements in the use of wind and water energy had increased the capacity for milling, and such information was eagerly sought.

4.7 Stradanus, *Nova Reperta*, printing press, 1580s. Artist Johannes Stradanus worked with the engravers of Philip Galle's Flemish publishing firm to produce a series of popular prints with the title *Nova Reperta*, or *New Discoveries*. In them, Stradanus inventoried the technological innovations that had contributed to the invention of modern life. Stradanus devoted entire plates to printing, arms production, eyeglasses, windmills, water mills, the compass, and the astrolabe, among other technical achievements. In this plate, the entire workings of a print shop are exposed. Apprentices work alongside **typesetters**, proofers, and press operators pulling prints from a wooden press. The youngest person in the shop was called the "printer's devil" (just one of many terms in a jargon as specialized as the trade that spawned it) because of the black ink on his hands. Although not shown here, women were frequently involved in tasks associated with printing, and print shops were often the inherited property of surviving widows or daughters.

Military weaponry, now assisted by gunpowder, had become more effective. Designs for building these weapons, and for improved fortifications to resist them, also took graphic form. Among the technological innovations of the period, those in the field of metallurgy were most relevant to the printing arts. Techniques for mining copper, silver, lead, and various forms of antimony improved. And the production of alloys for minting currency and other metalwork honed casting and handling skills that were applied to the manufacture of printing types and plates. Working parts in all sorts of machines and devices—including guns, watches, clothes, and scientific instruments—became more precise. Their production was based on the

Models for their construction were spread through print media.

same principles of modularity and standardization that were essential to letterpress technology. Models of their construction spread through print media. The knowledge industry was booming, and graphic designers gave form and style to disseminated texts that were commodities in a new market of literate consumers (Fig. **4.7**).

With the growth of European cities came cosmopolitan communities that challenged the exclusive right of the Catholic Church to intellectual enterprise and expertise. Universities continued to flourish, as did courtly life, and a taste for entertainment complemented the habits of study. In the visual arts, the invention of **perspective** in the fifteenth century radically changed techniques of composition and visual illusion. Oil paint added new dimensions of realism and luminosity to the canvas, but the **rationalization of space**—its depiction as a projection on a flat screen as seen from a single point of view—was a distinctly Renaissance development. The idea of drawing the world from an individual viewpoint was more than a technical innovation: it marked a shift in attitude. Perspective encoded rational conventions that brought the visual world into an ordered system. Meanwhile, private patronage grew among the nobility and merchant

4.8 Albrecht Dürer, *Draftsman Drawing a Reclining Nude*, 1538. The technique of perspective was outlined in a treatise by Leon Battista Alberti in 1435, about twenty years before letterpress printing was invented. This drawing method formalized a system of optical projection onto the picture plane. The result was a rationalized ordering of space that took the point of view of a single, unmoving eye as its point of origin. In Albrecht Dürer's image, the cliché of the male artist's gaze and the objectified female form, long taken for granted in Western art, is already inscribed in this system. The power relations that **monocular** perspective introduced into visual imagery coincided with the dawn of a subjective, humanistic viewpoint. Perspective became so naturalized within Western art and image-making that its artifices are almost imperceptible. But thinking of the visible world *as if* it were a projection onto a flat screen is only one way to encode experience into images. Maps and architectural plans and sections, for instance, are based on other conventions.

classes, and new subjects, such as the still life, the genre scene, and portraiture, gained popularity. Even pious individuals saw no impropriety in having their own image painted in recognition of their position or importance (Fig. **4.8**).

Print technology and type design
The capacity to reproduce texts and images in hundreds of consistent copies allowed ideas and information to circulate to an unprecedented degree. But the impact of print technology was not merely one of quantity. Print technology embodied and disseminated a model of standardization for content as well as production. The technical advancement of movable type was achieved by casting techniques that permitted individual pieces of type to be made squarely enough to be set and locked up together in a form. Johann Gutenberg is generally credited with the invention of letterpress printing. He was a metal worker who developed an adjustable mold to accommodate the difference between, for instance, an *i* and a *w* in a given **point size**. He may also have printed with type, and several documents produced in the early 1450s are attributed to him. Gutenberg's **typefaces** were based directly on existing manuscript styles, and though they were a remarkable technical achievement, they did not immediately advance letter or page design (Fig. **4.9**).

Printing spread from its origin in Germany into the Netherlands, Italy, France, Belgium, and England. Seeking new markets and clients for their skills, printers had established no less than sixty-five print shops in European cities by 1480. At first, printers were involved in all aspects of their trade. They cut letters on steel punches, made copper **matrices**, and cast their own type, as well as set and printed pages. Although the **point system** as we know it came later, the standardization of punctuation and spelling was a by-product of typographic conventions. Printing types may have assumed the familiar forms of local hands, but they also imposed greater regularity on these forms than could have been achieved by scribes. The model of a letter became embodied in metal. First, the letter was carved on a steel punch. Then, this punch was used to make a copper matrix, which, in turn, was used to cast the softer metal, lead. The hard steel punches and copper matrices could be used over and over again. By the mid-sixteenth century,

4.9 Type developed by Gutenberg, 1450s. The types made by Johannes Gutenberg for printing the forty-two-line Bible included several variants of most letterforms. Whether for practical purposes of fit, for variety of style, or because of technical limitations, close to three hundred different letters were cast by Gutenberg. Some scholars interpret the variants of letters as an attempt to preserve elements of handwriting. The imprecision of early casting technology might explain some of the variation, although accents and other alternative forms were clearly deliberate designs, not accidental effects. As in so many cases, the "new" printing technology was actually an ingenious combination and innovative use of existing elements, rather than a completely original invention.

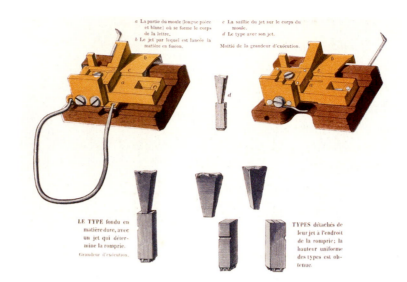

punch cutting, typecasting, and printing had become separate industries. Matrices could be ordered from the Netherlands and used to cast type in England or France. The sale of cast types lagged far behind the spread of printing, and the need to replace letters as they wore out meant that a foundry had to be close at hand (Fig. **4.10**).

The first breakthrough in type design came in the work of Aldus Manutius, a scholar and publisher who worked with the punch cutter Francesco Griffo. Under Manutius's direction, they created designs that took advantage of the physical properties of metal. In the 1490s, just fifty years after the invention of letterpress, the punches cut by Griffo produced faces that were no longer entirely indebted to manuscript models. Smaller,

Print technology embodied and disseminated standardization.

4.10 Type mold showing technology first used in the fifteenth century. The creation of metal (or movable) type relied on casting molds that could be set to accommodate varying letter widths while keeping the height standard. Letterpress type was made in a multistep process, beginning with hand carving the letter design onto a steel punch. The skill of **punch cutters** in making the letters of a font match and fit was remarkable. Most worked with only their naked eye and tested their work by blackening the end of the punch with a candle, then pressing the carbon onto a surface to see where fine adjustments were needed. By striking such punches into a softer metal (copper), a matrix was created into which an even softer metal with a lower melting point (lead) could be cast. Every letter had to be cast by hand, trimmed of its mold residue, filed, and examined for flaws before it could be used. For almost four hundred years, all type was made in this way. Not until the nineteenth century did any significant advancements take place in these technologies.

narrower, and more elegant than their predecessors, the Aldine types became widely known and imitated, as publications by Manutius's press circulated in Europe. The flowering of Venetian printing was followed by a golden age in French typography in the mid-sixteenth century, featuring the work of Robert Estienne, Simon de Colines, and others. Major French printing houses were established before censorship by the Catholic Church caused a number of printers to seek more tolerant publishing conditions in the Netherlands. The Dutch and Flemish printing industries thrived—thanks, in part, to the presence of the French printers. One of these was Christophe Plantin, a major force of innovation in type design and production techniques. By the late sixteenth century, Plantin's Antwerp printing house had twenty-two presses going nonstop, staffed by a small army of printers, typesetters, and other technicians. What are now known as **Old Style** faces prevailed throughout Europe and were exported to the Americas and other colonies. Meanwhile, in Germany, the tradition of **blackletter** types split into two main traditions: the rounder Schwabacher and the more pointed, often decorative Fraktur. Many faces designed by Renaissance typographers are still renowned and revered (Figs. **4.11a–f**).

luptatibus:suáq; ipe sentéti
est ut ostendimus:in cælu de
smortalitaté quę i cęlo ē. Et
pingui materia teneaĩ in qu
iustitia:qua teneĩ ad nitã. P
posuit in paradiso:idest inĩ
orientis omni genere ligni a
aleretur. Expersq; oĩm labo
ei certa mãdata quę si obserĩ
afficereĩ.Id auĩ preceptũ fuĩ
non gustaret.in qua posueĩ
inuidens opibus dei:oēs faĩ

4.11a Conrad Sweynheym and Arnold Pannartz, Subiaco, 1465. Germans Conrad Sweynheym and Arnold Pannartz were among the first printers. They settled near the monastery of Subiaco in Italy. Scribes there were known for their humanist hand, which the printers imitated in the types they designed. Considered the first "roman" faces, these typefaces were named for a proximity to the Italian city rather than for any relation to earlier classical letters.

reprehensa:& quo contra modo
    Multis & eruditis.
In hisce uerbis Ciceronis ex orat
sperant præsidio futuṛ:neq; mẽ
qui bonos uiolant libros:& futu
Ciceronis uerbo dictum : quod
aspera quædã de modulis nume
est.   Caput septimum.   In o
Historia in libris Phocionis phi
Demosthene rhetore.   Caput
Qui modus fuerit:quis ordo dif
imperatum obseruatúq; sit dicer
    Caput nonum.   Ordo.
Quibus uerbis cõpellauerit Pha
nimis:& prisce loquenté.   Cap

4.11b Nicolas Jenson, Aulus Gellius, *Noctium Atticarum,* **1472.** The typefaces of Nicolas Jenson are open, legible, and elegant. They grace the page with a combination of delicacy and robustness that is versatile enough to be used for a wide variety of texts. Derived from humanist minuscule hands (see Fig. 3.9b), Jenson's faces epitomize the Renaissance sensibility's engagement in a classically rooted but urbanely sophisticated aesthetic. They have inspired many imitations since their invention.

POLIPHILO QVIVI NARRA,CHE GLI PARVE AN
CORA DI DORMIRE,ET ALTRONDE IN SOMNO
RITROVARSE IN VNA CONVALLE,LA QVALE NEL
FINE ERA SERATA DE VNA MIRABILE CLAVSVRA
CVM VNA PORTENTOSA PYRAMIDE,DE ADMI·
RATIONE DIGNA,ET VNO EXCELSO OBELISCO DE
SOPRA.LA QVALE CVM DILIGENTIA ET PIACERE
SVBTILMENTE LA CONSIDEROE.

LA SPAVENTEVOLE SILVA,ET CONSTI-
pato Nemore euaso,& gli primi altri lochi per el dolce
somno che se hauea per le fesse & prosternate mébre dif-
fuso relicti,me ritrouai di nouo in uno piu delectabile
sito assai piu che el præcedente.Elquale non era de mon
ti horridi,& crepidinose rupe intorniato, ne falcato di
strumosi iugi. Ma compositamente de grate montagniole di non tro-
po altecia. Siluose di giouani quercioui, di roburi, fraxini & Carpi-
ni, & di frondosi Esculi, & Ilice, & di teneri Coryli,& di Alni,& di Ti-
lie,& di Opio, & de infructuosi Oleastri, dispositi secondo laspecto de
gli arboriferi Colli. Et giu al piano erano grate siluule di altri siluatici

4.11c Aldus Manutius, *Hypnerotomachia Poliphili,* **1499.** Aldus Manutius was a publisher and printer whose works are prized for their design. *Hypnerotomachia Poliphili,* Francesco Colonna's dreamlike narrative set among ruined fragments of classical sculpture, is considered one of the most beautifully conceived books of all time. In particular, it is praised for the harmony of its illustrations and type. Aldus was a smart businessman whose invention of the **octavo** volume helped establish a market for pocket books. Book sizes were named according to the fraction that they represented of a printed parent sheet. Thus, the pages of Manutius's octavo volumes were one-eighth the size of a standard sheet—or approximately the size of contemporary paperbacks.

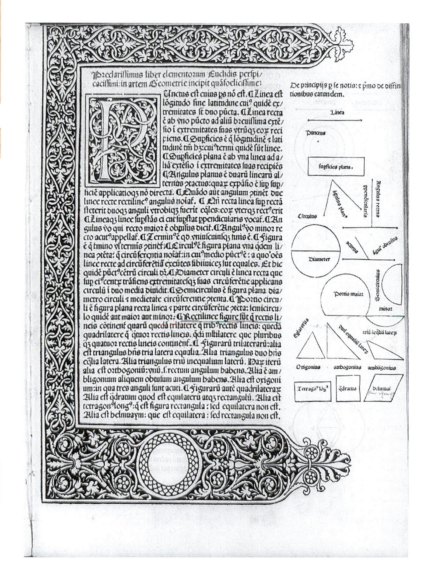

4.11d William Caxton, *The Recuyell of the Historyes of Troye*, page and detail, 1474. William Caxton learned the printing trade on the Continent but returned to England to set up shop. His types were robust interpretations of an English bastarda hand with tapered descenders and energetic shapes. The curved-back strokes of many majuscules (such as *E* and *T*) derived from much older uncial forms. Caxton's successor was his wonderfully named assistant Wynken de Worde. The English printer's designs are deemed less elegant than those of his contemporaries in Italy and Germany. His efforts brought Chaucer's *Canterbury Tales* and Thomas Mallory's legends of King Arthur into print, along with most of the other major works of English literature then extant. This distinctive typeface served as the graphic equivalent of a vernacular tongue, distinguishing English from other languages by its appearance.

4.11e Schwabacher, 1490s. German type designers continued to invent variations of two traditional forms: Schwabacher and Fraktur. Germany maintained the use of blackletter types longer than other European countries. As a consequence, blackletter came to be associated with Germany. To this day, these faces have an air of medievalism, although their designs by Renaissance punch cutters were sophisticated and depended as much on letterpress technology as did those of their contemporaries.

4.11f Erhard Ratdolt, *Euclid*, 1482. Erhard Ratdolt's publication of *Euclid* contains initial letters and borders that are used and reused throughout the book. The figures are elegantly constructed from what appear to be lines of cast rule, rather than carved wood. The graphic sensibility that informs these borders and initials makes aesthetic use of relief printing, skillfully exploiting its ability to create intricate black-and-white patterns in a single print **run**. A book whose layout is as organized as its contents, this work expresses the combination of aesthetic and rational values that linked Renaissance thinkers with classical culture. Geometrical principles became the foundation of architectural design and the basis for harmonious proportions in page layout, painting, and sculpture. Whereas Medieval scribes reveled in the capacity of a page's surface to support decorative arrangements, Renaissance designers related elements on the page according to a system governed by principles of order.

The idea of modularity that gave rise to letterpress technology also influenced graphic design. Modularity required that letters fit together physically and visually in various combinations. This requirement of *fit* constrained the relation of the letter to the body of type. Overlapping tails or **swashes** were delicate, and variants added cost and time to production. More generally, the basic structure of letterpress printing reinforced the concept of interchangeable visual units. Like letters, ornaments and

Images were often treated as generic, reusable representations.

decorative initials comprised a system of elements that could be used and reused, set in one line, then broken down and recombined in another. Images were often treated as generic representations of types of things— criminals, virgins, monsters—that could also be recycled without any diminishment of value or effect. Modularity reinforced the advantages of mechanical production, placing it at odds with the values of craft-based production. Efficiency was bought at the price of attention to each copy or even to details of letterform and layout, since the structure of type forms was rigid. Line lengths were set in metal, and flexibility was limited to variations in spacing and leading. No equivalent to the compression of letters in handwriting existed in print. The variations of individual, handmade objects became a technical liability in an industry that required standard sizes and regular shapes to function. Renaissance printing technology made a substantial contribution to establishing principles that were crucial to later industrialization. Although the technology of letterpress changed very slowly, the printing industry grew to support many specialized subindustries and skills, such as typographic composition, ornamentation, engraving, binding, and papermaking (Figs. **4.12a–c**).

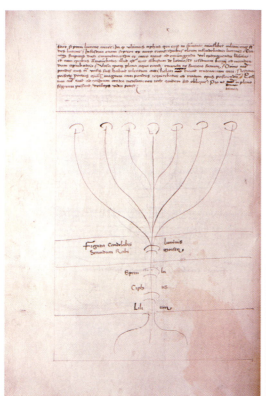

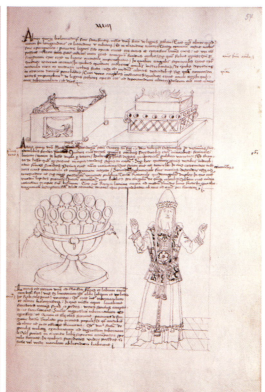

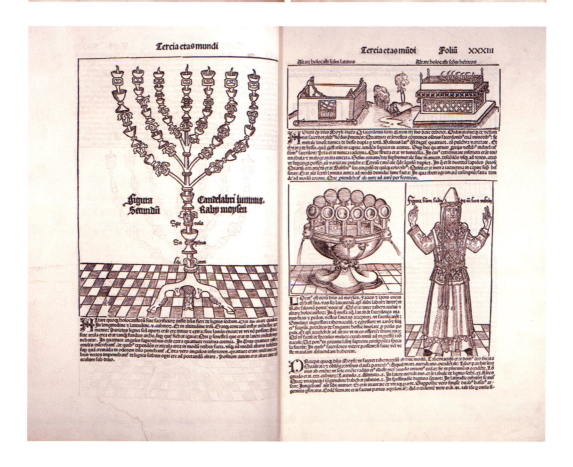

4.13 Pierre Metlinger, *Arbolayre*, 1487.
In the Renaissance, botany remained as important as it had been in the Middle Ages. The difference was that printing had arrived to assist the spread of its findings. Plants had to be accurately recognized if herbals were to function as guides to the practice of medicine. Images were not decorative but crucial to this and other disciplines. Plant knowledge was the basis of medical remedies until the advent of modern chemistry and the production of synthetic compounds. The ability to distinguish one plant from another could be a life-and-death issue. The blocks used in the printing of this herbal were used in a number of other books that treated the same topics. This particular volume went into more than two dozen editions.

The first medium for making copies of images was the woodcut.

Graphic forms of knowledge The idea of standardization affected the content of texts and images as well as their production. Knowledge that could not be conveyed in language became standardized through the publication of images, extending a dependence on visual information that had been integral to Medieval sciences, such as botany. The repeatability of printed images was critical to establishing a consensual knowledge-base in many fields. The first medium for making multiple copies of images was the **woodcut**. It was a relief form that could be printed side by side with typographic texts. In a **relief print**, negative spaces are carved away from the block, and what remains is inked and printed. Thus, fine lines require tedious labor and significant skill. The art of creating tonal values through line patterns became part of the graphic vocabulary of Renaissance art (Fig. **4.13**).

Copperplate engraving permitted finer and more intricate drawings to be reproduced with accuracy. In **intaglio** printing the plate surface is wiped clean, leaving ink in the engraved lines. The lines that are carved are the ones that print, so the effect is closer to drawing. In the letterpress era, the disadvantage of intaglio engravings was that they had to be printed

4.14 Albrecht Dürer, *The Four Horsemen of the Apocalypse*, 1498. Albrecht Dürer's immensely popular woodcuts were printed on broadsheets, collected into suites, and published as illustrations in books. His ability to achieve spatial and lighting effects through tonal variation and to organize complicated groupings into legible forms demonstrate tremendous graphic skill. His work gains its force from a combination of this technical virtuosity and the emotional and spiritual energy of its imagery. This depiction impressed the popular imagination with indelible figures of the biblical Apocalypse.

separately from type. As visual imagery achieved cultural currency, artists' skill levels increased, and sophisticated tonal methods for achieving spatial effects of volume and atmosphere developed. Albrecht Dürer's sixteenth-century scenes of the Apocalypse and Revelation take full advantage of the specific technical capacities of woodcuts. Dürer is renowned for his line work that produced tonal differences through density. Another technique for varying tonal value in woodblocks was invented in his lifetime: *chiaroscuro* printing used multiple blocks to lay down areas of variable shades upon which a final line block was printed. **Etching** methods were also developed in this period. Acid, rather than a cutting tool, carved the lines and shapes of an etching. It was discovered that by "stopping out," or covering, areas of the plate between acid baths, subtle effects of light and darkness could be achieved. Major artists, such as Rembrandt van Rijn and Peter Paul Rubens, created prints that contributed to their fortunes and celebrity but also displayed the excellence of print technologies. The capacity of these technologies to transmit not only beautiful but also accurate images of plants, landscapes, beasts, bodies, inventions, routes, and other objects of study brought visual communication into a new position of cultural prominence (Fig. **4.14**).

Graphic images also found uses and audiences in popular culture. Although textual literacy was growing, visual literacy was more accessible and widespread. Broadsides served to entertain and instruct and to foment subversive activity. Popular prints were circulated in sixteenth-century

Beliefs were formed by exposure to graphic representations.

4.15a Broadside, 1521. This German broadside satirized the Pope and other enemies of Martin Luther by giving them animal faces with less than positive attributes. Such imagery became standard fare, and these public caricatures came to be as recognizable as the names of the people they portrayed. For an image to have a shared and understood value, visual conventions must be fixed in graphic form.

Germany and Holland as a way of shaping political opinion and fanning the flames of controversy. Anti-Catholic sentiments were promoted by images that mocked the Pope and his representatives within the church. Images of class identity, such as depictions of the rural peasant as crude, bloated, and ignorant—or innocent and natural—became agents of ideology. Images generated stereotypes as much as they reflected them. Beliefs were formed by exposure to graphic representations of public figures and clichés in early forms of tabloid **broadsheets** that interpreted current events with inflated rhetoric meant to provoke inquiring Renaissance minds (Figs. **4.15a** and **4.15b**).

The Renaissance fascination with antiquity inspired an interest in hieroglyphics and a belief that images could communicate more directly than writing. **Emblem** books and **allegorical** prints used imaginative visual devices to engage a broad public. Many of these books contained moral messages and Christian teachings, but suggestive, humorous, irreverent, and erotic images and tales were also issued in multiple editions. Superb examples of these genres were produced in the sixteenth and seventeenth centuries (Fig. **4.15c**).

While illustrated books flourished in technical fields, improved
cartographic techniques fostered consequential changes in mapmaking.
European monarchs sponsored global exploration that led to far-flung
colonization of the Americas, Africa, and Asia. Conceptions of the world,
and of Europe's place within it, were reflected in the visual structure of
maps. The Medieval Christian vision of a flat earth with Jerusalem at its
center gave way to more modern geographical models. The Ptolemaic
worldview was revived from antiquity as a mathematical and rational
approach to mapping space. Ptolemy's *Cosmographia* was published in
the 1470s. His system of dividing the globe into evenly sized sections to
chart coordinates was based on geometry and uniform approaches to
measurement that were essential to exploration (Figs. **4.16a** and **4.16b**).

4.16a Isidorean T-O Map, 1472 *(above)*. The *T* and *O* map formula presented a Christian image of the world. In this image, the perfection of God's creation was reflected in the bounded form of a circle. A crosslike form divided this world among the sons of Noah. Although only crudely related to geography, such maps were the visualization of a worldview that bridged Medieval and early Renaissance sensibilities at a time when empirical observation was only beginning to challenge received wisdom. In many T-O map designs, the geometrical center of the circle is Jerusalem, and the continents are surrounded entirely by water.

The mathematical complexities of projecting the round shape of the Earth onto the flat surface of a map were given a new solution by the Dutch mathematician Gerard Mercator. Distortion proved useful in the design of navigation maps that showed nautical distances in a single scale. Many graphic conventions carried ideological values, such as those that inscribed Europe as the center of the known world. An iconography of

Many graphic conventions carried ideological values, such as

4.16b Ptolemaic map, 1482 *(above right)*. Although the writings of Hellenistic geographer Ptolemy synthesized existing knowledge of the world, his account did not include maps. When his ideas were discovered in the Renaissance, they were visually interpreted with remarkable accuracy. The geographical reach of these ideas included Europe, North Africa, the Middle East, India, and Asia. The Ptolemaic model dominated mapmaking until the early sixteenth century.

mythical monsters and unknown territories at the edges of knowledge made European culture appear superior and advanced by contrast. With exploration came exploitation. The wealth of Europe was bolstered by trade as well as by the crimes of slavery and the wholesale destruction of New World indigenous populations. The Portuguese slave trade shifted enormous numbers of African people into the Atlantic region of the Americas as forced labor in the cultivation of sugar cane and other crops. This labor contributed to increased trade and the rise of a wealthy merchant class. The production of exotic images of newly encountered civilizations contributed to the processes of cultural identity-formation, through which Europe normalized itself by declaring the rest of the world its "other." Colonial expansion took European values into new territories with an unquestioned assumption of their superiority. Printed images played an important part in the creation and spread of these ideas. At the same time, encounters with unknown animals and unfamiliar customs were often so disorienting that they could not be assimilated with any accuracy. The portrayal of novel environments often combined observation with mythology (Fig. **4.17**).

Renaissance Design: Standardization and Modularization in Print

4.17 Henricus Hondius, world map, 1630. In the early sixteenth century, global exploration began to revise the image of the world presented by maps. By then, methods for calculating the projection of the globe's complex shapes onto a flat surface with minimum distortion had been developed—most notably by Gerhard Mercator. As a mathematician, geographer, publisher, engraver, and calligrapher, Mercator had a unique combination of skills. His maps transformed the European understanding of the world. Geographical knowledge grew enormously during the sixteenth and seventeenth centuries, and the Dutch cartography industry became renowned. Improved engraving methods were essential to these advances, as were designers and artists trained to work with mathematical rigor.

Graphic representations advanced the natural sciences in concert with technological developments. Improvements in lens grinding and other **optical** inventions extended the reach of the human eye. The invention of the microscope, telescope, and reading glasses sharpened and broadened the visual realm. The work of Copernicus in the sixteenth century and Galileo in the seventeenth century introduced a revolutionary model of the universe and of the place of the Earth within it. Medieval cosmic hierarchies

those that inscribed Europe as the center of the known world.

4.18 Nicholaus Copernicus, *On the Revolutions of the Heavenly Spheres*, detail, 1543. The Renaissance intellectual revolution is exemplified by the works of Galileo and Copernicus. Although Copernicus's construction of a perfectly spherical and hierarchical universe drew on the work of the Greek mathematician Ptolemy, it was different in at least one major respect: It placed the sun, not the Earth, at the center. This move was so radical that it was deemed a heresy by the Catholic Church. Despite his efforts to forestall critics by introducing his theories as speculations, Copernicus saw his books banned and discredited. The publishing history of *On the Revolutions of the Heavenly Spheres* is a case study in the repression of scientific knowledge.

had been overturned, although controversies about modern astronomy were intense and persistent. The design of the universe, like the design of books about the heavens and the earth, began to embody notions of reason and order. Modern science was grounded in inquiry and the establishment of principles of observation and repeatability. But ideas that were deemed knowledge in one quarter were considered heresy in another. Instructions calling for the replacement of paragraphs or phrases were issued by the Catholic Church, and slips were printed to be pasted over the offending portions of scientific texts. Copernicus's book (1543) on the movements of the heavenly spheres contained many such passages and was issued in various editions to avoid condemnation. In the 1620s, Galileo was tried for heresy and forced to renounce his own work or face execution (Fig. **4.18**).

Since the twelfth century, the Catholic Church, in concert with its political allies, had administered the suppression of heresy through the authorities and tribunals of the Inquisition. This institutional persecution was alive and well in the Renaissance. The promotion of points of view that were antithetical to Catholic teaching could result in torture or death. Censorship became common, and lists of banned and acceptable books

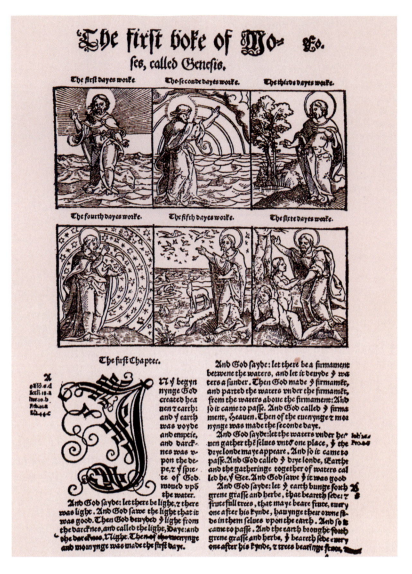

4.19 William Tyndale, Coverdale Bible, 1535. Shown here is the first page of an anonymous reprinting of William Tyndale's English translation of the Bible, published by Miles Coverdale on the Continent and smuggled into England. This translation was considered tainted by Protestant heresy, and Tyndale's unfortunate fate served as a cautionary tale to printers who struggled with censorship of biblical texts and interpretive commentaries, many of which were controversial. An image of the printer being burnt at the stake was included in James Foxe's popular *Book of Martyrs,* issued in 1563.

divided print culture into good and bad objects. The stakes were high. William Tyndale, for instance, was strangled and his body burnt at the stake in 1536 for publishing an English translation of the New Testament that was considered to have heretical overtones. In the 1530s, the British Star Chamber decreed that no work could be printed without official review and permission from the Crown. Their repressive techniques extended to the trade in print-related materials, resulting in the restriction of British type production, a dependence on Dutch imports, and even smuggling. In 1557, King Philip and Queen Mary chartered the British Stationers' Company as a professional organization charged with the self-regulation of printed discourse. By "self-regulation" the Crown really meant that the printers should keep Protestant propaganda out of print. The printers involved obtained monopoly control of printing in England as a beneficial by-product. "By permission of the King" was a common phrase on title pages, even as books were smuggled across national borders and issued in pirate editions to avoid royalties or censors (Fig. **4.19**).

Renaissance Design: Standardization and Modularization in Print

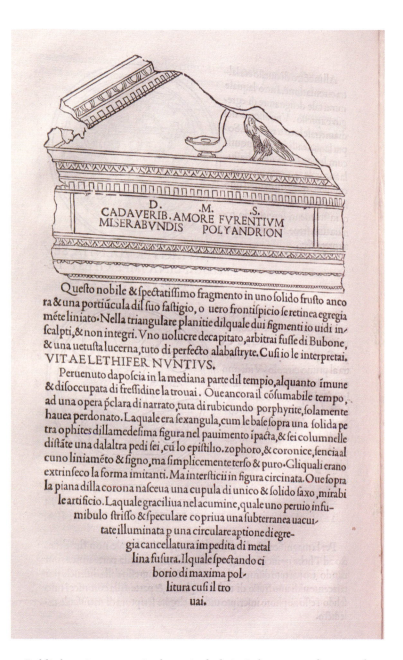

4.20b Michelangelo, inscription and detail, 1538. This inscription on the base of Michelangelo's equestrian statue of Marcus Aurelius in Rome was made in 1538. More uniform than their classical antecedents, these Renaissance letters take their Roman models' softening of constructed curves and strokes one step further, reflecting a recognition that too mechanistic a rendering would result in a sterile design. These highly legible and elegant letterforms remain in use, continuing a tradition of encoding public statements in a monumental graphic style that adds weight and seriousness to whatever content it presents.

Public lettering was revived, particularly in Italy, as part of a general rebirth of classical art and architecture. Monumental inscriptions became popular again. Churches, monuments, public squares, and buildings displayed their texts in a conspicuous proliferation unseen during the Medieval period. A sense of the urban landscape as an important site for civic communication informed commemorative and declarative inscriptions. The city had again become a text. Classical letterforms, particularly the capitals that had been refined by Roman carvers, were chosen for their grandeur and legibility as the models best suited to inscribe civic discourse. The use of such letterforms persists in Europe and the Americas, and their cultural meaning encompasses the associations that they held for their Renaissance revivers (Figs. **4.20a** and **4.20b**).

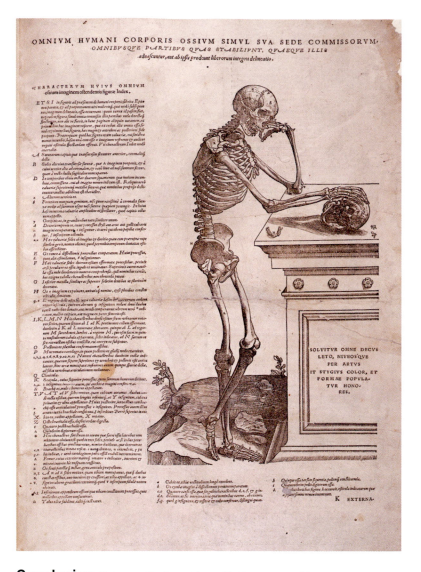

4.21a Andreas Vesalius, *De humani corporis fabrica*, 1543. The aesthetic of Andreas Vesalius's *De humani corporis fabrica* casts Renaissance humanism in a macabre light. To display his knowledge of human anatomy, Vesalius posed his skeletons, partially flayed bodies, and exposed organs in graceful versions of living poses. The design of these pages is as rational and calmly ordered as their illustrations. Every line, letter, and white space serves to structure the information presented. The rigorous linear geometry of letterpress informs an elegant aesthetic. The type is set in solid rectilinear forms that function as scaffolding for the presentation of information in a clear hierarchy.

Conclusion Between the invention of letterpress and image reproduction technologies in the mid-fifteenth century and the final decades of the seventeenth century, printing's many uses established the place of visual and typographic texts in European culture. Although only a small portion of the population could read, visual literacy rose rapidly. Through its ability to produce "exactly repeatable statements," printing brought information into being and into circulation in forms and formats that would ensure a shared reference-base for the development of knowledge. In the Renaissance, graphic arts embodied notions of standardization and modularization in the very technologies of their production. Graphic descriptions of the world spread assumptions, conventions, and standards. Every printed image and text expressed ideological values and reinforced cultural attitudes toward gender, national identity, the right of rulers, the power of the church, bodies, faith, and knowledge. Printing as a technology had an impact, but printed artifacts

4.21b Robert Granjon, Philippe Gautier, *Alexandreidos*, 1558. One hundred years after the invention of letterpress printing, the skills of punch cutters and designers had increased dramatically. Granjon created his elegant Civilité typeface as a tribute to national hands that he felt suited the Gallic sensibility. German textura and Italian roman faces had served as the basis of metal type production in its first decades, but French scripts, with their swash ascenders, small **x-height**, and colorful variation of thin and thick strokes had not found their way into letterpress. The name of this face derived in part from the subject matter of the book for which it was first designed: a work instructing young women in matters of etiquette or civility—the cultivation of manners suitable for individuals of refined taste.

4.21c Christophe Plantin, *Polyglot Bible*, 1569–1572. Christophe Plantin's *Polyglot Bible* was conceived on a monumental scale. Its Hebrew, Latin, and Greek typefaces, cut to mechanical and aesthetic perfection, mark the considerable distance print technology had come in a little more than one hundred years since its invention. The **textual apparatus** of the book is fully established—with running heads, page numbers, attribution of authorship, glosses, line numbering, cross references, and other scholarly elements functioning as integral parts of the graphic scheme. The scope of this undertaking and the complexity of its pages almost disappear in the artful elegance with which the whole is achieved. The work is a tribute to Plantin's prowess as a businessman, designer, and printer.

also had a powerful effect through both their forms and their contents. Ideas and their expression became regularized in print. The rationalization of production that made this communication possible was itself an outcome and a statement of modern sensibilities grounded in humanistic concepts of reason, scientific approaches to knowledge, and the revival and surpassing of classical learning. As the Renaissance gave way to the Enlightenment, rational approaches to government would challenge the long-standing monarchies of Europe and bring political change to the Western world. Print would have an important role to play in these developments, and the visual rhetoric of graphic design would continue to be integral to print's transmission of socially transformative ideas (Figs. **4.21a–c**).

Renaissance Design: Standardization and Modularization in Print 1450–1660

1436 Alberti's *On Painting* outlines laws of perspective

1452 Earliest dated metal engraving

Birth of Leonardo da Vinci

1455 Gutenberg's forty-two-line Bible completed

1462 Ivan the Great crowned in Russia

1464 Conrad Sweynheym and Arnold Pannartz introduce printing to Italy

1470 First printing in Paris

Nicolas Jenson casts his first font of type

1476 William Caxton sets up first print shop in England

William Caxton publishes Chaucer's *Canterbury Tales*

1481 *Pseudo Apuleius*, a ninth-century botanical manuscript, printed

1483 Birth of Martin Luther

1486 Thomas à Kempis's *Imitation of Christ* printed, becomes best seller

1488 Dias sails around Cape of Good Hope, South Africa

1490 First use of running heads in a printed book

Table Bay, South Africa, first seen by European explorers

1491 Wynkyn de Worde inherits Caxton's print shop

1492 Columbus's first voyage to America

La Reconquista: Christian forces defeat Muslims and conquer Granada, Spain

Jews expelled from Spain

1493 *The Nuremberg Chronicle* published

1497 John Cabot arrives in Newfoundland

1498 Columbus explores South America

1499 Amerigo Vespucci sails from Spain, later discovers Amazon River

Aldus Manutius publishes *Hypnerotomachia Poliphili*

1500 Portuguese sailors land in Brazil

1501 Italic type, cut by Francesco Griffo, first appears in Manutius's Virgil

First black slaves brought to Santo Domingo

1503 Leonardo da Vinci completes *Mona Lisa*

1509 Erasmus writes *In Praise of Folly*

Mechanical watch invented in Germany

1512 Michaelangelo completes Sistine ceiling

1513 Machiavelli writes *The Prince*

Balboa finds Pacific Ocean

1514 Nicolaus Copernicus claims sun (not the Earth) is center of solar system

1516 First edition of Ludovico Ariosto's *Orlando Furioso* published

Thomas More's *Utopia* published

1517 Martin Luther posts his ninety-five theses, which launch Reformation

1519 Cortes enters Mexico

1521 Martin Luther excommunicated

Lucas van Leyden first uses copper for etching

1522 Magellan's crew completes circumnavigation of globe by ocean voyage

Arrighi designs italic type with swash letters

Luther's German translation of New Testament published with Lucas Cranach's woodcuts

1526 Simon de Colines establishes print shop

1529 Geofroy Tory's *Champfleury* published

1534 Pizarro conquers Peru

English church declares its independence from Rome

Luther's German translation of Old and New Testaments published

1540 Cardenas first encounters Grand Canyon

1543 Andreas Vesalius's *On the Workings of the Human Body* published

Copernicus's *On the Revolutions of the Heavenly Spheres* published

1545 First engraved title page

1546 Etienne Dolet, Erasmus's publisher, burnt at stake for heresy

1547 Ivan the Terrible crowned in Russia

1557 Charter granted to Stationers' Company in London

1558 Elizabeth I crowned in England

1559 Pope Paul IV inaugurates Counter-Reformation

1560 *Puritan* first used (as term of abuse)

1564 Death of Calvin

1565 Graphite pencil invented

1568 Beer first bottled in London

1569 Mercator's projection method inaugurates modern maps

1570 Japanese allow foreign ships to visit

1572 Saint Bartholomew's Day massacre: 31,000 Protestants killed in Paris

1578 *Massacre*, meaning to butcher, first used in English

1586 Star Chamber decree prohibits printing outside London

1588 English navy defeats Spanish Armada

1590 Compound (double-lens) microscope invented

     Galileo's theory of falling objects developed

1595 Shakespeare completes *Romeo and Juliet*

1603 Death of Elizabeth I

1605 Cervantes's *Don Quixote* published

     The Relation, first newspaper, published by Johann Carolus

1607 Jamestown, first permanent European settlement in North America, established

1609 Johannes Kepler calculates elliptical orbits of planets

1616 Catholic Church condemns Copernicus

1628 William Harvey publishes study of blood circulation

1629 Elzevir firm's duodecimo books epitomize golden age of Dutch printing

1633 Galileo condemned by Inquisition for believing in Copernicus's theories

1635 French Academy founded by Cardinal Richelieu

1637 René Descartes's *The Discourse on Method* published

     Printing and type founding separated by decree in England

1640 Imprimerie Royale established in France

1642 Death of Galileo

     Puritans ban theatrical productions in England

     Birth of Isaac Newton

     English Civil War begins

1643 Louis XIV, The Sun King, crowned in France

1644 John Milton writes *Aeropagitica*, a bid to Parliament for "unlicenc'd printing"

1648 Taj Mahal palace completed

1649 Charles I beheaded by English Puritans led by Cromwell

1650 Tea introduced in England

Tools of the Trade

Powdered pigments

Oil-based ink

Chalk

Silverpoint for drawing

Lead and graphite sticks (after 1570)

Breadcrumbs as erasers

Watercolor and wash

Oil paint

Glazes in oil and varnish

White lead primer

Metal pens

Ruling pens

Full-sized cartoons for tracing

Prickers, pounce, chalk for copying

Adjustable compasses

Burin

Etching needles and burnishers

Engraving tools and gouges

Copper and steel plates for engraving

Wood palettes

Ivory panels

Slate panels

Canvas

Vellum

Paper

Woodblock

Metal type

Camera obscura

Ground glass with grid for drawing

Perspectival drawing system (1450s)

Orthogonal drawing (later)

Clay models

Wet cloth drapery studies

Magic lantern projection (1600s)

Pocket watch

Eyeglasses, magnifying lens

Waxed linen window panes for daylight

Water in globes to amplify candlelight

Oil and tallow lamps

Candles

THE
HEADS OF
SEVERALL PRO-
CEEDINGS IN THIS
PRESENT PARLIAMENT,

from the 22 of *November*, to
the 29. 1 6 4 1.

VVherein is contained the
ſubſtance of ſeverall Letters ſent
from *Ireland*, ſhewing what diſtreſſe
and miſery they are in

With divers other paſſages of moment touching the Affaires of
theſe Kingdomes.

London, Printed for *I. T.* 1641.

5. Modern Typography and the Creation of the Public Sphere
1660–1800

- In the Enlightenment era, an increase in the variety and distribution of printed matter helped establish communities among readers who were connected by common interests and beliefs, rather than geographical proximity; and distinctive designs made these media visually identifiable.

- Refinements of copperplate engraving provided greater accuracy and detail in images that helped advance engineering and science and enhanced the pleasure of illustrated works of fiction, drama, and poetry.

- Administrative needs in government and business gave rise to visual forms of statistical analysis.

- **Baroque** and **rococo** styles raised standards of graphic elegance and artifice in the visually rich print culture of the seventeenth and eighteenth centuries.

- The design of "modern" typography expressed Enlightenment attitudes that prized rationalism and objectivity, but style changes also reflected shifting ideologies and cultural transformations.

- The rise of the popular press fostered partisan interests and political activity, demonstrating the influence of media networks.

5.1 First printed diurnal, 1641. Newspapers were a new form of publication defined by their regular appearance, timeliness, and uniformity. This weekly publication of the daily events of the British Parliament would have been recognizable to its readers by the design of its title page, which remained consistent from one issue to the next. The layout of this page is not hierarchical but simply uses type in descending point sizes, breaking lines haphazardly. Although no **masthead** is present, the standardization of this format served the same branding function as titling type soon would in papers with names like *The Gazette*, *The Post Boy*, or *The Intelligencer*.

The Enlightenment period was characterized by the rise of nationalism, reason, and scientific **empiricism** in Europe and North America. In the course of this era, styles passed from the grandeur and flamboyance of baroque and rococo embellishments to the sometimes austere simplicity of **neoclassicism**. These cultural forces and aesthetic directions all took graphic forms. At the same time, a dramatic expansion of print production changed the way communities were made. Not only did the book trade continue to grow and serve as a powerful instrument of Enlightenment thought, but also newspapers brought a new social and temporal dynamic to publishing. Their design played a part in the creation of what is known as the **public sphere**, a virtual space made through the exchange of ideas and information. **Communities of belief** were built on shared reading and thought rather than common location. **News sheets** circulated with an air of relevance and even urgency, and the design of these media helped define what was current and important. Newspapers and journals attracted specific readerships that identified with distinct and often inflammatory points of view. Such reader partisanship could also be moved as a political force. The shift of power from absolute and personified rule to states defined as nations, managed by administrations and, eventually, governed by elected representatives, brought another aspect of modernity into being. New typefaces and approaches to graphic design expressed the increasing rationalism, secularism, and commercialism of the era. Novels, essays, and other literary texts were written in modern languages and printed—often with illustrations—alongside classics. Readerships

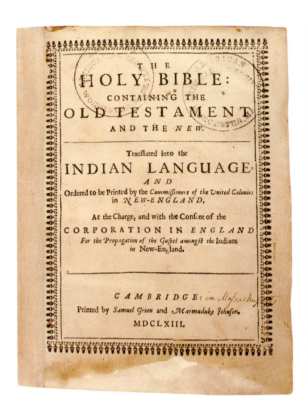
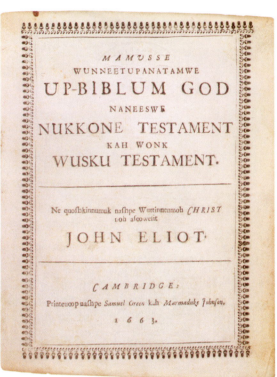

5.2a Holy Bible, Cambridge, Massachusetts, 1663. Printing arrived in the New World with colonial settlements. The first press was established in Mexico City in the mid-1500s. Printing was imported to New England in 1638. Almanacs and psalm books were among the earliest works printed in the colonies. This Holy Bible was printed in 1663 in English and "the Indian Language." Its production tested the limits of type and paper stock for its printers Samuel Green and Marmaduke Johnson. The book was meant to help spread the gospel by providing transliterations of it (phonetic versions of the indigenous translation in roman type). The page is organized by a clear hierarchy. The text is centered as was the norm. But the type is thickened, bent, and broken with wear. The acorn border adds a folksy touch, and the scale of such a project demonstrates the investment being made to foster cultural exchange. This publication is an example of an attempt to use print to mediate between communities.

grew, scientific and technical publishing increased dramatically, and the accuracy and reliability of statistical, geographical, and industrial information benefited from improved image production technologies and greater technical skill among artists and printers. An ever-increasing variety of printed forms of communication fostered distinct graphic vocabularies. Although still a function of the printing trade, graphic design on the eve of industrialization was beginning to be seen as a force for shaping public opinion. The persuasive power of graphic forms participated in the production and consumption of ideas (Fig. **5.1**).

Printed matter and the public sphere
The public sphere in seventeenth- and eighteenth-century European and American culture depended on the availability of printed matter. A virtual rather than literal or physical space, the public sphere is an arena where opinion and values are created. The social order—the sense that the structure of society is natural and that individuals should behave according to norms and expectations set by their position and status—is mediated through public discourse. Print plays an active role in this mediation. Thus, the modern period is characterized by changes in the ways that graphic media operate culturally, not just by changes in their style and form (Fig. **5.2a**).

In the Enlightenment era, empiricism and quantitative methods moved to the center of intellectual life. Scientific inquiry provided the basis of rational thought. Tensions arose between religious and secular belief systems. A truth grounded in empirical observation and one based in religious faith could not always be reconciled. Concepts like the **social**

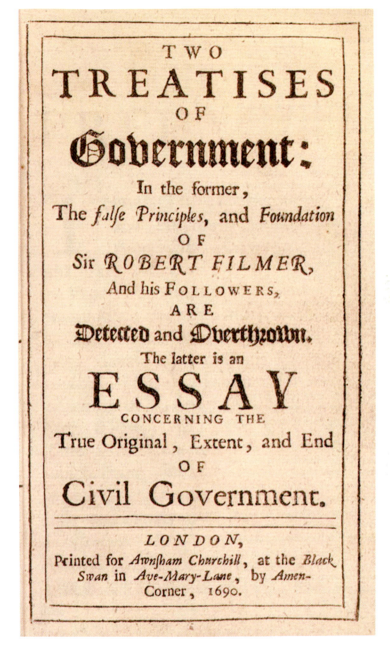

5.2b John Locke, *An Essay Concerning the True Original, Extent, and End of Civil Government*, 1690. Enlightenment philosophers laid a new foundation for thinking about the nature of government. They inherited humanistic ideas from the Renaissance, but they promoted reason over faith as the basis of individual and social action. By posing fundamental questions about knowledge, John Locke and others swept away the final remnants of a Medieval worldview and challenged the authority of monarchs and the Catholic Church. This title page contains a mix of faces and type sizes that reflect the state of English printing in the late seventeenth century. Blackletter types remained in use for emphasis. Note the way they link the words *Government*, *detected*, and *overthrown*. Robert Filmer, here being refuted, was an advocate of the divine right of kings. The bent rule that forms the border has obviously been much used, and the types show varying degrees of wear, sophistication in design and cutting, and skill in alignment and fit. The small format, mix of faces, and well-**leaded** lines of this title page are typical of the period.

contract and the free will of individuals challenged previously held assumptions about human nature, the divine basis of power, and the task of education. The relations of power between people and governments were beginning to be seen as reciprocal. The old aristocratic bases of monarchy were being threatened. New institutions for the validation of knowledge had arisen in the form of Academies established in Italy, France, England, and elsewhere in Europe. The Academies promoted and regulated debates and study in fields as diverse as architecture, geology, letters, astronomy, painting, and medicine, and helped draw the boundaries defining such disciplines (Fig. **5.2b**).

5.3 Denis Diderot and Jean le Rond d'Alembert, page from the *Encyclopédie*, 1751–1772. The publication of a work that would inventory all human knowledge in an orderly and systematic way is completely consistent with Enlightenment efforts to banish superstition and replace it with scientific knowledge. French philosophers Diderot and d'Alembert undertook this remarkable project. The resulting thirty-five-volume work, produced between 1751 and 1772, provided technical information in detail. Here, the elements of typesetting are clearly shown. Letters and spacers are shown in a composing stick; a *form* is shown with differences of type size filled in by spacing material; and **compositors** are shown setting type at the case and on a stone *(right)*. Printed sheets are hung to dry from racks above, but no presses are shown in this plate. More than fifty such engravings depicted all phases of printing, including papermaking, typecasting, and presswork, and all were accompanied by explanatory texts.

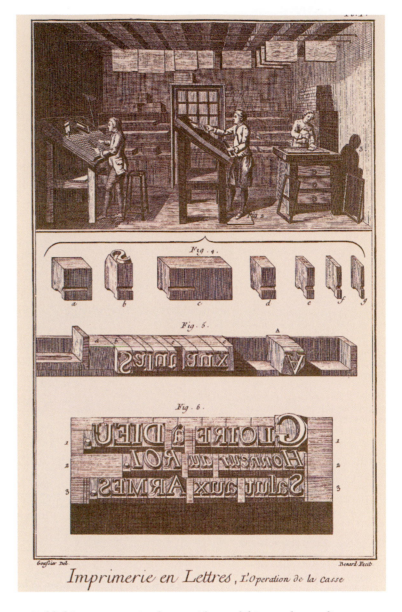

Imprimerie en Lettres, l'Operation de la casse

Publishing was perceived as an aid to codifying and spreading scientific knowledge. But it was also essential to administrative and bureaucratic structures. Accounting systems, statistical comparison and mathematical evidence, rules, regulations, and laws depended on graphic forms of printed communication. The numbers and kinds of objects that needed to be designed expanded exponentially. An intellectual project of ambitious scope, the French *Encyclopédie,* was edited by philosophers Denis Diderot and Jean le Rond d'Alembert. This publication realized the eighteenth-century idea of the book as a repository of human knowledge— systematically organized in a format well suited to express its philosophical commitment to rational order (Fig. **5.3**).

Arguments can be made for the **agency** of print as an instrument of social change in any period. But print is opportunistic, and cultural changes brought about by expanded markets, nation building, and new

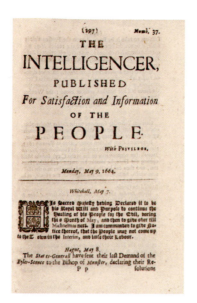

5.4 *The Intelligencer*, London, 1664.
This paper presents a notice from the king to the people, telling them not to come to town and "loose their labour." This injunction was issued at a moment of struggle between Anglicans, Puritans, and other groups whose sectarian affiliations had political ramifications. The newspaper served as an instrument of control in the face of civic unrest, as well as a place where events of the day were reported. This dual role as both shaper of opinion and action and record of events is essential to newspapers that mediate, rather than merely communicate, among various opinions and groups. Type that was set and kept standing was used for mastheads and introductions to subjects. This practice was efficient, and it offered readers a familiar object with a graphically marked identity. Note the phrase "with privilege," indicating official sanction for the publication.

5.5 *The Crying Murther*, 1624.
Newsbooks, named for their folded format, were often prompted by gruesome crimes or scandals, such as this brutal murder of a man on the highway. The victim was taken home, disemboweled, parboiled, and salted in a "most strange and fearfull manner." The graphic images on such sheets were often recycled: The depiction of a criminal was a matter of stereotyping rather than portraiture. But, in this instance, the crime clearly provoked a macabre interest in depicting specific details. These sheets were graphically crude, inexpensively produced, and widely circulated. They helped construct categories of criminality through their verbal and graphic vocabularies and cultivated an appetite for scandal.

forms of participatory government (wrought by the American and French revolutions) created arenas in which printed communication could operate with unprecedented effectiveness. Book production continued to account for about three-quarters of all printed matter well into the eighteenth century. At the same time, newspapers extended readership to include those interested in business and current affairs. The idea of timely content became significant as an aspect of publication. The relation of print to authority was thrown into relief, as the press became an agent of revolutionary movement. Political, financial, academic, and scientific sectors experienced a distinct expansion from physical spaces as the exclusive centers of public life—such as the Roman forum, the Medieval marketplace, or the Renaissance city plaza—into spaces of discourse created by print media. Print became a site of contestation and debate, not just a means of reporting (Fig. **5.4**).

Newsbooks, broadsheets, and newspapers
The origins of newspapers can be traced to basic human curiosity about passing events. But news publications also generate an appetite for information, producing a commodity that feeds public priorities with what has been made to seem important. For example, interest in scandal and crime has as much to do with entertainment value as with utility in most readers' lives. Ideas about what is newsworthy have always come hand in hand with vested interests in outcomes—and, in the case of newspapers, in sales. **News ballads** published in broadsheet form began to appear in the sixteenth century. The defeat of the Spanish Armada by the English navy in 1588 provoked one such poetic publication, but grisly tales of murder illustrated with crude, graphic images were more common subjects than political events. News sheets focused on a single tale or theme and appeared only as occasions arose. They offered moralizing commentary on the crimes that they reported, thus satisfying the taste for both scandal and propriety. In print, notoriety and renown became categories that justified public attention (Fig. **5.5**).

By contrast to these occasional sheets, the publications we would recognize as newspapers were distinguished by their regular and frequent appearance, their standard format, and the variety of stories featured in their pages. One type of forerunner to the newspaper was a system of private letters on matters of interest to a particular group. In the late sixteenth century, bankers and diplomats began to circulate such letters among themselves. Fostered by the shipping trade and by diplomatic communications, seventeenth-century newspapers spawned a culture of the press that quickly joined forces with another emerging institution—the coffeehouse. Public venues were established for the consumption of newly prized products of colonial exploitation—coffee and chocolate brought from the New World. These venues also provided a place for sharing newspapers that passed from reader to reader. The stimulating effect of caffeine coincided with the urge for conversation and exchange. The image of the coffeehouse as a place where time was wasted in endless chatter became common. Every era identifies its vices, and, in this period, idle intellectual pursuits seemed to threaten the moral order as much as cards and sensual pleasures had in earlier centuries. The 1667 ballad, "News from the Coffee House," caricatured the endless jabbering in which hours of productivity were lost (Fig. **5.6**).

The *Avisa Relation oder Zeitung,* published in Augsburg, Germany, in 1609, is considered the first newspaper to establish conventions of the medium. It presented an identifiable masthead, promised a regular appearance, and printed information of a timely nature. By 1621, two-page

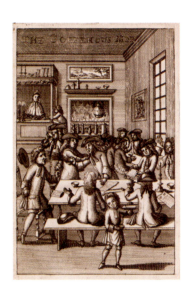

The public sphere is a virtual arena where opinion is created.

5.6 Ned Ward, *The Coffehous Mob* from *Vulgus Britannicus*, 1710. A coffeehouse is shown with newspapers open on its tables and heated arguments being fueled by a combination of caffeine and inflammatory journalism. Entitled *The Coffehous Mob*, the image depicts a real community's response to the papers—with their differing opinions and points of view. In *News from the Coffee House* (1667), Thomas Jordan wrote, "Here Men do talk of every Thing/with large and liberal Lungs." The essayist Joseph Addison, who wrote regularly for *The Spectator,* described scenes in which "Knots of Theorists" fed by "steams of the Coffee Pot" would dispose of monarchies and governments "in less than a Quarter of an Hour." Although it may be true that a lot of hot air was exchanged in such environments, the role of newspapers in creating communities of discourse was recorded in these remarks as clearly as in this image.

courantos began to run serially in England. The titles of these periodicals were protected by licensing laws passed in parliament in the 1650s: Branding had arisen simultaneously with news production. Seventeenth-century Amsterdam, a bustling cosmopolitan center, supported eight weeklies and biweeklies by 1645. Consumption of news proved to be habit-forming. In a merchant culture dependent on shipping for its wealth, information about piracy, shipwrecks, war, and other disrupting events was crucial. But newspapers became a commodity in their own right, and the groundwork was laid for the reader to become a consumer. Higher degrees of literacy existed in urban populations than in rural settings (and in the American colonies than in England), so as increasingly available materials brought printing costs down, **pamphlets** and broadsheets found a wide audience in these areas (Fig. **5.7**).

In the earliest news publications, or "intelligences," paragraph after paragraph was presented without typographical division. News and commentary were intermingled. Lines between fact and editorial opinion were even less clearly drawn than they are now. In 1690, the first North American newspaper, *Publick Occurrences,* was published, but it ran for

Modern Typography and the Creation of the Public Sphere

5.7 *The London Gazette*, 1687.
This paper's masthead remained in place for centuries. Its design served several purposes. Visible from afar and conspicuous among other papers, the masthead signaled its brand to prospective buyers and readers. The format allowed all articles to flow continuously without having to be broken into separate columns and continued elsewhere. A single column could be set by a compositor and then broken to fit the available space on each page. Here, a long address to the king that has been circulating in the city of London is presented as the first text. Following it are stories about Poland, the death of a count in Vienna and the distribution of his estate, and connections between these facts and military conflicts with Tartars and Turks. No headlines announce the stories, and display faces are limited to the masthead and drop capitals.

5.8 *Publick Occurrences*, 1690. The first newspaper printed in the North American colonies announced its intention in the opening lines: "It is designed, that the Country shall be furnished once a month (or if any Glut of Occurrences happen, oftener) with an Account of such considerable things as have arrived unto our Notice." Italics were used for editorial comment and emphasis, whereas a roman face was used for the actual report. Paragraph breaks demarcated stories, although themes and connections wove through the accounts of Thanksgiving, Indian activities, smallpox, and other affairs of note in the colonial environment. News bound the colony together as an identity, since its stories gave readers the sense that they were sharing in the same experiences, even when these were not immediately present.

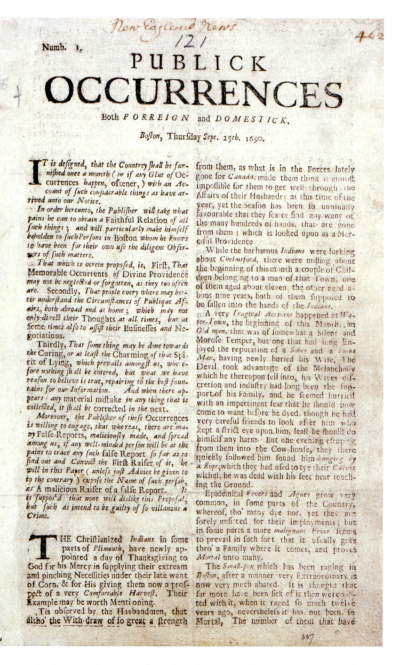

only a single issue. Its suggestions that the king of France was guilty of adultery provoked censorship. Reports from correspondents in dispersed locations quickly became a mainstay of newspapers, as did news of parliamentary proceedings and the machinations of other governing bodies. Sometimes the text was set twice, and the two versions—with inevitable minor differences between them—were printed simultaneously to speed production (Fig. **5.8**).

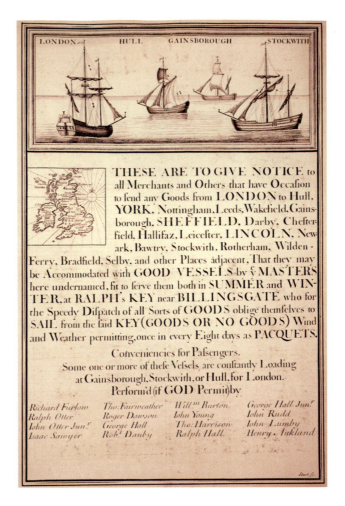

5.9a Sailing notice, 1680. Printed **ephemera** created a public space for the exchange of information. A **notice** like this one advertised available routes and services for shipping goods and "conveniences for passengers." Its images communicate immediately, and information about ports and schedules is given in the text. This notice is engraved rather than typeset. All of the letters are written out by hand, including the capitals. Organization and hierarchy of information are clearly structured into the format, and the text is laid out with care—although not without split words at the ends of lines. The labor of engraving such a notice, rather than setting it in type, may have been offset by the advantages of having its images on the same plate.

The solid gray stream of news was soon broken into columns

From their beginnings, newspapers revealed the interconnections of commerce and politics. Advertising notices and shipping news were essential to the well-being of colonial economies. Announcements of imports occupied prime spots on the front page. The solid gray stream of news was soon broken into columns and then departments, separating local politics and foreign reports into recognizable patterns of print and regular schedules of publication. As competition for readers' attention grew, the design of advertisers' notices demanded greater investment, and the visual differentiation of newspapers themselves became a matter of economic consequence (Figs. **5.9a** and **5.9b**).

Politics and the press In their capacity to shape public opinion, newspapers played a vital role in the revolutionary upheavals of North American and European politics in the seventeenth and eighteenth centuries. Patterns of protest and censorship make clear that newspapers were perceived to be a potent instrument in national power struggles. In 1640, at a time of civil war in England, poet John Milton had called for a free press in his *Areopagitica*. The English Licensing Act of 1695 allowed

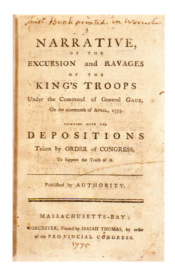

5.9b *Lloyd's List*, February 17, 1740.
While the columns of a newspaper like *The London Gazette* regularly featured shipping news, more specialized publications were created specifically to serve commercial interests. In the 1690s, the proprietor of a London coffeehouse, Edward Lloyd, decided that it would be advantageous to publish a weekly bulletin of information of interest to his clientele who were mainly commercial shippers. News of the arrival of goods into port was of interest to many sectors of the population, since it signaled the safe passage and return of vessels and their crews and opportunities for merchants to acquire new stock. The trade in imports and exports was a chief engine of colonial economies, and such notices were equivalent to the business reports of the day. In later versions, this publication carried information about exchange rates for currency, stocks, and commodities, helping to standardize this information by making it public in a form that served as a reference.

and then departments, separating local and foreign reports.

5.10 Isaiah Thomas, *A Narrative*, 1775
(above right). Books participated in the creation of communities as much as newspapers did. Colonial publishers took considerable risks printing texts like this one, which called the British to account for actions taken by their troops. Printed in Worcester, Massachusetts, the title page of this text bears the statement that it is printed by order of the Provincial Congress. The conditions for revolution were ripe, and printed matter helped justify and inflame passions in the struggle for American independence. Isaiah Thomas's newspaper, *The Massachusetts Spy*, had begun in 1770 with the intention of neutrally presenting loyalist and patriot views, but soon it had taken the side of the revolutionaries. Commercial competition and partisan politics coincided, and customs officials refused to give Thomas the shipping news essential to the success of his publication. For safety's sake, Thomas had to move his operation from Boston to Worcester.

a new freedom of the press that promoted the careers of early journalists Joseph Addison and Richard Steele. Their publication, *The Tatler*, was launched in 1709. They followed this with *The Spectator* a few years later. John Adams observed that the American Revolution was fought in the minds and hearts of the people long before the war began—in part because newspapers had established an idea of "The Colonies" as an entity with a right to self-government. Printers' design work contributed to the creation of an image of independence by branding newspapers and broadsheets with a national identity. One of the colonies' strongest protests arose when the 1765 Stamp Act imposed a tax on every sheet of printed newspaper, dramatically increasing their cost (Fig. **5.10**).

Democratic forms of government were a novelty, and they depended on new models of political engagement. A public sphere of consensus and exchange was a significant component of this engagement. The concept of civil society was central to the French Enlightenment. Jean-Jacques Rousseau's idea of the social contract was that it set limits on power and responsibility between a state and its people. But participatory democracy relied upon a well-informed population. Newspapers played a critical

LIBERTÉ DE LA PRESSE

role in fomenting partisan fervor throughout the French Revolutionary period, when the posting of public notices was highly controlled. The French Declaration of the Rights of Man (1789) and the American Bill of Rights (1791) both contained provisions to protect the "freedom to communicate thoughts and opinions." Freedom of the press remains fundamental to the operation of a democratic government. Not surprisingly, one of Napoleon's first acts following his seizure of power in 1799 was to

Printers learned their trade through an apprentice system,

5.11b Jean-Paul Marat, *L'Ami du Peuple*, **August 13, 1792.** Before the revolution, the press in France was tightly controlled by the government. Unofficial news was circulated in handwritten letters and sheets. Rumors spread by word of mouth, and the distribution of newspapers was not always adequate to satisfy the demand for information among rural populations. The *Gazette de France* did not mention the storming of the Bastille, since it was not in the interests of the king of France for such news to be in print. But one of the tenets of the Declaration of the Rights of Man issued in 1789 was the freedom of the press. From four French newspapers in 1788, the number rose to 335 in 1790. Factions abounded, and, by 1792, leaders of the revolutionary government were trying to suppress publications by those loyal to the monarchy. Jean-Paul Marat expressed his own views in his paper, *L'Ami du Peuple*. He was assassinated in his bath, and this copy of his paper is stained with his blood.

restrict that freedom. Increased production of newspapers demanded rapid turnaround in the tasks of compositors and printers. Efficient methods involved **templates** and other formulaic, repurposable solutions, as well as coordinated tasks that allowed many hands to contribute to meeting short deadlines (Figs. **5.11a** and **5.11b**).

Graphic arts and design
The rationalization of production that marked the initial invention of movable type was further honed in the seventeenth and eighteenth centuries. The specialization of tasks and refinement of each aspect of graphic design was reflected in the organization of the printing industry and in aesthetics of the period. The graphic arts were still part of the trades throughout the seventeenth century. Although the burgeoning industry introduced high degrees of specialization, the tasks of design work were not yet defined by an independent professional identity. Nonetheless, aptitudes for fine engraving and printing, artful layout, and elegant type design were all recognized and prized. Printers learned their trade through an apprentice system or were brought up in a family business. **Journeymen** printers, having

Modern Typography and the Creation of the Public Sphere

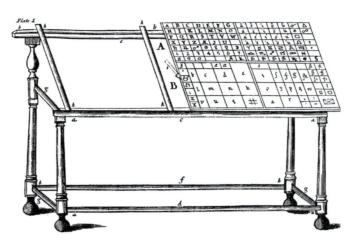

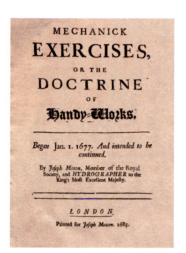

completed their apprenticeships but lacking the capital to set up their own shops, were permitted to work for wages. The traditions of secrecy that cloaked Medieval guilds had continued to hold sway over many trades through the Renaissance. Printing was often a dynastic business, with ownership and control passing among family members. This structure meant that women—widows and daughters—could come into powerful positions in the trade. Women's roles changed as patterns of family life, education, and work shifted. Meanwhile, certain professions allowed women to operate outside the confines of the domestic sphere, and even within that sphere, the division of labor between husbands and wives often gave women primary control over financial management.

Training in the design of printed matter was informal and took place in shops and workrooms. Typography, book design, and illustration had each reached a high degree of artistry in the Renaissance when a single

whereas training in the design of printed matter was informal.

5.12a and 5.12b Joseph Moxon, *Mechanick Exercises,* **title page and illustration, 1683.** British printing was in a poor state in this period, having improved little since the days of William Caxton and Wynken de Worde almost two centuries earlier. Moxon had spent time in the Netherlands and was impressed with the quality of Dutch type design and printing. He decided the best solution for his country was to write a textbook that treated every aspect of the printing industry in great detail, providing guidelines for excellence. Engravings showed the layout of the compositor's case, the structure of the **tympan** that fed paper through the press, the way to lock up a form, and other steps of the printing process. The book supplied all of the information necessary to a printer, from advice on purchasing a forge to explanations of press construction, casting and finishing type, and setting forms effectively. The title page uses both blackletter and roman types in a manner typical of the era. Centered, symmetrical typography was the dominant convention in both title page and broadside design.

shop usually carried out all aspects of print production. When Joseph Moxon published his *Mechanick Exercises* in 1683, his instructions were meant to encode correct procedures for every aspect of the trade and to establish standards of production. But along with social and political transformations in the period from 1660 to 1800 came structural changes in the work of printing and graphic design. Typecasting, printing, papermaking, engraving, binding, and book publishing became separate enterprises. The printing trade became an industry, and a range of occupations developed within its ranks. For instance, the **foundry** sector was separate from the composing room and pressroom. The design, casting, and finishing of type required very different skills from those of composing type, setting it up on the press, inking it, or pulling **proofs**. Proofreading required a higher level of literacy than tasks associated with collation, **imposition**, and the preparation of sheets for binding. Although the category of graphic designer did not exist, certain individual printers achieved celebrity among discriminating consumers on the basis of the excellence of their type design, their punch cutting, or the overall beauty of their books (Figs. **5.12a** and **5.12b**).

5.13a William Playfair, "Chart Representing the Increase of the Annual Revenues of England and France," *The Commercial and Political Atlas*, **1786.** Playfair's images were not only informative, but also they were elegant and beautiful. He is considered one of the first designers of **information graphics**. Condensing statistical information into legible graphic form was an expression of the administrative sensibility of eighteenth-century culture. Basic issues in **information design** took shape in Playfair's work: how to group and divide **information** and what can be measured or **parameterized** as data and thus presented by a **graphic metric**. The arches used to clump decades into centuries, heavy and light line widths to subdivide amounts, and hand coloring to mark an area between lines as an entity are all graphic codes that became standard elements of information design.

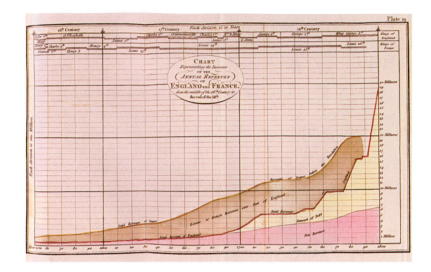

Information design gained sophistication, as administrative tasks for secular governments and business relied increasingly on statistical methods. The advantages of presenting information in condensed visual forms promoted the use of tables, graphs, and charts. One aspect of the tremendous social change that took place during the Enlightenment period was the development of forms of administered culture. The elaborate scaffolding of civil service and business management depended on the abstraction and analysis of information. This abstraction made statistics graphically presentable. The effect of such visualizations was to lend the authority of empirical science and its methods to the management of human situations and cultural affairs. Statistical facts have a very

Administrative tasks relied on the abstraction of information.

5.13b Letterpress trade card, 1770. Thomas Williams's **trade card** is set in a form of Baskerville and printed with great clarity. Despite the decorative border and somewhat quaint capitalization of nouns, this design feels considerably more contemporary than engraved cards of the same period. The clear layout of textual information, without fussiness or devices, reveals the influence of a modern sensibility, one that rests on principles of order and organization rather than flourish and decorative distraction.

different face than individual people, and decisions made on the basis of rational analysis of information are not always compatible with values of compassion. The rise of a market economy grounded in global empires and trade shifted eighteenth-century Europeans out of older land-based and agricultural models and into new patterns of wealth, in which capital accumulated and circulated more freely. Currency and stock shares, rather than goods, became the instruments of financial activity, introducing yet another level of abstraction into the relationship between graphic representation and material realities (Fig. **5.13a**).

Established tradespeople, catering to the bourgeoisie in towns and cities, also found uses for printed matter. Business cards and letterheads advertised services, and generic graphic attributes identified different professions, as visual conventions for signage developed. Printed ephemera included death notices and other personal announcements, generally within stock frames that were recycled from customer to customer. Standard forms that could be used repeatedly embodied efficiency and convenience, both principles that reinforced administrative approaches to graphic design. Printed matter found its way into private and public life with increasing

Modern Typography and the Creation of the Public Sphere

Double Pica Roman.

ABCDEFGHIKLMNOPQR
STVUWXYZ ABCDEFGHIK-

PAter noſter qui es in cœlis, ſan-
ctificetur nomen tuum. Veniat
regnum tuum: fiat voluntas tua, ſicut
in cœlo, ita etiam in terra. Panem noſtrum quotidianum da nobis hodie.
Et remitte nobis debita noſtra, ſicut
& remittimus debitoribus noſtris.
Et ne nos inducas in tentationem,
ſed libera nos ab illo malo. AMEN.

Double Pica Italick.

AABCDEFGHIJKLMM
NOPQRSTVUWXYZÆÆ

PAter noſter qui es in cœlis, ſanctifi-
cetur nomen tuum. Veniat regnum
tuum: fiat voluntas tua, ſicut in cœlo, ita
etiam in terra. Panem noſtrum quotidia-
num da nobis hodie. Et remitte nobis de-
bita noſtra, ſicut & remittimus debitori-
bus noſtris. Et ne nos inducas in tentatio-
nem, ſed libera nos ab illo malo. Amen.

5.13c Engraved tobacco label, 1675.
Copperplate engraving allowed the flourishes of the writing master to find their way into printed artifacts. The carefully controlled lines in the lettering of the tobacconist's name replicate pen strokes and finishes, and the address is an example of *drawn* type. The overall design combines lettering and imagery to create a decorative composition that effectively communicates the product and its relation to colonial practices and locations. Images of the New World carried exotic associations that concealed the more brutal aspects of plantation culture.

5.14a Bishop John Fell's types, 1690s.
The story of the Fell types demonstrates the technological discrepancies that existed in different parts of Europe in this period. During a visit to the Netherlands, Bishop John Fell, vice chancellor of Oxford University, perceived that greater excellence distinguished the types there from those in use in England. He took type, punches, and matrices back with him to England and, eventually, hired a Dutch **punch cutter** to work at the Oxford University Press. The faces cut by Peter Walpergen for Fell contain a number of idiosyncrasies but, in many ways, anticipate eighteenth-century English transitional faces.

variety and refinement of purpose, and the graphic forms by which print announced its various roles became conspicuous elements of **visual culture** (Figs. **5.13b** and **5.13c**).

Modern type design By the seventeenth century, type design and casting had become highly specialized skills. **Matrices** were regularly bought and sold, and printers were well aware of the benefits of exclusive possession of certain types. Styles of type followed fashions, and national tastes varied along with conventions for use, but Old Style faces prevailed until nearly the end of the seventeenth century. Dutch foundries had supplied much of the material used by English and European presses. But around the turn of the eighteenth century, styles began to change. **Transitional faces** (so-called because they marked a shift toward "modern" type design) stood more upright and featured higher contrasts between thick and thin strokes. These took advantage of the capability of smoother paper surfaces to print more delicate lines and ornaments. By the end of the eighteenth century, a vogue for neoclassical faces (with highly constructed letterforms, hairline thin strokes, and **unbracketed serifs**) was fostered by French and Italian designers. They cut designs for ancient and exotic scripts and modern languages (Fig. **5.14a**).

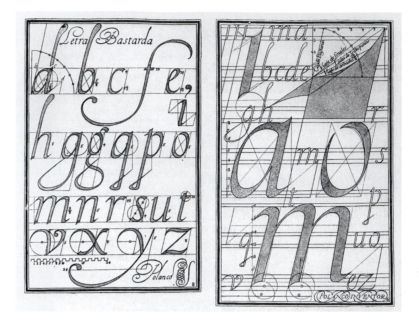

5.14b Juan Claudio Polanco, *The New Art of Writing*, 1719. These **specimen sheets** present the construction of all lowercase letters, according to a single system of strokes, proportions, angles, and shapes. Polanco presents his system as well as its products, and the two are equally important. Simply making fine letterforms is only half of the writing master's art. The other half lies in demonstrating that the hand has been disciplined to conform to a logical system. Writing specimens became elaborate exercises and extended displays of skill, with labyrinthine flourishes, both penned and engraved.

The form of these faces reflected the greater technical sophistication of eighteenth-century punch cutters. But the cultural meaning and ideological value of the new letterforms went beyond a display of improved techniques and expertise. The identity of a typeface resides not only in its look, but also in what its formal sensibility expresses. Modern types emphasized intellectual ideals in forms that marked their distance from the physical act of handwriting. Body and mind were distinguished, the trace of the hand was banished, and rationality prevailed

The identity of a typeface resides not only in its look, but also

over gestures and feelings. Humanistic models based in manuscript brush and pen strokes were displaced by a calculated approach to measure and proportion. Even handwriting was subject to a new rational discipline. The virtuoso productions of writing masters in this era demonstrated systematic methods and elaborately choreographed movements of the hand. Such trained handwriting flourished and became ornate in a manner consistent with baroque and rococo styles in furnishings, fashion, and the fine arts (Fig. **5.14b**).

A unique experiment in type design occurred at the end of the seventeenth century. Designs for the Romain du Roi were prepared by a committee convened in 1692 by the French king, Louis XIV, and engraved by Louis Simoneau. The committee's charge was to achieve a formal perfection in type design. This perfection was to be based in a rational consistency that would embody the king's absolute power, his divine right to rule, and his definitive authority as arbiter of taste for the civilized world. The designs were engraved according to mathematically precise formulas in a tightly gridded scheme. This approach was aesthetically removed from the humanist tradition and followed quantitative rather than organic principles

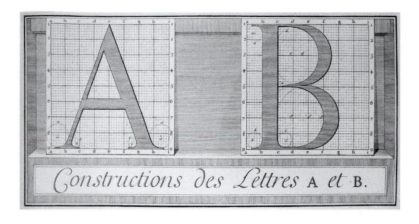

5.15a Romain du Roi designs for *A* and *B*, 1690s. Louis Simoneau's copperplate engravings show the unitary system for generating mathematically perfect letterforms in great detail. Modularity and precise measure governed the designs of the Romain du Roi, which were static and mechanical in their original form. But when interpreted by punch cutter Philippe Grandjean, the letterforms were subtly modified. Had they been produced to conform to the original designs, the absolute verticality and evenness of measure in each stroke would have been deadening. This stateliness had been an intentional aspect of the designs, conceived according to the majestic sensibility of the baroque style epitomized by Louis XIV.

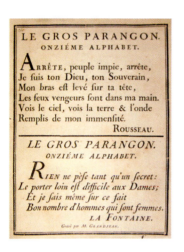

of proportion. In this respect, the Romain du Roi designs anticipated the neoclassical forms of modern type that came into vogue fifty years later. They exemplified an attitude toward design rooted in the notion of expertise as a function of intellectual knowledge rather than craft experience. The Romain du Roi's design was also a representation of royal splendor that was essential to baroque culture. The types were controlled entirely by the Imprimerie Royale (royal printing house), and their use for any but officially sanctioned purposes was a criminal offense. They encoded the very image of the state as a centralized authority. Because they could not be licensed for use, they were widely imitated in spirit as well as form (Figs. **5.15a** and **5.15b**).

Typefaces and graphic designs were also influenced by exchanges in visual and decorative arts prompted by global trade. Early eighteenth-century rococo design sensibility in Europe drew on exotic motifs

in the ideas and ideals that its formal sensibility expresses.

5.15b Philippe Grandjean, Romain du Roi, 1702. The final form of the typeface reveals considerable modification by Philippe Grandjean. He softened the mathematical rigidity of the models into forms that had some of the variation and liveliness of more traditional type designs. The contrast between ideal designs on paper and realized letters in metal demonstrates the difference between theoretical and practical knowledge. Although the original designs were all based on a square, Grandjean took liberties with these absolute proportions. The flat serifs, with almost no bracketing, are one of the striking departures from Old Style designs that would become characteristic of neoclassical faces at the end of the eighteenth century.

from the Middle East, Africa, and Asia (conceived as the *Orient*), and a vogue for **chinoiserie** appeared in elaborately decorated type and border designs. Paradoxically, some of the same designers involved in adorning these delicately complex devices were also responsible for advancing the logical basis of type production. Pierre-Simon Fournier le Jeune extended the rationalization of type design by standardizing **point sizes** and the height of type to paper, so that types cast by one foundry could be used in coordination with those produced by another. Fournier's 1737 *Table of Proportions* proposed uniform measures to be shared by a community of printers, and his imitations of the royal typefaces put their forms into wider circulation. His 1742 *Modèles des Caractères* displayed modern faces based on the formal system that was so conspicuous in the design of the Romain du Roi. These innovations were part of a larger shift toward administered culture. The same logical principles that governed the management of production were those that prevailed in the coordinated management of populations and resources. Fournier's typographic ornaments, or **fleurons**, were flowery forms designed to be used with the same **combinatorial** regularity as any other font. Although modularity had been a feature

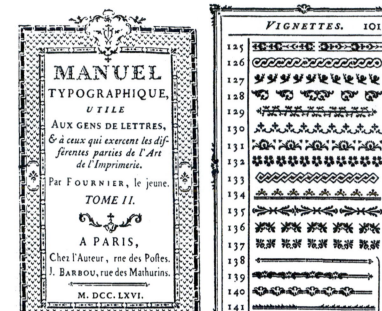

**5.16 Pierre-Simon Fournier le Jeune,
Manuel Typographique, 1766.**
Fournier's typographic specimens
contained ornaments that could be
combined as elements of a consistent and
logical system. These metal decorations
were known as printers' flowers, and
they brought symmetry and harmony
to eighteenth-century page designs.
Rococo arabesques and floral tendrils of
the period are immediately recognizable.
Lacelike curves create a lively pattern that
depends on an underlying grid to order
its combinations. Although the use of
display faces began in earnest only in the
nineteenth century, eighteenth-century
taste in book design was receptive to
elaborately decorative letterforms.

of Renaissance print technology, the idea of a system as an overarching
principle of organization was a new and characteristic feature of eighteenth-
century approaches (Fig. **5.16**).

In the 1770s, François Ambroise Didot perfected the 72-points-to-the-
inch system elaborated in Fournier's *Manuel Typographique*, first published
in 1764. The Didot firm was also instrumental in bringing a neoclassical
sensibility to late eighteenth-century typography that banished much of the

The aesthetic effect of letterforms depends, in part, on layout.

rococo excess associated with the monarchy. The spare elegance of Didot's
page designs echoed the intellectual coolness ushered in by a revival of
Greek art. Symmetry and clean lines replaced the effusive floral patterns
of a generation earlier. The technical skill of late eighteenth-century punch
cutters rose to the challenge of producing hairline serifs and strokes. The
minimal page designs of Didot's monumental publications appear almost
severe in their elimination of all but typographic elements. Although
industry roles were increasingly distinct, a certain number of printers, like
Didot, were publishers as well. Others primarily did work for hire. Large
firms had the economic advantage of in-house type production, whereas
smaller firms were supplied by foundries. Many printers could not have
sustained their business if they had to cast all of their own typographic
material (Fig. **5.17**).

In eighteenth-century England, William Caslon and John Baskerville
brought distinction to British type design for the first time. Caslon's types
were issued in specimen form in 1734 and were immediately adapted for
use in any and every kind of printed matter. Their round sturdiness showed
signs of influence from Dutch Old Style faces. Caslon's letters were so

Modern Typography and the Creation of the Public Sphere

BIBLIORUM
SACRORUM
VULGATÆ VERSIONIS
EDITIO.
TOMUS PRIMUS.

JUSSU CHRISTIANISSIMI REGIS
AD INSTITUTIONEM
SERENISSIMI DELPHINI.

PARISIIS,
EXCUDEBAT FR. AMB. DIDOT NATU MAJ.
M. DCC. LXXXV.

5.17 François Ambroise Didot, *Bibliorum Sacrorum*, **1785.** The Didot family were publishers and expert type founders. F. A. Didot's two sons Pierre and Firmin continued the work of the family firm into the nineteenth century. The types used on this page were designed in the neoclassical style that became popular in the period following the French Revolution when Greek and Roman models were fashionable in dress and decoration as well as government. Didot's finely balanced design is distinguished by the upright quality of the letterforms, the harmonious proportions of the page, and the careful leading and letter spacing of the lines. Nothing extraneous or superfluous is present, either in the letters or on the page. Didot's designs set a style for French literary publishing that signaled high **cultural value**, and his faces continued to be a hallmark of fine content and quality production.

5.18 William Caslon, type specimen, 1734. The overall evenness of Caslon's strokes gives his letters a uniform character that is legible and robust. The uppercase is considerably higher than the lower, and the letters do not have elaborate swashes, tails, or curves (with the exception of the *Q*). The bar on the lowercase *e* is horizontal, and the type has very little slant to it. This verticality distinguishes Caslon from a true Old Style face. Note the peculiar fit of the letters and word spaces and the space before the question mark. **Orthography** and punctuation were being standardized by printing, and conventions of composition established in the pressroom had a real influence. Caslon's faces had enormous practical value, and, although letter by letter the designs are somewhat homely, when set, they are comfortably readable in many sizes, leadings, and line lengths.

popular that they were practically considered the English national face, even as they were being exported to the New World. Caslon was a type designer, not a publisher, and he had little control over the use of his faces. Novels, broadsides, journals, newspapers, public notices, trade cards, menus, and advertisements of every sort were set in Caslon. Caslon's faces were robust, and they were versatile. But if worn and battered, ill-set or poorly laid out, they could also seem banal and inelegant. The aesthetic effect of letterforms is not merely a function of shape but also of layout and printing skill (Fig. **5.18**).

John Baskerville's career embodied an aesthetic sensibility and entrepreneurial imagination characteristic of his era. He had apprenticed to a writing master but went into the business of decorating vases, fans, and screens using a lacquer technique known as "japanning." These elegant objects met with enthusiasm among the rising British professional and business classes. Having made his fortune, Baskerville turned his attentions

5.19a John Baskerville, type specimen, 1762. Baskerville's faces sparkle with a perfection that made them seem alien and chill to his contemporaries, many of whom complained that they were hard to read. The phrase "Baskerville pains" became synonymous with difficulty in reading. What distinguished Baskerville's type was the influence of copperplate engraving and the delicate line quality it sustained. Baskerville's earliest training had been in penmanship, and his approach to letterforms was rooted in that discipline, rather than in the experience of punch cutting. Each letter is exquisite on its own, and every formal detail is tended.

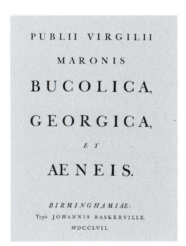

5.19b Virgil, *Bucolica, Georgica, et Aeneis*, designed and printed by John Baskerville, 1757. The austere clarity of Baskerville's design anticipates the neoclassical typography that appeared in French and Italian publishing at the end of the eighteenth century. The spacing and leading of the type alone confer a commanding authority upon the page. The argument can be made that this type breaks up, that its forms do not hold together as words, that the overall effect is one of strokes and spikes rather than letters and lines; however, the decision to dispense with ornament and concentrate entirely on the text of the Latin poet established a typographic ideal that would find enthusiastic followers in the early twentieth century, when these typefaces were revived alongside older humanistic faces.

and resources to the design of type. He invented a blacker, denser ink and pioneered the use of **calendared** paper that was rendered smooth and shiny by being pressed between hot plates. During his lifetime, Baskerville made exclusive use of his types for publications of his own design. A scholar with an international circle of correspondents, he worked in the mode of the **private press** publisher, and the effects of his type were exquisitely controlled in layout and production. But when he died, his types and punches only found a buyer in France. They had been mocked in England for their supposed illegibility, but Baskerville's types found favor with the French dramatist and publisher Pierre A. C. Beaumarchais, who bought them from the designer's widow in 1775. Although the purchase effectively removed them from circulation, it also preserved them. It would be more than a century before Baskerville's designs were revived, but they have subsequently remained in continuous use as standard text faces (Figs. **5.19a** and **5.19b**).

Adria, Città antica d' Italia, che diede il nome al Golfo Adriati.

Another major figure of modern typography was the Italian printer and publisher Giambattista Bodoni. His letters reflected the late eighteenth-century neoclassical interest in order and brought modern type design to maturity. Whereas seventeenth-century academic quarrels had pitted the "Ancients" against the "Moderns" in a contest of aesthetic virtue, the eighteenth-century faces that we now call "modern" are grounded in geometrical proportion, which was an outstanding trait of classicism. Bodoni's early hero had been Baskerville, but his approach to design extended a highly rational manner even further. He distilled letterforms into basic elements of serifs, straight lines, and curved strokes, as if they were units to be recombined, rather than integral parts of a gestural whole.

Bodoni distilled letterforms into recombinations of basic units.

Bodoni's designs earned him international success and celebrity. He was honored by royalty and esteemed by the publishing world. In addition to his editions of classical and biblical texts, he designed books by contemporary writers, both in their original language and in Italian translation. His career demonstrates the extent to which print design was esteemed as an art and rewarded as a service (Figs. **5.20a** and **5.20b**).

The durable versatility of typefaces designed by Caslon, Baskerville, and Bodoni was proven when they were reinterpreted for mechanized production by **Linotype** and **Monotype** machines in the nineteenth century. Digital versions are testimony to the continuity between their "modern" sensibilities and contemporary graphic design. The development of modern typography depended on more than this handful of designers, but their stories exemplify the relationship between graphic design and the business of printing and publishing in the eighteenth century. Contributions of aesthetic value also had commercial value, and artistic achievement was compensated in a successful industrial undertaking. The craft of printing and the work of graphic design were intimates of the business world, and commerce was more than a mere handmaid to the artistic spirit.

5.21a Joseph Highmore, illustration for Samuel Richardson's *Pamela*, 1744.
Illustrated editions of novels popularized reading in the eighteenth century, and the consumption of fiction increased with print runs. Tales of innocent young women corrupted by adventurous and predatory men provided cautionary instruction about the price of virtue. The engravings featured in Richardson's epistolary novel were based on twelve paintings by Joseph Highmore. In this one, the action is static, and the picture space mimics a theater stage in its flat presentation of figures brought to attention by highlighting. Yet the audience for such images grew to support separate sales of narrative illustrations as suites of prints.

5.21b William Hogarth, *Gin Lane*, 1751.
Hogarth's prints epitomized the spirit of the age of Enlightenment. His mastery of production is evident in his sweeping narrative range, while the moral of his tales was unmistakably conceived within the highly gendered and class-based values of the time. Vice and virtue were distinct categories and absolutely defined. Wisdom and folly were a matter of will and character. Hogarth often made superbly witty exposés of the greed and hypocrisy that he perceived among the bourgeoisie. The complex, crisscrossed composition, multitonal divisions of space, and symbolic moments in this print demonstrate his skill as a draftsman. With it, Hogarth was able to conjure dramatic impact and social criticism in the same work. His caricatures helped fix particular types in the public mind. Hogarth's work was widely pirated. In response, he lobbied aggressively for the Engraver's Copyright Act in England, which passed in 1735. Sometimes referred to as *Hogarth's Act*, it was a significant—if not always effective—milestone in the protection of **intellectual property** in print culture.

On the edge of industrialization
Eighteenth-century type and book design continued to enrich the range of faces and formats in print. Books illustrated with copperplate engravings became far more common, and major artists created drawings for publication. The appeal and utility of courtly handbooks, military and martial arts treatises, garden books, guides to gallant behavior, and works of entertainment relied on such illustrations. Scientific and technical fields depended increasingly on the skill of engravers to produce maps, plans, schemes, diagrams, and renderings. Engraved title pages that framed a reader's entry to a text with architectural motifs became fashionable, as did garlands and wreaths for chapter headings and borders. In the eighteenth century, the novel emerged as a major literary form, distinct from poetry, drama, and other genres. Illustrated works by celebrated authors created visual archetypes alongside descriptions of characters. Such entertainment engaged a broadening readership. Meanwhile, specialized communities were served by publications that sustained and advanced professional discourse (Figs. **5.21a** and **5.21b**).

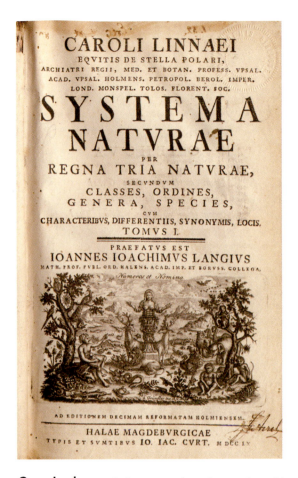

5.22 Carl Linnaeus, *Systema Naturae*, 1758. The study of natural sciences leapt forward with the work of Carl Linnaeus, a Swedish scientist who developed a **taxonomic** system based on scientific principles. His classification system established the hierarchy of phylum, class, order, genus, and species that is still used. Based on empirical observation and **morphology**, it was the first fully inclusive and organized taxonomy. The engraving on the title page depicts the natural world as a kind of Eden. The idea of nature as an innocent condition was an eighteenth-century concept that was used to justify many distinctions and actions. The ideal of an original uncorrupted purity is exemplified in this design, even as the ordering system, so elegantly described and laid out on this title page, brings nature under the control of reason. One of the goals of Enlightenment rationality was to banish superstition from the natural world, allowing nature's ways to be understood by the empirical means of science. One effect of the removal of the sacred by these forays of reason was to render nature's resources entirely testable and exploitable. The development of descriptive systems to identify the forms and processes of nature was an essential part of this effort, since language defined the world.

Conclusion Enlightenment thought was shaped by the use of print to disseminate information, manage power, and administer resources. Landmark publications by Blaise Pascal, John Locke, Robert Hooke, Isaac Newton, Denis Diderot, Carl Linnaeus, Thomas Paine, and others helped define geology, anthropology, history, mathematics, astronomy, biology, politics, and other fields. The allegorical imagery of these publications' **frontispieces** often stood in striking contrast to their sober interior pages. Renaissance humanism had been replaced by Enlightenment reason. The era was characterized by a commitment to social and technical progress, a conviction that scientific knowledge should be freed from religious doctrine, the establishment of democratic forms of government, and the rise of markets that generated—and were dependent on—the flow of capital. The intellectual, legal, and economic liberations of the Enlightenment cleared the way for a massive change, as industrialization shifted into gear. Printing, which had helped bring about the Enlightenment, was, in turn, to be affected by its fruits: Production would be boosted by mechanization and industrial methods at the beginning of the nineteenth century. Newspapers, fine and popular press books, scientific publishing, and information design had established graphic conventions that could be clearly identified. As audiences and readerships grew, niche markets and specialized functions would propel graphic design toward previously unimagined variety (Fig. **5.22**).

Modern Typography and the Creation of the Public Sphere 1660–1800

1660 Charles II restored to English throne

Birth of Daniel Defoe, author of *Robinson Crusoe*

1661 Robert Boyle's *The Sceptical Chymist* inaugurates modern chemistry

1662 John Graunt publishes first work on statistical methods of studying mortality

1663 Royal Academy of Inscriptions and Belles Lettres founded in France

Missionary bibles printed in Algonquin language in Cambridge, Massachusetts

1664 New Amsterdam becomes New York

Robert Hooke's *Micrographia* published in London

1665 Great Plague in London

Publication of *Philosophical Transactions of the Royal Society*, first scientific journal, begins

1666 Academy of Sciences founded in France

First Stradavarius violins made

1667 Publication of John Milton's *Paradise Lost* begins

1669 Death of Rembrandt

Blaise Pascal's *Pensées* published

1670 Dom Perignon perfects Champagne production

Anton von Leeuwenhoek sees animals through a microscope

1677 Death of Spinoza

1678 John Bunyan's *Pilgrim's Progress* (written in jail) published

1679 Death of Thomas Hobbes

1682 William Penn founds Philadelphia

1683 Joseph Moxon's *Mechanick Exercises* published

Ottoman Empire fails siege of Vienna

1689 Peter the Great crowned Czar of Russia

1690 First paper mill in U.S. established near Philadelphia by William Rittenhouse

John Locke's *An Essay Concerning Human Understanding* published

1692 Romain du Roi designs completed

Salem witchcraft trials

1694 Freedom of the press laws enacted in England

1697 Charles Perrault's *Tales of Mother Goose* published

1702 Romain du Roi types, cut by Philippe Grandjean, first published

1704 Isaac Newton's *Opticks* published

1709 First Copyright Act passed in Britain

Bartolomeo Cristofori makes first piano

The Tatler launched by Addison and Steele

1711 Tuning fork invented

1715 Rococo style of Louis XV and his mistress Mme. de Pompadour becomes popular

1717 Diving bell invented

1718 First English banknote

1719 Daniel Defoe's *Robinson Crusoe* published

René Réaumur conceives of producing paper from wood pulp

1721 Bach composes Brandenburg concertos

1725 William Ged invents stereotyping method using papier-mâché

1726 Jonathan Swift's *Gulliver's Travels* published

1728 Vitus J. Bering, Danish explorer, finds Alaska

Benjamin Franklin sets up print shop in Philadelphia

1734 Caslon's first type specimen sheet

1735 Carolus Linnaeus's *Systema Naturae* founds modern biological classification systems

1737 Fournier le Jeune standardizes type sizes and height to paper

1742 Fournier's *Modèles de Caractères* published

James Lind discovers cure for scurvy in citrus

1751 Publication of Diderot and d'Alembert's *Encyclopédie* begins

1752 Benjamin Franklin invents lightning rod

1755 Samuel Johnson's *Dictionary* published in London

1757 Baskerville publishes Virgil's *Aeneid*

Horace Walpole establishes Strawberry Hill, early private press

1759 Voltaire's *Candide* published

1760 George III crowned King of England

1762 Jean Jacques Rousseau's *The Social Contract* published

1764 Horace Walpole's *Castle of Otranto* introduces gothic theme in literature

Death of William Hogarth

Fournier's *Manuel Typographique* published

Spinning Jenny invented by James Hargreaves to automate production of yarn

Johann Winckelmann's *Art of Antiquity* published

1766 Gotthold Lessing's *Laocoon: An Essay on the Limits of Painting and Poetry* published

1769 James Watt patents steam engine

1770 Captain James Cook goes to Australia

1775 Postal service established in North America

More than fifty printers in the thirteen American colonies

Flushable toilets invented

1776 Adam Smith's *The Wealth of Nations* published

American colonies declare independence

First volume of Edward Gibbon's *Decline and Fall of the Roman Empire* published

1779 Franz Mesmer's *Animal Magnetism* published

1781 British surrender at Yorktown

Immanuel Kant's *Critique of Pure Reason* published

1783 Didot perfects Fournier's point system

Ludwig Beethoven's musical scores first published

1787 Mozart writes *Don Giovanni*

1789 French Revolution begins

Guillotine invented

William Blake publishes *Songs of Innocence*

1790 George Vancouver explores western coast of North America

Thomas Bewick's *General History of the Quadrupeds* published

HMS *Bounty* mutineers establish a colony on Pitcairn Island

1791 Thomas Paine's *The Rights of Man* published

1792 Mary Wollstonecraft's *A Vindication of the Rights of Woman* published

1793 Louis XVI and Marie Antoinette beheaded

1795 Metric system adopted in France

1796 First smallpox vaccinations

Alois Senefelder invents lithography

Napoleon marries Josephine

1798 Thomas Malthus's *Essay on the Principle of Population* predicts explosive growth

Gaspard Monge develops basis for orthographic projection

1799 Baskerville's widow sells his printing materials to French playwright Beaumarchais

Rosetta stone found in Egypt

Tools of the Trade

Powdered pigments

Chinese ink and India ink

Color ink

Sugar and gum arabic medium

Chalk

Chalk pastels

Crayons

Graphite stylus

Black and red pencils

Stumps for smudging

Duck feather quills

Quill-ferruled brush

Sable brushes

Gum eraser

Rubber erasers (1770s)

Scissors

Knives

Fine drafting tools

French curve

Standard metric rulers

T-square

Metal rulers

Compasses

Bladders to hold mixed paints

Canvas

Transparent papers for tracing

Cotton wove paper

Ruled paper

Soft-ground etching

Aquatint (late 1700s)

Stipple etching

Mezzotint rockers

Drawing board

Portable easel

Wood portfolio stand

Flayed model casts for life drawing

Study collections of drawings

Transparent papers for color mixing

Lettering manuals

Silhouettes and shadow tracing

Squaring-up grids for enlarging

Pantographs for reproduction

Anamorphic lenses (optical distortion)

Coal gas lamps (late 1700s)

6. The Graphic Effects of Industrial Production 1800–1850

- The industrialization of print production expanded graphic and typographic vocabularies.

- Promotional uses of printed images helped produce **mass** markets and, incidentally, a new visual culture.

- Publications served to mediate social values across readerships and classes to an unprecedented degree, as literacy rates grew within an increasingly mobile workforce.

- **Lithography** and **photography** altered the aesthetic and conceptual codes of imagery, and printed images assumed social and practical functions in education, entertainment, politics, and science.

- Mass-produced graphic media became objects of consumption in their own right, and the line between commercial art and fine art defined the status of graphic design in modern visual culture.

6.1 Poster advertising Honoré de Balzac's *Petites Misères de la Vie Conjugale* (*The Little Miseries of Married Life*), 1845. Lithography was used for color printing, but approaches to the *design* of lithographic color were still closely tied to woodblock practices. In this image, separate areas of flat color were carefully registered in a series of press runs from individual blocks. The fluidity of image and text relations in lithography stems from their being drawn in the same way and printed from the same surface (although in this case, the black type seems to have been added on a letterpress). The appearance of a new Balzac novel was an event worth publicizing. The plight of a husband, bearing his idle wife with her lapdog (in imitation of an aristocratic lady) while carrying an infant and struggling with a toddler twisted around his leg, promises to unfold under the influence of a devil who hovers, whispering into his ear. The scene is contemporary, the narrative is poised for action, and the poster promotes its consumption. Many of Balzac's novels were published in serial form in daily newspapers, reaching a broad audience to whom this advertisement was meant to appeal.

Industrialization reconfigured practices that were fundamental to every area of European and American culture, including graphic design. In 1800, printing was still done on presses with wood mechanisms similar to those first used by Gutenberg. Every impression had to be inked and pulled by hand, one sheet at a time. The invention of the cast-iron press around 1803 allowed for a larger printing area and greater pressure, both of which were necessary for effective reproduction of images. The first papermaking machines increased paper production. The speed and efficiency of mechanized punch cutting and typecasting generated decorative **display types** in abundance. Industrial scaling methods produced larger point sizes in an enormous array of designs. By the 1820s, the combination of steam power, iron presses, and **endgrain** wood engraving released a stream of illustrated weeklies for public consumption. Entrepreneurial and democratically inclined publishers promoted educational and entertaining printed materials that sold cheaply to a growing spectrum of the population. Literacy rates increased, prompted by the need for a workforce that could read, write, and calculate, and driven by an ideology that promoted self-improvement. Lithography brought new flexibility to image production, while photography brought new codes of realism. Under industrial conditions of production and distribution, **mass culture** flourished: Images circulated more readily, advertising grew, and type design was stimulated. Folk and popular traditions endured alongside new cultural forms in which the centralized production of print media played a major role. **Compositors** and **layout** artists took on design tasks as workers in the printing trade. Their contributions to the rising advertising and publishing industries begin to look familiar to contemporary eyes (Fig. **6.1**).

6.2a Engraving of George Gordon (Lord Byron) by Henry Meyer, after a drawing by George Harlow (second version), 1816. George Gordon—Lord Byron—was the first and most celebrated figure of romantic poetry. The 1812 publication of the first sections of his long poem, *Childe Harold*, made him famous. His reputation for being "mad, bad, and dangerous to know" made him infamous. But the demand for mass-produced images of the poet could barely be satisfied by the printing technology of the day. As a model of mass-culture celebrity, he was unparalleled in the early nineteenth century. His curls, striking profile, and white throat exposed by the open collar of a flowing shirt became the defining image of the romantic poet and were much imitated by his followers. That "Byronic" image came before the public eye with its own attractive force, even as Byron's poetry gained instant and far-flung renown.

Industrialization and visual culture In the cities of Europe and the United States, printed artifacts took their place within the increasingly prolific realm of visual culture in the early industrial era. Hand-painted signs remained a vivid feature of any environment where tradesmen operated shops, pubs, or agencies. Paintings, tapestries, and sculpture had long adorned the churches and homes of the upper classes. But a combination of new production and importation capabilities made elaborate textiles, decorated china, fancy housewares, and painted furnishings more affordable, even as the economic basis for this

Romanticism took flight, partly in response to industrialization.

6.2b Illustration for *The Byron Gallery*, 1833 *(above right).* The demand for illustrated versions of Byron's poems provided a pretext for many images of the poet to show up in engraved prints. The male figure in this image is an example of *Byronism*, the fad of mimicking the poet's distinctive features. A subsidiary graphic industry arose on the force of Byron's fame, aiming products at a mainly female readership. Deluxe editions designed for drawing rooms and boudoirs offered sumptuously printed drawings of the characters in his works. The capacity of industrial production methods to meet this demand helped create media stardom and make it an integral part of the romantic movement.

affordability shifted more workers into the anonymity and flux of urban centers. The social and technical changes that define this era occurred in the context of a cultural shift from the rationalism of eighteenth-century neoclassicism and empiricism to the emerging spirit of **romanticism**. Nature, passion, and unbridled imagination took swift flight—partly in response to the perceived numbing effects of industrialization. In the world against which the romantics rebelled, progress was seen as synonymous with the engines of industry, and knowledge was acquired in order to be profitably applied. Publishers justified their entrepreneurial activities with the rhetoric of democratic idealism. They promoted broader public education in popular journals and illustrated books. Printed matter became abundant, and changes in the sites and uses of posters, ephemera, and publicity introduced images and texts into the daily environment in unprecedented ways. Stimulated by **mass media**, **celebrity culture** intensified. Standards of beauty and style were reinforced. Fashion was no longer simply the concern of an aristocratic elite but became part of the lives of the middle and working classes who saw themselves newly represented and addressed in print (Figs. **6.2a** and **6.2b**).

6.3a Vauxhall Gardens, bill of fare, 1826.
The design of this bill of fare reveals that sufficient business was being transacted consistently enough to merit setting and printing the menu. The design is unadorned, but Robert Thorne's **fat face** letters provide a solid heading for itemized refreshments and their prices. These faces echoed those likely to be seen on posters for entertainments at Vauxhall. The layout is long and clear, legible to the waiter and client alike. The receipt shows the public character of this commercial transaction: Everything is as systematized and organized as goods on stock shelves. Although the connection may be subtle, the relation between the consumption of entertainments and the production of goods is marked in such a design. Disposable income and leisure time spent in Vauxhall were earned in urban settings where industrialization concentrated working populations and structured the use and economics of free time.

6.3b Coach notices, 1820 and 1830
(right). These coach notices feature two variants of a woodcut that serves as a motif or icon, rather than a depiction, of the conveyance being advertised. Image production in everyday print shops remained limited in the early nineteenth century. Although fine engravings were used for book illustrations, and lithography was beginning to find its way into poster production, the convenience and cheapness of woodblocks kept them a standard element of print culture. Imagery in advertisements remained crude, and cuts were often worn and clogged with ink, but bold typography made a graphic match for rough woodcuts and battered borders.

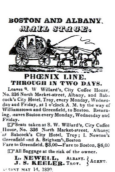

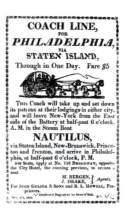

6.3c Grocer's label, 1820. Coarse woodblock cuts, much worn and generically suggestive, adorn this label but provide very little specific information about the grocer's wares. Woodblocks came in for repeated use and functioned more as a sign language than as pictorial images. Tea is represented as a commodity that connects the Orient and the West by way of the sea, and the shape of the three-masted vessel rhymes with that of the pagoda. The reach of empire was extensive in the nineteenth century. British and European colonies supplied raw materials for industrial production alongside spices, textiles, and—importantly for graphic design—prints and other artworks.

The participation of printed matter in the business of daily life also marked a change in the function of visual culture. Ephemera such as tickets, **billheads**, **bills of fare**, menus, and other momentarily useful items began to make their appearance. Public notices and posters made use of the rapidly expanding vocabulary of display types when they were not expressively composed on a lithography stone. Competition for viewers and readers intensified. Skilled design of printed materials contributed to the economic value of competing services and products in a growing commercial landscape. Illustrators and caricaturists made their own contributions to the vicissitudes of industrial and political activity. Boom and bust cycles, partisan struggles and labor shortages, hardships and surfeits all prompted rhetorical strategies: to seduce hesitant customers, promote bargains, reach a specific audience—or have a joke at the expense of a public figure. Print culture was both an industrial product and an instrument through which markets and opinions were mediated (Figs. **6.3a–c**).

Illustrated papers The most radical change in the media landscape came not in books or prints—although these were certainly modified by industrialization—but in the development of illustrated papers. At first, broadsheet publishers continued the tradition of the scandal-centered news sheet by publishing sensational tales of crime and relying on stock images. An 1823 publication that described a notorious murder sold 500,000 copies. Whether they preached moral values or radical politics, or merely provided entertainment, these papers used new illustrational techniques to appeal to their readers. Soon, however, democratically inclined entrepreneurship reshaped the mission and design of these papers. Industrialism had brought with it the goal of universal education (with both the controlling and the empowering effects that public education implies). This promise was contingent on the availability of affordable books and reading materials, and

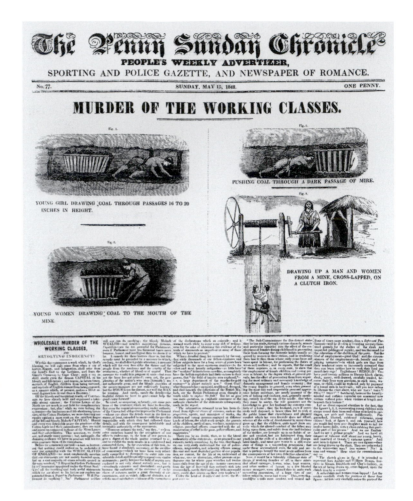

6.4 *The Penny Sunday Chronicle*, "Murder of the Working Classes," 1842. The development of newspapers to address the interests of the working class was a significant feature of nineteenth-century industrialization. The small type size on this well-printed and proportioned, multiple-column page suggests that its readers were expected to be capable of sustained reading. Although only a small percentage of the British population could read, write, or even sign their own names in 1800, that number grew rapidly. Basic literacy skills produced workers essential to the administration of industrial growth, but **cultural literacy** and the exchange of opinions also fostered independent thinking and political organizing. The subtitle of this paper lists the entertainments and distractions it features to indulge readers' appetites, but the front page story and images are far from amusing. The engravings publicize working conditions in the mines with dramatic graphic impact.

Newspapers began to address the interests of the working class.

this is what some publishers sought to provide. Anyone spending a penny of his or her wages to purchase a paper certainly measured that outlay against the cost of other choices, such as a cup of tea or a pound of flour. Still, the value of print was symbolic, as well as economic. The consumption of information and stories fueled imaginations and stimulated fantasy. In their pursuit of mass education, newspapers were a major cultural force, shaping opinions, identities, and audiences (Fig. **6.4**).

Organs like *The Penny Magazine* in England were conceived with the aim of purveying pictorial information in affordable formats. Editor Charles Knight, taking seriously the mission of his sponsor, the Christian philanthropic Society for the Diffusion of Useful Knowledge, sought to inform his readers about the natural world and foreign lands in a generously illustrated publication that sold for a penny a copy. Between 1832 and 1845, *The Penny Magazine* established the viability of the illustrated weekly. It sold well to a faithful audience and was circulated to numbers far in excess of its edition size (it was estimated that every copy had four or more readers) before it was driven out of business by competitors keen to copy its techniques. Didacticism was both overt and subtle in the editorial stance

DALKEITH.—THE DUKE OF BUCCLEUCH'S.

6.5 *The Penny Magazine*, "The Dying Gladiator," 1833. *The Penny Magazine* was published by the Society for the Diffusion of Useful Knowledge. This reproduction of a Roman sculpture is artfully drawn and rendered in a steel engraving. The precision of its line work presents the classical nude as an object worthy of contemplation for its graceful proportions and dignified representation of the human form. The nobility of the figure reinforces a moral tale of commitment to duty. It is glossed by a caption emphasizing the valor of perseverance under duress. The arts were supposed to be uplifting, and classical sculpture and verse were seen as a counterpoint to novels, romantic poetry, and scandal sheets. *The Penny Magazine* maintained a tone of superiority and pedagogical correctness designed to advance its readers beyond their humble origins.

6.6 *The Illustrated London News*, 1842 *(above right)*. Queen Victoria's travels to Scotland supplied the topic of this travel feature showing scenes of the northern landscape toured by the monarch. Vignettes sketched from observation portrayed local costumes and customs while celebrating particular events. Depictions of "the royal party on Loch Tay" or the queen and prince landing in some specific spot were meant to integrate them with the landscape to the point of conflation. The pageantry and pomp accompanying their arrival at any particular site could be extrapolated to present an image of unified support. Populations throughout the British Isles could thus be imagined welcoming their queen in any and all circumstances. The sense that the reader was being invited to share in the experience broadened participation; a diverting feature such as this was also a means of building loyalty among British subjects by making them feel they were all part of a common narrative.

of these weeklies. The virtues of hard work and honesty were praised in animal and insect species, while a reproduction of a great work of art might occasion a caption commending moral character. Images sold, and editors and advertisers were happy to satisfy their readers' appetites for instructive illustration (Fig. **6.5**).

Other publishers were less moralistic. Benjamin Day's slogan for the New York-based paper *The Sun*—"it shines for all"—was first and foremost an unabashed bid for a broad audience. Changes in print technology were well-timed for such ambition. Frederick Koenig, a German inventor living in England, filed a patent for the first automated press in 1811. When this press was put to work at *The London Times* in 1814, the paper boasted of its capacity to produce 1,100 sheets an hour. By contrast, a **hand press** would have produced 125 sheets an hour. When Day purchased his steam-driven press in 1835, it could print 4,000 copies an hour. By 1851, the rate was 18,000 copies. When *The New York Herald* was founded in 1835, its publisher, James Gordon Bennett, aimed for 20,000 copies a day. Bennett set in motion some of the basic operations of modern journalism. He promoted investigative reporting, extended coverage of world events, and depended on maximal sales rather than political patronage to finance his enterprise. A growing market spawned dozens of provincial and urban newspapers, all vying for circulation and advertisers. The introduction of images as a regular feature of the penny press created new journalistic genres, such as travel narratives and features evoking local and exotic scenes, rather than simply reporting events. The illustrated press was as much a product for consumption as it was a means of communicating information (Fig. **6.6**).

Specialty publications began to cater to selective tastes of consumers, playing on their self-perception as discriminating audiences. *Godey's Lady's Book* was launched in 1830. This and other women's journals fostered a fashion-conscious sense of self-image through visual reproductions. The subject of beauty, which had been the province of poets and painters, now had a place in mass media. Here, beauty was not a timeless ideal but an ever-changing set of norms. The ephemerality of fashion generated a

6.7 *Mechanic's Magazine*, 1823. This publication promoted the ideal of applied knowledge as a benefit to industry and a key to society's advancement. The contributions of scientist-engineers, like James Watt, inventor of the steam engine, were celebrated and held up as models. Practical use of learning and the idea of self-improvement were part of the ethos of such journals. This ethos also drove the publication of encyclopedias filled with detailed articles on specific machines and industrial processes. Whether or not an aspiring engineer could learn enough from such publications to actually fabricate working machines, a reader would certainly absorb the lessons of hard work and study.

subsidiary industry in publications meant to keep one as up-to-date as a "fashion plate" (a term used figuratively to mean a fashionable person but which literally referred to the engravings reproduced in such publications). The *Mechanic's Magazine*, first published in 1823, reached a steady and loyal base of 16,000 subscribers who had a use for the diagrams and technical illustrations contained in its pages. Factual information found its audience, although, perhaps, never so successfully as entertainment and scandal. The concept of self-improvement and education indicated a newly mobile workforce with a sense of its capacity for self-determination. Media helped construct this concept as well as gratify the desires it generated (Fig. **6.7**).

Book design for mass production
Novels and poems found wider readerships at the beginning of the nineteenth century, as literacy rates rose in Europe and the United States. But the volume of print production remained limited until steam-powered presses came into use. Production capabilities varied by location, and the industrialization of printing did not advance at the same rate in all areas. With it came engraved frontispieces and charming illustrations that graced the pages of poetry and fiction. Mass-market publishing escalated, and the fashion for gift books, Christmas books, and other albums catered to a middle class with an appetite for sentimental imagery and decoration. Tales of adventure and travel supplied entertainment. Illustrated Bible stories delivered lessons of moral values and faith. The culture of children's education expanded, and alphabet books with amusing rhymes and colored engravings made their appearance in response to a ready market. Mass media had become a cultural industry that drove styles and set consumption patterns. Reputations were rapidly made through its instruments, and dreams and desires were spread on a grand scale (Figs. **6.8a** and **6.8b**).

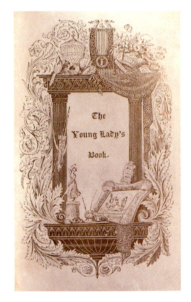

6.8a *The Young Lady's Book*, title page, 1829. Books of instruction on topics ranging from morals to practical arts and crafts became popular among the middle class. They were a means of establishing expectations about behavior and setting limits, however subtle, on gender roles in polite society. This book was extremely popular and went almost immediately into a second edition. The design of its title page presents the range of arts that a young lady must possess—dancing, flower gathering, painting and penmanship, and the care of caged birds. In fact, the book also contains rudiments of ornithology and botany.

A
COLLECTION
OF
JUVENILE BOOKS.

U stands for Umbrella, that
upset Sammy Snub.

6.8b Alphabet book, 1832. John Catnach and his son Jemmy published a wide variety of street literature and inexpensive editions, among them many books for the instruction of children. While learning the alphabet was essential to reading, the moral lessons encoded in these books also provided social and behavioral instruction. That these books were produced by a publisher who also printed (and himself engraved) images of gruesome crimes and violent murderers may or may not have given pause to his readers. Catnach was a commercial success. His presses ran twenty-four hours a day; one account he furnished of a particularly heinous crime ran to over a million printed copies.

Virginie, voyant la mort inévitable, posa une main sur ses habits, l'autre sur son cœur, et, levant en haut des yeux sereins, parut un ange qui prend son vol vers les cieux.

Illustration helped make romanticism a popular concept.

6.9 Jacques-Henri Bernardin de Saint-Pierre, *Paul et Virginie*, 1838. The tale of innocents Paul and Virginie was an immensely popular subject for illustration. The sad plight of the young heroine, here shown casting her eyes to the heavens in advance of an inevitable fate, is about as romantic as an image can be. The human spirit is about to be inundated by forces of nature, a small life lost before the eyes of her beloved. Her modesty prevents her from being saved from a shipwreck, since it would entail stripping and being carried to safety by a sailor. *Paul et Virginie* is considered a gem of early nineteenth-century book design, although the choice of a **neoclassical** typeface links it to the first appearance of the story, originally published in 1789.

Yet the standards of book production were low in this period. Long print runs and worn type produced smeared pages. High-volume production often meant compromised design. The economics of printing did not often include the costs of careful layout, wide margins, well-leaded lines, and other features that improve legibility and enhance aesthetic appeal. Graphic production proliferated, but the role and value of design within it were not yet firmly established. Meanwhile, illustration brought fame to many artists whose work helped make romanticism a popular concept or furnished sentimental imagery that idealized childhood, motherhood, family life, and virtue (Fig. **6.9**).

Publishing and editing were respectable fields for a middle-class man. Printing, although a useful trade, was a form of manual labor and thus a working-class occupation. The gentleman scholar and producer of fine press books in privately issued editions enjoyed an altogether different status, and such individuals rarely did their own printing work. The ranks of printers and engravers were largely filled through apprenticeship rather than formal schooling. The French distinction between *beaux arts* ("fine arts") and *métiers* ("trades") marked a difference of class and employment

6.10 *Lady Willoughby's Diary*, Chiswick Press, 1844. Industrialization lowered publishing production standards dramatically in early nineteenth-century Britain. The use of high-speed presses and machine-made paper, and the rapid release of large editions for a mass market, meant that the care and craft of hand press production disappeared under commercial pressures. The literary publisher, Chiswick Press, was an exception to this rule. By its example, Chiswick Press showed that book design could be expertly executed even in an industrial era. They revived Caslon's excellent book types after several decades of neglect and had them recast and set with regard for the shape of the page and the text upon it. The results became a model for other **fine press** productions and artistic engagements with book design in the late nineteenth century.

1. Geospiza magnirostris.
2. Geospiza fortis.
3. Geospiza parvula.
4. Certhidea olivacea.

> *Lady* Willoughby.   77
>
> we wept together at the thought that we ſhould   1655.
> ſee his little merrie face no more.
>
> Madame,   *Letter from the Earle of Winchelſea.*
>   It is with unſpeakable Griefe that I have to
> informe your *Ladyſhipp* of the Deceaſe of
> my *Sonne*, who departed this Life at 9 o'
> Clocke this morning. The *Infant* is no
> better, but the Feaver is not ſo greate as was
> the little *Boyes*, and my deare *Wife* doth con-
> tinue to hope it will be ſpared to comfort
> us for our heavy Loſſe: I beg your *Ladyſhip*
> to excuſe more at this time from
>   Madame your *Ladyſhips*
>   Affectionate and humble Servant,
>   *Winchelſea.*
>
>   To-day have received another Letter from   *April 2, Monday.*
> my Lord *Winchelſea*, the little Infant is releaſed.
> My poore *Daughter's* ſorrow unexpreſſable,
> both her precious Babes taken! *Heavenly Fa-*
> *ther*, comfort and ſupport her under this afflict-
>   ing

Fine printers started the vogue for revivals of historical styles.

6.11 Charles Darwin, diary from his voyage on the *Beagle*, 1839. This careful drawing of finches from the Galápagos Islands is reminiscent of earlier biological studies, but the implications of the design of this page offer something else: comparative meaning. Darwin's research depended on the collection, observation, and accurate **rendering** of specimens. In this case, a visual comparison highlights differences in the thickness and shape of the finches' beaks. Rather than confirming that each species had been created independently, Darwin's findings suggested they were versions of a common ancestor. His analysis of these adaptations gave rise to a theory of the natural world's historical dimension. The discovery and classification of fossils, geological layers, and other remains during this same era affirmed belief in this dimension.

expectation that prevailed throughout Europe and the United States. Fine printers and specialized publishers, however, were the ones primarily responsible for starting and supplying the vogue of period style revivals. These connoisseurs oversaw the elaboration of graphic vocabularies meant to signal historical associations (Fig. **6.10**).

The business of scientific publishing expanded. Illustrations by and for major naturalists, such as John James Audubon and Charles Darwin, set high standards for image reproduction and accuracy in drawing. But processes that were only partially visible to the eye also began to find their way into technical drawings and information displays. Although encyclopedic approaches to knowledge were a legacy of eighteenth-century Enlightenment principles, a demand for pages that provided detailed descriptions of industrial procedures and equipment continued to justify the high cost and intense labor of engraving. The design of information framed comparisons and visualized processes as well as presented forms and structures. Geology became a central focus of nineteenth-century study, and the science and practice of archaeology shed light on human history, as well as that of the earth and its flora and fauna (Fig. **6.11**).

6.12 *The Laughers' Museum*, ca. 1840. Consumption of mass-produced prints is portrayed as a popular pastime with passersby pausing to take an entertaining look rather than to make a purchase. Satiric works caricaturing everyday situations were common, and viewers saw their own follies reflected in the images they gazed at, as well as those of others. Political figures had a public life in images. The myth of Napoleon, for instance, was continually reworked. He took on the aura of a heroic martyr through the embellishments of the press. The viewing circumstances evoked in this image offer an opportunity for exchanging ideas provoked by graphic media. These dallying figures are clearly engaged in sympathetic glances and commentary that mediate their responses to the prints.

6.13 Thomas Bewick, *Quadrupeds*, **1790.** Thomas Bewick's illustrated book of quadrupeds vaulted him to prominence and commercial success, although his work was endlessly copied without credit or royalties returning to him. The widespread publication of these images made him a household name. The clarity and precision of his draftsmanship were enabled by carving blocks on the endgrain—the hard, smooth surface of wood cut across the grain. Unlike woodcuts, which relied on raised areas for definition, endgrain blocks could be carved with engraving tools that incised fine, uninked lines. Bewick's white-line wood engravings sparkle with detail. Although he belongs to the end of the eighteenth century, it was industrial levels of reproduction that allowed his imagery to gain a popular following.

Printing images Although prints had been popular for centuries, they had never been so abundant or affordable as they became in the nineteenth century. In the eighteenth century, the cost of a single copperplate print had been beyond the reach of the general population in the United States and Europe. Books illustrated with engravings had been luxury items for an elite market. Relief woodblocks and metal intaglio plates were the only ways of reproducing images until the end of the eighteenth century. In the first half of the nineteenth century, steel engraving, endgrain wood engraving, and lithography dramatically expanded printing capabilities, while photography introduced its own terms for realism defined by mechanical processes. Industrialization had a direct impact on image reproduction techniques, but it also had an indirect impact on traditional visual media, shifting their status and influencing their aesthetics. The public display of images made for the sole purpose of consumption helped codify visual **stereotypes** (the term is derived from an industrial process) and increase the appetite for pictures (Fig. **6.12**).

Image production was still slow and laborious at the beginning of the nineteenth century. But the innovation of endgrain engraving offered an improvement. Since they were printed relief, endgrain wood engravings could be printed at the same time and on the same press as type, just as woodblocks could. But because they were carved into hard endgrain blocks, wood engravings held finer lines and more detail than plankwise cuts and could stand up to larger print runs than copperplate engravings. Stereotyping, and later **electrotyping**, produced multiple casts of original blocks, further increasing print runs. Wood engravings were popularized by Thomas Bewick, whose 1790 *Quadrupeds* was an immediate success. Bewick's graphic talent appeared at an opportune moment and met a huge demand in the publishing industry. His illustrations were copied and used in literary and reference books, broadsides, and anywhere else a printer could find to put them. Versions of his blocks proliferated. This kind of pictorial recycling remained a standard feature of everyday print jobs. But a discerning public was beginning to constitute a market for freshly, specifically, and even lavishly illustrated books (Fig. **6.13**).

6.14a Honoré Daumier, *The Daguerreotype Portrait*, lithograph, 1844. The splendid immediacy of Daumier's drawing anticipates the spontaneity that would characterize photographic images. Although the lithograph has a conspicuously hand-drawn quality, with vigorous strokes everywhere in evidence, the strength of the overall composition and attention to expressive detail show how carefully the image has been developed. Lithography allowed such drawings to be reproduced directly—with all of the characteristic marks of their authors.

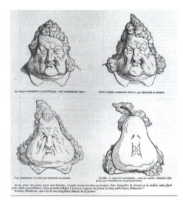

Another new means of printing images arrived with the invention of lithography in 1796 by Alois Senefelder. Lithographic drawings could be made directly on a stone by artists who did not want their work to suffer transformation by an engraver's hand. Even when an original was copied onto a stone by a skilled artisan, the transfer did not entail such differences in tools and effects as engraving required. It took more than a decade for lithography to come into widespread use. The equipment and materials were novel, and training was required in the succession of steps needed to grind, draw on, treat, and print stones. In lithography, the receptive surface of limestone was used and reused as the basis for grease or wax

In lithography, freeform letters could interact with figurative

6.14b Charles Philipon, *Les Poires*, pear caricatures, from *Charivari*, 1832. Satire and **caricature** were highly popular visual forms, and their dependence upon graphic recognition shows visual literacy at work. Following political upheavals, Louis-Philippe ascended to the French throne in July 1830. He became known as the "bourgeois monarch," and his image was quickly codified. Stringent censorship laws made it impossible to ridicule him outright, but the pear shape to which his head devolves in Philipon's 1831 cartoon was crudely reproduced all over the walls of Paris. By reducing the features of the king to a simple, recognizable image, Philipon created a sign that functioned effectively across various media and modes of visual culture.

pencil drawings that were much quicker to print than intaglio. Lithographs were printed on different presses than type, but lettering could be drawn on stones in the same way as images. The possibilities for integrating text and images were, in this sense, much greater than in the side-by-side relationship of woodblocks and text blocks on letterpresses. Freeform letters could interact with figurative compositions with an ease unknown in intaglio engraving. Not until the development of photographic processes of relief engraving would this intimacy of words and visual forms be matched by letterpress (Figs. **6.14a** and **6.14b**).

Photography was invented in the 1820s when Frenchmen Nicéphore Niépce and Louis Daguerre, working independently, found ways to produce an image by exposing metallic salts to light. Their inventions were patented in the 1830s as industrial techniques. When British inventor Henry Fox Talbot published his album *Pencil of Nature* in 1844, the images it contained made a convincing argument for the beauty as well as the wonder of the new medium. From its beginnings, photography struggled for recognition as an art form, not just a mechanical process. Photographic methods were not adapted to mass production until later in the nineteenth century, but

The Graphic Effects of Industrial Production

6.15 Daguerreotype. The kind of image Daumier's subject was showing off to his audience would have resembled this portrait. Because of required exposure times, a sitter was obliged to hold a supposedly candid pose at length to achieve a casual look such as this. Photographic portraits quickly gained popularity. The affordability of **daguerreotypes**—named for the inventor of the process—brought portraiture within the reach of the middle class who found the novelty of sitting for a camera irresistible. From the start, photography had a complex relationship with the visual arts. Daguerreotypes were often used as the basis of compositions in traditional media. Their high-contrast tones introduced a new visual code that painters worked with and against in equal measure. Painting sought to distinguish itself from the mere mechanics of the photographic image but also took advantage of the technique as a visual reference for realism.

compositions with an ease unknown in engraving or letterpress.

the standard of realism set by photographic imagery brought challenges. The clash of fine art and mass media placed all the value of originality and creative imagination on the side of individual artists who made unique works. Yet photography provided the early nineteenth-century public with images of itself at a relatively low cost—especially by contrast to traditional portraiture. Fascination with a medium that seemed to draw with light itself (*photo* meaning "light," *graphy* meaning "written") took hold of the public imagination. Travel albums of editioned prints were one of the first genres of photographic publishing, as bourgeois clients yearned for views of exotic sites associated with the fashionable "Grand Tour" of Europe and areas of North Africa and the Middle East. Such souvenir tourist imagery did not usually register the political and social tensions underlying cross-cultural exchanges. Instead, carefully posed images framed picturesque views of other cultures as "exoticized" people and places. Although photographic reproduction was not part of the printing process until about 1850, the early impact of photography on visual culture was profound. An image made entirely from light and chemistry seemed to have a claim to unquestionable truth and infinite accuracy (Fig. **6.15**).

6.16a Announcement of sale, 1829. A cruel irony underlies the use of a rational, neoclassical **titling face** to promote a sale of human beings. Display faces were invented for advertisement and designed to be used hierarchically in a range of sizes and styles. The delicacy of the serifs and relatively small size of this titling face confirm that it is metal type. The wear on the type and relatively poor quality of the printing situate this piece within a service-oriented job shop, rather than a fine printing environment. The development of specimen books to showcase the wares of such a shop allowed clients to choose their own typefaces.

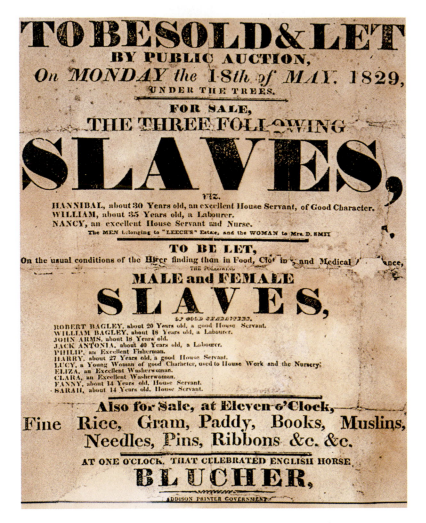

6.16b "3 Guineas Reward," 1829. Reward signs and other public notices were often composed with little planning, as if taken down verbatim from a customer. A typesetter might, as in this case, identify the most important facts—the size of the reward, the nature of the lost item. But, in other cases, the composition—the choice of line breaks or use of display faces—seems almost arbitrary, merely an attempt to break up the monotony of the page and meet a customer's expectations of graphic impact. Typesetting and layout conventions followed familiar norms but were not governed by explicit rules or self-conscious design principles. The habit of capitalizing nouns was reinforced in public language by the graphic style of notices like these. Although the text is written in the third person, the poster's graphic language directly addresses its audience.

Advertising design and typography Public notices were once issued only by figures of authority as proclamations of law or decree. But in the nineteenth century they were widely produced for anyone who could pay to have them set and printed. Notices served to alert the public to sales of property, lost children or possessions, or the presence of criminals in a neighborhood. Many such notices were produced for ephemeral purposes and local populations, and their numbers attest to the availability of print shops as a regular feature of urban and small-town settings. The text of these notices also provides information about the way printers and typesetters worked, since they often seem to be simply a transcription of an oral account rather than a carefully composed message in a calculated design. Taking the extra steps of writing out a text, choosing line breaks, and introducing graphic hierarchy into the setting was not yet a common practice in the composition of ads or ephemera. It also was not a skill someone would pay for. This situation changed, however, as the advertising industry grew and as printers began to invest effort in designs meant to showcase their talents and attract clients (Figs. **6.16a** and **6.16b**).

6.17a *Daily Chronicle*, **Philadelphia, 1831.** Advertising pages represent the best and worst of nineteenth-century design. For sheer efficiency and density of communication, they were unparalleled. But they had to be set quickly and used cuts so worn they were often immediately clotted. **Rule** was battered, type was over-inked, and design choices were more likely to be dictated by whether something fit than by how it looked. But the overall effect, in fact, was very legible and quite engaging to the eye, despite faults at the microlevel of individual letters and lines. These dense pages served their purpose: to advertise goods and services in a concise and direct manner.

Rapid transportation of goods made advertising more critical.

6.17b "Wares," poster, 1830. The balance in this advertisement is finely achieved. Large sizes of display type are explained and supported by small texts below. Variation in color and tone ensure legibility at a distance as well as up close. The range of faces used is sufficient to provide interest but not so outrageous as to cause confusion. A clear hierarchy of content has been established and reinforced by secondary design choices. A professional hand has clearly taken a dense and multifaceted text and turned it into a poster display. Such projects were the stuff of everyday print-shop work, and, although this is a skillful piece, it suggests a job done regularly and competently rather than fussed over.

Industrialization brought new patterns of production and consumption that created opportunities for **graphic art**. In the streets, shops, and fairs of Europe and the United States, producers and purveyors sought a share of the market for their goods and services through the new medium of advertising. As the railroad system spread in the 1830s, new possibilities for rapid distribution of goods made branding and advertising increasingly useful. Of course, the same increased transportation meant that printed materials were more widely disseminated. Urban centers were not the only places in which newspapers and journals circulated. As advertising reached more people, there was increasing competition for readers' attention. Typographic design became a critical factor that shaped communication, and, in the early 1800s, an abundance of new typefaces came into use. Poster designers indulged in riotous displays of sizes, shapes, and varieties of letterforms. A vogue for novelty overcame any residual decorum or sense of restraint. Classified ads ran in newspapers and increasingly occupied the back pages of journals, as patented and trademarked items were produced and distributed. Typographic rhetoric for editorial and advertising purposes acquired a profuse new formal range (Figs. **6.17a–c**).

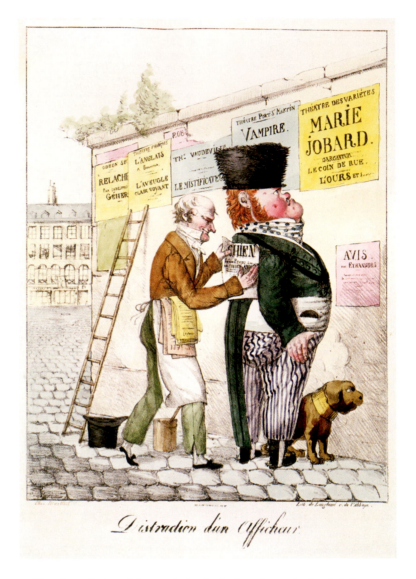

Distraction d'un Afficheur

6.17c Circus bill, 1844. This large poster, originally printed in two colors in Lambeth, London, shows the amount of variety that wood and metal type had developed for publicity purposes. The press on which this would have been printed had a large bed and was capable of considerable impression. Setting a form this big was almost as spectacular a production as the entertainments it described—such as Modern Chinese Warriors! The design creates an expectation that the evening will be varied and active, featuring one amazing performance after another.

6.18 *The Amusement of a Bill-Sticker*, 1820. Rules about posting notices changed continuously, as it became clear that public venues had commercial value and political uses. The struggle to keep certain neighborhoods publicity-free, to claim their walls for official purposes, would only intensify. Meanwhile, the job of the bill-sticker became a subject of humor in the nineteenth century. The absorbed reader hardly notices his surroundings, and the fast-acting bill-sticker uses his pot of glue and brush to paste over any available surface. The size of posters shown remains relatively modest by modern standards, but these must have seemed enormous typographic displays to their audience.

Typefaces designed for use in books had rarely reached point sizes much greater than an inch during the eighteenth century. But this limit vanished at the beginning of the nineteenth century. The freedom of graphic expression afforded by lithography had injected a variety of creative letterforms into public spaces. Lithographic posters, **handbills**, and advertisements were a vivid part of the urban scene. Professional **bill-stickers** plastered the walls, competing for the eyes of the crowd. Typefaces had to follow suit if letterpress printers were to vie for their share of the newly burgeoning market in advertising. Competition stimulated invention, and technical advances enabled it (Fig. **6.18**).

In 1803, Robert Thorne's *fat* faces were produced in metal. The first **sans serif** types appeared in a specimen book published in 1816. In 1817, Vincent Figgins's foundry in London produced *Egyptian,* or **slab serif**, faces that had a square, flat look. But it was the invention of the pantograph in 1828 that ignited an explosion of floral, decorated, **historiated**, and otherwise ornamented faces. The pantograph mechanized scalability of

type design drawings, greatly facilitating the multiplication of elaborate faces. The graphic imagination of type designers had been given a means of production. The arduous task of cutting punches had been replaced by machine labor. Typographic invention was a genie let out of a bottle, never to be repressed again by technical constraints. To reduce the weight of metal in presses and **galleys,** large type was made of wood. Letters used to print posters for public display ranged from a few inches to a few feet in height. Designs for two- and three-color typefaces were devised to compete with **chromolithography,** which brought color processes to lithography in the 1840s (Figs. **6.19a–c**).

Fine art and graphic art

Paintings and prints had been rare and expensive when the nineteenth century began, but by mid-century images in advertising and printed journals became affordable items of mass consumption. The habits of advertising transformed the tone of public language from admonition to seduction. The effects of this shift could be seen in the persuasive character of texts and the ubiquitous presence of imagery. The names of certain graphic artists and illustrators of the early nineteenth century were well known to their audiences. Many had gained reputations and followings for their work. On the other hand, the fields of type, book, and journal design were driven by anonymous workers. The

6.20 F. O. C. Darley, *Scenes from Indian Life*, 1843. Felix Darley was a young illustrator in Philadelphia when he produced the elegant line drawings for this book. His inspirations were British and French neoclassical illustrations, but he popularized their style by using it for subjects other than Greek and Roman poetry. Native American life was a popular, romantic theme, and Darley's images portray these figures as natural—unspoiled and unaffected—as if they had spontaneously appeared on the page. (Throughout the nineteenth century, the living conditions of Native American populations, who continued to lose ground to westward expansion of the United States and to the federal government's aggressive "Indian Removal" policy, were actually far from idyllic.) The simplification of Darley's images and backgrounds gives them a universal, almost ahistorical look, although this drawing style was directly linked to a late eighteenth- and early nineteenth-century appreciation of classical vases and friezes.

design of printed ephemera hardly counted as anything but skilled labor of a general character. In earlier centuries, artists whose work involved prints had enjoyed popular success as well as exclusive patronage. The identity of these figures had not been contradicted by oppositions between high art and mass culture. But as steam-powered mechanical means of reproduction brought images into widespread circulation, a cultural change took place. The fine artist acquired a status very different from that of the graphic worker in the printing industry (Fig. **6.20**).

Industrialization drew a line between high art and graphic work.

Fine art was handmade and, to borrow the critic Walter Benjamin's term, *auratic*—that is, its unique presence had a special air or **aura** of authenticity that linked it to the original artist. The use of mediating machinery to transfer images from drawings to wood, steel, and copper surfaces, and the intervention of engravers trained to exploit the properties of their printing media rather than to express themselves, shifted the very identity of mass-produced images into a new and separate category. Woodblock engraving was considered a comparatively humble, commercial skill, not an art. Work was often compensated according to the size of the area carved. Large blocks were divided for more rapid production and then assembled, their joints and discrepancies smoothed before printing to efface any difference between individual engravers. For all of their artfulness, graphic images were not considered high art. Debates about the border between these realms still affect the identity and status of graphic designers today. Client-driven, commissioned work is made within very different constraints than pieces created primarily to express a personal point of view. Yet the mass production and consumption of images and texts are an important part of the larger culture in which modern art functions, and the rich productions

6.21 Johann Wolfgang von Goethe, *Faust*, illustrated by Eugène Delacroix, 1828. Eugène Delacroix was a major figure of French romantic art. His imagery had the emotional impact and exotic grandeur of the work of great romantic poets. Johann Wolfgang von Goethe's *Faust* is a quintessential tale of human weakness that found an eager audience in the 1820s. The combination of Delacroix's images and the tale of a man who sells his soul to the devil caused an immediate sensation when the book was published. Certain areas of the dark, moody lithographs reveal the artist's vigorous drawing style. This publication helped define romanticism, giving it a concrete graphic style in the popular imagination.

6.22 William Blake, *Jerusalem*, 1804–1820. William Blake's highly individual view of God, humanity, and the values of the world was given form by his equally idiosyncratic printing methods. He made relief copper plates through an etching process that he perfected himself. Although he made his living as a traditional engraver, he used this technique in the books he wrote, illustrated, and printed on his own. His vision of a human spirit born innocent, guileless, and capable of bliss was a pointed counter-argument to the teachings of the Catholic and Protestant religions. Blake's works were not well known in his lifetime, and he was not a popular artist. He made his living from his commercial commissions. But his inspired designs reveal his belief in the liberating power of the imagination in a way that has come to be seen as emblematic of the romantic spirit.

of graphic design play at least as significant a role in mediating the values of modern life as do works of fine art. The two have a complex, highly synergistic relation to each other that we inherit as part of the cultural legacy of early modern attitudes (Fig. **6.21**).

Almost from the onset of industrialization, the aesthetic spirit of romanticism arose in protest to the effects of mechanization on modern life. Imagination and creativity were perceived as a rebellious antithesis to the regimes of order and discipline essential to producing well-behaved workers whose bodies and minds conformed to the rhythms of machines. The images of nature and of passionate energy evoked by romantic painting, poetry, and music surged against this repetitive order and the dulling effect of its routines. The early nineteenth-century artist William Blake embodied this attitude. He gave voice to an alternative, visionary sensibility in his handmade books of illuminated poetry. Making his living as an engraver and illustrator, he also lived the paradox of an age in which fine art's imagination was conceived as the necessary "other" of industrial production. Modern life, industrial capitalism, and the image of the artist as a free spirit involved in a form of unalienated activity are all of a piece. Graphic arts and mass media made expressions of the romantic spirit highly attractive commodities through which to imagine a life of excitement and passion at odds with working-class dreariness or middle-class decorum. A gothic revival brought back blackletter types and ornaments associated with Medieval romance. Elements of aesthetic platforms antithetical to industrialism were in place. These would be fully constructed in the second half of the nineteenth century (Fig. **6.22**).

6.23 John Leech, "Specimens from Mr Punch's Industrial Exhibition of 1850," 1850. Industrial exhibitions gained popularity in the nineteenth century. These brought new products to market and provided a platform for industry and public to meet in a showcase that promoted technological progress. The sharp tone of Leech's image for the satiric magazine *Punch* is unmistakable. The exhibition of types of exploited workers was meant to make clear that human beings, not machines, were the agents of production. The mythology of industrialism tended to obscure the human element in mechanical work. The types defined in this image have physical characteristics that identify their class but also the long-term effects of their repetitive labors. The grotesque face of Mr. Punch contrasts with the body language of the middle-class gentleman taking in the exhibition with sober decorum.

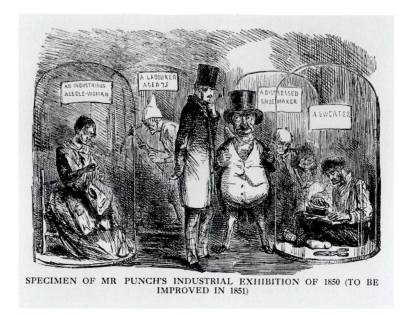

SPECIMEN OF MR PUNCH'S INDUSTRIAL EXHIBITION OF 1850 (TO BE IMPROVED IN 1851)

6.24 *The Poor Man's Guardian*, August 20, 1831. Partisan politics created specialized markets in publication design. This paper's audience is named in the title, while the motto states its political aim. The woodcut, "Knowledge Is Power," features an old-fashioned hand press, but the design of the *Guardian* is contemporary in its clean legibility and businesslike in its sobriety.

Critical issues

The popular press is often seen as an instrument of social control through which the masses consume ideas and values that may run counter to their own interests. Belief in hard work and submission to discipline is communicated in subtle but effective ways that transform the working classes, allowing them to be exploited. But newspapers and journals can also organize a base for political action. Mass culture clearly plays an active part in ongoing negotiations of power through symbolic representation. The rise of industrialization shifted a large agrarian population into factory work in urban circumstances. Living and working conditions were often poor, wages were low, and the difficulties encountered by laborers or reformers who wished to change these circumstances were daunting. But the way individuals perceive themselves depends, in part, on the way they are represented. Conceptions of virtue or vice, of normal behavior and expectations for a satisfying life, are taken from and returned to the public sphere through media. The role of graphic design cannot be reduced to manipulation, but designers and their work are participants in complex cultural systems. The social construction of reality is always realized by symbolic means and shared perceptions. The first mass media offered readers reciprocal glances across class boundaries through images and texts (Fig. **6.23**).

The power of the press could be harnessed for radical progress as well as for numbing relief. The mid-nineteenth century was marked by upheavals and revolutions. Social unrest was on the rise among the working classes. Early nineteenth-century political theorists advocated utopian socialism. The potential of labor as a political force was trumpeted by the 1848 publication of German political philosophers Karl Marx and Friedrich Engels's *The Communist Manifesto*. Voices of resistance and opposition to established interests used graphic media to stir partisan support but also to forge a common understanding of social goals and cultural ideals (Fig. **6.24**).

6.25a Jean-Ignace Isidore Gérard, known as Grandville, *A Parisian Lion*, 1842 *(above)*, and 6.25b George Cruikshank, *A Free Born Englishman*, 1819 *(right)*. Cruikshank and Grandville were the graphic stars of their age. They were both artists of great range and flexibility, masters of various media. Both were consummate print artists, fully aware of what communicated well in graphic terms. Each of their drawings handles shape, line, tone, and contrast of planes with a precision that appears effortless. Both demonstrate complete control over their draftsmanship and a capacity to create caricatures with imagination and humor. Grandville's was the more eccentric vision, and some of his work seems as fragmented and strange as a dream. Cruikshank's imagery referred to real people and political events. His ability to conjure a scene made him an ideal illustrator and cartoonist.

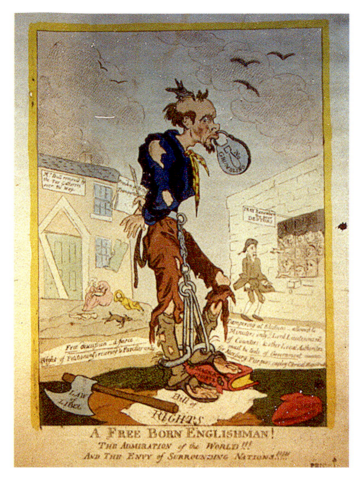

A FREE BORN ENGLISHMAN!
THE ADMIRATION of the WORLD!!!
AND THE ENVY of SURROUNDING NATIONS!!!!!

Conclusion The graphic effects of mass-media production involved changes in print technology and the publishing industry and their impact on the look and kinds of materials available to consumers. The nineteenth century began with an artisanal printing trade still catering largely to the upper classes in an era when production and consumption of many goods remained local. The movement of raw materials and products was only possible by ship or wagon. But by the mid-nineteenth century, iron and steam had combined to produce powerful new modes of production and transportation. Increased production and distribution of goods, in turn, gave rise to a modern advertising industry that met manufacturers' need to compete in expanded markets. New concentrations of mobile laborers changed urban landscapes and formed a demographic eager for education and entertainment. Mass-media culture had become established. Printed images created an audience for the news within a changing social structure, but they also contributed to that change, regulating and challenging notions of class and status. Critical debates over the role of mass-media in modern culture started to take shape, as the dangers of reading novels—or the virtues of being informed—were propounded. But these debates had just begun. In the second half of the nineteenth century, the coming of steel and electricity would bring new capabilities to production that would, yet again, alter the structure and systems of modern life (Figs. **6.25a** and **6.25b**).

The Graphic Effects of Industrial Production 1800–1850

1800 William Wordsworth and Samuel Coleridge's *Lyrical Ballads* published
Library of Congress established
Alessandro Volta's first electrical batteries
Earl of Stanhope designs first all-iron printing press
1801 Robert Thorne's first fat face
1802 William Bulmer prints Boydell's editions of Shakespeare
1803 First English papermaking machine in use
Robert Fulton's first steamboat
Louisiana purchased from France by U.S. for $15 million
1804 Napoleon crowned emperor
Haiti, first black colony to become nation, declares independence from France
Lewis and Clark expedition begins
1806 *Webster's Dictionary* published
1807 Gaslight first used in Pall Mall, London
1810 Sir Walter Scott's *Lady of the Lake* sells 25,000 copies in eight months
Peter Durand invents tin can
1812 Britain and U.S. fight war over freedom of seas
1813 Jane Austen's *Pride and Prejudice* published
1814 First steam-powered press used at *The London Times*
1815 Napoléon defeated at Battle of Waterloo
1816 Stethoscope invented
First sans serif typeface in a specimen book of William Caslon IV
1817 First slab serif typefaces brought out by Vincent Figgins foundry in London
1818 Lord Byron's *Don Juan* published
Mary Shelley's *Frankenstein* published
Bodoni's *Manuale Tipografico* published by Stamperia Reale
1819 Grimm's *Fairy Tales* published
Simon Bolivar liberates Colombia, Venezuela, and Ecuador from Spain
Ink rollers replace pelt balls
1821 Champollion deciphers hieroglyphics using Rosetta stone
1822 Nicéphore Niépce's first photographic experiments on glass plates
First typecasting machine
1823 Charles Babbage's calculating machine
Mackintosh raincoat invented in Scotland
1824 Portland cement, modern building material, produced
1825 First passenger railway in Britain
1827 Wood type developed as alternative to heaviness of large metal letters
Modern matches invented
Rodolphe Töpffer creates first comic book
1828 Pantograph used to produce wood type
1829 Firmin Didot becomes last Imprimeur du Roi in France
Louis Braille invents raised letter code for the blind
Greeks win war of independence from Turkey
1830 French King Charles X overthrown
Eugène Delacroix paints *Liberty Leading the People* to commemorate July Revolution
Railway links Liverpool and Manchester
1831 Faraday discovers electromagnetism
1832 Faraday devises basic principles of electric motor
The Penny Magazine, first weekly illustrated paper, launched
1833 Slavery abolished in British Empire
1834 Charles Babbage begins work on analytical engine, prototype of digital calculator
Braille shown at Paris Exposition of Industry

1835 *The New York Herald* launched, aims for 20,000 copies a day

1836 Battle of the Alamo fought

Samuel Colt invents revolver

1837 Victoria crowned queen of England

Samuel Morse invents telegraph

Isaac Pittman's shorthand system published

1838 Charles Wilkes sets out to explore Antarctica

The Illustrated London News launched

Charles Dickens's *Oliver Twist* published

1839 Daguerre invents photographic method

Charles Goodyear begins commercial rubber production

First electric printing press

1840 China resists English introduction of opium trade in first Opium War

Wood pulp paper produced by machine

Chromolithography introduced

Standard time adopted in England

1841 Horace Greeley founds *The New York Tribune*

Adolphe Sax invents saxophone

Augustus Pugin's *The True Principles of Pointed or Christian Architecture* published

1842 Crawford Long uses ether as first anesthesia

1844 First installment of Henry Fox Talbot's *Pencil of Nature* published

Chiswick Press prints William Pickering's edition of *Lady Willoughby's Diary*

1845 Texas annexed as state

Robert Besley designs Clarendon typeface

Edgar Allen Poe's *The Raven* published

1846 First rotary press perfected by Richard Hoe

Irish potato famine begins

1847 Emily Brontë's *Wuthering Heights* published

Charlotte Brontë's *Jane Eyre* published

John Ruskin's *The Stones of Venice* published

Frederick Douglass launches abolitionist newspaper, *The North Star*

1848 Marx and Engels's *The Communist Manifesto* published

Revolutions in Europe

Harriet Tubman escapes slavery on underground railroad

1849 California Gold Rush begins

Speed of light first calculated

Safety pin invented

Tools of the Trade

Tusche

Gum arabic

Milk as fixative

Chalk dust

Watercolor in dry cakes

Conté crayons

Oil sticks

Graphite of different hardnesses

Mass-produced pencils

Machine-made steel pens

Self-filling fountain pens

Metal ferrule brushes

Pin fasteners

Portable paint boxes

Precision drafting instruments

Architect's linen with special surface

Tracing paper

Wood pulp paper

Carbon paper

Leather rollers

Gelatin rollers

Rubber rollers

Lithography stone

Daguerreotype

Wet plate photography

Stereotyping

Ellipsograph

Pantograph

Gas light

Electric arc lamp

KALENDAR 1885

JANUARY					
S	-	4	11	18	25
M	-	5	12	19	26
T	-	6	13	20	27
W	-	7	14	21	28
T	1	8	15	22	29
F	2	9	16	23	30
S	3	10	17	24	31

FEBRUARY				
S	-	1	8	15	22
M	-	2	9	16	23
T	-	3	10	17	24
W	-	4	11	18	25
T	-	5	12	19	26
F	-	6	13	20	27
S	-	7	14	21	28

MARCH					
S	-	1	8	15	22	29
M	-	2	9	16	23	30
T	-	3	10	17	24	31
W	-	4	11	18	25
T	-	5	12	19	26
F	-	6	13	20	27
S	-	7	14	21	28

JULY					
S	-	5	12	19	26
M	-	6	13	20	27
T	-	7	14	21	28
W	1	8	15	22	29
T	2	9	16	23	30
F	3	10	17	24	31
S	4	11	18	25

AUGUST					
S	-	2	9	16	23	30
M	-	3	10	17	24	31
T	-	4	11	18	25
W	-	5	12	19	26
T	-	6	13	20	27
F	-	7	14	21	28
S	1	8	15	22	29

SEPTEMBER				
S	-	6	13	20	27
M	-	7	14	21	28
T	1	8	15	22	29
W	2	9	16	23	30
T	3	10	17	24
F	4	11	18	25
S	5	12	19	26

APRIL				
S	-	5	12	19	26
M	-	6	13	20	27
T	-	7	14	21	28
W	1	8	15	22	29
T	2	9	16	23	30
F	3	10	17	24
S	4	11	18	25

MAY					
S	-	3	10	17	24	31
M	-	4	11	18	25
T	-	5	12	19	26
W	-	6	13	20	27
T	-	7	14	21	28
F	1	8	15	22	29
S	2	9	16	23	30

JUNE				
S	-	7	14	21	28
M	1	8	15	22	29
T	2	9	16	23	30
W	3	10	17	24
T	4	11	18	25
F	5	12	19	26
S	6	13	20	27

OCTOBER					
S	-	4	11	18	25
M	-	5	12	19	26
T	-	6	13	20	27
W	-	7	14	21	28
T	1	8	15	22	29
F	2	9	16	23	30
S	3	10	17	24	31

NOVEMBER				
S	-	1	8	15	22	29
M	-	2	9	16	23	30
T	-	3	10	17	24
W	-	4	11	18	25
T	-	5	12	19	26
F	-	6	13	20	27
S	-	7	14	21	28

DECEMBER					
S	-	6	13	20	27
M	-	7	14	21	28
T	1	8	15	22	29
W	2	9	16	23	30
T	3	10	17	24	31
F	4	11	18	25
S	5	12	19	26

NORRIS & COKAYNE,
Manufacturing Stationers & Printers,
ST. PETER'S SQUARE,
Nottingham.

7. Mass Mediation 1850–1900s

- The volume and variety of printed media escalated dramatically in this period, as changes in print technology broadened the range of type, images, and production methods available to graphic design.

- The demand for graphic skills and services rose, as the specific value of their contribution began to be understood in a competitive business environment.

- The more that printed matter came to mediate social transactions, values, and communication, the more it was taken for granted as "natural."

- Commercial artists faced new ethical challenges, as they provided graphic interpretations of information in a growing media network that integrated telegraphy, journalism, advertising, political discourse, and private communication.

- **Graphic art** was at the center of debates about control of public display space and censorship of visual imagery that sometimes pitted commercial interests against civic groups.

7.1a Trade calendar, 1885. This elaborate design is remarkable not only for its graphic effect, but also for its controlled use of printing techniques. In the late nineteenth century, printers produced such pieces to advertise their skills. A calendar was useful but also enduring, and a printer could imagine that a client might look at it throughout the year. Every color was a separately printed and registered press run. The composition shows off the printer's rich stock of borders, type, and other decorative blocks and motifs. The stylish imagery of a dragon, lotus flowers, and interlocking patterns reveals a vogue for exoticism.

More printed matter was produced in the second half of the nineteenth century than ever before. Electricity replaced steam, offering an abundant energy source to industry. Further automation accelerated presses and paper manufacturing—and every page, every public notice, every slip of printed paper had to be designed. For the first time, the tasks and responsibilities of visualizing a layout or sketching a composition were separated from those of printing. Commercial artists began to develop a recognizable professional identity. Trade journals and advertisements of graphic services appeared with increasing frequency in the last decades of the nineteenth century. Graphic skills began to be valued for the way they grabbed readers' attention in a visually cluttered environment. Along with the increase in the volume of production came an expansion of the functional range of materials being printed. Printed **ephemera**, such as tickets, programs, checks, receipts, and schedules, helped transact the business of everyday life. Printed paper soon mediated so many aspects of modern existence that it came to be taken completely for granted. Advertising grew, as mass-produced goods and new marketing strategies proliferated. Photography and chromolithography changed the look of printed images, while automated methods of casting and setting type increased the speed and volume of text production. Graphic artists who worked in the commercial realm began to face ethical questions of truth in information and advertising. The urban landscape was papered with posters and notices. Journals and newspapers were commodities with their own markets, but they were also venues for advertising. Mass-circulation magazines, such as *The Atlantic Monthly, Ladies Home Journal,* and

7.1b Alphonse Mucha, Job cigarettes poster, 1897. The color scheme and lavish decoration in this poster have much in common with the trade calendar, but Mucha's sensual drawing takes advantage of the flexibility offered by lithography. Like other talented artists of the period, the Czechoslovakian Mucha went to Paris to study fine art but found his consumable style suited to commercial work. His painterly effects and soft palette were hugely successful. The forms are organic, and the drawing style is free and open, catching the figure in the midst of action. The "new" woman was conceived as a consumer, and smoking and bicycle-riding were profitably represented as expressions of her freedom. Printing these posters required preparation of a drawing and a stone for every color. Skilled registration and consistent inking are evidence of the sophistication of late nineteenth-century craftsmanship.

7.2 Department store poster, Au Moine St Martin, 1875 *(above right)*. Department stores originated in the late nineteenth century as a way to market goods to a new type of urban, middle-class consumer. The fantasy of consumption was fed by these environments and by the posters that advertised them. Beautiful showcases were filled with every conceivable variety of goods. Display techniques were intimately related to graphic design: Arranging and picturing commodities were both ways of making them seem available and desirable. Buying ready-to-wear clothing was still a novelty, and acquiring even a single object seemed to be a way to participate in a whole universe of gratifying possibilities. Likewise, the image of variety offered by promotional materials gave consumers a sense of unlimited options, each of which was part of a vast system of satisfaction.

Harper's Bazaar, came into vogue, and popular imagery began to compete with fine art for a share of audience interest. Illustrators developed high-profile careers and mass followings, and established artists began to take commercial jobs (Figs. **7.1a** and **7.1b**).

Printed mass media The tremendous increase in the volume of printed matter in the late nineteenth century was part of larger industrial changes. High-speed automation leapt ahead of mere mechanization. Graphic art and printed media were active participants in new **communication systems**. These **networks** of production and distribution had unprecedented geographic reach and both diversifying and homogenizing effects. Not only did mass production mean *more*, but also it meant more of the same. The rhetoric of **commercial art** became a distinctive feature of mass culture. Printed matter was a site of cultural production (of shared customs, images, meaning, and aspirations), not just a vehicle for delivering practical messages. The late nineteenth century was the last era in which printed matter enjoyed almost exclusive command of mass communication, and the medium registered many tectonic shifts and tremors, as photographic innovations, electrical applications, and commercial radio appeared on the horizon in the 1890s and early 1900s. Meanwhile, the identities and practices of graphic design underwent significant change. Professional and educational institutions were established that helped define the field as we know it, and increasing specialization within that field separated the tasks of layout, illustration, composition, typesetting, and **touch-up work**, among others (Fig. **7.2**).

Industrialism shifted not only the scale of printed matter but also the cultural values encoded and communicated by it. No longer an isolated or unusual experience, mass media became a part of daily life. Early industrialization had produced an abundance of innovations in type design for display. Now new methods of image production succeeded each other rapidly, bringing unprecedented appearances to printed media. Whether

7.3a Train tickets, 1880. Train tickets may have been humble and familiar objects, but the production of this type of ephemera became a staple of commercial printing as the nineteenth century progressed. Expectations and habits of use can be read from even a simple design. The business of setting fares in relation to distances between destinations, for instance, is part of a rational, centrally controlled system. The operation of such a system was mediated by graphic objects. **Standardization** of activities, environments, and forms became a norm, and coordinations of time and space were regularly represented in grids that governed daily life. Printed mass media formed an entire social infrastructure. Graphic design participated in this formation by configuring the use of printed matter in everyday life, and these simple objects are manifestations of complex and interrelated social systems. The same is true of other ephemera used for transacting daily business.

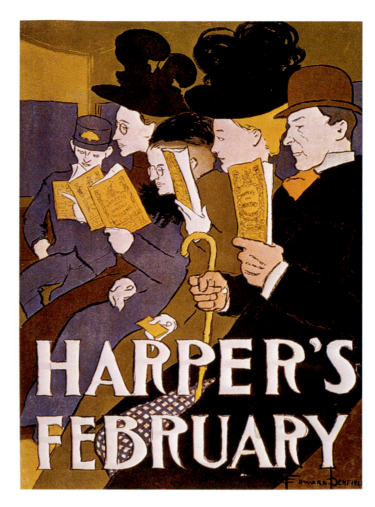

Standardization of activities and environments became a norm.

7.3b Edward Penfield, *Harper's* ad, 1895. The flat color and black outlines of this ad emulate Japanese art, but its message—that *Harper's* is everywhere and being read by everyone—was for Americans. The omnibuses and trolley systems that developed along with urban industry in the late nineteenth century provided an opportunity for reading—and for advertisements to be displayed on the inside and outside of cars. Public space was increasingly inscribed, as advertisements took over every available surface. But this poster has a subtle subtext: that persons of good breeding observe the rules of decorum, even while they are absorbing a mediated experience. In fact, the journals form a screen between the passengers and their surroundings. These people are as much involved in the reading experience, which is private and interior, as they are in the immediacy of riding the trolley. They are quite content to take in whatever *Harper's* has to offer, and to submit to the regimes of good behavior dictated by social norms inside and outside its covers.

in the guise of news or entertainment, advertisement or information, images saturated the culture. The novelties of color lithography on a large scale, photographic detail on a smaller one, and ever more sophisticated techniques for reproducing tone and fine line work helped define modern media. The result was a world in which images shaped opinion about style and form, behavior and decorum, social priorities and prohibitions in ways that were more integrated with the habits of daily life. Sites and venues changed, as outdoor advertising and mass-circulation publications endeavored to reach local and national audiences. The concept of an **advertising campaign** as a coordinated communication strategy across multiple media and contexts was still in a formative stage. But mastheads and **logotypes** already served as markers of social and commercial territory, as well as signs of a commodity's origin and quality. As rail transport and shipping increased the speed and range of the distribution of mass-produced goods, customer loyalty was fostered by identifiable graphics. In the cultural momentum of the late nineteenth-century era of industrialism known as the Gilded Age, printed mass media provided the common symbolic currency of business, political, and domestic life (Figs. **7.3a** and **7.3b**).

7.4 Excursion notice, 1873. As the century wore on, the crude flamboyance of early display type was mostly brought under control, although faces and decorative elements continued to exhibit amazing variety. In this instance, the delicacy of the typefaces points to the influence of engraving. Their fine metal lines are meant to signal elegance by contrast to the chunky faces that flaunted themselves on posters for public entertainments. Class distinctions are coded into graphic formats. Paper choices, type settings, and production standards embody these class differences in material terms that were certainly legible in their time.

7.5a Linotype machine, 1880s. The invention of machines for setting and casting type was a technical triumph that had a tremendous impact. Wood type production made use of automated techniques beginning in the early nineteenth century. Stereotyping (a molding method) had made it possible to make multiple copies of a single block of type and print the same text on several presses simultaneously. But Linotype and Monotype casters were the first major innovation in metal type production since Gutenberg, almost four hundred years earlier. The technology was elaborate and required the replication of many very precise movements. Thus, the machines themselves were remarkable pieces of industrial design. They made a huge leap forward in the speed and efficiency of letterpress composition. Ottmar Mergenthaler's Linotype machine was patented in 1884. Tolbert Lanston's Monotype caster appeared a year later. Both machines used molten lead and were operated with a keyboard. Linn Boyd Benton's punch-cutting machine, introduced in the same decade, further advanced the production of metal typefaces by automating the most difficult task of all, making steel punches and brass matrices for casting. As a result, the manufacture of type families that comprised a wide range of sizes, proportions, and styles was made considerably easier, if more mechanistic.

Changes in print technology

Changing methods of generating and processing text and images, improvements in the speed of printing presses, and a new source of paper fiber all contributed to advances in print technology in the later part of the nineteenth century. These advances, in turn, produced a torrent of printed matter. In addition to books, broadsides, and newspapers, there were posters and prints, journals, reviews, albums, and a whole range of ephemera. Until mid-century, almost all paper was produced in sheets from cotton and linen rags. These conditions were expensive and limiting, and pressure to find a cheaper alternative led to the invention of processes for turning wood pulp into paper fiber. Paper was soon machine-made in rolls as well as sheets, and, although much of it was of poor quality, it was abundant, inexpensive, and smooth enough to work on high-speed presses (Fig. **7.4**).

Type styles continued to proliferate to meet the demands of advertisers more eager than ever to distinguish their goods and services in a rapidly expanding marketplace. Innovations in the production of **wood type** had radically altered the design of display faces, but, until the 1880s, longer text production still entailed the laborious processes of casting and composing

7.5b and 7.5c Type families. The basic families of nineteenth-century display type can be distinguished, in part, by their serif shapes. **Tuscan** had bifurcated serifs, **Egyptian** had flat or slab serifs, **Gothic** and **grotesque** had no serifs, and many fat faces featured the hairline serifs of neoclassical "modern" designs. Other variations included bell-shaped serifs, shaded and decorated bodies, shadows and dimensional illusions, and whimsical shapes of people, animals, and flowers. This profusion of styles is a testament to the inventiveness of nineteenth-century type designers and their willingness to push the limits of taste or habit in the name of innovation. It is also evidence of a market driven by opportunistic forces, convinced that novelty was worth the price.

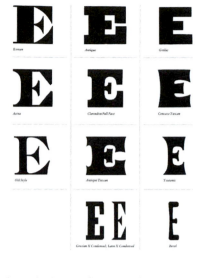

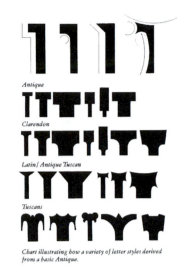

Chart illustrating how a variety of letter styles derived from a basic Antique.

letter by letter. Then, metal type production technology changed for the first time since Gutenberg. Handset type could not keep pace with popular demand for books and newspapers or sustain the dependence of business and government sectors on printed forms and published documentation. Faster, automated methods were needed. The precision required for manufacturing machinery to replicate the complex actions involved in typecasting and composition relied on sophisticated engineering. The **Linotype** and **Monotype** casters are marvels of nineteenth-century industrial design. These machines transformed the printing industry. New faces could be designed and cast in metal in a fraction of the time taken by traditional methods (Figs. **7.5a–c**).

In a market driven by opportunism, novelty was worth the price.

7.6 Lithographed menu heads, 1897. These beautifully drawn standard designs are ready for use and reuse on any job a busy shop might get, rather than conceived for an individual customer. They show the extent to which commercial art was becoming standardized. Client needs fell into established categories. A billhead or logotype became a necessity because it was a possibility, and alternatives became more limited and more expensive because a custom format would have had to be developed from scratch. Improved transfer techniques, including photographic processes, meant that designs could easily be copied from samples to engraving plates and lithographic stones. The curves, flourishes, and dynamics of these designs echo the arabesques that continued to characterize Victorian decorative style and would come to be seen as excessive by the next generation.

Many inventions affected image production and reproduction in the nineteenth century, as printers struggled to find efficient ways of printing images with texts. Relief printing, the basic technology of letterpress, dominated newspaper, book, and magazine production at mid-century. Although endgrain wood engraving had improved line and tone quality, it could not compare to the lush effects of lithography that had become widespread by the 1830s. In the late 1840s, chromolithography (color lithographic printing) became an industrially viable method with the invention of metal plates flexible enough to wrap around the cylinder of an automated press. Lithography was used extensively for commercial work in which image, text, and decoration were combined. Its direct and integral methods meant that these combinations were less constrained than letterpress compositions and less mediated than artwork interpreted by engravers. In the 1880s, as we shall see, a handful of innovative artists experimented with chromolithography and developed a vivid, painterly aesthetic that made use of the medium's specific capabilities (Fig. **7.6**).

Photography was a popular way of producing images by mid-century. But in the history of graphic arts, photography has not only been a

7.7a Engraving, 1880, and 7.7b Halftone techniques for printing photographs, 1909. The white line engraving of this portrait shows how much value was attached to rendering photographic qualities. The halftone version suggests an effortless realization. Wood engraving was highly developed in the final decades of the nineteenth century, and skilled practitioners of the craft were justifiably worried that their work would be replaced by photographic techniques. An enormous variety of technical processes that involved positive and negative casting, transfers, gelatin, metal, and other media was being tried as ways to translate the continuous tone of photographs into a printable form. While the engraving maintains many of the high-contrast features of a photograph, the lined shading reveals the workings of a hand. The halftone process was not entirely mechanical, but the screen pattern expressed an objective translation that distanced photographic reproduction from hand engraving, with its evident interpretative qualities of line and style. Halftone engraving translated the gradated tones of photographic images into a relief form. The difficulty of printing remained because optimal pressure, inking, and paper surfaces for images were not always the same as those for printing type. The solution to these difficulties would eventually come in the form of photo-offset technology.

technology of image production; it has also been a **meta-technology** that has facilitated reproduction. For example, photographic transfer techniques, in use by the 1860s, enabled engraved images to be replicated using lithographic stones and machine-made plates. A series of experiments did seek viable industrial methods for translating photographs themselves into mass-productive forms, but there were also consequential efforts to apply photographic processes to other printing procedures. When photolithography was perfected in the 1880s, commercial artists' compositional range expanded to include basic photographic manipulations of scaling, cropping, adjusting contrast, and so on. In the 1890s, **photogravure** and **rotogravure** further boosted the rise of illustrated magazines that had begun more than a decade earlier. **Halftone** screens were perfected only at the turn of the twentieth century, but the graphic sensibility that late nineteenth-century techniques had cultivated was poised to take advantage of the invention when it came (Figs. **7.7a** and **7.7b**).

Late nineteenth-century graphics teemed with elegant illustrations and type designs by highly trained artists. The decades from 1890 through 1910 were a golden era for illustration and a time when many graphic artists achieved fame. But there were many more who worked steadily and anonymously to satisfy the demand for illustrated magazines and books. The Sunday papers began to include color supplements, and, by the turn of the century, comic strips and cartoons had gained a broad following. Imagery had come to be taken for granted as part of daily habits

7.8 Color comic in *The World*, 1902.
Many illustrations in the latter half of the nineteenth century continued to rely on engraved relief blocks that could be printed on the same presses and at the same time as type. Relief halftone printing on high-speed machines introduced color to mass-circulation magazines and newspapers. Cartoonists and illustrators exploited the compositional and stylistic possibilities of the new technology. Visual narratives caught the public eye, as paper became a cheap commodity, and color printing satisfied consumers' appetites for amusements in print. The panel format became standard for comics and short narratives with punch lines. Combinations of yellow, red, blue, and black print runs enlivened designs. In the comics' pages, these colors might be flat or patterned, but with mechanical separation techniques, the same colors could create painterly and photographic effects as well.

of reading. The next significant shift in visual communication came when halftone technology was adopted. Photographic codes of realism would come to dominate news reporting, and, within decades, photography in advertisements and journals would be seen as the essence of twentieth-century **modernism**. But just before this occurred, nineteenth-century illustrators produced some of their finest works (Fig. **7.8**).

Photography enjoyed wide public appeal from the moment it was marketed in the late 1830s. The subsequent ability to produce multiple copies of photographic images expanded their audience exponentially. Postcards, portraits, travel albums, and all manner of exotica and erotica were common in the second half of the nineteenth century. Commercial artists would not make extensive use of photographic imagery in advertising work until the twentieth century, but photographic processes played a part in type design, illustration, and fine arts. Photography influenced the ways tonal values were rendered, and line-work techniques developed in etching and engraving were replaced by approaches that mimicked the high-contrast patterns of photographic compositions. Photographic technologies underwent rapid development as well. More portable cameras replaced the heavy equipment and elaborate chemistry required in the early decades of photography. The invention of celluloid film in the late 1880s was a major breakthrough. By the century's end, the practice of photography was no longer restricted to professionals and die-hard amateurs. Attitudes toward the composition of images expanded to embrace the spontaneity of ever decreasing exposure times and the incidental quality of snapshots. Modern vision was linked to photographic terms, and photography was increasingly used to record and mediate aspects of contemporary life (Figs. **7.9a** and **7.9b**).

7.9a Jessie Wilcox Smith, Kodak ad, "A Christmas Morning," 1904. Just as their labor entered other sectors, women joined the printing workforce in the late nineteenth century as typesetters and binders. But women also rose to prominence as publishers, editors, writers, and illustrators with careers and reputations of their own. Smith was one of the most beloved and successful illustrators of the era. Her work combined strength of composition with a touch of sentimentality, as in this sweet picture of a girl and her new doll being photographed with a Kodak. Introduced to the market in 1889, the Kodak made photography available without special skills or elaborate equipment. Smith's scene reinforces the message that photography is now for everyone and that the medium mediates memory as well as personal interactions. The illustration softens this message, making it familiar and consumable.

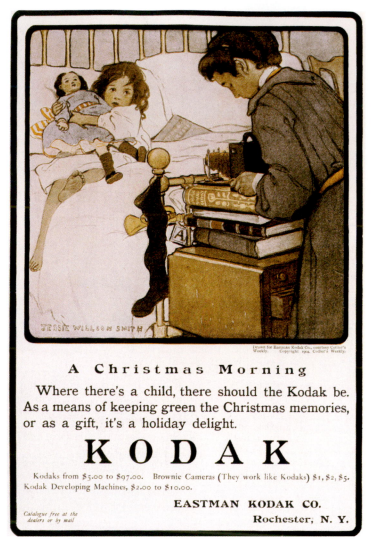

7.9b Eadweard Muybridge, motion study. The photographic image defined late nineteenth-century codes of realism. But photographs also became a currency and a means of establishing identity and authority. Photography became an instrument of the criminal justice system and of scientific documentation, establishing categories of pathology in medicine and psychology. The range of photography was extended, as cameras were adapted for use on airplanes and under water. But the medium also lent itself to the visual exploration of phenomena that could never be seen by the naked eye, such as rapid movement. Gradually, photographs began to replace illustration in reporting news and social events. Although much debated even in the nineteenth century, the authority of photographs was a distinct part of public perception of the new medium. It seemed unable to lie. Muybridge's photographs of a horse in motion were used to settle a bet about whether all four of a horse's feet were ever off the ground at the same time. By breaking movements into visible units, Muybridge made it possible to reassemble photographed movement as well: The motion picture was just a small step away.

Changing patterns in the use of graphic media

Technological advances in print technology did not occur in isolation. The rapid industrialization that had transformed manufacturing in the United States and Europe created a new social order. The practical administration of modern life was organized by printed artifacts. A paper trail assisted the manufacture, shipping, tracking, ordering, and selling of products. Advances in universal education turned out an increasingly literate workforce in the nineteenth century, while office work produced a new labor profile: the white-collar worker. Business became its own industry with its own products, equipment, and services. Organizations had to be managed, and printed graphics helped with every administrative task. The upper-middle-class and professional strata of society expanded, changing the demographics of urban centers, extending suburbs, and creating markets for products that had once been consumed only by an elite. Industrial expansion also had its downsides. Pollution became a feature of the industrial urban landscape. Working and living conditions for factory workers were often inhuman and unregulated. Class divisions assigned

7.10 Invitation to a soirée, 1884. Printed ephemera became a commonplace, and job shops were everywhere. On a daily basis, the printing trade provided services priced to fall well within range of a middle-class household. The formality of this piece is an important part of its function because it sets the tone for an event, framing it within conventions and social norms. The invitation does as much work by its design as by the information it contains, and the printed object produces the event in advance through its graphic codes. Although the type is centered, the border is placed only on the top and left, creating an asymmetrical accent that echoes patterns on china and textiles of the day, which were influenced by newly discovered Japanese decorative designs.

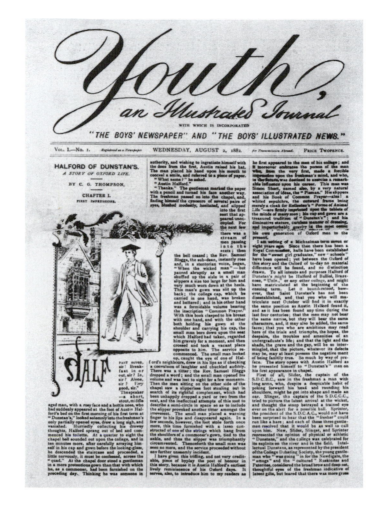

Social categories were generated and reproduced in print media.

7.11 *Youth, An Illustrated Journal*, 1882. Mass-circulation magazines for specialized audiences helped construct the identity of these readers in their own minds. The gradual transformation of childhood into a category with clear boundaries and needs, for instance, was a phenomenon furthered by the design of publications catering to this age group. Boys and girls were highly differentiated, and part of the effect of these journals was to signal the activities appropriate to each gender. Print media were sites and agents of the genesis and reproduction of social categories. Magazines were a potent force for mediating individual identity in relation to cultural norms.

those at the lower end of the economic spectrum to whole new kinds of risk and forms of exploitation, even as the rhetoric of entrepreneurialism promoted the myth of rags-to-riches self-determination (Fig. **7.10**).

Many wage earners enjoyed some leisure time and discretionary income. The titles of mass-circulation magazines attest to the changing demographics of readership: *The Saturday Evening Post, A Boy's Own Paper, Vanity Fair*, and *Cosmopolitan* were all launched by the 1880s. They catered to an audience interested in fashion, entertainment, and the passing scene. Newspapers were designed to suit a variety of readers. Serious-looking pages set in regular columns of small print appealed to men of business, while the celebrity-studded pages of gossip sheets broke their text columns into readable, liberally illustrated bits. Books and newspapers were printed in larger editions, as the range of tastes to which they catered grew. These changes were part of larger cultural shifts, not merely the result of new production methods. But the net effect was an increase in the appetite for printed ephemera. As demand increased, so did variety and specialized readerships, all sensitive to—and addressed by—the codes of graphic design (Fig. **7.11**).

7.12 Paper money, "shinplaster," 1870.
The increasing use of paper money as a basic medium of exchange in the nineteenth century is a telling example of the extent to which printed materials came to function as a means of doing daily business. The embodiment of value in a printed surrogate makes production a powerful act. Although silver certificates were backed by reserves, the bill itself would only work if accepted as a bona fide promise of its worth. Collective belief systems supported this premise. The use of paper money is so widespread that its novelty in the nineteenth century is hard to imagine. These engraved bills were issued in economically unstable frontier communities and earned the name "shinplaster" because they were so devalued that soldiers used them to line boots or wrap wounds.

7.13 Cover image, *Science for Everyone*, 1909. The illustrator of this striking cover has taken full advantage of the image of a chic, eye-catching young woman to set off the effect of a scientific perspective that is far more arresting. While we see her body, we also see right through it, to her bones. The promise of science as superior knowledge is given a clear graphic form. The tension between visible and invisible information gives graphic communication a role. By providing an image of what would normally be unseen (and unseeable), the design mediates with potent authority, extending the realm of knowledge by visual means.

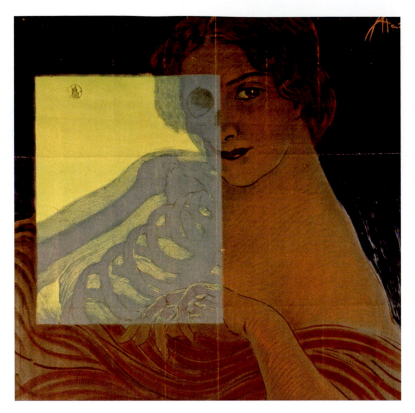

Money, stamps, official documents and papers, police records, census forms, and many other graphic artifacts served the bureaucracy generated by an increasingly administered culture. All of these artifacts had to be designed, and, by their designs, they came to be identified with—and to perform—their many functions. Paper money is one of the most dramatic examples of graphic design operating in and through symbolic value. But postage stamps and other exchangeable printed materials also came to serve specific functions. In 1847, the United States Post Office required postage be paid and affixed in advance for the first time, although stamps had served tax and other official purposes much earlier. Interestingly, antiforgery techniques had to be invented at the same time, and these posed their own design challenges (Fig. **7.12**).

Direct person-to-person communication through printed matter increased. The movement of goods and people by rail and ships to meet production schedules in an industrialized economy put pressure on communication to be quicker and on management to be more tightly coordinated. Business and scientific publishing also underwent a boom and transformation. The empirical bases of knowledge production were supported by tables, maps, and graphs. But printed media performed ritual functions as well, forging community bonds and prompting social exchanges around shared values. Popularization of knowledge brought technical information to a general audience. Scientific discoveries and medical advances were promoted by appealing publications. Ideas enjoyed vogues just as much as goods and styles did. Information became an item of consumption produced by printed media (Fig. **7.13**).

7.14 "His Master's Voice," 1900.
Transatlantic cables connected the United States, Great Britain, and Europe in a system of near-instantaneous communication by the early 1870s, producing an altered perception of the relations between time and space. The telephone became a part of social life in the 1880s—albeit mainly among the upper middle class. The novelty of instant contact connecting remote locations shook the nineteenth-century sensibility. Many boundaries, including class distinctions and the division of public and domestic space, seemed threatened by these new media. The invention of the gramophone introduced recorded media into the home and, with them, one of the most memorable **brand** images.

Media networks The roles of printed matter were related to the duties performed by other emerging media. Before the 1840s, the only way to get a message from one place to another was to have it physically carried. Communication depended on transportation. But this situation changed dramatically between 1840 and 1900, as electricity was applied to new purposes, and telegraphy, telephones, and, finally, radio radically altered communications infrastructure. In the North American context, territorial—commercial, political, and military—expansion stretched communication lines. In Europe, increased activity in dynamic markets, such as national stock exchanges, made the speed of information delivery financially critical. The telegraph had been invented in the 1840s and

The "here" and "now" were redefined by telecommunications.

a decade later was used for business, news, and personal messages. Instantaneous communication between geographically remote locations became a reality. The use of **wire services** for reporting the news hastened the rate at which events were known and put into print. The "here" and "now" were redefined by a geographically diffuse system of points linked by telecommunications. Wire photos came into wide use in the first decade of the twentieth century. Such innovations overturned conventional limitations of time and space (Fig. **7.14**).

The telegraph was intimately linked to newspaper activity. Wire services coordinated the transmission and distribution of news but also turned news into a commodity. Journalism barely existed as a profession before the nineteenth century, but the use of telegraphed communication created the possibility—and then the expectation—that information about events would be rapidly transmitted in digest form for redistribution in newspapers. An interlinked network of "lightning lines"—as telegraph wires were known—ran along the roadbeds of the railroads. In the middle of the century, the Associated Press gained a near monopoly on news distribution by entering into an exclusive agreement with Western Union.

7.15 Winslow Homer, *The Army of the Potomac*, 1864. War reporting galvanized journalism, and the call for graphic reporters offered an opportunity for young artists to acquire experience in the high-pressure, short-deadline world of publishing. Changes in graphic codes for reporting were dramatic in the latter half of the nineteenth century. Artists sometimes worked from observation, but they might also work from description to recreate an imagined scene. Such remote and artificial techniques were considered acceptable even in photographic renderings well into the twentieth century: Studio sets were used to simulate major events for newsreel footage. Winslow Homer was an artist whose skills as a draftsman and as an observer of human subjects were honed by his work as a reporter. Homer's compositions reveal the narrative conventions of his day. The emotional impact of this drawing derives from Homer's choice of the moment to be represented with all that it implies about the events preceding and following it.

7.16 President McKinley's funeral, 1901. Newspapers reproduced photographs with increasing frequency after halftone screens were invented. Crises drove innovations in reporting. The assassination of President McKinley prompted photographic attention. Note the framing and distance in the image and the graininess of the print quality. These are characteristics of early photographic printing. However, even lacking detail, photography seemed to communicate reality with more authenticity than drawings—as if the blurs and blobs registered by film carried an accurate record of real events. The formal contradiction between this image and the Victorian border that surrounds it is a reminder that change in visual conventions rarely happens all at once.

Visual reporting became a part of the late nineteenth-century media landscape. Commercial illustration was commonplace: A news reporter at the turn of the century might as easily be an artist as a writer. The appearance of Frank Leslie's illustrated weekly in 1864 not only reflected an increased capacity for printing images, but also for reporting breaking news—in this case, events of the ongoing Civil War. Leslie's was the first newspaper to rely on images as up-to-date news. The look and purpose of practical visual reporting were distinct from the sensational use of pictures in broadsheets and the uplifting, educational, and entertaining illustrations in the penny press (Fig. **7.15**).

Graphic journalism quickly became established in the illustrated papers, and soon more direct and spontaneous reporting styles arrived, influenced, in part, by the capabilities of photography. The shift from static depictions of people and scenes to lively renderings of action was marked by compositional changes. Photography altered expectations, not only about technique but also about the basic conception of visual documents. The major change that occurred in late nineteenth-century newspaper illustration was from generic images and stereotypes to highly specific visual records. Often this degree of specific detail was achieved with the direct aid of photographs that were exposed or mounted on endgrain blocks as guides to carving. By the time photography could be printed effectively in the daily news, the public was already disposed to accord a higher truth value and authenticity to photographic images than to drawn ones (Fig. **7.16**).

The industrial machinery that had been mobilized in the American Civil War effort was retooled for peacetime activity in the 1870s. Office machines with multiple moving parts were manufactured by companies with names like Remington, long associated with rifles and munitions. The typewriter, the mimeograph machine, and the punch card calculator became commercially available. As business technology changed, so did entertainment media. The phonograph, for instance, permitted music and voices to be recorded and replayed. American inventors—Thomas

7.17 Typewriter advertisements, 1889.
In the United States, commercially
viable typewriters were patented in the
period just after the Civil War, as arms
manufacturers retooled for peacetime
industries. The challenge of mass
producing precise movable parts was
met by refinements of earlier industrial
methods. The typewriter and other
office machines automated the business
environment in new ways but also
helped standardize communications and
behaviors. Women entered the workforce
as clerks and typists, their roles and tasks
defined, in part, by these mechanized
processes and protocols. Typewritten
documents replaced handwritten ones
as the accepted medium of professional
exchange. The modern proverb, "time is
money," succinctly encodes the attitude
of the business sector at a time when the
virtues of the machine reinforced ideals of
efficiency and standardization.

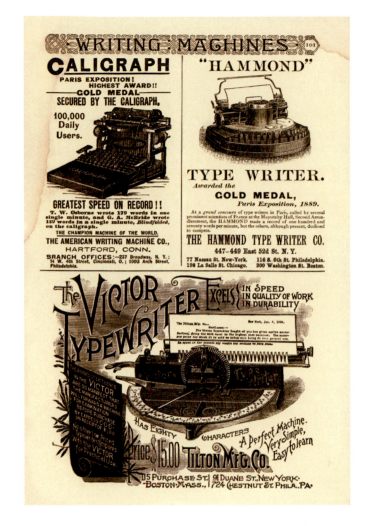

**7.18 "Edison Records Echo All Over the
World," early 1900s.** Organic background
motifs suggest the graceful movement
of sound, while the banner headline
curves with elegantly modern freedom.
A photograph of the inventor, whose
name was synonymous with innovations
of the period, is reproduced in halftone.
This combination of graphic elements
reinforces the message that phonographs
are stylish, up-to-date consumer items.
The more subtle subtext relates to the
expansion of North American industries
to markets overseas. By the turn of the
century, more goods were being mass-
produced than could be consumed
domestically. Standardization of media
formats became an international matter,
as did control of intellectual property.

Alva Edison foremost among them—caught the wave of late nineteenth-
century economic expansion and rode it with successive innovations.
Advertisements had an important role to play in representing these
products to the public (Fig. **7.17**).

Everyday uses of electrical power heralded the start of the twentieth
century. Electrification introduced large-scale changes in manufacturing
and permitted longer working hours, but it also supplied urban
entertainments. In the 1890s, film was invented, with its strange novelty
of recorded movement and projected light. At the same time, electrical
signs added a new display medium to the advertiser's palette. Commercial
artists produced the images that would promote, familiarize—and
even glamorize—these new inventions. Like other popular mechanical
devices, including the camera, the success of the motion picture and other
electrical novelties relied on the development of a significant middle class.
Campaigns to acquaint consumers with electrical inventions demonstrated
the importance of graphic communication in mediating between new
technology and its market. Advertisements did not just sell electricity;
they created images of enhancement that were synonymous with modern
life (Fig. **7.18**).

7.19a Merchant's Gargling Oil ad, 1894. Advertising was largely unregulated until the early twentieth century. Promotions used outrageous rhetoric to claim the virtues of drugs, cures, products for health, beauty, or virility. Until the Pure Food and Drug Act of 1906, virtually no standards for mass-produced goods existed in the United States. Any enterprising soul could make, bottle, label, and sell something that promised to renew lost vigor, promote longevity, cure baldness, or treat hysteria—often all with the same tonic or ointment. In this case, the potion is not even specified.

7.19b *Sunset* magazine cover, 1904. *Sunset* magazine was launched in 1898 by the Southern Pacific Railroad, the largest landowner in the state of California to which it had recently constructed a direct railway line. To change California's image from a rough-and-ready territory of questionable morality to a wholesome destination, the company published *Sunset*. It promoted images of the Golden State as a sunshine-filled paradise of fruit orchards and flowering bowers ripe for development. The journal created an image of a developer's paradise but also a place of youthful pleasure and adventure.

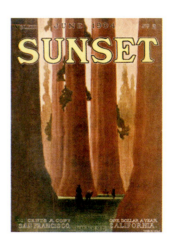

With the growth of the advertising industry, graphic art became

Graphic design and advertising The ethos of industrial capitalism went hand in hand with the rise of advertising. Business directories published in the late nineteenth century used variations in type size to distinguish one company from another, and the benefits of an identity that carried through from storefront to stationery were becoming evident. Ads sold more than goods and services; they also promoted values and lifestyles. By suggesting that products might improve or correct a condition, they set norms and expectations. They could also sway public opinion, confirm identities, and open new territories, both real and imagined. The boom that followed the discovery of gold in California in 1849 exemplifies the way graphic art and publication could hop on a movement and then help bring about a transformation through publicity. The *image* of California was an important component of what lured people to settle there. The promotional efforts of newspapers and prospective real-estate developers brought many towns into being. The collective imagination was sparked, and lives were mobilized, by the promise of new opportunities, as the expansionist mood of nineteenth-century business extended the reach of commerce and industry (Figs. **7.19a** and **7.19b**).

7.20a Georges Massias, Gladiator bicycles ad, 1905 *(right)*, **and 7.20b Will Bradley, Victor bicycles ad, detail, 1900** *(below)*. The freedom of bicycling is interpreted very differently in these two images. Will Bradley's design features a woman in a dignified posture—her social conformity signaled by the echoes between her body and the vines that organize the background space. The Massias image, on the other hand, offers an outrageous fantasy. Bradley's Japanese-inspired abstraction plays on a two-dimensional pattern of positive and negative shapes, while the fantasy image, paradoxically, is more literal in its rendering—perhaps to make it more believable, certainly to make it more engaging. Many artists became actively involved in the commercial world at the end of the nineteenth century. Will Bradley's skills extended to typography, layout, and illustration and exemplify the range of graphic services on offer in his day. But design as a programmatic approach to visual communication was just coming into focus and had not yet taken root as a profession.

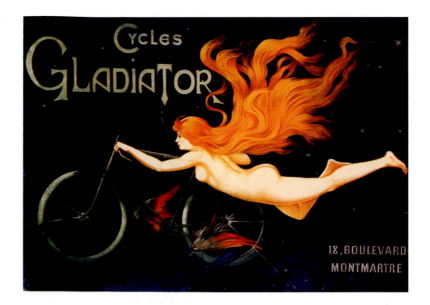

As mass media became more complex, graphic skills became more specialized. Advertising, which began as the business of selling space for publicity in newspapers, gave rise to the purveyance of ad copy and artwork as a professional service. The first American advertising agency opened in 1841, and, by the 1860s, twenty such agencies were operating in New York City alone. N. W. Ayer, one of the most famous, was established in 1869. The same year, John Wanamaker's Philadelphia department store commissioned a full-page ad in a local newspaper. The new emporium catered to middle-class consumers. Putting real goods on display while advertising them in a virtual (print) setting reinforced the links between media and actual

an integral part of the way products reached their consumers.

7.21 Products and brands. Coca-Cola®, Quaker® oats, UNCLE BEN'S® rice, and Campbell's® soup are among the long-lived brands whose identities were created in the late nineteenth century. Each had a logotype, and many spawned characters with whom to identify. Although these have been updated over time, the basic icons have persisted in the graphic landscape. Industrial methods of food production combined with networked transportation to make branding and packaging useful for attracting and keeping customers. The graphic identity of these familiar brands relied on color schemes and lettering as well as images to make products recognizable on crowded shelves and among competing advertisements.

experience. J. Walter Thompson and other agencies that would dominate the industry well into the late twentieth century were also established in this era—along with mass production and distribution of many of the products they promoted: cigarettes, automobiles, bicycles, soft drinks, and alcohol (Figs. **7.20a** and **7.20b**).

With the growth of the advertising industry, graphic art became an integral part of the way products reached their consumers. Along with branding and labeling, package design played a crucial role in fostering product recognition when consumer goods began to be distributed nationally rather than consumed locally. Getting buyers used to the idea that they should buy a particular company's oatmeal, rice, or soap flake required a change in habits and attitudes from those that had governed purchases from the local merchant selling flour from a sack. Brands themselves became valuable assets; government regulation of **patents** and **trademarks** increased (Fig. **7.21**).

By the 1880s, full-service ad agencies were buying and selling space in journals and on walls and billboards. As brokers for such space, advertising firms could conveniently coordinate use of their services at the

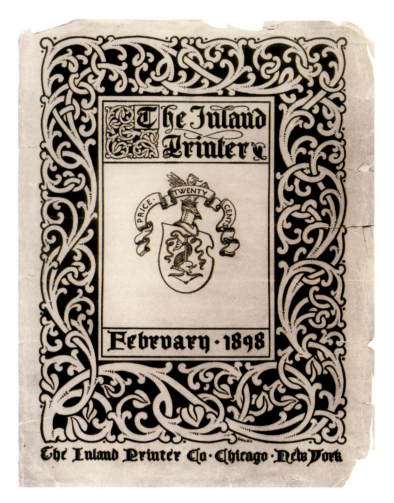

7.22 Frederic Goudy, *The Inland Printer*, 1898. In the 1880s, *Printer's Ink* and *The Inland Printer* were among the first publications designed to serve the graphic industries with technical information as well as advertisements for products and services. In 1905, American advertising pioneer Earnest Elmo Calkins and his partner Ralph Holden published *Modern Advertising*. Advertising gained definition and status as an art and science by distinguishing itself from printing.

Possibilities for making a name in the graphic arts increased.

same time. Publications that addressed the print and advertising industries began to appear. The first issue of a French journal about poster art, *L'Affiche Illustrée*, appeared in the 1880s, as did other trade journals that served the advertising industry. Through the successes of advertising, commercial art had passed a major milestone: From that point onward, the profession would be aware of itself and the value of its skilled practitioners. The field of graphic design was poised for full-fledged emergence (Fig. **7.22**).

Possibilities for making a name and a career in the graphic arts increased, as industry roles became more numerous. Many practitioners were still trained on the shop floors of the printing industry and remained tradesmen. Others became aspiring young professionals in agencies that promoted advertising as a new science of mediation between producers and consumers. Training for illustrators and commercial artists began to be institutionalized in trade schools in the 1880s. Artists were taught to draw specifically for reproduction, and basic printing techniques could be acquired by following a series of courses. Illustration was a trade in which women were allowed to work, as was typesetting. Independent classes, and even schools, were established to train women. With few exceptions,

7.23 John Everett Millais, Pears Soap ad, 1886. When British artist John Everett Millais sold a painting to the manufacturers A. and F. Pears, it was reproduced as an advertisement for their product, Pears Soap. Both the soap and the picture thereby gained a popular following. The product's name was discreetly added as lettering on Millais's bar of soap, but it was the titling type to which the soap bubble seemed to attach that placed the image squarely in a commercial frame. Some of Millais's contemporaries thought he had degraded himself through this association. Competing advertisers, however, were keen to find images that would promote the same recognition for their own products. A tension arose over distinctions between fine art and graphic art. It was argued that a moral purpose of spiritual improvement belonged to the former, while crass commercial motives drove the latter. But many illustrators and poster artists saw themselves as creating democratic art that was readily available and affordable but still of high quality. Such questions involved not only style and technique, but also the expression of points of view. Use of Millais's sentimental image of a child making fragile soap bubbles linked Pears to purity, innocence, and gentleness, which appealed to female consumers.

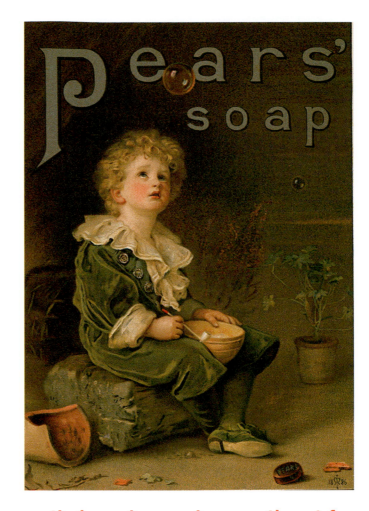

Many poster artists saw their work as a democratic art form.

however, the pressroom remained an exclusively male domain. Printing manuals of the late nineteenth century contained lessons in layout for cost-saving and effectiveness. Trade journals offered critical discussions of specific advertisements and campaigns. Customers began to see graphic design as a skill separate from typesetting, and professional agencies distinguished between layout and print production (Fig. **7.23**).

Posters and public space By the late nineteenth century, lithography was in common use, but it took an artist's vision to push poster production to the aesthetic heights that we associate with the golden age of poster art. In the late 1860s and 1870s, Jules Chéret made important technical and aesthetic contributions to the medium's refinement. Approaching color as a fundamental of composition rather than an addition, he perfected separation and registration methods and developed gradated and splattered inking techniques. Chéret and other poster artists, such as Eugène Grasset, Henri de Toulouse-Lautrec, and Alphonse Mucha, were as well known as the painters and poets of their day. Industrialized production promoted many of these artists to a position of celebrity. Their

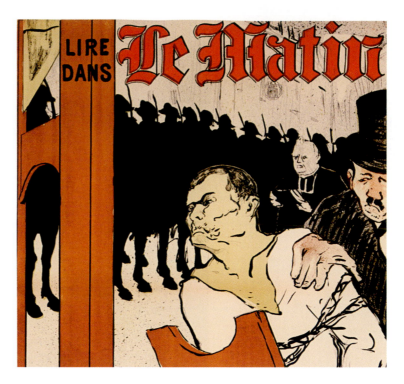

7.24 Jules Chéret, lithographed poster of dancer Loïe Fuller, 1893. Jules Chéret proclaimed that the ideal height for a woman was 8 feet tall—the size of the enormous litho stones used for posters. This dynamic drawing of modern dancer Loïe Fuller conveys the full effect of Chéret's images of flamboyant sensuality. These images celebrated the fine art of lithography almost as much as they showcased their subjects. Chéret's exploration of painterly technique was supple and fluid. Catching dancers and their costumes in midair created an image of ebullience and pleasure that was designed, precisely, to promote entertainments. Entertainment imagery, shot through with erotic undertones and intimations of carefree indulgence in the pleasures of contemporary urban life, had a definite impact on cultural values. But the image of the 1880s and 1890s as a gilded age of joyous spirit and vivacious fun had a counterpoint in the labor struggles and unrest, anarchist activity, and other social difficulties brought on by industrialization and its demographic shifts.

7.25 Henri de Toulouse-Lautrec, poster for Abbé Faure's memoirs in *Le Matin*, detail, 1893. This advertisement for a serialized account of the confessions of prisoners who awaited execution presents a very different image of *La Belle Epoque* than the flashing legs of can-can dancers usually associated with Toulouse-Lautrec. Graphic design's legacy has played an important role in sustaining the mythic image of the 1880s and 1890s as a period of spectacular entertainments, outdoor pastimes, and pleasant moments in gardens and beer halls. It was also a violent period in which public executions were common.

posters became collectable objects, and the line between mass-produced and unique works of art became blurred. Individual styles in poster design were associated with approaches to the use of color, line, composition, and iconography. In the late nineteenth century, the poster became a fully developed art form through the efforts of these superbly talented graphic artists. Many commercial artists remained largely anonymous, their identities swallowed or erased by the system of production. But famous or nameless, professional graphic artists introduced a new scale of images into the public landscape. These images were not pointed responses to industrialization but works that took full advantage of its capabilities. Every aspect of the printing trade had been changed, and the vivid inks, large format, photographic and mechanized separation and reproduction methods of the late nineteenth century offered artists the means to make striking works of commercial art (Fig. **7.24**).

The distinction between fine art and advertising became difficult to maintain. An artist like French painter Henri de Toulouse-Lautrec was able to express significant political and personal views in the posters and journal covers he designed. Posters were not only reflections of nineteenth-century life, but also very much a part of that life and its culture. They reached a large audience in city streets that functioned as mass visual cultural sites. Some poster designers and advertisers took their role as public artists seriously (Fig. **7.25**).

As graphic artifacts continued to proliferate, so did debates about what was acceptable for public consumption and who should control visual uses of public space. Throughout the century controversies arose, but, by the final decades, regulation seemed essential. Rocks and other natural features were covered with promotional images and messages—as were walls, trucks,

7.26 Posters in city space, 1905. The publicity sector was so successful and the activity of bill-stickers so aggressive that disputes arose over the use of public space for advertising. Civic-minded reformers often found themselves at odds with the imperialist spirit of enterprise that flourished in this era of rapidly expanding industrialization. The use of thoroughfares, walls, storefronts, and empty lots for advertising display came to be seen as a problem that required regulation. City districts were contested ground, and shifts in the use of visual space marked class divisions among neighborhoods.

7.27 Lucian Bernhard, poster for Adler typewriters, 1908. Bernhard was a skilled artist whose *Sachplakat* ("object poster") style took full advantage of the richly saturated color that turn-of-the-century printing techniques made possible. The images Bernhard created were striking and pleasing to the eye. His posters were as consumable as the objects they advertised. Anticipating modern abstractions of space and color, Bernhard's **plakatstil** compositions isolated objects as highly aesthetic commodities removed from any connection to systems of production, or even use. They were given an **aura** of desirability for their own sake, as objects—as if in their perfection they had always existed or had sprung into being without effort or cost.

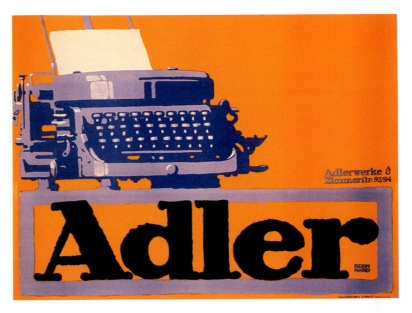

and other available surfaces. To advance their own business interests, members of the advertising industry founded a precursor of the Outdoor Advertising Association of America in 1891. The question of who owned visual public space became important, as licensing rules and censorship restrictions tightened. In New York, the Municipal Art Society formed in the 1890s to set standards for public imagery that reflected civic values. By the early 1910s, more formal control emerged in the form of a Billboard Advertising Commission, with clout and backing from the New York City government. Public debates continued, but the outbreak of World War I shifted opinion again—this time in favor of outdoor wartime information and mobilization campaigns (Fig. **7.26**).

Conclusion Highly visible, imaginative print productions added their own notes to the cacophony of graphic voices in **kiosks**, newsstands, stations, stores, and reading rooms at the turn of the century. Civic debates about the control of public space revealed concerns about the influence of ever-spreading graphic media. But deeper tensions surrounded the impact of industrial production, in general, and the purpose of art in light of it. The identity of modern design fields would be forged in the many social and aesthetic forms that responses to industry took. For graphic design, the groundwork for a distinct professional identity had been laid by increased specialization of tasks in the printing business and the emergence of advertising as a separate and valued service. Printed matter would never again have so exclusive a claim on the role of mediating responses to contemporary life as it had in the final decades of the nineteenth century. But aesthetic responses to mass production and the modern movement that grew out of them would ensure that the nascent field of graphic design would not be limited to any one medium and would have an even more critical part to play in the cultural conflicts and alliances that defined the twentieth century (Fig. **7.27**).

Mass Mediation 1850–1900s

1848 Associated Press founded
1851 Great Exhibition at Crystal Palace in London
Livingstone explores Zambezi River
Herman Melville's *Moby Dick* published
1852 Harriet Beecher Stowe's *Uncle Tom's Cabin* sells 150,000 copies in six months
Singer sewing machine invented
1853 W. F. Stanley markets architectural drawing instruments
1854 Henry David Thoreau's *Walden* published
Commodore Perry establishes trade with Japan
1855 Alphonse Louis Poitevin patents commercially unviable photolithography technique
First edition of Walt Whitman's *Leaves of Grass* published
European discovery of Victoria Falls in Zimbabwe
1856 Owen Jones's *The Grammar of Ornament* published
John Wanamaker's Philadelphia department store commissions first full-page newspaper ad
1857 Elisha G. Otis introduces passenger elevator
1858 Nadar takes first aerial photographs
Lenoir invents internal combustion engine
1859 Charles Darwin's *On the Origin of Species* published
Suez Canal begun
First oil well drilled in Pennsylvania
1861 Bicycles produced in France
Rotary presses begin to use curved stereotypes
American Civil War begins
1863 Emancipation Proclamation calls for an end to slavery in U.S.
Edouard Manet presents *Luncheon on the Grass* to scandalized public
Defeat of Confederates at Gettysburg marks turning point in Civil War
1864 Frank Leslie's illustrated newspaper launched
General Sherman's Atlanta campaign devastates American South
1865 Thirteenth Amendment abolishes slavery in U.S.
Abraham Lincoln assassinated
Civil War ends
1866 Tin cans with key openers mass-produced
Alfred Nobel invents dynamite
1867 Joseph Lister establishes principles of sterile hygiene
U.S. purchases Alaska from Russia for $7 million
1869 N. W. Ayer establishes first advertising agency
1870 Heinrich Schliemann begins excavation of Troy in Turkey
1871 Bicycles catch on in England
1872 Thomas Edison invents duplex telegraph
Jules Verne's *Around the World in Eighty Days* published
Yellowstone Park established
1873 Zanzibar slave market, once world's largest, closed
Typewriters mass-produced
Barbed wire invented
1875 Mimeograph machine invented
First Kentucky Derby
Henry Stanley explores Congo River
1876 Mechanical windup alarm clock first produced
1877 Bell Telephone Company founded, telephones introduced
Edison patents phonograph
Electric arc lamps installed outside Paris Opera House
1878 Eadweard Muybridge begins motion study photographs

1879 *A Boy's Own Paper*, a weekly magazine for boys, launched
George McGill patents stapler
Edison's first usable electric lightbulbs produced

1880 British Perforated Paper Co. makes toilet paper
Edison Electric Illuminating Company of New York founded
First solar power electric cells created

1881 Jewish pogroms in Eastern Europe
American Red Cross established
Automatic player piano produced
Halftone blocks used in letterpress printing of images

1882 First wire photos sent by telegraphy
Standard Oil Trust establishes first industrial monopoly
First rabies vaccine

1883 Brooklyn Bridge completed after thirteen years

1884 Flexible celluloid film on a spool first produced
Waterman fountain pen produced
Pantographic punch cutter perfected

1885 Death of Victor Hugo
Coca-Cola invented

1886 Ottmar Mergenthaler produces Linotype machine
Sears and Roebuck start mail-order business
Les Affiches Illustrées, French journal focused on poster art, launched
Susan B. Anthony founds women's movement
Apache chief Geronimo surrenders
John Everett Millais's *Soap Bubbles* appears in Pears Soap ads

1887 Tolbert Lanston perfects Monotype machine
Arthur Conan Doyle's first Sherlock Holmes tales published

1888 *Printer's Ink*, first advertising industry journal, launched
Kodak box camera developed by George Eastman
Revolving door patented
Jack the Ripper murders in London

1890 Hollerith's punch card tabulator used for U.S. census
Photogravure and rotogravure image printing processes perfected
Sioux fight Battle of Wounded Knee under Chief Sitting Bull

1891 Zipper invented
Peep shows introduced as popular entertainment
Edison invents kinetoscope camera

1892 First portable typewriter produced

1893 Coca-Cola trademark registered

1894 Linn Boyd Benton cuts Century typeface

1895 Sino-Japanese war ends with defeat of China
X-rays discovered
Lumière Brothers make their first movie camera and exhibit films
Safety razor introduced
The Penrose Annual launched

1896 Typhoid vaccine created

1897 General Electric establishes corporate identity department
Diesel engines produced
Theodor Herzl founds Zionist movement

Tools of the Trade

Semi-moist cake watercolors
Watercolors in tubes
Oil paints in tubes
Fountain pen (reliable)
Pencils with erasers attached
Airbrush
Typewriter
Brass fasteners
Preformed staples
Staplers
Cardboard
Scratchboard
Solid sketch blocks
Canvas boards
Dry plate photography
Paper film photography
Electrotyping
Photogravure
Halftone screens
Copying inks
Synthetic dyes
Aniline dyes for duplicating machines
Hectographic duplication
Gestetner duplicating machine
Gelatin duplicator
Mimeograph
Stencil duplicators
Rubber stamps
Transfer presses (pressure only)
Linotype typecasting
Monotype typecasting
Silkscreen
Collotype
Chromolithography
Chromoxylography
Embossing
Zinc plates for relief printing
Relief halftones
Type specimens
Stock art catalogs
Kerosene lamps
Electric lamps

8. Formations of the Modern Movement 1880s–1910s

- Modern trends in graphic design arose in response to the social and aesthetic effects of industrialization.

- Approaches to style addressed the relationship between aesthetic form (shape and decoration) and production (materials and methods).

- Integration was a goal that united many otherwise disparate movements in their approaches to process, form, and composition.

- The impulse to return to **craft** traditions evolved into a productive dialogue with industry.

- Historical revivals and **folk** styles combined and conflicted with new forms of abstraction, both **organic** and **geometric**.

- An international spectrum of movements contributed to the explicit assertion of a modern identity for graphic design.

8.1 Owen Jones, *The Grammar of Ornament*, 1856. Owen Jones's milestone publication presented an exhaustive inventory of historical and cultural styles. But by its organization and layout, it signaled alignment with the modular and systematic approach that was essential to industrial production. The richly colored book made masterful use of the newly perfected technology of chromolithography. Each of Jones's twenty sections presents motifs of distinct historical moments and cultural groups—from "Savage Tribes" to "Greek," "Celtic," and "Hindoo." Jones's use of the term *grammar* invokes language as a model for graphic design. Jones called attention to the specific qualities of organic, traditional, ethnic, and nonindustrial ornaments. But he also created an extensive pattern book for mass-produced decoration. This tension between historical recovery and industrial application permeated the Arts and Crafts movements of the late nineteenth century.

Artists had actively contributed to mass culture in the latter part of the nineteenth century. Many had simply assimilated technical advances that affected their media. But modern tendencies in graphic design emerged as self-conscious responses to the structural changes produced by industrialization. Taking their impetus from the mid-century British Arts and Crafts **movement**, late nineteenth-century designers redefined the nature of their work. Industrialism had brought the gap between **aesthetics** (form and surface) and production methods (means and materials) into focus. Designers saw their role as bridging this concrete and conceptual gap. A new designer emerged, intent on addressing broad social and cultural issues through deliberate principles of design practice. On the basis of a distinction between things that were *made* (in the traditional sense) and those that were *designed* (for production), design became an explicit field for the first time. Design, in this modern sense, was international and multidisciplinary in spirit and reach, cutting across architecture, furniture, decoration, and print. Graphic design publications provided a forum for proposing and embodying new aesthetic ideas. Tensions between historical styles and contemporary realities came into sharp relief, as designers mined the graphic inventory of earlier periods and diverse cultures. Trying to resolve the apparent contradictions between fine art and mass production meant reconciling traditional modes of production and those of the industrial era. Designers looked to formal expression as a way to model ideals of social transformation. The result was a sophisticated approach to stylistic innovation rooted in the conviction that graphic design served a cultural purpose distinct from that of fine art (Fig. **8.1**).

Responses to industrialism In the late nineteenth century, the idea of craft-based guilds attracted graphic designers eager to participate in

8.2 John Ruskin, *The Nature of Gothic*, Kelmscott Press, 1892. William Morris's design for the Kelmscott Press edition of a chapter of Ruskin's 1853 treatise on Venetian architecture demonstrates the relationship between influence and interpretation in his work. The layout and borders are meant to invoke the craft traditions of Medieval manuscript production. The type is adapted from fifteenth-century Italian letterforms. But for all his attention to historical sources, Morris was not an imitator. His border interlacings are complex and contemporary. The regularity of spacing and nearly mechanical perfection of shapes are modern. The *idea* of a Medieval interlace, rather than a copy of it, informs his design. A rigorously structured effect distances his work dramatically from the sentimental floral vignettes and page decorations that had characterized early nineteenth-century and Victorian book design. (See Fig. 6.8a for a comparison.) Ruskin's work was polemical and widely influential. His drawings were gleaned from notebooks full of studies he made on site. The recovery and appreciation of historical styles carried an agenda that passed from Pugin to Ruskin to Morris in a direct line. Morris designed graphic evocations of Medieval imagery for a late nineteenth-century eye, while Ruskin had been intent on recapturing and preserving an authentic architectural legacy.

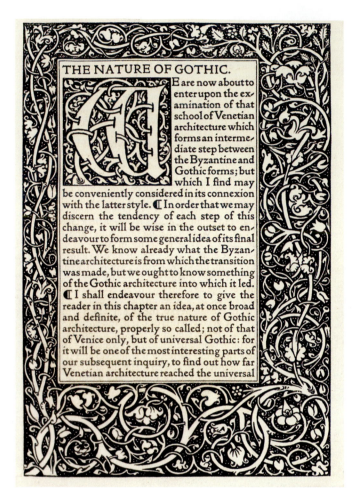

The shoddiness of everyday objects was seen as a moral failing.

the socially conscious enterprises begun by the Arts and Crafts movement. At the time, criticisms of labor practices and industrial pollution were accompanied by visions of socialist alternatives. The influential theories of Karl Marx and Friedrich Engels had expanded debates about the condition and power of the working classes. For their part, artists and designers sought an aesthetic response to the perceived fragmentation, degradation, and exhaustion brought on by industrialism. Throughout England, the United States, and Europe, artistic impulses and movements seized on pre-industrial forms and processes as keys to a mythic past of integrated lives and healthier spirits. The conviction that graphic design could help shape contemporary life was fostered by the writings of two significant architecture historians, Augustus Pugin and John Ruskin. Both suggested that design style and production methods expressed the quality and values of a culture. To them, the shoddiness of everyday objects and environments in the mid-nineteenth century indicated a moral failing and cultural weakness. Ruskin had a direct influence on William Morris, an independently wealthy artist, poet, and designer who helped found the British Arts and Crafts movement. Along with others who likewise

Formations of the Modern Movement

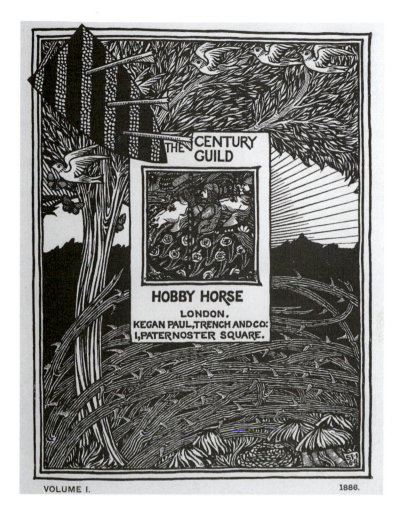

8.3 Selwyn Image, *The Century Guild Hobby Horse*, title page, 1886. Artist Selwyn Image, along with writer Herbert Horne and other founding members of the Century Guild, used the *Hobby Horse* to represent an ideal of collaborative work that integrated graphic design and fine art. The Century Guild workshop was formed with the conviction that by approaching the trades as arts, a revival of the pre-industrial guild could provide an alternative to modern production. This cover design features Medieval trappings in an idealized image of pageantry and heraldry. Somewhat mythic yet powerful in their imaginative force, these ideas took hold, in part, because the publications that presented them embodied the aesthetic they promoted. The Century Guild advanced the notion that all visual arts, including applied design, should be equal to sculpture and painting. This exemplary production, supervised by Emery Walker and masterfully printed at the Chiswick Press, supported such claims.

perceived debased conditions of production as having devastating spiritual effects, Morris sought to restore the dignity of labor, the pleasures of craft, and the basic beauty of useful objects and domestic spaces that he believed had existed in an earlier era. The historical revivals he encouraged were grounded in the study of decorative and graphic arts from remote and often idealized ages and cultures (Fig. **8.2**).

Arts and Crafts publications
The Arts and Crafts movement had an enormous impact on the design of fine press and trade books and independent artists' journals. The influence of Arts and Crafts styles and ideals was linked to the economic force and cultural reach of the British Empire. It was also the result of the powerful rhetoric of Morris and his peers. To spread the principles that inspired Arts and Crafts workshops, artists produced their own publications. Although often short-lived, these journals helped internationalize aesthetic movements. Artists and writers took control of every practical aspect of these publications, seeking handmade paper and collaborating with printers through every phase of production. These artist-initiated ventures were virtually unprecedented. Their integration of graphic design, aesthetic program, and imaginative art offered a new model of independent expression (Fig. **8.3**).

8.4 *The Studio*, cover, 1893. Launched in 1883, *The Studio* was the first and most influential among a flurry of independent publications that arose in the last decade of the nineteenth century. The linkage of fine and applied arts in the magazine's description reinforces the vision of an integrated approach to design. The lettering echoes the illustration's floral motifs whose stylized quality borrows from Medieval tapestry work. The effect is a sinewy organicism, sensual and seductive rather than disciplined or systematic. Illustrated journals such as *The Studio* were essential vehicles for spreading visual ideas and styles but also contained critical essays about fine art and poetry.

8.5a William Morris, *Canterbury Tales*, Kelmscott Press, 1896. Morris had studied Medieval illuminated manuscripts in the 1850s during his undergraduate days at Oxford. Beginning in the 1860s, he produced studies and tests for deluxe books in the Medieval spirit. He collaborated with the **Pre-Raphaelite** artist Edward Burne-Jones, creating page prototypes for several illustrated editions long before he established the Kelmscott Press. In his publications, Morris followed the guild model of collaborative production that he endorsed, engaging highly skilled artisans. He commissioned handmade paper as well-crafted and durable as sheets made in the fifteenth century. He also found sources for vellum and leather-binding materials. Every Kelmscott book was designed to suit its text. In this case, the work of the great Medieval author Geoffrey Chaucer is set in the adaptation of a Gothic typeface that bears his name. Morris's approach to book design was widely imitated in trade publishing, with mixed results. Arts and Crafts decoration became formulaic, and pseudo-medievalism was applied to all sorts of purposes. Morris's integration of elaborate production techniques enriched the unity and legibility that he structured into his pages.

Distribution networks that had been established for commercial and **popular** press publications brought these artistic journals into public view in kiosks and bookstores. Despite their alternative sensibility, artistic journals thus benefited from the mass-culture infrastructure. In turn, the design sensibilities of these independent publications were taken up by trade journals and even commercial magazines. Such appropriations were still a novelty in the late nineteenth century (Fig. **8.4**).

Most mass-produced books in the nineteenth century were of appalling quality, careless design, and poor workmanship. The challenge to cultivate new visual sensibilities and production values gave rise to the concept of "the book beautiful." This ideal was formulated in conversations between the ubiquitous William Morris and his colleague Emery Walker in the late 1880s. When, toward the end of his career, Morris established the Kelmscott Press, his book and type designs set a standard of production that extended his influence for decades. The elaborate decorative elements that bordered

Formations of the Modern Movement

Morris became interested in reviving blackletter typefaces that would invoke the broad-edged quill-based letters of the Gothic period. He designed 18-point Troy as a semi-Gothic, modern adaptation of blackletter. Morris based his designs on samples of early German printing but simplified and expanded them, avoiding the spikiness that he believed rendered later blackletter faces illegible to a modern reader. The designs are clearly revivals rather than copies of historical models. The Troy types were ready for use by 1892 when they were first printed on handmade paper for Kelmscott's edition of *The Recuyell of the Historyes of Troy*. Morris's techniques for reworking historical typefaces inspired other typographic revivals.

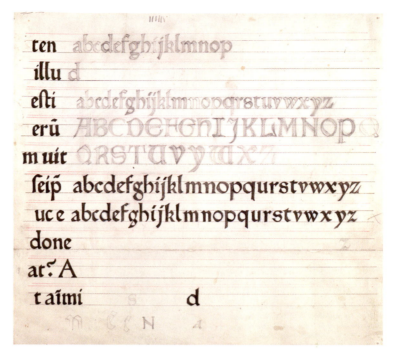

his pages and his commitment to the revival of Venetian and Gothic typography laid the foundation for a range of styles. These included Arts and Crafts emulations and imitations throughout Europe and the United States, and elements of Art Nouveau. Even the reactions of later innovators who rejected Morris's overwrought motifs and relentless patterns were *positioned* by his influence. Morris thought very differently about design than his predecessors. Successive movements took up his challenge to

After Morris, movements took up the challenge of social design.

8.6 Elbert Hubbard, *The Philistine*, **1895.** Elbert Hubbard was a charismatic and zealous American missionary who promoted social reform through common sense, honest work, and entrepreneurialism. After visiting Morris on his deathbed, he practiced a style of printing that would make his Roycroft Bibles treasured objects in thousands of middle-class American households. His workshops produced finely made yet affordable lamps, chairs, and other household objects conceived and designed in the spirit of Morris's work. Hubbard had succeeded in translating an aesthetic movement into a popular, consumable line of products. But it was his personal character and rhetoric that made him a celebrity. *The Philistine* boasted a loyal subscriber base in the hundreds of thousands. This cover design reveals an Arts and Crafts influence, but the magazine's contents celebrate an attitude that is homespun and folksy rather than studied, elaborate, or refined.

approach graphic design as a social and cultural activity and a serious engagement with production—not just a set of formal principles (Figs. **8.5a** and **8.5b**).

Arts and Crafts dissemination
British Arts and Crafts affected the evolution of graphic and other design disciplines throughout Europe and the United States well into the twentieth century. Arts-and-Crafts-inspired movements sprang up in California, the Midwest, and the Eastern United States. Architecture, furniture, textiles, glassware, metalwork, jewelry, fashion, literature, and fine art took up the ethos and aesthetic of the Arts and Crafts movement. The effect on print culture was widespread and conspicuous. This work shared a belief in design's capacity to envision alternatives to industrial forms and methods that would reconcile everyday life with human and organic values. Arts and Crafts may have become aesthetically banal and politically diluted as it spread, but its popular success must also be counted as a measure of its importance (Fig. **8.6**).

Arts and Crafts movements and their offshoots had been reactions to industrialization, yet these movements were popularized by mass-produced

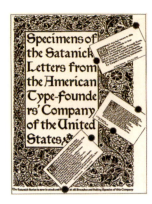

8.7 Satanick type sample, *The Inland Printer*, 1896. Morris's Troy and Chaucer types inspired far-flung imitators. But the name and design of this typeface resulted from a direct exchange between the Dickinson type foundry and Morris. When Dickinson said they wanted to produce and distribute his typefaces in the United States, Morris refused, telling them to go to the devil. They responded by creating a version of his type named accordingly. This sample appeared in *The Inland Printer*, where its design may have been supervised by Will Bradley, a major figure in the American diffusion of the Arts and Crafts style. The announcement cleverly imitates Kelmscott-style typesetting without regard for word or line breaks. The *trompe-l'oeil* cards and seals in the margins are a cruel joke on Morris and his integrated page designs. Here the border is treated as mere background pattern.

8.8a J. Herbert McNair, Margaret and Frances MacDonald, The Glasgow Institute of the Fine Arts poster, 1898. The Glasgow style is attributed to the work of J. Herbert McNair, Charles Rennie Mackintosh, Margaret MacDonald, and Frances MacDonald, known in their day as "The Four." Designed by McNair and the MacDonalds, this exhibition poster demonstrates a shift from the botanical organicism of English Arts and Crafts to a more geometric style. The elongated forms that lend this poster its elegance were characteristic of the Glasgow group and echo Mackintosh's architectural and interior designs. Medievalism and religious associations persist in the stylized costumes and beneficent postures of these figures. The design is organized according to linear patterns that divide the entire surface into carefully proportioned units. This graphic modularity and repetition reflect an abstract sensibility. The symmetry of positive and negative spaces within the composition gives figures and ground equal substance. Their shapes are harmoniously integrated into an overall design that continually shifts between abstraction and illustrational or decorative motifs. The hand-drawn lettering varies and enlivens the graphic space of the poster.

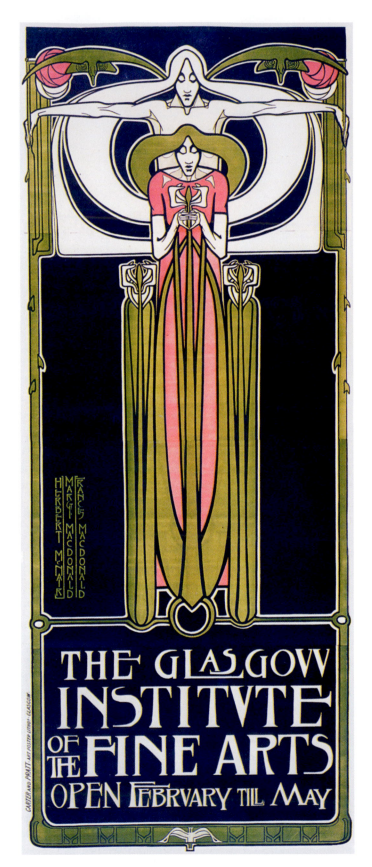

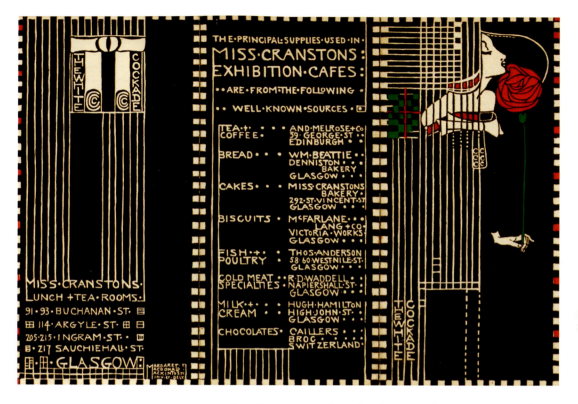

THE·PRINCIPAL·SUPPLIES·USED·IN
MISS·CRANSTONS·
EXHIBITION·CAFES·
··ARE·FROM·THE·FOLLOWING·
··WELL·KNOWN·SOURCES·

TEA·+· COFFEE·	AND·MELROSE+Co 59·GEORGE·ST EDINBURGH·
BREAD	WM·BEATTIE DENNISTON· BAKERY GLASGOW
CAKES·	MISS·CRANSTONS BAKERY 292·ST·VINCENT·ST GLASGOW
BISCUITS	McFARLANE· LANG+CO VICTORIA·WORKS GLASGOW
FISH·+· POULTRY	THOS·ANDERSON 58·60·WEST·NILE·ST· GLASGOW·
COLD·MEAT·+ SPECIALTIES	R·D·WADDELL NAPIERSHALL·ST· GLASGOW·
MILK·+· CREAM	HUGH·HAMILTON HIGH·JOHN·ST· GLASGOW·
CHOCOLATES·	CAILLERS BROC SWITZERLAND·

MISS·CRANSTONS· LUNCH +TEA·ROOMS·
91·93·BUCHANAN·ST·
114·ARGYLE·ST·
205·215·INGRAM·ST·
217 SAUCHIEHALL·ST·
GLASGOW

THE·WHITE COCKADE
THE·WHITE COCKADE

8.8b Margaret MacDonald, The White Cockade tea room menu, 1911. This menu design for a tea room at the Glasgow Exhibition shows the evolution toward geometric and modular form. The composition of motifs, borders, and delicately defined solid volumes establishes a language of interlaced lines and flat shapes that works abstractly. The attention to order and arrangement of forms moves dramatically away from illustration, although the female face, rose, and hand hint at sensuality. The degree of abstraction in this work indicates a readiness for the repeatable modularity essential to design in an industrial context. The patterns are adaptable to stencils, weavings, and wallpaper production and echo the geometric systems that Mackintosh used to organize his architectural elements.

artifacts. Late nineteenth- and early twentieth-century print culture teemed with bad copies of Morris's designs—ill-drawn, poorly printed, and designed by artists who grasped only the surface features of Morris's work, leaving its aesthetic and social principles by the wayside (Fig. **8.7**).

As Arts-and-Crafts-influenced movements were formed in the late 1880s and 1890s by artists in Glasgow, Vienna, London, Paris, Berlin, and other European cultural centers, they diverged in attitudes and goals. Stylistic innovations moved away from historical sources, and two poles of abstraction—organic and geometric—came into vogue. Posters, publications, and publicity for major industrial exhibitions showcased the graphic styles of these groups, which often translated architectural approaches into visual motifs. An increasingly vital dialogue developed between industrial methods and fine art. Unlike the original Arts and Crafts impulse, which was firmly rooted in a romantic socialist agenda, late nineteenth-century movements often combined a mystical spiritualism with nationalist undertones. Scottish Arts and Crafts invoked Celtic roots that were as mythic as they were historical. These ethnic motifs resonated with themes of renewal and rebirth that were central to the *Zeitgeist*. Scottish Arts and Crafts practitioners shared their English counterparts' aesthetic concerns and progressive commitment to material integrity and honesty of production (Fig. **8.8a**).

A new preference for clean lines and clear organization banished the excesses of Victorian domesticity. Although generalizations about style are debatable, British designers tended to create spare, geometric forms and well-structured empty space, while those on the Continent tended to fill their formal arrangements with decoration (Fig. **8.8b**).

8.9 *Artistic Japan*, 1888. In 1888 Siegfried Bing launched a publication titled *Artistic Japan*, which was printed in both English and French. It contained informative articles and images that capitalized on the vogue for Japanese prints and paintings that had begun in the 1850s with the opening of that country to trade with the West. The use of a Japanese print in the poster that advertised this journal demonstrates Bing's commitment to putting these images directly into circulation. The influence of Japanese aesthetics had been felt in high-art circles before *Artistic Japan* began publication. But Bing did not just cater to the extremely wealthy private and institutional patrons whose collections he supplied. He wanted to educate a broad audience of consumers who found his imports in department stores. Japanese art's oblique angles, dramatic use of white space, and compositional flow were radically different from Western notions of symmetry and stable balance. Adopted, though not always successfully translated, the techniques of this tradition inspired new approaches to layout. Japanese prints, in particular, orchestrated surface and spatial effects in graphic forms that lent themselves to imitation in poster designs and decorative arts.

Art Nouveau's practitioners aimed to cultivate bourgeois taste.

Art Nouveau *Art Nouveau* was a general term applied to the work of many artists and designers in the 1890s and 1900s. It was originally the name of a Paris gallery established in 1895 by Siegfried Bing, a German importer of Asian objects. The term was soon applied to any work that seemed to reject historical reference in favor of a "new" sensibility. The commercial origin of Art Nouveau's name spotlights the basis of its phenomenal popular success as a style. Unlike the socialist theories and rarefied consumption that characterized many Arts and Crafts undertakings, Art Nouveau's goals were mainly anti-elitist. Most of its practitioners aimed at cultivating and gratifying bourgeois taste with comfortable expressions of contemporary affluence. Art Nouveau designs integrated novel shapes into the overall form of objects and structures. In its graphic versions, this style shaped book and type design and transformed the treatment of decorative elements in packaging, poster, and logo design. Art Nouveau designers drew conspicuously on Japanese techniques of asymmetrical composition and flowing spatial organization (Fig. **8.9**).

Art Nouveau attracted considerable public attention at the 1900 Paris Exposition Universelle and began to be seen in art posters and

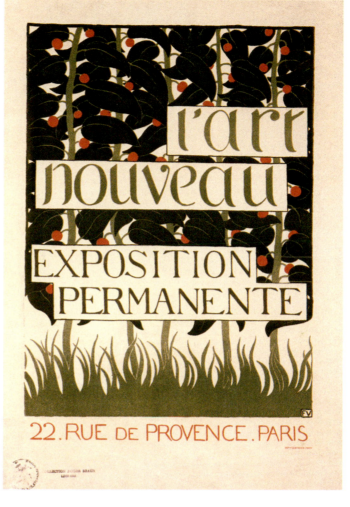

8.10a Félix Vallotton, poster for l'Art Nouveau gallery, 1895. Hand-drawn lettering and simplified and patterned floral motifs are characteristic of the Art Nouveau sensibility. The colors in this design are also typical of the organic tones used in turn-of-the-century applied arts. The lettering has been somewhat awkwardly set off from the background. This distinction between background and foreground is unusual in Art Nouveau graphics, which more commonly sought to integrate type and decoration.

8.10b Will Bradley, *The Inland Printer*, 1894. The American designer, Will Bradley, imported a new graphic sensibility to the United States, imprinting its expression with his own style. In 1895, he established the Wayside Press, which published works of his own design, including the art journal, *Bradley: His Book*. His association with *The Inland Printer* brought his designs to a trade readership. This hand-drawn masthead with its curved-back *E* reveals an Arts and Crafts medievalism, while the black-and-white line drawing indicates the influence of Walter Crane and Aubrey Beardsley. Bradley's graphics are more conventional and less erotic than those of his British counterparts. An innocence prevails in his chaste treatment of nude figures.

advertisements that associated commodities with a freer, modern **lifestyle**. Images of women with flowing hair, soft curves, and streamlined forms in positions of flight introduced a mildly erotic undertone to much Art Nouveau style. Its motifs are so distinctive that it has become in itself a historical referent, appropriated to express nostalgia for a turn-of-the-century abandon to fantasy. This fantasmatic mode luxuriated in a casual use of nude figures intertwined with vines, flowers, insects, and animals in exotic and elegant designs. In architecture and industrial design, Art Nouveau took advantage of technological improvements to mold materials into free-flowing forms. While such technological changes were only incidental to graphic work, designers invented visual corollaries to the new industrial capabilities, translating physical properties into alluringly fluid and tensile motifs. Suggestive without causing offense, this indulgent style became a great favorite among upper-middle-class consumers (Figs. **8.10a** and **8.10b**).

Jugendstil In the last decade of the nineteenth century, designers struggled to find a solution to the relations between form, function, and decoration. Graphic designers translated lessons learned in architecture

8.11a GE logo, 1890 *(above),* **and 8.11b motifs from** *Ver Sacrum,* **1899** *(below).* The familiarity of the GE logotype obscures its historical origin in the late nineteenth century. But set alongside these motifs and decorative devices from Jugendstil publications, its formal connections to them are immediately striking. The integration of shape and ornament into a functional whole is typical of Art Nouveau design. Organic unity and curvilinear forms characterized the graphic work of designers in the 1890s, but geometric motifs and modular approaches also made their appearance. The significance of such abstraction went beyond mere style choice. Although machine aesthetics belong to the twentieth century, late nineteenth-century graphic designers were increasingly interested in industrial methods of production as models for their practice and as sources for their forms and compositions.

8.12a Otto Eckmann, *Jugend,* **1897** *(above right).* The title of this publication, which gave Jugendstil its name, translates as "youth." The journal was first published in 1896 by Georg Hirth. Every cover and masthead for *Jugend* was different. All attempted to appear contemporary to a youthful culture whose values they helped define. As a result, *Jugend* became a forum for advancing the cutting edge of style and a showcase for designers eager to exhibit their unique approaches and new sensibility. Otto Eckmann was an artist who gave up painting in favor of design. His designs for *Jugend* magazine demonstrate the attention to letter and image relations that distinguished the style of the period. *Jugend* was published from 1896 to 1914, years of determined cultural optimism in the face of political struggles that led to the devastation of World War I.

and other applied arts into concise visual forms. For architects, the idea of *gesamtkunstwerk* ("total, unified work of art") called for fully integrated spaces, including furniture, wall treatments, fixtures, and textiles. Graphic design popularized the patterns and models of such approaches. Typefaces, decorative motifs, and page layouts all shifted away from the piecemeal miscellany of the Victorian era toward systematicity (Figs. **8.11a** and **8.11b**).

The popular and influential German movement Jugendstil took its name from a publication that portrayed and promoted a contemporary lifestyle. Its practitioners were artists whose embrace of industrial production included designs for type and mass-produced furniture, as well as posters for the industrial exhibitions that displayed such designs. Jugendstil and Art Nouveau, like Arts and Crafts before them, had specific sources. But they quickly became generic terms applied to a range of locations, artists, and works. All were characterized by expressions of sensual freedom, signaled by female forms, floral and organic motifs, and suggestions of primal eroticism as a liberating force from the bonds of convention. The stylistic grace cultivated by these movements was an asset to commercial interests staked on consumption rather than social reform (Figs. **8.12a** and **8.12b**).

8.12b Otto Eckmann, Eckmann-Schmuck, 1900–1901. Eckmann's skill as a designer is evident in his typographic adaptation of Jugendstil devices. These organic letterforms are drawn with a brush and contain echoes of Medieval and floral forms. Each is a modular element of a design system, as are the units of his border motifs. The flowing links between positive and negative spaces forge the same dynamic movement in borders and type. The legibility of the letters is all the more striking given the tight fit of their lively forms. Their swollen lines and bulbous shapes bridge organic and geometric vocabularies, and the repetition of formal elements reveals the industrial sensibility that underlies this approach. These ornaments were readily adaptable to production in various media. Their appearance in graphic form allowed them to be copied and stenciled, woven, molded, inscribed, or printed in any number of applications.

8.13 Gustav Klimt, first Secessionist exhibition poster, 1898. Klimt's work combines elements of classicism and exoticism yet tends toward **modernism** in its striking geometric organization. The male figure was nude in the first version of the poster. Trees were added to cover his naked genitalia, a sign of the conservatism of a world enamored of Greek and Roman classical traditions but shy about fully embracing them in their historical authenticity. Such compromises were typical of the ways in which inspirations from the past—or from other cultures— were applied in graphic designs. Lip service was paid to the ideal of cultural exchange, but the domestication and normalization of imagery and designs "inspired" by exotic sources betrayed a colonial attitude. The structure and line work of this composition anticipate later Secessionist design developments.

Viennese design The Vienna Secession was formed in 1898 to simplify, distill, and modernize design. The name *Secession* derives from the decision by the founding artists to exhibit their work outside the fine art academy. While other Arts-and-Crafts-inspired activities had been anti-industrialist in orientation, these artists' rejection of academic constraints represents another crucial realignment in early **modern movements**. Initiated by Gustav Klimt, the Vienna Secession attempted to forge fundamental links between fine and applied art, an approach that ran counter to prevailing distinctions between high art and the trades. Klimt was the intellectual leader and first president of the fledgling Secession. His poster designs helped establish the public profile of the group, which included Koloman Moser, Alfred Roller, and Josef Hoffmann. Their first exhibition garnered public acclaim and recognition, as well as support from the emperor who was keen to consolidate Austrian national identity in an increasingly shaky political context (Fig. **8.13**).

9. Innovation and Persuasion 1910–1930

- A basic tenet of modernism in design was that new realities demanded new approaches to form. Seeking a formal rupture with the past and a transcendence of stylistic relativity, modern designers embraced functionalism, geometric formalism, and machine aesthetics, even as more traditional approaches persisted in commercial contexts.

- Formal experiments in the early decades of the twentieth century were fueled by a belief in the power of design as an agent of social change.

- The development of graphic design was informed by an exchange between commercial publicity and fine art conventions, despite the polarization of these realms by definitions of high and mass culture.

- Graphic design education took institutional forms, and curricula were developed based on the notion of a visual language that marked a turn away from historical styles in favor of a pursuit of "universal" principles and systems.

- The effectiveness of graphic design as a shaper of public opinion prompted questions about the nature of propaganda and the social responsibility of designers.

9.1 Herbert Bayer, Bauhaus poster for Kandinsky exhibition, 1926. The functionalist aesthetic that characterizes modern design is exemplified by the approach developed at the Bauhaus. This poster was designed by Herbert Bayer, a teacher at the school and a strikingly accomplished designer, for an exhibition of the modern abstract painter Wassily Kandinsky. Like Bayer, Kandinsky was affiliated with the Bauhaus, and his theoretical writings defined the universal language of visual form embodied in his abstract paintings. Kandinsky aspired to a graphic mode that would be analogous to musical composition, its formal arrangements based in properties of rhythm, tone, and harmony. The belief that such approaches would transcend context and be free of historical associations was, eventually, caught in a contradiction: The formalist, geometric graphics of the 1910s and 1920s came to be completely identified with their period. Bayer's design expresses a similar sensibility. All of the elements are geometric, except for the photograph which is machine-made. The decade preceding this design had been filled with experimental work that contributed to the development of its modern style. But the systematic quality of Bayer's approach shows modernism in a mature phase of development. The bold formalism of rule, type, and blocks sets up an active dialogue with the sheet's edge at every point that registers an angle.

Industrial production radically altered everyday realities in the nineteenth century, but not until the early twentieth century did graphic designers engage modernity as a new cultural phase. Modernism was an embrace of the new that required a break with the past, but many commercial graphic design commissions depended on evoking a sense of comfortable familiarity and cultural continuity. This contradiction meant that machine aesthetics, **functionalism**, and abstraction replaced organic and historical sources of style in some dedicated circles, while illustration persisted in most popular contexts. Many modern approaches began with **avant-garde** artists committed to formal and conceptual experimentation. By the 1910s, these experiments had begun to upset traditional attitudes in architecture and had given rise to the newly defined disciplines of industrial and graphic design. Artistic movements that combined radical political and aesthetic agendas gained visibility in the years leading up to and following World War I. These movements were sustained by a belief that design in all of its forms could be an active agent of social change. Their graphic inventions came to have an enormous impact on commercial practice, as the visual forms of avant-garde art from the 1910s were assimilated, systematized, and defined in professional settings of the 1920s. Perhaps at no other moment in the history of graphic design have innovators had such a high public profile in artistic and commercial circles simultaneously. Some graphic artists who had participated in the fervor of aesthetic revolution transferred their skills to information campaigns that supported the national efforts of World War I and the social transformations that followed. After the war, graphic

9.3a El Lissitzky, *Beat the Whites with the Red Wedge*, 1919. El Lissitzky used abstract forms to symbolize conflict between revolutionary and counter-revolutionary factions in this famous poster. The red wedge represented the Communist armies organized against the conservative "white" forces of aristocratic landowners. The dynamic red triangle comes from the left and breaks into the white circle that symbolizes stability. Lissitzky was committed to the goals of the Russian Revolution, a civil war that had resulted in the abdication of the czar in 1917. In 1919, when Lissitzky composed this piece, power struggles among anarchists and other revolutionary forces were still ongoing. His attempt to communicate a political meaning in a new graphic language demonstrated his conviction that aesthetic direction could change the world by providing new forms for imagining society. Placed in public view outside a factory entrance where it would fall under the daily gaze of workers, the poster was meant to signal a new social order to those toiling to bring it about.

designers helped found new educational and cultural institutions dedicated to the applied arts and developed approaches to a "**universal language** of form." And just as theirs was becoming a recognized profession, graphic designers saw their work—and the **propaganda** produced during and after World War I—become the focus of a new scrutiny of mass media, public opinion, and persuasion (Fig. **9.1**).

Visual culture and avant-garde design
By the beginning of the twentieth century, an amazing variety of typographic and visual materials were available to editorial and advertising design. Display and

It was not until the early twentieth century that designers

text faces in metal and wood, custom engravings, and standard cuts stocked the cases and shelves of letterpress print shops. Mechanical production techniques gave designers enormous freedom, and print media thrived on the novelties it produced. Photographic images were becoming increasingly commonplace. Illustration persisted, enhanced by color printing techniques. Motion pictures added a new dimension to mass entertainment, and the posters that promoted them showcased signature graphic styles. Modern visual culture was prolific, and printed matter abounded. Books, newspapers, magazines, posters, packaging, and ephemera supplied designers with an inexhaustible stock of ideas and imagery to draw from in their work (Fig. **9.2**).

In spite of the profusion of nineteenth-century technical inventions, it was not until the early decades of the twentieth century that designers purposefully exploited and revealed their capabilities. Such self-consciousness about media and materials was typical of the modern movement's desire to expose, present, or portray the devices of art and language. The artists who identified with the most adventurous visual experiments are known as the avant-garde. They did not have to make

9.3b El Lissitzky, self-portrait, *The Constructor*, 1924. Lissitzky's montage self-portrait pictures him as an engineer. His approach to design is revealed in the composition and production of this image, both of which were boldly unconventional for the period. The compass, a tool for making perfectly rational geometric forms, long associated with the work of architects and masons, is presented in a modern photographic rendering. Stencil letters and a gridded surface that suggest a mechanical drawing table reinforce the image of design as an industrial activity (rather than a fine art or an old craft), while Lissitzky's own closely cropped hair and turtleneck sweater are a far cry from the flowing locks and floppy ties of an earlier generation.

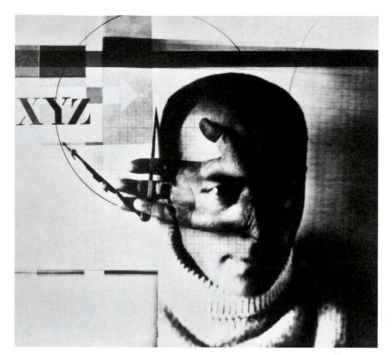

radical changes in technology (commercial uses of the printing industry had already prompted these), but they tried to find a visual language to translate the social meaning of these changes. In pursuit of this goal, they altered the look of graphic design for the rest of the twentieth century. They adopted a functionalist, antihistorical approach in which organic, hand-drawn, and ornamental forms were replaced by sans serif faces, geometric designs, and photographic imagery (Figs. **9.3a** and **9.3b**).

purposely exploited and revealed new technical capabilities.

9.4 Ilia Zdanevich, *Soirée du coeur à barbe* (The bearded heart evening) poster, 1923. This poster advertises an intentionally strange-seeming artists' performance in Paris and contains all the characteristic elements of the avant-garde sensibility. Created by Ilia Zdanevich, an expatriate Georgian poet and typographer, it combines various languages, signs, and images in a seemingly chaotic composition. In fact, the work is carefully arranged. In its use of multiple sizes and styles of type, it is also a technical achievement of intricate letterpress construction. This "ransom note" typography was typical of the first wave of experimental impulses in avant-garde poetry and art that appeared in the 1910s. It breaks with the decorative sensibility of Arts and Crafts publications and fine printing and brings the verbal and visual languages of advertising into the world of art.

Exposing and subverting the powers of mass-media rhetoric and the pretenses of middle-class culture, avant-garde artists and designers appropriated the slogans of advertising to create publicity for their outrageous events and performances. Their posters and announcements made visual and verbal jokes that were often shocking. Their poetry and artwork deployed phrases, images, and typefaces designed for commerce, as they cut and tore publications to produce jarring new meanings in disturbing **collage** compositions. Their graphic annihilation of literary and high art conventions deliberately distanced their agitations from mainstream and fine press publishing. They wanted to scandalize the **bourgeoisie**, so they staged events that baffled the public. *Disorientation* and *defamiliarization* were catchwords for the idea that art and design could change the way people understood the world (Fig. **9.4**).

The graphic impact of Futurism and Dada Futurism

and **Dada** were international movements. In 1909, the Italian poet Filippo Marinetti burst into the spotlight when his *Futurist Manifesto* was published on the front page of the popular French newspaper,

9.5a Filippo Marinetti, *Zang Tumb Tumb*, 1914. Marinetti's **manifestos** may have had more influence than his poems, but the publication of *Zang Tumb Tumb* was a remarkable achievement. The book celebrated the Battle of Tripoli with expressive typographic methods that combined sound poetry and visual prosody. The repetitive drumbeat of war was represented in syllables whose graphic repetition suggested a powerful machine rolling with inevitable momentum. *Zang Tumb Tumb* combined a love of machines, militarism, and violence. Marinetti's later support of the Italian dictator Mussolini reinforced the impression that his Futurist aesthetic had fascistic implications, although these were not necessarily evident in the 1910s.

9.5b Filippo Marinetti, *Mots en Liberté*, 1919. Among the most famous typographic experiments of the avant-garde, this poem portrays the sounds of battle in an image that explodes off the page. The graphic effect is powerful and unprecedented. Tremendous visual imagination was required to conceive of such a work and to integrate its visual-verbal-tactile effects so thoroughly. It is a prime example of poetic **synesthesia**—an aesthetic carried over from Symbolism—in which one sense perception (e.g., sound, sight, smell) was expressed in terms of another. In the last decades of the nineteenth century, Symbolist artists deplored direct expression and sought to create esoteric symbols for the richly cloaked presentation of ideal forms. In Marinetti's Futurist sensibility, the crashing violence of war is rendered by a visual equivalent. His language is direct, his methods abrupt, and his aesthetic represents an about-face from the mystical world of transcendence that occupied artists a generation earlier. The modern world in all of its immediacy is the target of Marinetti's aim.

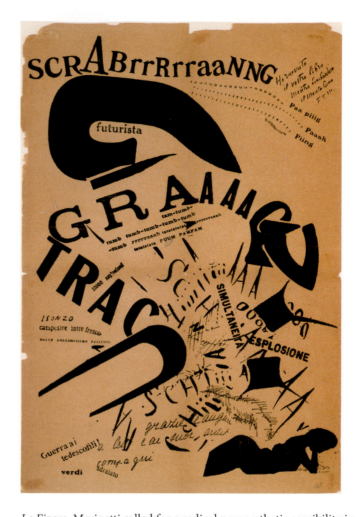

Le Figaro. Marinetti called for a radical new aesthetic sensibility in all arts. The moment was ripe and the impact was explosive. Avant-garde activity erupted simultaneously all over Europe and in Russia and America in the 1910s. This internationalism was one of the distinctive features of modernism. Almost overnight, far-flung artists felt compelled to define their work by a dramatic rejection of all inherited aesthetic values. Marinetti claimed that a racing car was as beautiful as the Venus de Milo and celebrated the machines and industrial products of modern life. He exhorted artists to express the "wireless imagination" associated with the new medium of radio. His phrase "words in liberty" became a rallying cry to break the habits of poetic thought. His incitement to do away with conventional punctuation in favor of mathematical symbols and more direct and concrete means of relating textual elements was an assault on bourgeois propriety. He also called for graphic innovations that would banish the last of the late nineteenth-century stylistic sensibility that still cluttered pages with elaborate motifs and borders. Marinetti's attacks on the decorative typography of old-fashioned books were as rabid as his proclaimed hatred for the soppy first-person of lyrical poetry. Modern meant new and new meant machine-made or at least machine-like, and sometimes nihilistic and antihumanistic (Figs. **9.5a–c**).

9.5c Fortunato Depero, *Depero Futurista*, 1927. The strongest link between Futurism and commercial design appeared in the work of Fortunato Depero. An avid follower of Marinetti, Depero was also an advertising artist. His 1927 book combined Futurist techniques and promotional campaigns. The punched cover reveals the bolts that bind the book. Streaking cones of light break the type into active fragments that have nothing to do with letterpress forms. Active diagonal elements combine with angular lettering (albeit hand-drawn) to convey a mechanical design. The graphic sources of much experimental artwork had been publicity. In turn, graphic design was revitalized by the flow of artistic energy into mainstream advertising. The exchange was circular, the direction of influence often hard to pin down. Yet distinctions between high and low art were firmly maintained by different values and venues.

9.6 Natalia Goncharova (with text by Velimir Khlebnikov and Aleksei Kruchenykh), *A Game in Hell*, 1912. Russian painter Natalia Goncharova looked to traditional sources to distinguish the spirit of the Russian avant-garde from that of France and Italy. She sought inspiration in woodblock books of Russian folktales and used powerfully drawn imagery to illustrate works by experimental poets such as Velimir Khlebnikov and Aleksei Kruchenykh. The bold expression of her graphic compositions signaled a break with nineteenth-century sensibilities, conventional influences, and European academic styles. The text is equally direct and deliberately forceful. Publications such as this were issued in tiny editions and circulated among artists rather than in a broader, commercial market.

Marinetti's ideas spread rapidly, as the *Futurist Manifesto* was translated and published in newspapers throughout Europe. Artists had never used the media more effectively. Forms of Futurism appeared everywhere. In Russia, artists took up the term and applied it to any and all experimental work in poetry, art, or design that seemed to embody modern forms and utopian visions. These included indigenous sources and homegrown varieties of anti-academic work among poets and painters in Moscow and Saint Petersburg. Russian artists conceived of books as tactical media to be circulated broadly. By making books themselves, they felt they could escape some of the controls of publishers who were more interested in money than original ideas. Using block cuts, hand lettering and drawing, primitive office **duplicating machines**, and any other ready means of production, Russian artists made books of an unprecedented boldness. Deliberately crude, with shocking titles like *A Slap in the Face of Public Taste*, *A Game in Hell*, and *World Backwards*, these books contained poetry and imagery that was unsentimental, brash, and far from the preciousness of an earlier generation (Fig. **9.6**).

Not all avant-garde activity was directly inspired by Futurism. In 1916, artists of various nationalities gathered in neutral Switzerland to protest the war. They took a nonsense word, *Dada*, as their name to symbolize

9.7a John Heartfield, *Neue Jugend* (New youth), 1917. From Cubism to **Constructivism**, collage practices made imaginative use of mass-media materials. These were extended by the skilled photomontage work of Dadaists Hannah Höch and John Heartfield. Experimental compositions and dynamic typography set off shocking combinations of image fragments. Mass-produced visuals were reworked into artistic and graphic expression. Heartfield, in particular, understood the effective translation of a camera-ready paste-up into a printed image. His originals were often filled with carefully painted, erased, and reworked contours. He knew how to manipulate value and tone in a composition and how to make the most of mechanical prepress processes. The pages of *Neue Jugend* confront their reader with high-contrast colors, bold sans serif display faces, and photographic and decorative devices in unusual combinations.

9.7b Hannah Höch, *Cut with a Kitchen Knife Dada through the Last Weimar Beer-Belly Cultural Epoch of Germany*, collage, 1919–1920. One of the most original and striking graphic talents of the Dada movement, Hannah Höch introduced issues of gender and ethnicity into her collages. As her richly supplied composition suggests, photography had made the cultural shift from one-off darkroom prints to mass-produced, readily available, visual material. Höch's satiric edge combined with her uncanny eye to produce peculiar hybrid images. Although such work is commonplace today, at the time it was disturbing and controversial. Women were major figures and active innovators in the twentieth-century avant-garde, particularly in Germany and Russia. Höch's work aggressively attacked stereotypes of women, as well as the distinctions between Western and non-Western cultures. Her ethnographic interests turned inward toward German culture as well, and her recombined images of athletes, politicians, and other public figures contain a record of her nation and times, edited and illuminated by her searching eye.

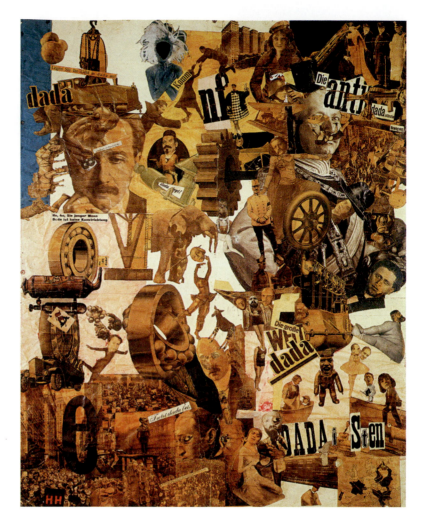

the outrageous attitudes of their movement. Dada publications and performances appeared in Berlin, Paris, and New York among other cities and embraced nonsense as an antidote to what artists considered a monstrous use of reason to justify the bloodshed of the war. A curiously mixed group, the Dadaists included pacifists, anarchists, and radicals. Their aesthetics raised a cry of protest. Their behavior was meant to shake the citizens of Zurich—and later, other major capitals—into a reaction against the horrors of the conflict. Dada designs had to be tamed before they could be adapted for commercial purposes, but their style was distinctive. Eventually, many Dada techniques became part of the standard repertoire of modern graphic design, particularly mixed-face typography, hodgepodge cuts and figures, and high-tension collage. Indeed, in the hands of advertising designers, collage was to become one of the most versatile and reliable methods for activating visual energy and condensing complex messages. But at the time of their development by Dadaists, collage and **photomontage** were techniques of disruption—of the illusion of pictured space, of the cultural expectations of public discourse, and of the political effects of familiar directives (Figs. **9.7a** and **9.7b**).

III

DIE KUNSTISMEN

1924
1923
1922
1921
1920
1919
1918
1917

HERAUSGEGEBEN VON EL LISSITZKY

1916
1915

UND HANS ARP

1914

LES ISMES DE L'ART

1924
1923
1922
1921
1920
1919
1918
1917

PUBLIÉS PAR EL LISSITZKY

1916
1915

ET HANS ARP

1914

THE ISMS OF ART

1924
1923
1922
1921
1920
1919
1918
1917

PUBLISHED BY EL LISSITZKY

1916
1915

AND HANS ARP

1914

EUGEN RENTSCH VERLAG
ERLENBACH-ZÜRICH, MÜNCHEN UND LEIPZIG

1925

9.8 El Lissitzky, *The Isms of Art*, 1925. Lissitzky designed and coedited *The Isms of Art*, a trilingual book presenting a seminal decade's succession of modern movements through the work of representative artists. The order and structure on the title page establishes a systematic program that is maintained throughout the book. Lissitzky's approach to overall organization of content and form set a completely different course for book design. Rather than thinking page by page, or in terms of word and image relations within a single design, he established the hierarchy and structure of a book as a whole and exposed that systematic structure as an explicit part of the design. This operative concept—of a form calling attention to itself and its functions—distinguishes Lissitzky's work from traditional book design, which strives to perform its task self-effacingly, with the transparency of a "crystal goblet," as American type critic Beatrice Warde would later write.

Geometric abstraction was adopted as a sign of functionality.

From experiment to principles Another dramatic development in the early twentieth century was the adoption of geometric abstraction and flat, hard-edged forms as signs of a contemporary sensibility. These became distinctive, defining features of modern graphic design. British and American Arts and Crafts, the Vienna Secession, and Deutscher Werkbund had begun this formal simplification. But in the early 1910s, Kasimir Malevich's painting of a single black square defined **Suprematism**, a new aesthetic based in nonrepresentational imagery that distilled visual forms to an essential grammar. In the broader Russian-based movement known as *Constructivism,* these formal developments were combined with a proactive orientation toward production. The idea that artists should seize the tools of industry and become engineers of a new sensibility established a powerful foundation for applied art, including graphic design. Constructivists' desire for the social benefits of mass production found expression in an appreciation of the look—as well as the principles—of functionality derived from machines (Fig. **9.8**).

By the 1920s, an international community of artists began to formalize the tenets of these early experiments as a design method. Among them

9.9 Alexander Rodchenko, *Novyi LEF*, back and front covers, 1928.
Alexander Rodchenko's photography exploited dramatic angles as disorienting perspectives from which to view the world. These perspectives were facilitated by the Leica he bought in 1928. The first mass-produced 35-mm camera, the Leica was small, light, and easy to use, freeing the photographer to go anywhere and assume any position. Rodchenko's designs for the post-revolutionary Soviet journal *LEF,* and its successor *Novyi LEF,* depended heavily on photographs but not as straight-on, squarely composed documents. The effect of "defamiliarization" was crucial to Rodchenko, as was attention to the subject matter of built, man-made forms, rather than natural or traditional portraits and scenes. Text is placed at points of tension and transition. Traditional black and red inks have been modernized by hard-edged geometry. Such designs expressed the utopian basis on which a new society could be structured: It should be striking, functional, and, above all, dynamic. By the end of the 1920s, the utopianism that originally inspired Rodchenko and other Russian avant-garde artists was considerably dampened by the disciplinary measures of the communist government and its rising leader Joseph Stalin. In 1928, the first in a series of centrally dictated Five Year Plans set the agenda for Russia's transformation into a world industrial power. This agenda would impose limits on consumption and quotas on production that no one could ignore or challenge.

were Russians Alexander Rodchenko and El Lissitzky, Hungarian-born Laszlo Moholy-Nagy, and Dutch artist Theo van Doesburg. Russian painter Wassily Kandinsky's *Point and Line to Plane*, published in 1921, provided a theoretical model for an abstract visual language. Kandinsky attempted to formulate a set of universal principles to explain the graphic elements of composition and the rules governing the interaction of visual forms as a set of forces. Constructivism bridged the early avant-garde unruliness of

Constructivists blurred the line between fine and applied art.

the 1910s and a new spirit of order that took shape in the 1920s. In their practice and pedagogy, Constructivists blurred the lines between fine and applied art and between theoretical concepts and their use (Fig. **9.9**).

These artists were impatient to change the world and overturn its repressive structures. Architecture, graphic and industrial design, film, literature, and dance all showed signs of the revolutionary spirit. The stylistic and conceptual impact of the avant-garde on graphic design was both immediate and long-lasting. Avant-garde artists approached design as a cultural force and a discipline according to which ways of thinking were theorized in advance of practice. The progressive ambition and methodological contributions of this generation cannot be overestimated (Fig. **9.10**).

Modern graphic language was characterized by geometric forms, high-contrast black, white, and red inks, and boldly structured typographic arrangements. Some designers combined collage with abstraction. Others united word and image in shared formal terms. These inventions were filled with an exuberant purpose that was to meet with crushing disappointment, as repressive political forces took control in the late 1920s (Fig. **9.11**).

9.10 Georgii and Vladimir Stenberg, poster for *The Eleventh*, 1928. The boldness and dynamism of this poster typify the Russian Constructivist movement. It was composed by the Stenberg brothers for a film celebrating the eleventh anniversary of the October Revolution that had brought the Bolsheviks to power. For all of its cutting-edge industrial references, its design reveals the extent to which technology was lagging in the Soviet Union. Its areas of flat lithographic color combine with photomontage to create a powerful and complex image, but its masking and lettering have been worked by hand. The photographic sources, geometric typography, and strongly organized vertical spaces are all characteristic of the exuberance with which Russian avant-garde graphic design promoted the new social order of the Soviet Union as the essence of modernity.

9.11 El Lissitzky, Vladimir Mayakovsky's *For the Voice*, 1923. Mayakovsky's rousing poems were often read aloud to crowds. Lissitzky's placement of icons representing each title on the tabs of a thumb index was meant to facilitate such readings. While this engagement with the physical form of the book is striking, it is Lissitzky's design of the poems' opening pages that make *For the Voice* one of the monuments of modern poetic and graphic imagination. Of his design Lissitzky wrote, "The book is created with the resources of the compositor's type-case alone." The suggestion of a figurative image is made with printer's rule in weights and forms that are closely related to those of the sans serif type. The unified aesthetic of geometry succeeds in overcoming graphic differences between elements so all appear to belong to the same register. The trick of using **rule**, wood **furniture**, and other technical components of letterpress also suited the goal of producing an aesthetic value from functional objects. A unique work, *For the Voice* embodies elements of formalism in its typographic approach that bridge Constructivist and imaginative worlds. It also anticipates much of the poster and publication design that would make Lissitzky's style so influential.

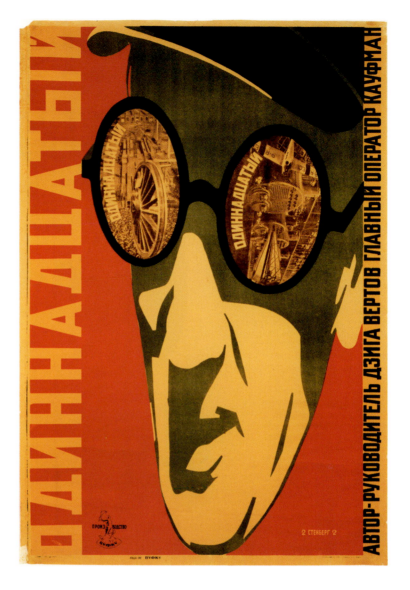

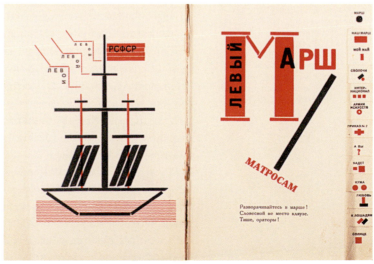

9.12 Lucian Bernhard, loan campaign, poster, 1915. Blackletter and a mailed fist were meant as positive images of German identity. Strong, simple imagery and direct messages in Fraktur lettering came to be associated with German nationalism. Bernhard's design was unmistakably nationalistic. Even the style of the drawing, with its reference to wood engravings perfected in Renaissance Germany, suggested a deep tradition and mythic roots of identity. Flat colors and lithographic printing further simplify the design's reductive imagery.

Familiar poster styles allowed the transition to armed conflict to

9.13 Hans Rudi Erdt, *U-boats Out!*, 1916. The flat graphics and simplified imagery in this propaganda poster reiterate a style used to advertise vacations and leisure activities. This familiarization of war activity allowed the transition to armed conflict to seem more like a continuity than a disruption of everyday patterns of life. Using designers whose work had already become recognizable in the promotion of commodities was a subtle way of eliding the difference between war and peacetime cultures.

Propaganda and mass-communication studies The
early twentieth century avant-garde's internationalism stemmed in part from social upheavals. Political shifts caused large groups to move across national boundaries, and émigré communities fostered artistic exchange. Accelerated technical advances in radio, telecommunications, radar, and mass media outstripped nineteenth-century industrialism and provoked revisions of beliefs and values. The avant-garde was one symptom of the violent political, economic, and technological changes in Western culture. The development of mass-persuasion techniques was another (Fig. **9.12**).

While the avant-garde promotional machine advocated anarchism and revolution, other propaganda campaigns were being mounted by national governments to build support among civilian populations for the "war to end all wars," as President Wilson would later call World War I. Also known as "The Great War," WWI devastated large areas of Europe and maimed, killed, and traumatized millions of soldiers between 1914 and 1918. Fought mainly in trenches, it pitted the Allied Powers (Russia, France, Britain, Italy, and, eventually, the United States) against the Central Powers (Austro-Hungary, Germany, and the Ottoman Empire) in a battle for military

9.14 Ludwig Hohlwein, *Red Cross*, 1914.
The figure in this image is rendered with dignity and pathos on a heroic scale. The poster presents the military campaign in metaphoric terms as a human struggle without any reference to the political circumstances or specific policies of the war. This iconographic approach to communication manipulates the viewer with emotional force rather than information, aligning the audience with a cause without revealing what that cause is. Ludwig Hohlwein's draftsmanship combined with a striking ability to distill iconography for maximum emotional impact. His muscled figures would become Aryan supermen in the decades to follow. Germany's army was maintained by conscription, so there was no need to recruit. Rather, ongoing cooperation and enthusiasm were the goals.

seem more like a continuity than a disruption of everyday life.

domination over territories and resources. World War I signaled and caused many of the cultural ruptures that defined modern life. It also prompted the development of mechanized military technologies and mass-propaganda strategies. Artists of every stripe lent their graphic skills to promote readiness, recruitment, sales of bonds, discipline on the home front, and other war-related efforts. The contributions of accomplished illustrators and established advertising and editorial designers were tremendously effective. Avant-garde styles were rarely absorbed directly into mainstream propaganda which, by contrast, sought to reach a broad audience through familiar formats and imagery. The vivid flat color and bold lines that had characterized an effective commercial poster style (*plakatstil*) were pressed into the service of German propaganda (Figs. **9.13** and **9.14**).

A painterly approach to illustration also found its way into poster design, particularly in England and the United States. Images of heroism and military valor were accompanied by hand-lettered texts in a humanist mode. An end to the conflict would require international cooperation; meanwhile, war and nationalism fed each other. Images of domesticity reminded soldiers what they were fighting for and gave women, children,

9.15a James Montgomery Flagg, *Uncle Sam Wants You,* **1917.** The American designer James Montgomery Flagg used his own image to create a famous version of Uncle Sam for a recruiting poster whose iconography included red-white-and-blue bunting and other symbols of nationalism. The strategy of binding nationalism to symbolic images goes back to antiquity, but the use of mass media to incorporate elements of a patriotic code into several graphic levels simultaneously reached new levels of sophistication in the propaganda of the twentieth century. New verbal and visual rhetoric came into use. Direct graphic address in the second person—*you*—and a confrontational visual engagement with the viewer resemble both advertising and avant-garde techniques. The decorum of an earlier era would never have allowed such directness.

9.15b Joseph Leyendecker, *USA Bonds,* **1917.** Illustrator and designer Joseph Leyendecker rendered his mythic image of American Liberty in a monumental style that was as persuasive by its graphic strength as it was by its themes. Like the work of his German counterpart, Hohlwein, this imagery set the tone for civic art for decades to come, peopling it with superhuman, overdeveloped bodies. The giant figure of Liberty is masculine and muscled. The boy's gaze and the massive sword he holds effortlessly both point to higher values.

and older people role models of steadfast patience and courage. Gender roles were clearly demarcated, and stereotypes of bravery and sacrifice reinforced the sense that the Allied cause was the preservation of humanity itself. Critics saw the war as an offensive waged by the rich against the poor of all nations. But propaganda posters portrayed the struggle as that of democratic civilization against the forces of destruction (Figs. **9.15a** and **9.15b**).

Graphic persuasion and its effects Public relations campaigns were essential to maintaining the effort to win the war, and they included a new form of public communication: information graphics. Posters were designed to familiarize the public with the various shapes of planes and ships so that enemy craft and military insignia could be readily identified. The capacity to recognize the enemy relied on visual cues for which graphic rehearsals were the best education. Information campaigns

9.16 *Public Warning*, **British poster,
1917.** Posters that displayed silhouettes
by which to distinguish friendly and
enemy aircraft were distributed to the
public. The urgency and importance of
the information on these posters made
boldness desirable. In the tradition of
the public notice, the communicative
impulse dominates here, rather than any
self-conscious aesthetic. But the starkness
and clarity of the design are in keeping
with modern functionalism.

in post-revolutionary Russia had the task of educating a broad class of
workers, many of whom were illiterate. Public announcements combined
schematic forms and photomontage to communicate visually. Artists and
designers set about changing hygiene habits and social behavior, increasing
productivity, and projecting an image of collective ownership (Fig. **9.16**).

Meanwhile, in the United States and England, the women's suffrage
movement, which had been an organized political force since the
1890s, launched its own campaigns to get women the right to vote. War

The concept of the "new woman" was embraced by marketers.

9.17 Suffragist poster, 1913.
Unflattering images depicted suffragettes
as unfeminine, shrill, strident, ugly, and
even demonic—or else as dowdy and
old-maidish. These images contrasted
with those of the domestic mother and
young beauty who sought male approval
and were happy to remain subject to
patriarchal power. Even if she raised
eyebrows in conservative circles, the
"new woman" was a concept embraced
by marketers because her liberated
condition and control over disposable
income made her a consumer of such
new luxuries as cigarettes, bicycles,
and stockings.

work placed women in positions left empty by mobilized men. Their
contributions as nurses, drivers, and civil servants helped change attitudes
about women's rights; so did images. In progressive publications, protests
against abusive power were shaped by the successes of commercial and civic
design. By the time laws were passed, giving women over age 30 in England
(1918) and white women in the United States (1920) the right to vote, the
image of the "new woman" had become a significant icon in marketing and
advertising as well as politics (Fig. **9.17**).

The political situation remained unstable in Europe and Russia in the
decade after World War I. Economic and human devastation had left many
newly reconfigured states with only a tentative grasp on civic government.
The war had not solved problems of unrest among the working class and
had not fully refashioned political structures within each nation. Radical,
energetic artists seized the opportunity of uncertainty to contribute their
aesthetic vision to the fashioning of a new social order, particularly in
Weimar, Germany, and the newly formed Soviet Union. Graphic designers
of all persuasions tested modernist techniques of engagement in public
discourse. By the end of the 1920s, the rising tide of German fascism

9.18 Gustav Klutsis, *Under Lenin's Banner*, poster, 1930. This poster imposes the image of the dead Soviet leader Vladimir Lenin onto that of the reigning Soviet leader Joseph Stalin. The intended effect is to blend the two figures in the eyes of a populace quite familiar with both faces from photographs. Fragments of industrial factories symbolize progress, the energy of which is expressed by diagonal arrangements of red and white elements. The Russian avant-garde had been successful in creating a graphic language associated with revolution, but it had not anticipated the totalitarian direction that Soviet communism would take under Stalin. Thus, formal means devised for utopian use are shown here in the service of a political and ideological agenda that is far from their purpose.

provoked graphic protest. Artists and officials on all sides of the political spectrum recognized the power of graphic communication to shape public opinion. Their sophisticated conceptions and uses of symbolic language went far beyond literal depiction and into communication designed to influence the political system by subtle, psychological means (Fig. **9.18**).

The power of graphic propaganda had come home with abrupt and shocking vividness in the aftermath of World War I. Social analysts and policy makers in the United States and Europe grappled with the effects of the media on public opinion and the potential of mass communication as a political tool. The field of propaganda studies was born. American sociologists such as Walter Lippmann and Paul Lazarsfeld struggled to understand the mechanisms by which print media encoded and delivered their messages. The concept of "public opinion" (Lippmann's phrase) was

Policy makers grappled with the effects of the media on opinion.

9.19 One million mark note, Herbert Bayer, 1923. German political and economic vicissitudes of the 1920s involved tremendous inflation. Herbert Bayer was given the task of designing currency in large denominations. This design makes use of Bayer's preferred black and red ink, rule, and sans serif type, overprinted in bold orthogonal arrangements. A currency without portraits or **allegorical** imagery seems strikingly modern, as if all extraneous information has been stripped away, so that only a bare statement of value and an identification of the issuing authority remain. But an aesthetic of functionality could not keep the bills from becoming useless when political conditions shifted. Although these currency designs may not constitute propaganda, they circulated on the basis of belief systems that were subject to rapid change and reconsideration.

amplified in phrases like "engineered consent" and "voluntary complicity." Theorists of what became known as the Frankfurt School in Germany took a slightly different approach, examining how values could so permeate a culture as to make their manipulation almost invisible. Marketing surveys, polls, and other instruments for measuring subjective response were developed for the first time to analyze the effects of propaganda, news, and advertising. Perversely, the burgeoning advertising sector would become a powerful client for communication theories. Edward Bernays, the nephew of the inventor of psychoanalysis Sigmund Freud, founded the field of public relations in the United States. Bernays used strategies of unconscious motivation and manipulation in highly successful campaigns for products and politicians. Critical studies of media, like the graphic forms of expression that initially provoked them, remain relevant cultural instruments (Fig. **9.19**).

Institutionalizing graphic design One of the most enduring legacies of early twentieth-century experimentation came in the form of novel approaches to the pedagogy of graphic design and other applied

9.20 Alexander Rodchenko and Vladimir Mayakovsky, state tobacco ads, 1923.
In the 1910s, Alexander Rodchenko and poet Vladimir Mayakovsky were major avant-garde figures in Russia. After the revolution they applied their talents to concrete projects. They designed workers' clubs, news kiosks, publications, and advertising campaigns for Soviet goods, including these advertisements for the state brand of tobacco. In the late 1910s and early 1920s, their ideas were incorporated in curricula that blended industry, craft, and radical aesthetics at the new art and technical schools VKhUTEMAS and InkHuk. Their brightly colored ads struck a modern Soviet note, but their production tools were limited in the post-revolutionary context. Most of their designs were made using pens and paint, while their counterparts in the United States and Western Europe had access to photographic techniques.

Novel approaches to graphic design pedagogy were instituted.

arts. A number of important institutions were established in the 1920s. In post-revolutionary Russia, InkHuk (the Institute for Artistic Culture), VKhUTEMAS (the design school in Moscow), and the Popular Art Institute (in Vitebsk) were established to synthesize art, culture, and technical knowledge for the application of design to industry. These institutions trained young designers according to Constructivist principles. Major figures of the prewar avant-garde sought to link the euphoric ideals of the new state to reforms by which design could be taught effectively (Fig. **9.20**).

The Bauhaus, first established in 1919 in the short-lived Weimar Republic of Germany, became the most legendary of the new institutions for graphic design research and pedagogy. Although not a revolutionary state, the Weimar government was progressive enough to support a proposal for a radical experiment in design education, a visionary project that was allowed to establish a firm base of operations. In the spirit of an avant-garde movement, the school was founded on a manifesto by architect Walter Gropius. But in Gropius this spirit went back to nineteenth-century sources. He had been an assistant to Peter Behrens and a member of the

German Werkbund, and strains of the Arts and Crafts ideal of aesthetic integrity appeared in his program for the school. The manifesto's call for a return to craft and the integration of art and architecture might not seem, on the surface, to have ushered in modernism. But this call marked the

The Bauhaus established a concept of design as a discipline.

beginning of a fourteen-year curricular evolution aimed at involving art in production and thus, in a sense, inaugurated design as we know it. From the *Bauhaus Proclamation* until the school's closure by Nazi policy makers in 1933, from an early emphasis on handwork to inspiration by industrial processes, the Bauhaus established a concept of design as a discipline that meaningfully closed the gap between formal ideas and material conditions. A spiritual tone permeated its early years, particularly in courses taught by Johannes Itten. But the hallmark of the school was its development of foundation courses in principles of composition, construction, and appreciation of materials. These were useful to designers working in textiles, architecture, furniture, and metalwork, as well as graphics. *Design* became a highly elastic term, extending to include everyday objects and their industrial production (Fig. **9.21**).

The Bauhaus provided a pedagogical laboratory in which the formal innovations of early avant-garde experiment were absorbed and systematically applied to architecture, graphic design, and industrial design. The year 1923 marked a shift from Arts and Crafts to art and industry: "Art and technology—a new unity!" became the school's motto. Conspicuous

9.22a Edward Johnston, London Underground typeface, 1916 *(top left and below)*, **and 9.22b Herbert Bayer, alphabet, 1926** *(top right)*. Bayer took over the typography workshop from 1923, when the Bauhaus moved to Dessau, until he left in 1928. During that time, as he was developing his own vision of graphic design, his influence as a teacher was far-reaching. Few designs apply the rules of a system in strict allegiance to modern principles of reductive functionalism to the same degree as Bayer's design for a single-case alphabet. Derived from the same set of streamlined elements that defined his earlier "universal" type designs, the alphabet was meant to serve any and all printing and writing purposes. The letters retain their elegance and consistency throughout. The quest for pure, minimal, and universal typefaces was not unique to Bayer or the Bauhaus. Edward Johnston's 1916 typeface design for the London Underground had similar aspirations and certain formal resemblances. After the clutter of late nineteenth-century typography, the visual simplicity of these designs was striking. But their aspiration to transcend history by using geometric forms was misconstrued.

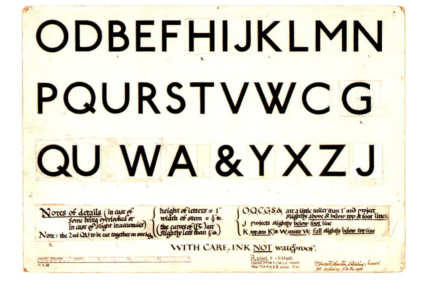

9.23 Laszlo Moholy-Nagy, *Painting/Photography/Film*, 1923. Books published by the Bauhaus helped codify and disseminate the school's pedagogy and research. The division of page space by black-and-red rule, the construction of a letterform using geometric elements, a sans serif face, and a carefully weighted composition demonstrate the principles of balanced tension. An implied grid rationalizes the organization of information while suggesting that an architectonic form undergirds this design. Diagonals have been eliminated in this example in favor of the stability afforded by vertical and horizontal elements. The rule is very heavy and overwhelms many of the images and the type. It had become such a given of the contemporary approach that it appeared in the work of almost every self-consciously modern designer of the period.

stylistic features characterized this attitude. Formal reduction, dynamic asymmetry, and systematic structuring of graphic space crystallized in Moholy-Nagy's typographic workshop. His introduction of a more streamlined modernism unified the designs of the Bauhaus books. Two younger designers, Joost Schmidt and Herbert Bayer, extended the principles of Bauhaus style and publicized a functional, systematic approach. Their influence as practitioners and teachers was to be profound (Figs. **9.22a**, **9.22b**, and **9.23**).

9.24a Kurt Schwitters, *Merz*, 1924 (right), and 9.24b Kurt Schwitters, Pelikan ad, 1924 (above). The red-and-black rule, implied grid, asymmetric arrangement, and use of arrows, white space, and compositional tension show Schwitters's assimilation of the principles of modern design. This eleventh issue of *Merz* is dedicated to advertising design ("Typoreklame") and draws attention to Schwitters's client Pelikan, whose logotype appears in the bottom right corner. *Merz* was an independently published artists' journal, yet its cover uses the same graphic language as the ads that it features. The line between fine art and commercial work has been fluidly crossed: The publication presents designs for the ink company to demonstrate the "Thesis on Typography" that is printed on its back page. Schwitters was a collage artist and experimental poet but also an active advocate of modern design.

Foundation courses derived from those developed at the Bauhaus became a standard feature of graphic design education by mid-century but were particularly influential after the 1950s, as we shall see. The concept of a formal language of visual communication came to be a commonplace. Although freighted with a modernist—and contested—belief in the universal nature of graphic forms, the Bauhaus approach to composition, based on principles of dynamism, balance, harmony, and asymmetry, has been absorbed into every area of graphic design.

Many influential modern graphic designers had no official connection to the Bauhaus. In the 1920s, designers whose styles and attitudes had been formed by earlier movements made a transition from experimentation to applied design, from art groups such as **De Stijl** to offices and studios that professionalized design as a field independent from print shops and publishing houses. One of the more seminal associations formed during this period was the Circle of New Advertising Designers. It was founded in 1927 by Dadaist Kurt Schwitters to advance the conceptual cause of the New Typography. Its membership was small but multinational, and contributors to its exhibitions included such luminaries and advocates as Jan Tschichold, Paul Schuitema, Piet Zwart, Ladislav Sutnar, and Karl Tiege (Figs. **9.24a–d**).

9.24c Theo van Doesburg, *De Stijl*, 1921.
Artist and architect van Doesburg was never officially part of the Bauhaus, but the visits he made to promote the agenda of the Dutch avant-garde movement, De Stijl ("The Style"), certainly had an effect there. During the war, Holland had remained neutral. Thus, it was a place where prewar aesthetic investigations could continue uninterrupted. De Stijl, a group of artists and designers that included Piet Mondrian, was the most influential development of this continuity. De Stijl sought a spiritual vocabulary capable of describing modernity and found it in primary colors and neoplatonic forms. From 1917 to 1928, van Doesburg published a journal called *De Stijl* to disseminate the group's ideas. His "Elementarist" revision of De Stijl's program in 1924 maintained the movement's faith in primary forms and colors but allowed the use of diagonals for dynamic effect, whereas Mondrian's Neoplasticism accepted only vertical and horizontal lines. Van Doesburg's explorations of geometric simplification were readily translated into commercial work by his contemporaries, including Piet Zwart whose affiliation with De Stijl, although not official, was formative.

9.24d Vilmos Huszar, De Stijl logotype, 1917. Huszar's design for a logotype for De Stijl wraps letter parts around each other in imitation of printer's rule and machined forms. Curiously organic, it is also highly geometric, and the way the text breaks down into abstract forms only to recombine as a readable word reveals the influence of **Gestalt psychology** on this design approach. The emphasis on the relationship between parts that creates the perception of a whole is typical of a gestalt conception. As a guiding graphic principle, this approach was conducive to the design of logos or letterhead in which an aggregate entity (such as a corporation, group, or school) wanted to present itself as a single visual identity.

DE STIJL

MAANDBLAD VOOR NIEUWE KUNST, WETENSCHAP EN KULTUUR. REDACTIE: THEO VAN DOESBURG. ABONNEMENT BINNENLAND F 6.-, BUITENLAND F 7.50 PER JAARGANG. ADRES VAN REDACTIE EN ADMINISTR. HAARLEMMERSTRAAT 73A LEIDEN (HOLLAND).

4e JAARGANG No. 11. **NOVEMBER 1921.**

LETTERKLANKBEELDEN (1921)

IV (in dissonanten)

U^I	J—	m^I	n^I
U	J—	m^I	n^I
V—	F—	K^I	Q^I
F^I	V—	Q^I	K^I
X^I	Q^I	V^I	W^I
X^I	Q^I	W	V
U^I	J—	m—	n—
	g^I		
A—	O—	P^I	B^I
A—	O—	P^I	B^I
D—	T—	O^I	E—
d	t	o	e
	O^I E^I		
	B^I D^I		
Z^I C S		B P D	
	j		

Aanteekening: te lezen van links naar rechts. Voor de teekens zie men Stijl no. 7.

Among these advocates, Jan Tschichold ultimately achieved the greatest impact through his writing. His 1928 outline for a "new typography" (*Die Neue Typographie*) was a foundational text and is still read and used. His design principles swept away the muddle of earlier commercial approaches and demanded typography that was as strictly functional as the engineered structures that defined modernity. At the same time, his views expanded the definition of typographic function to encompass visual expression of the logic and thrust of content. Although ideological in the sense that it attached a social meaning to modern design, Tschichold's program was aesthetic rather than political. But by the 1930s, his work was seen as antinationalist. Like many others, he chose to emigrate after being targeted by the police. Not all experimental designers were so fortunate. The brilliantly innovative, politically vocal H. N. Werkman was imprisoned

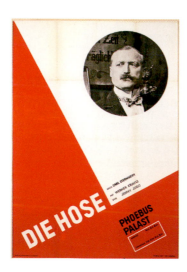

9.25a Jan Tschichold, poster, 1927.
Tschichold's influence derived from
his published writing on typography as
well as his startlingly elegant designs.
By the time *Die Neue Typographie* was
published in 1928, Tschichold's designs
had already helped define the "new" style.
The bold diagonal, white dropped-out
title, and typographic minimalism of this
poster exhibit a refinement of principles
in widespread use. Tschichold had an
unsurpassed capacity to reduce a page
to essential-seeming elements in delicate
but dynamic balance.

**9.25b Hendrik Nicolaas Werkman,
The Next Call, 1926.** While other
figures whose sensibilities had been
formed by the avant-garde became
involved in advertising and commercial
art, Werkman retained his commitment
to the experimental and poetic use of
letterpress. His typographic compositions
drew on the material richness of wood and
metal letters, and his dedication to the
artistic potential of modern design kept
its innovative spirit alive long after much
of the original impetus for avant-garde
experiment had been absorbed and
exploited by commercial interests.

for "seditious typography" and executed by the Nazis in 1945. Still, the
experimental spirit of the avant-garde did not disappear entirely from the
Continent. Eastern and Western European designers continued to produce
seminal work throughout the 1930s and 1940s (Figs. **9.25a** and **9.25b**).

Despite political pressures, the influence of the avant-garde was long-
lasting and profound. The International Typographic Style arose from its
roots, as did approaches to corporate identity and branding campaigns.
The teaching of graphic design as a set of formal principles remains
suffused with terms and concepts that can be traced to the work of early
twentieth-century practitioners. The idea of a language of graphic design
came from this period when influential individuals and institutions
formulated the bases of a modern practice. Almost incidentally, but no
less importantly, they also invented the graphic designer as a figure both
formally and conceptually skilled, for whom style was the expression of a
point of view on the world, not merely an expression of individual taste
or disposition (Fig. **9.26**).

9.26 Joost Schmidt, catalog cover, 1924. Produced while he was still a student at the Bauhaus, Schmidt's cover design represents graphic design at the intersection of Constructivist experiments and Bauhaus systematicity. Horizontal and vertical forms organize this design, while the slightly distorted letterforms become graphic elements whose shapes and contrasts create interest and surprise. The way that black and red are used translates a printing tradition into a modern idiom. The composition is kept in balance by attention to repeating motifs, and the sans serif face lends itself to visual rhymes with the other lines and blocks.

Conclusion Design became a major social and cultural force in the 1910s and 1920s. Avant-garde artists borrowed the techniques of advertising to promote their aesthetic principles in the 1910s. New forms of graphic communication served utopian artistic programs and propagandistic campaigns alike in the politically volatile European context. The quest for a stable system of rules that governed the communicative effect of graphic form fed the period's fascination with abstraction.

A violent moment of stylistic change characterized the avant-garde before, during, and after World War I and the Russian Revolution. But the features that had come to define modernism—geometric abstraction, asymmetric dynamism, and nontraditional sans serif type—caused it to be branded as subversive in Germany. Artists and designers became targets of persecution, and a wave of emigration began.

In the 1920s, early experiments settled into a modern style.

9.27 Piet Zwart, Nutter margarine wrapper, 1923. Piet Zwart's capacity to compose a well-organized design with varied sizes and styles of type in a densely packed space shows his understanding of visual timing and rhythm. Zwart absorbed the lessons of Constructivism and the principles of systematic graphic communication and became one of the leading figures of modern Dutch design. His work pointed almost immediately toward the kind of corporate identity and branding that would come to be the standard at mid-century.

In the 1920s, early experiments settled into a modern style that marked its distance from Arts and Crafts influences by replacing historical and organic motifs with dynamic geometric abstraction. Designers took their well-honed skills into the service of the new Soviet state as well as corporate and public information campaigns in the United States and Europe. The alarm caused by the success of wartime propaganda gave rise to a new field of academic study devoted to understanding mass communication. New institutions devised design curricula in a systematic manner, taking into account the changed role of graphic communication in industry, popular culture, business, and artistic expression. As a whole parade of illustrious teachers and students made their way through its courses and classrooms, the Bauhaus shaped graphic design as a discipline and a profession. A sophisticated theoretical discussion of design principles became codified in publications that stated and exemplified their aesthetics for an increasingly international audience. As booming economies brought new commercial challenges in the 1920s, graphic designers would find that they had modern techniques and professional structures with which to address them (Figs. **9.27**, **9.28a** and **9.28b**).

9.28a and 9.28b Paul Schuitema, Berkel campaigns, late 1920s. In his work for the major scientific instrument manufacturer Berkel, Schuitema communicated the precision of the company's machines through the careful calibration of his designs. By the late 1920s, his integration of photographic and typographic elements into tightly organized arrangements was adventurous and successful. Borrowing from *neue sachlichkeit* developments in photography, he took the idea of an objective document revealing an essential form and applied it to products. The objects to be promoted became icons, their own manufactured shapes serving as the basis of a system of visual forms worked carefully through the designs. Whether in fine art or commercial applications, modern graphic design signaled a sensibility grounded in the present and the new, rather than the past. That it became a highly recognizable and historical movement in its own right is one of the ironies of modernism's aspiration toward universal and transcendent form.

Innovation and Persuasion 1910–1930

1909 F. T. Marinetti's *Futurist Manifesto* published in *Le Figaro*
1911 Crisco invented by Proctor & Gamble
Gold found in Alaska
U.S. Navy gets its first airplane
General Motors truck company founded
1912 Marcel Duchamp paints *Nude Descending a Staircase No. 2*
Paper cup (Health Kup, later Dixie cup) invented
Soviet Communist Party paper, *Pravda*, launched
U.S. Army mounts first machine gun on a plane
Fenway baseball park built in Boston
First prizes in Cracker Jacks
Russian Futurists form the Donkey's Tail group
Archbishop in Paris says, "Christians must not tango"
Peppermint lifesavers introduced
1913 Edison and others receive patents for synching sound to film
Suffragist march in Washington, D.C.
Geiger counter for detecting radiation developed
Albania becomes sovereign nation
First crossword puzzle in *New York World*
The Adventures of Kathryn, first movie serial, released
Brillo pads produced
1914 Panama Canal completed
35-mm cameras produced
Assassination of Archduke Ferdinand sparks start of WWI
Marinetti's *Zang Tumb Tumb* published
AIGA founded
Lee DeForest's "audion" vacuum tubes pave way for radio
Tinkertoys invented
Charlie Chaplin debuts "The Tramp" character
1915 Panama Pacific International Exposition in San Francisco
First stop signs introduced in Detroit
Design and Industries Association formed in Britain
Mexican revolutionary Pancho Villa signs treaty with U.S.
D. W. Griffith's *Birth of a Nation* opens, causes riots
British passenger liner, *Lusitania*, sunk by German torpedo
Fox Film Corporation founded
1916 Edward Johnston designs typeface for London Underground
Martial law declared in Ireland by British
Slang word "jazz" appears in *Variety*
Norman Rockwell's *Saturday Evening Post* covers begin to appear
Dada artists create Cabaret Voltaire in Switzerland
Margaret Sanger opens first birth control clinic in Brooklyn
Einstein's *General Theory of Relativity* published
1917 U.S. enters WWI
Mata Hari arrested for spying in Paris
Russian Revolution; Czar Nicholas abdicates
First British women's military unit, WAAC, established
Felix the Cat character invented
Marcel Duchamp signs urinal as R. Mutt
Shortwave radio invented
1918 Ludwig Wittgenstein writes *Tractatus Logico-Philosophicus*
Flu epidemic kills 20 million people in one year

Armistice ends hostilities between Germany and Allies
Germany declared a republic; Kaiser Wilhelm II abdicates
Leon Trotsky becomes head of Red Army in Russia
Poland declares independence from Russia
Daylight saving time adopted in U.S.
Child labor deemed unconstitutional by U.S. Supreme Court
Warner Brothers builds first film studio on Sunset Boulevard
Tarzan of the Apes premieres on Broadway

1919 Fascist party founded in Italy by Mussolini
Prohibition law passed in U.S.
Bauhaus founded
RCA founded
Afghanistan becomes sovereign nation
News kiosks designed by Alexander Rodchenko

1920 Women get the vote in U.S.
League of Nations established
Joan of Arc canonized by Pope Benedict XV
First radio compass used for air navigation
VKhUTEMAS, technical design school, founded in Russia
Ireland divided in two
Good Humor Bar marketed
First tractors in common use in U.S.

1921 First sports and weather radio broadcasts
Western Union develops wire photo service
Polygraph (lie detector) invented

1922 BBC begins radio broadcasting in Britain
Howard Carter discovers King Tutankhamun's tomb
T. S. Eliot's *The Wasteland* published
Hays Office introduces its code of Hollywood censorship

1923 Rodchenko begins designing ads for state companies, often with Mayakovsky
Kurt Schwitters launches *Merz*

1924 Electric loudspeaker introduced

1925 Portable Leica camera mass-produced
El Lissitzky designs *The Isms of Art* (*Die Kunstismen*)

1926 Adolf Hitler's *Mein Kampf* published
Chiang Kai-shek appointed Chinese revolutionary commander

1927 Der Ring (Circle of New Advertising Designers) formed
Newsreels use sound
Werner Heisenberg's uncertainty principle developed
Farnsworth's television patented
Pez candy marketed

1928 Magnetic tape patented
Bubblegum marketed
Jan Tschichold's *Die Neue Typographie* published
Jet engines developed
Penicillin discovered

1929 Le Corbusier completes designs for Villa Savoye
Fortunato Depero's *Futurism and the Art of Advertising* published

1930 *Fortune* magazine launched
Mahatma Gandhi arrested after Dandi Salt March for independence

Tools of the Trade

Oil pastels
Gouache
Paste
Rubber cement
Plastic tools, rulers, devices
Pro-film (knife-cut shellac stencil)
Ben Day textures
Portable Leica camera
Tabletop duplicators
Spirit duplicators
Flash powder (for photography)
Spiral binder
Type specimen books
Copy camera
Photomechanical printing
(See also Chapter 10)

Holeproof Hosiery

10. The Culture of Consumption 1920s–1930s

- Graphic design contributed to a culture of consumption, and modernism became a consumable idea, as once-experimental forms were popularized through style trends.

- Graphic designers were increasingly involved in creating **lifestyle** fantasies that were not inherently connected to the goods and services they sold. These fantasies often concealed production histories while promoting widespread consumption.

- **Brand** identities not only lent an appearance of difference to similar products but also became commodities themselves, demonstrating that a designed concept was a marketable one.

- Graphic design in the United States was ennobled by official praise for fusing democratic ideals and entrepreneurship, even as many innovative forms of visual modernism became contested political ground in Europe.

- **Art directors**, commercial artists, and layout designers began to see the value of professional organizations and trade publications that highlighted their respective roles and promoted their field as a whole.

10.1a Coles Phillips, Holeproof Hosiery ad, 1921. As sheer and draped as the material expertly rendered in Phillips's illustration, an aura of intangible but definite desirability attaches to women's stockings in this ad. Commodities served a symbolic purpose and satisfied a psychological need. Conspicuous display helped define social differences. The central myth of consumer culture was that anyone could purchase goods; because they were widely advertised, they seemed readily available. But this illusion was quickly checked by economic realities, and disparities in purchasing power had a stratifying effect. Still, consuming a fantasy—with the purchase of a pair of silk hose or a face cream—played an important part in the pleasure of possession. Creating a market for goods that were not essential required a very different approach from that of previous advertising strategies. Early advertisements had been little more than notices that alerted the public to the availability of goods or services. But as production increased, so did the competition for buyers' eyes and money.

Graphic design became a recognized economic, political, and cultural force by the end of World War I. Having demonstrated its power to sway public opinion during the war, graphic design in the 1920s and 1930s became the source of stylish fantasies that were crucial to the growth of consumer culture. Borrowing the innovative approaches of the avant-garde to shape these fantasies, graphic designers effectively sold modernism itself in the process, packaging its ideas as a fashionable aesthetic rather than a social project. Meanwhile, the graphic design profession grew, spawning many institutional forms that continue to the present. Advertising was praised as a boon to progress and celebrated with missionary zeal. Ad agencies provided a range of increasingly specialized services. Art directors took conceptual and aesthetic responsibility for the design of whole publicity campaigns and mainstream publications. Graphic styles changed, as commercial applications brought new life to a sophisticated legacy of modern art. The idea of creating and selling an **"image"** came to replace the simple notion of promoting goods or services. Fabricating an intangible aura of desirability, far beyond any real necessity, graphic designers produced perpetual longing for an imagined life. Subtle advertisers channeled attention toward purchases that indicated status rather than satisfied needs. This image-driven attitude was described as *conspicuous consumption*, a term coined by American sociologist Thorstein Veblen at the turn of the century (Figs. **10.1a** and **10.1b**).

10.1b Roger Broders, Vichy ad, 1926.
An unmistakable air of luxury is inscribed in this advertisement for the spa resort of Vichy, France. Taking the waters and bathing in mineral springs had been part of nineteenth-century medicinal culture. But in the 1920s, resorts focused on golf, dancing, water sports, racing, and other fashionable pleasures. This world lies far from necessity or labor. Consumption, not production, is its sole justification—or so we are to believe. The elongated bodies of the figures in this poster convey a sleekness and ease that is remote from work or industry, although their clean lines are inspired by industrial designs. The organic world is gone, vanished under the sheen of flat, geometric shapes and angles. Even the landscape is completely transformed, processed into a stylized backdrop. In the United States, disposable income rose almost 10 percent between 1920 and 1929. But three-quarters of that rise was enjoyed by investors in the top 1 percent. This bubble of capital gains made "on paper" by a select few contributed to the economic instability that resulted in the Crash of 1929, yet images of opulence in films, advertising, and mass-circulation magazines made this life seem within reach.

Designing the modern lifestyle
Modern lifestyle was an idea that designers helped invent and promote in all areas of material culture. At a time when American industrial production outstripped demand, graphic design earned new clout by its ability to push consumption beyond the satisfaction of needs. This push came in the form of a polished image of modernity as a desirable, ever-changing way of life whose attributes were embodied by the newest product and the latest style. Each new thing replaced an outmoded one whose **planned obsolescence** was the work of manufacturers. Industrial capacities made this surplus possible, but economic conditions were not all rosy. European countries, struggling to recover from World War I, experienced a series of boom and recession cycles before the crisis of global markets and the Crash of 1929. In the United States, economic expansion was accelerated in the 1920s by unregulated financing that also contributed to the devastating effects at the decade's end. But these were also years in which new energy sources and raw materials drove industrial innovation. The combination of natural resources, a labor pool fed by immigration, and a business-friendly political climate offered unprecedented opportunities for economic development. The delivery of electricity became reliable and petroleum readily available. This dependable availability of energy changed work routines, production parameters, transportation and communication networks, and

10.2a Franklin Car Co. ad, 1929 *(above)*, **and 10.2b Kaspar E. Graf, Swiss Grand Prix poster, 1934** *(right)*. Automobiles were among the most conspicuous new products in the 1920s and 1930s. A wide range of associations were devised to help potential buyers imagine scenarios for their use. Automobiles had only begun to be mass-produced a few decades earlier, but, by the 1920s, they were transforming patterns of work and leisure throughout the United States and Europe. The aesthetic contrast between these two advertisements reveals differences in European and American design of the era. Kaspar Graf's 1934 poster for the Swiss Grand Prix recalls Futurist art in its rendering of speed through streamlined and fragmented forms. The 1929 Franklin Car Company advertisement, designed for placement in a journal, is firmly rooted in a realistic illustrational style, even though it depicts driving as a fantasy of flying. The European travel poster trades on its association with fine art, whereas the American design exploits the easy legibility of a golden dream girl meant to be "everybody's" ideal. The copy in the Franklin ad describes the mechanical advances in this model, but the imagery of lithe young bodies against ocean waves reinforces the free-spirited gesture of the woman whose shadow appears to be turning into that of a gull. Commercial illustration and fine art remained distinct categories in the American context, and illustrators rarely exhibited their work in galleries or museums. European designers and artists, on the other hand, gained status from a synthesis of fine and applied art and often had careers that celebrated their artistry as well as their commercial work.

entertainment habits. Automobiles, cinemas, phonographs, electric lights, and radios created new markets. America became a significant force in an increasingly global economy, and graphic design became a potent engine for driving the machines of consumption (Figs. **10.2a** and **10.2b**).

In this new culture of **consumer capitalism**, ad campaigns equated style with currency and currency with success. To make spending glamorous, graphic designers developed an aesthetic that was **moderne**—cool, streamlined, sophisticated, and in tune with the jazz-age culture that thrived in the margins of a residual Victorianism and, in the United States, of Prohibition. Tourism and entertainment industries flourished, exploiting new degrees of mobility and leisure in a growing middle class and testing strategies for packaging *experiences*. As more aspects of everyday life were commodified, more products were sold by their association with a prestigious image. Style added value to a product, and graphic designers were actively involved in expanding the role that publicity played in affixing that value to brands. When the stock market crashed in New York in 1929, it triggered an economic depression that lasted in the United States and Europe until the beginning of World War II. But throughout the 1930s, graphic designers continued to shape the notion of a contemporary life of abundance in the popular imagination. The gap between reality and imagery was often striking (Figs. **10.3a** and **10.3b**).

10.3a Adolphe Jean-Marie Mouron Cassandre, sports cap ad, 1925 *(right)*, **and 10.3b Herbert Matter, Switzerland poster, 1935** *(above)*. Images of luxury invoked worldliness and refinement. This often meant associations with European culture, finely made goods, and elite vacation spots populated by a privileged few. French designer A. M. Cassandre hit the right style note to translate the more esoteric features of modern art into a graphic vocabulary with wider appeal. An echo of Cubism and modern abstraction permeates the advertisement he designed for a sporting cap. The image appeals to a viewer who recognizes references to great modern artists such as Pablo Picasso, Henri Matisse, Georges Braque, and others, in its outline, color blocks, and shadings. Advertising brought modern art before the public, and, if it made modern images less challenging, it also made abstract style more popular. Cubism and modern art in general were frequently mocked in the popular press, but they introduced a touch of chic urbanity to marketing campaigns. Herbert Matter's design depends on innovative photographic imagery to achieve its impact. Photography is associated with realism, but here the use of a dramatic angle has a disruptive effect. The contrast between the close-up and background portions of this poster divides the image into distinct icons. The design promotes an idea of Switzerland as a winter tourist paradise by manipulating images as signs, rather than for their literal depiction of Swiss mountains. Matter's training at the Bauhaus provided him with a strong foundation for formal invention in the modern mode.

Modern style in graphic design

European and American graphic design looked quite different in the late 1910s, but various historical factors contributed to a stylistic synthesis of regional trends by the 1930s. The avant-garde had left a conspicuous imprint on European graphic design. The spirit of innovation that charged Futurism, Dada, Constructivism, and De Stijl had fostered the use of abstract forms, heavy rule, black and red ink, strong shapes, and striking arrangements. Asymmetrical typography prevailed as the prescribed approach to dynamic layout. Sans serif typefaces, some designed with an engineer's precision by compass, straightedge, and drafting pen, expressed the new typographical thinking. European graphic designers also made photography one of the hallmarks of modernism and embraced a clean, "objective" style for books, magazines, and commercial work (Figs. **10.4** and **10.5**).

The legacy of Russian Constructivism was carried by émigrés to cosmopolitan European capitals in the 1920s. The tenets of a new formalism derived from early experiments took stylistic form. Following the 1917 revolution, Russian practitioners had designed campaigns to promote state production goals and a new social order. But when Joseph Stalin took

10.4 Piet Zwart, NFK Kabel Company ad, 1926. Zwart was one of several noted Dutch designers who applied the lessons of avant-garde experiments to advertising and commercial work. The red and black ink and diagonal emphasis in this advertisement betray the influence of Russian Constructivism. Use of these elements in a campaign for a utility company indicates how readily the radical concepts of the avant-garde were assimilated for commercial use. The ad's fragmented presentation of its message communicated modernity rather than functionality. This association with experimental, visionary design compensated for the absence of any concrete information with a dynamic charge to the company image. Style, more than substance, supplied the content of this campaign. In the course of his career, Zwart continued to synthesize experimental principles for use in corporate, commercial, and civic communication.

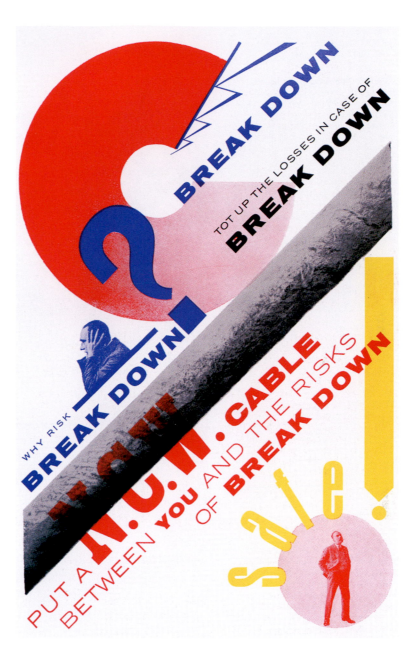

10.5 Jan Tschichold, exhibition catalog, 1933. Jan Tschichold was another designer who effectively translated early experiments into practical graphic work. The diagonal movement and extreme angle of the photograph in his design for this 1933 exhibition catalog cover are characteristically modernist in their emphasis and willingness to disorient. Bold shapes organize the overall design, while the typography is balanced through carefully measured axes, rather than within a single grid or central spine. The design communicates a commitment to clarity and dynamism as positive values. But the excitement of a contemporary vision also implied a rejection—of history. Jettisoning the past was an act that went against the German Nazi party's desire to ground its own legitimacy in an ancient, even mythic past. Freshness and novelty were an affront to these attitudes, and, for all of their apparent neutrality, embodied ideological positions.

control of the Soviet Union in 1929, it became an isolated, increasingly totalitarian regime. Dreams that the new state might provide a model of utopian socialism had all but vanished by the mid-1930s. The belief that formal innovation could help bring about social change had been premised on an understanding of graphic design as a political force. This belief was doubled by an inverse conviction: that without a new aesthetic, a new world could not be envisioned. The faith underlying this conviction began to wane in the face of changes in the Soviet Union but also under commercial pressures. Elements drawn from Constructivism, such as grid structures, dramatic photography, and emphatic diagonal compositions, had become established features of European graphic modernity. Ironically, the capacity of these design elements to reveal the inherent elegance of rational and

10.6a Max Burchartz, dance festival poster, 1928. Formal innovation reshapes photography and lettering in this poster for a dance festival designed by Max Burchartz. Its montage sensibility recalls Soviet posters of the same era, and its exuberant color and arrangement suggest a contemporary, athletic approach to dance in which movement, rather than classical postures, takes precedence. This emphasis on dynamism points to the continuing legacy of Futurism, but the poster's geometric and photographic realization aim at modern communication rather than defamiliarizing effects.

Consumerism absorbed the formal lessons of the avant-garde.

10.6b Max Bill, African art exhibition poster, 1931. In the late 1920s, Richard Lohse, Anton Stankowski, and Max Bill began to distill the rudiments of Swiss design. Max Bill's poster for an exhibition of African art relies on minimal means—black and a single color on white paper—to build an architectonic image. Solid, balanced, formally refined, it demonstrates the synthesis of earlier explorations into a systematic approach that appears to be content-neutral. The large white form is meant to reference African sculpture, but the design's organization is so strong that it could carry almost any information. The arrival at an appearance of stable neutrality marks a break with more experimental work, but the familiar elements of rule, grid, and bold type remain from the formative stage.

industrial forms was easily harnessed to the commercial task of presenting mass-produced objects as stylish. Consumerism absorbed the formal lessons of the avant-garde without its visionary ideals (Figs. **10.6a** and **10.6b**).

On the American scene, the high-profile innovator William Addison Dwiggins was helping define the field he called *graphic design.* His published work and public lectures gave voice to the idea that a systematic approach to design depended on rules and elements in combination—the syntax and semantics of graphic design. In Europe, this approach had been institutionalized in the curriculum of newly hatched design schools. But in the United States, the profession remained more pragmatic than theoretical. In articles, essays, and books like *Layout in Advertising,* Dwiggins helped bridge the gap, linking technical tips to larger questions of aesthetics and design philosophy (Fig. **10.7**).

In 1925, when the *Exposition Internationale des Arts Décoratifs et Industriels Modernes* was held in Paris, the United States did not participate. Symptomatic of the difference in attitudes on either side of the Atlantic, a statement by American officials included suggestions that their countrymen did not consider modern design important. But the term *Art Deco,* with

The Culture of Consumption

10.7 William Addison Dwiggins, *The Power of Print—and Men,* **1936.** This book displays W. A. Dwiggins's abilities as a type, ornament, and layout designer. Metro and Electra, both designed by Dwiggins, are featured on the title page, along with his moderne take on **printers' flowers** in an asymmetrical arrangement. Commissioned by Mergenthaler Linotype Company to celebrate fifty years of Linotype's contributions to printing and publishing, *The Power of Print—and Men* makes an unequivocal claim for progress that is embodied in the force of its design. Humanism and industry are reconciled in its modern aesthetic. The presence of machinery can be felt in the clean impact of type and seen reflected in the ornaments' hard-edged references to a press cylinder. Dwiggins was an influential critic who sought new terms and adequate distinctions to address rapid changes in the field of "graphic design"—a name he is credited with introducing.

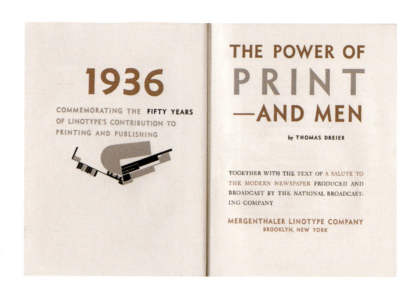

10.8a and 10.8b Alexey Brodovitch, *Harper's Bazaar,* **1935.** Modern editorial design came to the New York publishing industry under the direction of European émigrés. In Brodovitch's 1935 layouts for *Harper's Bazaar,* boldly shaped text blocks echo photographed forms, and overlapping images crop and fan the curve of a deeply shadowed body. The clothes are ultra-fashionable; their presentation is sculptural and formal. The design suggests that style is not about individual women or their narratives—but about shape. Objects and things, rather than people, command attention. This approach to design defines fashion as an abstract form and implies that bodies are to be subordinate to designed shape. Consumption is conformity, not only to a vogue or trend, but also to a body-type and a set of gestures that discipline the physical self.

all of its stylistic implications, entered popular usage after that event, and moderne motifs quickly found favor with American consumers. While Art Deco got its name from a trade fair designed to boost France's reputation as a purveyor of fine design, modern*ism*—in the sense of an embodied belief system—found its way across the Atlantic in the 1930s for quite different reasons. The rise of fascism and threat of war in Europe prompted many prominent graphic designers to emigrate. Some were escaping persecution on the grounds of ethnic identity, but modern design itself was also targeted for its political associations. Once in the United States, key figures such as Herbert Bayer, Mehemed Fehmy Agha, and Alexey Brodovitch were hired by publishers and ad executives eager to capture the sophistication of European style. Their work transformed *Vogue* and *Harper's Bazaar* and brought new ideas to leading agencies (Figs. **10.8a** and **10.8b**).

The formal and conceptual range of graphic design changed in the seminal years after World War I. The methods and discoveries of experimental art were successfully transferred to commercial work. The

10.9 Herbert Bayer, Breuer chairs ad, 1927. Bayer's photographic imagery vies with Breuer's tubular steel forms to be most conspicuously modern. Dramatic use of a photographic negative, simple text, diagrammatic arrows, and sans serif type are hallmarks of a streamlined look that claims to be functional above all. Yet these stylized design elements carry symbolic value. The "meaning" of this style is the idea that modern design is closer to engineering than to decoration. It implies that the industrial aesthetic is not only compatible with the human form but also actually superior to older, handmade, or traditional designs in meeting human needs. The emphasis on efficiency as an unquestionable benefit comes through this imagery clearly, as if any opposition to the virtues of modernity would be irrational and therefore unbelievable.

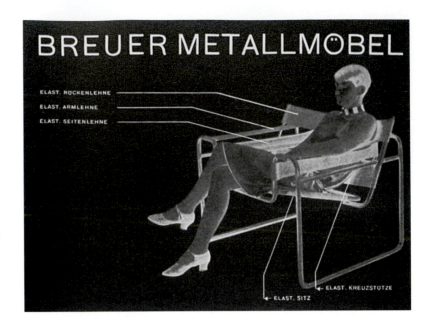

avant-garde legacy was absorbed in a rapid cycle of appropriation and obsolescence. In the process, much of its progressive intent was lost, but the association of a certain graphic vocabulary with modernity became consolidated in the public imagination. Through its dialogue with fine art, design helped define modernity as a social and personal ideal. By the end of the 1930s, this ideal was being linked to products and industries in the design of sophisticated ad campaigns. A generation of graphic designers formed by De Stijl, Constructivism, and other modern movements had come of age. Their synthesis of European avant-garde experiments and

A certain graphic vocabulary became associated with modernity.

American business models was characteristic of the dynamic cultural climate between the two world wars. By the end of those decades, a large part of mainstream advertising and editorial design followed the precepts of modern style (Fig. **10.9**).

Consumer culture
"Mass consumption," notes historian Daniel Boorstin, was considered "the great democratizing force in modern America." The advancement of an ideology of consumer capitalism in the early twentieth century was fueled by this equation. Graphic design was both an expression and an instrument of this ideology, and it was key to promoting consumption as an ideal, not simply a practicality. Advertising imagery sold goods by association with cultural values and class identities. In the 1920s, American advertising presented products as solutions to problems that might have emotional sources or social dimensions. Visual metaphors of the American dream invited identification with a vision of prosperity, even during the Depression. This collective fantasy of American opportunity may have seemed ironic, but it provided a powerful image (Figs. **10.10** and **10.11**).

10.10 Edward Steichen, photograph for cruise ad, 1934. Luxury imagery, whether in fine art or fashion photography, was a specialty of Edward Steichen. This ad for a cruise to Hawaii shows a glamorous woman, fully at ease in evening clothes, being seated for dinner. Her hair, curled in the marcelled waves of the day, delicate profile, and impeccable features suggest that her status and her beauty are perfectly matched, even naturally linked. Her fairness and face shape fulfill a stereotype, an image of aristocratic class that was coded to link ethnic identities and social values. Working-class women and people of color or distinct (non–Northern European) ethnic identity are rarely pictured in ads of this period. The Depression and its deprivations are also far from this scene, which represents a life secured against such difficulties rather than an escape from them.

10.11 Listerine ad, 1923. Not all images of glamour were meant to appeal to the most moneyed class. The narrative of middle-class daily life in this ad stands in contrast to the elitism communicated in Steichen's photograph. American advertising consistently offered vignettes with which a broad readership could identify. Listerine launched a series of advertisements in the 1920s that targeted young men and women anxious about their social success. The development of new products for personal hygiene subdivided the body into zones, each worthy of its own special attention and therefore capable of being targeted by ads. The departing figure is depicted in a voguish manner, but her style is powerless to compensate for her poor dental hygiene. The text reads like a **pulp** romance. Its narrative creates a natural-seeming segue between a social dilemma and the benefits of the product.

In the 1920s and 1930s, most of this American imagery was still rendered by hand. Illustration, hand-drawn logotypes, and serif display faces persisted. To anyone with a view of both continents, the contrast between the literal, narrative, and thematic emphasis of American commercial art and the formalism of European graphic design must have been striking. Yet some design phenomena were more universal. Advertisers on both sides of the Atlantic sought their audience in the pages of nationally distributed magazines rather than along sidewalks. Radio was on the rise as an advertising medium, absorbing promotion budgets into a new and competing form of public space. Poster production declined, but billboards introduced a new scale of graphic design to be viewed from automobiles or across large urban spaces. These monumental messages often focused on luxury products, such as cigarettes, automobiles, and branded processed foods. The business of outdoor advertising grew into its own subfield of graphic design (Figs. **10.12a** and **10.12b**).

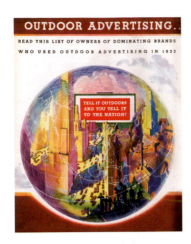

10.12a Outdoor Advertising ad, 1934 *(above)*, **and 10.12b Generic templates for gasoline billboards, 1930s** *(above right)*. Automobiles and roads for their use developed in tandem in the 1920s and 1930s. The creation of parkways for leisure driving led to a paved road system. Posters could effectively reach pedestrians, but billboards were the outdoor advertising mode for automotive zones. Urban, suburban, even rural sites offered new advertising spaces, and new skills were needed to translate drawings and paintings into roadside scale. Because billboards were produced by sign painters, flat color and simplified shapes were typical. More detailed paintings were less common because they were far more labor-intensive to produce. These **templates** were promotional tools, meant to show the strengths of associating products with iconic metaphors.

10.13 F. S. May, Schweppes Table Waters ad, 1931. Style codes function in vernacular imagery as well as through high art references. The Schweppes girl is clearly ready to have a good time. Her body language, dress, and facial expression are unambiguous. The softened modernism of her lines, the swirling pattern of her red shawl, and the blue vibrations that surround it underscore movement, but no distortion occurs in the image. The type is legible, the image is simple, and the bubbles in the glass suggest champagne as economically as the bobbed hair suggests a flapper. The persistence of such imagery into the Depression era had its own nostalgic attraction, offering the chance to recapture the roaring 20s in effervescent "table waters." Symbolic value, not literal description, sells the product through the pleasures of a consumable image.

10.14a Eduardo Benito, *Vogue*, 1926 *(left)*, and 10.14b Mehemed Fehmy Agha, Art Director, *Vanity Fair* cover, 1934 *(right)*. The eight years that separate these two images mark a shift from moderne style to the clubby realism of a new generation. The abstraction of Eduardo Benito's drawing proclaims style as a set of smoothly polished forms, while the realistic illustration on the *Vanity Fair* cover, under the art direction of M. F. Agha, is grounded in a new kind of contemporaneous look infused with a **technicolor** promise. The photographic quality of the image suggests that the scene is observed as much as imagined, and that reality can contain a fantasy, a dream can come true. The 1934 cover presents young sophisticates in flesh and blood, rather than an abstract symbol of worldliness, implying that theirs is a life to be lived, not merely an idea of modern culture. Agha's full-color covers became one of his trademarks.

Logos and brand names had worked to distinguish products in competitive markets, but a taint of P. T. Barnum-esque exaggeration and snake-oil quackery lingered in the mottos and claims that promoted these names. Advertisers shifted from extolling the virtues of products to picturing them in fantastic contexts to which their purchase seemed to promise access. Brand image production operated through visual codes in packaging, ad copy formulas, rendering style, and typographic reference. A new professional—the market analyst—was born. Armed with statistical methods and survey techniques, market analysts produced serious studies, proving that white evoked hygiene, black was sophisticated, sleek shapes were modern, stolid ones were old-fashioned, and so forth. The trim figures of young women, uncorseted and alluring, meant opulence and easy pleasure. Designs of bodies and gestures, particularly those of women, also tapped into style codes and came to be perceived by the public as standards of desirable beauty (Fig. **10.13**).

The notion that graphic design had a mission higher than mere presentation soon crept into the profession. Graphic designers were described as "product stylists" and "consumer engineers" whose task was to create an aura that had little to do with practical uses. The promotion of lifestyles as realms of self-realization and expression produced a curious side-effect—conformity. The mass production of fantasy channeled consumption into market-driven patterns. The industrial consumer was an engineered concept, a generic figure who followed trends with a personal interest (Figs. **10.14a** and **10.14b**).

10.15a Harry Beck, London Underground map, 1933 *(right)* and 10.15b Poster showing Eric Gill's alphabet in LNER signage, after 1929 *(below)*. Harry Beck's revision of the London Underground map set a new standard for clarity and efficiency in information design. His abstraction of the map streamlined graphic variations, straightening and color-coding lines, unifying angles, and evening spaces between stations. Beck was an engineering draftsman who borrowed the schematic configuration of his design from electrical circuit diagrams. His design complemented the spare elegance of Edward Johnston's typeface, which, like Beck's map, achieved a degree of legibility that has stood the test of nearly a century of continuous use. Eric Gill was Johnston's student. He designed letters that, like his teacher's, combined features of calligraphy with more systematic, mathematical foundations. Gill's alphabet was used by the London and North Eastern Railway in more than 2,000 stations, on train cars and locomotives, as well as in publicity materials, forming the basis of an overall identity system. A slight deviation from purely geometric design enlivens the letters with a humanistic touch.

Beyond the nineteenth-century concept of **trademarks** as guarantors of products, brands extended to complete visual identity systems and became marketable in their own right. These systems were applied to entire lines of goods and styles of communication. A company no longer simply had a logo or a letterhead, but a "look"—a harbinger of the corporate identity systems that would mature in the post-World War II years. As transportation and communication systems expanded, the idea of coordinated signage design followed, echoing the business sector's branding schemes and enforcing visual unity. For roads, legibility was the highest priority, especially at the higher speeds introduced by automobiles. Coordinated typography indicated authority, and its integration in a system

Coordinated typography indicated authority and oversight.

suggested that a guiding and benevolent oversight lay behind the design of the roadways as well. This spirit of organization, "spoken" through an identifiable graphic system, contributed to the "image" of a paternalistic government (Figs. **10.15a** and **10.15b**).

The profession In Europe, the Bauhaus provided an institutional framework for design instruction, while studios and firms founded by its faculty and students disseminated the spirit of modernism. By the time the Bauhaus was displaced from its original home in Weimar and relocated to Dessau in 1925, the foundation course and typography workshop had established a style as well as a set of formal and pedagogical principles. Focusing on the achievement of harmony, order, dynamism, stability, or excitement, these principles defined modern graphic design as attention to the striking arrangement of elements on a surface. When pivotal figures such as Josef Albers, Laszlo Moholy-Nagy, Georgy Kepes, and Herbert Bayer left the Bauhaus in the 1930s, they brought its curricular approach with them to the American and Swiss schools where they found positions. Moholy-Nagy established the New Bauhaus in Chicago in 1937, an

10.16 Herbert Bayer, *Bauhaus* cover, 1928. The Bauhaus came to symbolize modern design. This 1928 publication, produced in Dessau, brought the school's work into public view. Many of the cover design's ingredients can be traced to Russian and German avant-garde compositions and the abstract vocabulary of De Stijl. Abstraction was one of the hallmarks of modernism. The use of nonrepresentational elements as the formal basis of graphic design challenged traditional ideas about meaning and communication, particularly in the American context. Bauhaus-inspired design suggested that a universal visual language existed, which did not bear any relation to history or culture. In fact, such work was specific to its historical moment.

10.17 Laszlo Moholy-Nagy, *The New Bauhaus*, prospectus, 1937/1938. Similar observations may be made regarding this prospectus for the New Bauhaus, established in Chicago by Laszlo Moholy-Nagy. Its geometric solids suggest ideal forms without any cultural baggage. But these forms are Western, rational, and mathematical. They banish emotions associated with individual expression in favor of the values of an engineered universe.

experiment that succeeded two years later as the School of Design. In the American context, the Bauhaus aim of teaching students to *think* beyond immediate pragmatic or conventional considerations was meant to counter narrow professionalism and Beaux Arts traditionalism. Courses modeled on the Bauhaus foundation became standard fixtures in art school curricula (Figs. **10.16** and **10.17**).

In the United States, graphic design in the 1920s was seen as an aid to reaching economic and political goals. The Association of American Advertising Agencies was founded in 1917. Speaking to its members in 1926, President Calvin Coolidge praised the advertising industry for "ministering to the spiritual side of trade." Government rhetoric extolled American ingenuity and industry. But the trade generated by creating new

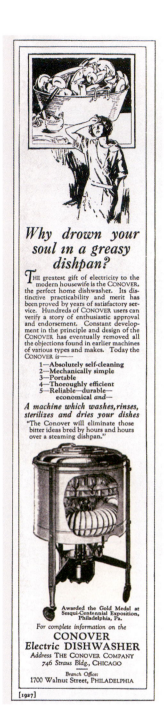

Why drown your soul in a greasy dishpan?

THE greatest gift of electricity to the modern housewife is the CONOVER, the perfect home dishwasher. Its distinctive practicability and merit has been proved by years of satisfactory service. Hundreds of CONOVER users can verify a story of enthusiastic approval and endorsement. Constant development in the principle and design of the CONOVER has eventually removed all the objections found in earlier machines of various types and makes. Today the CONOVER is —

1—Absolutely self-cleaning
2—Mechanically simple
3—Portable
4—Thoroughly efficient
5—Reliable—durable— economical and—

A machine which washes, rinses, sterilizes and dries your dishes

"The Conover will eliminate those bitter ideas bred by hours and hours over a steaming dishpan."

Awarded the Gold Medal at Sesqui-Centennial Exposition, Philadelphia, Pa.

For complete information on the

CONOVER
Electric DISHWASHER
Address THE CONOVER COMPANY
746 Straus Bldg., CHICAGO
Branch Office:
1700 Walnut Street, PHILADELPHIA

10.18a Conover's dishwasher ad, 1927 *(left)*, **and 10.18b James Haworth, Ransomes grass machine ad, 1928** *(above)*. The advertisement for Conover's electric dishwasher announces its virtues in a straightforward way. But the ad for Ransomes "grass machines" suggests a lifestyle of grace and ease. The older paradigm of promoting a product through literal description gradually gave way to associations that placed products, and thus their prospective buyers, in settings of personal fulfillment and cultural favor. Electricity was no longer in its infancy, but the organized delivery of well-regulated supplies to homes and businesses was still novel. In addition to providing light, electricity was used to power small appliances, creating a new market in devices that redefined domestic chores. Likewise, gasoline had become a readily available source of energy for small motors. This "grass machine" appears to be a push-model, rather than a power-model, but the ease of operation suggests that the labor involved does not raise a sweat. The denigration of physical labor is another subtext in these images: Polite society set itself at a distance from any form of hard work—even as athletics became a sign of middle-class leisure.

10.19a Young & Rubicam ad, 1930.
This ad for the Young & Rubicam agency appeared in 1930 in the first issue of *Fortune* magazine. It was still being used, unchanged, in 1946. The only amendments were additions to the list of offices in major cities that had increased from the original two. The effectiveness of the ad lay in its photographic image and direct message. Issues of race were not addressed, and the idea of a black boxer being the emblem of an advertising agency's capability provoked no commentary, apparently. Close cropping and bold type produce the ad's drama.

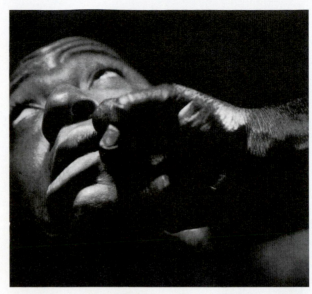

10.19b Young & Rubicam ad, 1935.
By contrast, this ad looks like elegant stationery and implies an exclusive club of insiders in the know, able to recognize quality through visual codes of expansive white space, spare type, and concise messages. For advertising firms to market themselves, they had to have an "image" that appealed to the business sector. Young & Rubicam was a pioneer agency that lasted through the twentieth century as a distinct entity before merging with other companies amid increasing consolidation of the advertising industry at the turn of the millennium.

markets and promoting American goods abroad was the real benefit. Many new products defined themselves as necessities. Personal hygiene devices such as hair dryers and electric razors were introduced, and the domestic environment was invaded by a host of electrical appliances for automating housework. Industrialization crossed from the factory into the home. At the same time, business machines extended into every corner of the office. White-collar work expanded, and professional categories multiplied. Graphic design was one such burgeoning field (Figs. **10.18a** and **10.18b**).

Graphic design acquired new institutional and professional forms in the decades between the world wars. The Art Directors Club was founded in New York in 1920. In 1921, its first *Annual* established yearly awards to recognize outstanding professional achievement in distinct categories such as direct mail, packaging, advertising, and point-of-purchase display. The American Marketing Association was established in 1931, another milestone marking increased professional recognition. By then, the phrase *Madison Avenue* had come to be associated with the advertising industry. Behind the scenes, the specialization of tasks generated new roles and skills and demanded ever more organized networks of interdependent practitioners (Figs. **10.19a** and **10.19b**).

10.20 Lester Beall, technical image from trade journal, 1938. Trade journals and professional annuals proliferated as venues for the graphic design industry to recognize technical and artistic achievements. In this two-page spread, Lester Beall shows readers the negative space that is required for overprinting photographs. The layout is striking: Its large organic shape frames the white space of the page, and a piece of black rule cuts across the foreground so that the cropped hand does not appear gruesome or macabre. The bold simplicity of the composition is deceptive. Its complexity lies in all the spatial layers that are articulated between edge and boundary, frame and overprinting, photographic dimensionality, and flat graphic space. Beall had absorbed the lessons of modern art. Yet he used them to develop a graphic vocabulary that organized printed space in lively ways that did not require his audience to know the sources on which he drew.

10.21a Lester Beall, Hiram Walker advertisement, 1937. Printer's cuts and clichés are combined in this ad for a Hiram Walker bourbon distillery. The energy of the composition clearly shows a European influence on the young designer from America's heartland. Beall eagerly digested the samples of avant-garde graphic art that he found in imported publications. But he translated these impressions into a strikingly American idiom by his use of such figures as the rifle-bearing pioneer in a coonskin cap. Primary red, blue, and black all strike the eye with equal intensity, and, despite being layered, the individual components remain thoroughly legible. Beall's designs demonstrate an extensive technical knowledge of printing processes. He maximized the impact of each element by considering its production possibilities. Color, shape, tone, and scale interacted with ink layering sequence, drop-outs, overlays, and other graphic processes that were carefully manipulated aspects

of his vocabulary.

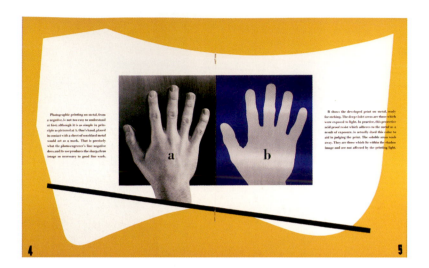

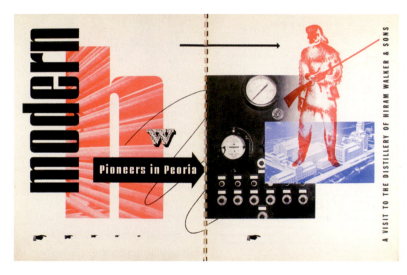

Ad agencies assembled teams to provide a range of services, replacing the older model of the individual designer working in a studio. In the 1920s, art directors began to assume editorial and aesthetic responsibility for shaping campaigns that assessed a client's identity and communication needs in a systematic way, rather than simply advertising goods as need arose. Major figures in the American scene, such as Ernest Elmo Calkins, Charles Coiner, and Lester Beall, pioneered a new professionalism in graphic design, giving it legitimacy and demonstrating the value of advertising in the modern business world. Alongside the organizational methods of **Fordism** and later **Taylorism**, strategies for marketing and measuring communication's effectiveness adopted statistical methods. A scientific approach to consumer research introduced questionnaires and opinion surveys. A flurry of new publications, such as *Advertising-Selling, Advertising Arts,* and *Commercial Art and Industry* sought to analyze the basics of successful campaigns (Fig. **10.20**).

Tools and media for the basic tasks of graphic design in the 1930s included scissors, tape, gum, mass-produced textures such as Ben Day dot

Seamless imagery embodied a rhetoric of easy consumability.

10.21b Jan Tschichold, *The Professional Photographer*, exhibition poster, 1938.
Jan Tschichold designed this striking poster for an exhibition of professional photographers in 1938. The negative does much of the communication in this design, suggesting an expert's experienced relation to production. The distribution of type is masterful, every element weighted and placed to strike a dynamic balance that echoes the structural division of the image. Type calls attention to the composition of the image without obvious reference, simply by arrangement and tonal value. Its shifts in scale and weight reinforce the vibrancy of the whole, while its sans serif clarity provides stability. This work would have been deemed decadent, even subversive, in Germany in the late 1930s: All of the signs of visual modernity that it displays were politically charged. Modern design's striving for universality through formal rules was, paradoxically, one of the grounds on which it met with the greatest cultural hostility.

patterns, gouache, india ink, straightedges, pencils, brushes, and technical pens. Increasingly, they also included photographs, cut and pasted into mock-ups and layouts. More significantly, graphic designers began to make sophisticated use of photolithographic methods and to think in terms of color separations, spot colors, metallic inks, and varnishes (Figs. **10.21a** and **10.21b**).

Graphic designers in the 1920s and 1930s could count on new reproductive techniques to produce glossy images with smoothly toned surfaces. Seamless imagery embodied a visual rhetoric of easy consumability. The manipulation of images or type through photographic prepress processes introduced flexibility into a repertoire that had previously been circumscribed by the limits of hot metal type and an engraver's skill. Shaping, layering, highlighting, reversing, and otherwise altering artwork became readily possible. Photomontage, a provocative technique in avant-garde artistic circles, became an eye-catching staple of commercial design. The airbrush, initially used for retouching photographs, was more widely adopted in the 1920s as a way to lend graphic art a machine-like finish that proclaimed modernity. Images became products,

10.22 Adolphe Jean-Marie Mouron Cassandre, Normandie poster, 1935.
A. M. Cassandre's work is practically synonymous with 1920s and 1930s popular culture. His airbrush techniques produced a surface that seemed to be machined. His image of the ocean liner—monumental, architectonic, and massively formalized—is a graphic icon. The capacity to simplify while creating elegant form was one of Cassandre's signature traits. The design's effect is a halcyon image of a perfectly running world, smooth as the surface of the transatlantic cruise ship. Modernity is pictured as a powerful machine, ensuring ease and grandeur on untroubled waters, stable and unsinkable.

10.23 Display lettering, *Commercial Art Advertising Layout*, 1938. Type and lettering styles of the period signal modernity—streamlined machine faces, scripts of greatly exaggerated elegance, and letters that seem to bear the mark of engineering tools. The names of typefaces resonate with associations from the era—Broadway, Vogue, Metro, and so on. Linotype and Monotype technologies contributed to the advent of such faces. Careful drawings that took into account the optical distinctions necessary for keeping consistency in a type family at different sizes and weights were used as patterns for production. Faces inspired by Garamond, Plantin, and Baskerville were made fresh, reinvented for a new generation and new purposes. As Frederic Goudy said, "The old guys stole all the good ideas." That may have been true, but the *new* guys designed a whole inventory of robust text faces. They also produced novelties of stylistic effect, such as shaded lettering and twisted ribbon forms, that came to epitomize the culture of the day.

well-made commodities in their own right that circulated as consumable forms. **Four-color** photographic separation and **offset** printing promised to stretch graphic capabilities beyond the limits of gravure and relief, bring costs down, and increase the volume of print runs. Relief printing would remain viable, in part, because of the capital investment in equipment made by many printers and publishers, but offset lithography was soon to become the industry standard (Fig. **10.22**).

Type design in the 1920s and 1930s reflected the diversification of the graphic design industry. Display faces for advertising and commercial work featured geometric designs, streamlined shapes, and names that encapsulated the era by reference to fashion, stylish entertainment, luxury settings, tourism, or technological innovations: Vogue, Broadway, Neon, Golf, Trocadero, and so on. For book publication, Monotype casting was most practical. Various foundries commissioned redrawings of traditional faces for contemporary use. The American Type Founders Company had consolidated many independent foundries and begun marketing type in coordinated families. Stanley Morison's design of Times New Roman for *The London Times*, completed in 1932, set a benchmark for robust versatility and legibility in text faces. Extensive use of sans serif **fonts** created demand for variety in style and weight. Paul Renner's Futura and Rudolf Koch's Kabel, both initially offered in several weights, became popular choices.

10.24 Nembhard Culin, World's Fair poster, 1939. The geometric solids and futuristic rendering of John Binder's poster for the 1939 New York World's Fair express a curious optimism. The Western world was on the brink of war, and the idea that rationality of any kind could prevail over fascism in Germany, Spain, and Italy was dubious. The poster's visual signs of modernity are clear: elongated rectilinear type, airbrushed forms, distorting angles, dramatic shadows, a graphic interplay of surface and depiction. But the conceptual flaws of this approach are also in evidence, as the very abstraction that gives the image its modernity simultaneously reveals it to be a fantasy. This is not the world of 1939 or its future, except in a graphic designer's imagination. In 1939, the utopian agenda of early modernism was subsiding under the pressure of political and social realities. Graphic design had been an expression and an instrument of that utopianism. But this image projects a future as already-antiquated as the radio-watch worn by the 1930s interplanetary comic-book hero, Flash Gordon.

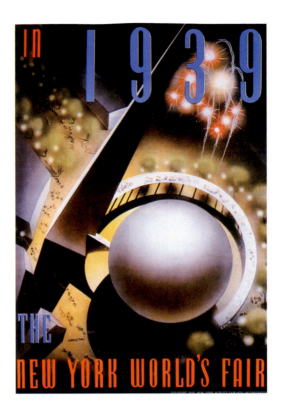

Their use supplemented that of standard turn-of-the-century Gothic typefaces. The specimen sheet designed to promote Futura mimicked industrial methods by presenting each light, regular, and bold variant as part of a coordinated product line (Fig. **10.23**).

Conclusion Increased consumption of standardized products and imagery structured conformity into patterns of modern culture. Entering the public imagination by ingenious means, advertising and editorial design planted and manipulated fantasies of lives defined and fulfilled by style. Mass-circulation magazines were bought for their sleek, consumable images of products, activities, and glamorous circumstances far beyond the means of their readership. And with the fantasy, a certain image of modernity was sold. Many sophisticated graphic designers, aware that a broad public, particularly in America, would never engage directly with modern art, considered commercial design to be a vehicle for introducing new styles, shapes, attitudes, and approaches to form. In intellectual circles, influential critics such as Van Wyck Brooks and H. L. Mencken paid attention to the iconography of advertising and commented on the broader phenomenon of a culture driven by fantasies of enjoying abundance. The two decades between the wars brought modernism to a practical maturity in fashion, commerce, and business. Traces of earlier avant-garde agendas remained, but they were increasingly relegated to formal devices and motifs. Graphic design had a profound impact on modern culture, but the impact was more aesthetic than political. Designed images disseminated concepts of what it meant to be modern and sold modern aesthetics in popular culture (Fig. **10.24**).

The Culture of Consumption 1920s–1930s

1917 Association of American Advertising Agencies founded
1919 J. Walter Thompson advertising agency adds marketing department
1920 Art Directors Club founded
Band-Aids marketed
Sinclair Lewis's *Main Street* published
Mark of Zorro film opens
National Negro Baseball League's first game
Wonder Bread marketed
First public radio broadcasts
1921 Rudolf Valentino stars in *The Sheik*
Black Sox baseball scandal
White Castle, first hamburger chain, opens
1922 W. A. Dwiggins writes "New Kind of Printing Calls for New Design"
Mussolini's march on Rome
Commercial Art launched in Britain
Emily Post's *Etiquette* published
Little Orphan Annie opens
Technicolor process developed for film
U.S.S.R. established
1923 Self-winding watch invented
Cecil B. DeMille's *Ten Commandments* opens
Chanel No. 5 perfume first issued
U.S. Steel Corp introduces eight-hour workday
1924 Greece becomes republic
J. Edgar Hoover named head of FBI
Gebrauchsgraphik launched in Germany to promote advertising art
Death of Franz Kafka
First transatlantic photo facsimile (picture of Calvin Coolidge) transmitted
International Business Machines Corporation (IBM) formed
1925 *The New Yorker* launched
Exposition Internationale des Arts Décoratifs et Industriels Modernes in Paris
F. Scott Fitzgerald's *Great Gatsby* published
Bird's Eye introduces frozen foods
John T. Scopes tried for teaching evolutionary theory
Birth of Malcolm X
Mount Rushmore proposed
Special Services (SS) formed by Nazis
1926 President Calvin Coolidge addresses Association of Advertising Agencies
NBC, first major radio network, founded by David Sarnoff
Cardboard packaging perfected by Container Corporation
1927 Herbert Bayer designs Breuer furniture ads
Nicola Sacco and Bartolomeo Vanzetti, anarchists, executed in U.S.
Charles Lindbergh flies nonstop from New York to Paris
First transatlantic phone calls
The Jazz Singer, first commercial sound film, opens
Kool-Aid invented
1928 Cellophane tape commercially available
Amelia Earhart's transatlantic flight
Walt Disney's *Steamboat Willie* with Mickey Mouse synchs images to sound
Amos 'n' Andy debuts on radio
A. A. Milne's *House at Pooh Corner* published
TWA (Trans World Airlines) incorporated

Felix Salten's *Bambi* opens

Schick electric razors invented

1929 Yo-yo fad in U.S.

Mehemed Fehmy Agha hired by Condé Nast for *Vanity Fair*

Limited Editions Club founded

Stock Market Crash

Death of Wyatt Earp

Saint Valentine's Day mobster massacre in Chicago

MoMA opened in New York by Alfred Barr

Birth of Martin Luther King, Jr.

Ernest Hemingway's *Farewell to Arms* published

Neon lights in Las Vegas

Dziga Vertov's *Man with a Movie Camera* opens

1930 *Advertising Arts* launched in New York

Alexey Brodovitch goes to New York

Pope approves use of rhythm method of birth control

Haile Selassi crowned king of Ethiopia

The Shadow broadcast on radio

Planet Pluto named

Twinkie invented

1931 The Studio Ltd publishes Alfred Tolmer's *Mise en Page*

Teletype introduced

American Marketing Association established

Electric guitar invented

Salvador Dalí paints *Persistence of Memory* with melting clocks

Eric Gill's *Essay on Typography* published

1932 Color photo printing in newspaper pioneered

1933 Prohibition repealed in U.S.

Bauhaus closed by Nazis

Roosevelt begins his regular "fireside chat" radio broadcasts

Black Mountain College founded near Asheville, North Carolina

1934 Charles Darrow invents Monopoly game

Machine Art exhibit at MoMA

Chinese Communists' Long March begins

1935 Associated Press wire service, first wire service for photographs, established

Mussolini's army invades Ethiopia

Kodachrome film introduced

Federal Arts Project starts in U.S.

First working radar

1936 W. A. Dwiggins decorates T. Drier's *The Power of Print—and Men*

Spanish Civil War begins

1937 Nescafé instant coffee invented

Kurt Schwitters declared "degenerate" by Nazis

MoMA exhibits Lester Beall's Rural Electrification Administration posters

New Bauhaus founded in Chicago

Polyurethane developed

1938 *Bauhaus 1919–1938* exhibit at MoMA

1939 School of Design opens, replaces New Bauhaus

Ladislav Sutnar designs Czech pavilion for New York World's Fair

Public demonstration of television at New York World's Fair

Electron microscopes produced

Gone with the Wind opens

Tools of the Trade

Mayline drafting table

Cellophane tape

Masking tape

Kodachrome film

Flashbulbs

Lettering sample books

Typewriter with changeable faces

Teletypesetter

Photolithography

Color separation

Photographic prepress processes

(See also Chapter 9)

11. Public Interest Campaigns and Information Design 1930s–1950s

- Depression-era programs and wartime dictates pressed designers into large-scale, publicly funded information campaigns that also exposed a broad audience to cutting-edge visual trends.

- Documentary photography became a mainstay of mass-circulation publications and established a general perception of photojournalism as a source of unbiased records.

- Information design emerged as a powerful means of condensing large quantities of complex data into highly legible forms, and designers aligned themselves with engineers in the belief that statistical graphics could communicate with objective rationality.

- Graphic designers began to think in terms of *programs* and systematic approaches to the flow of information, borrowing the metaphors and technology of electronic information management.

- Information design relied on an appearance of fact-based objectivity to present arguments as if they were simply **empirical** statements, rather than graphic forms of persuasion.

11.1 Harry Koerner, *Save Waste Fats*, 1943. Wartime posters sought to communicate with the broadest possible audience by using direct, dramatic means. Economic austerity was a central theme. Here, frying-pan fat becomes a source of molten energy, going directly into bombs. The iconographic image eliminates all subtlety. The link between domestic cooking and weapons production is compressed into a single event. The woman's manicured nails identify the target audience for the recycling efforts being promoted. But the war is very present and sinister in this imagery. The highlight on the woman's slender knuckles contrasts her feminine flesh with the dark power of the explosion.

In the mid-twentieth century, national information campaigns called graphic designers to public service. Educational goals and techniques of persuasion overlapped in this work, whether it took the form of a socially conscious photo-essay, a helpful poster, or a civic-minded advertisement. Graphic methods for presenting information gained clarity and impact when they were applied with a sense of urgency. Wartime design work to serve the common cause was often commissioned by government agencies whose directors cared little for aesthetics but placed a high premium on results. National mobilization during World War II depended heavily on effective public communication. Posters recruited soldiers and defense workers, promoted government bonds, and warned of security risks. They also produced images of patriotic cooperation in times of austerity. The rhetoric in these posters took the form of slogans and simplified iconography familiar from earlier **propaganda**. Public information campaigns had a political purpose and sought to be effective rather than subtle in order to move large groups of people to action. But such campaigns could also draw on a forceful visual vocabulary whose power of persuasion was less obvious: **information graphics**. Bar charts and flow diagrams seemed like straightforward presentations of fact. The overwhelming emphasis on communication in these forms obscured the fact that the arguments structured by grids and arrows were grounded in a system of beliefs and values. The hidden rhetorical strength of information design lay in the appearance of fact-based objectivity. Objectivity was also presumed to be inherent to documentary photography because of

11.2 Flowchart Westinghouse Radio ad, 1944. Flowcharts have an appearance of neutrality and efficiency. They can be generalized and adapted to depict almost any process or activity. They became a fixture in business contexts at mid-century when corporate organizational strategies demanded a seamless image. Flowcharts organize information according to an implied narrative of continuity. In a real work situation, each stage of a process is mediated by human beings. But such charts suggest that activity is independent of individual agency. This Westinghouse ad exemplifies the rhetorical component that necessarily enters graphic presentation of information or data. The sheer force of the arrows, their curved flow and forward momentum make the "process" seem inevitable and natural. This simplified flowchart connects the rational grid of the global map with a colonial-style house. Humans are conspicuously absent, and radio broadcasts travel through the light blue air with unhampered force.

Public interest graphics treated social norms as common sense.

the methods of the medium itself. Photographic essays served the public interest by seeming to report directly and gained cultural authority through their association with social responsibility. Information graphics and documentary photography both had power to shape public opinion. After the war, information designers adapted visual **lexicons** developed for military, scientific, and statistical applications to lend authority to the purposes of business and industry (Figs. **11.1** and **11.2**).

Public interest and education Graphic design in the public interest was already a well-established category of visual communication by the 1930s. The promotion of public safety and personal hygiene had been a feature of earlier twentieth-century campaigns, spreading middle-class assumptions and social values. In simplified graphics designed to elicit civic-minded participation, individuals were addressed with benevolent paternalism. The causes of poor people, children, and workers were often championed with condescension. The tone of these campaigns suggested that certain codes of behavior were universally accepted. Reformers interested in controlling the spread of disease in domestic and work

11.3 WPA Anti-syphilis poster, late 1930s. *Syphilis.... Six out of ten cured because they did not wait too long.* Repeated figures in this poster turn a statistical argument into iconography. The bold distinctions of red, white, and black inks combine with the almost mechanical shape of the bodies to create a visually effective presentation of information. Even without the text, the contrast between happy and despairing men is obvious. But the implication is that syphilis is a male problem. Women are nowhere in evidence, even though the disease is sexually transmitted. Prevention is not mentioned at all, only the benefits of swift action to aid recovery. Neither symptoms nor results of the disease are specified. Instead, infection is equated with a psychological condition of despair. Isolation of the word *Syphilis* at the top renders it concrete and autonomous—as if it were a thing, rather than an infection spread through a network of social interactions. The official "voice" of reprimand that comes through the poster is definitive in its judgment and blunt in its warning.

environments promoted cleanliness in compositions that aligned physical hygiene with moral virtue. Although the benefits to individuals and the public were indisputable, these campaigns contained many unexamined attitudes toward family, sexual identity, age, class, and other demographic categories. By contrast to advertisements that encouraged the consumption of new products for personal distinction and gratification, public interest graphics often attempted to regulate individual behavior by promoting social norms as common sense. Their presentation of information rode a delicate line between informing the public and prescribing conformity. Audiences were clearly identified. But the "speaker" was often lent authority by a façade of generalized, institutional identity (Fig. **11.3**).

From 1936 to 1943, an unprecedented program, sponsored by the United States government, brought graphic design into a new relation with the public. The Works Progress Administration (WPA) established by President Franklin D. Roosevelt produced over 3,000 posters in shops around the

11.4 Martin Weitzman, WPA fire safety poster, ca. 1936. This striking WPA poster advocates safety through a mix of artistic styles. The figure silhouetted against rising flames and smoke is poised in a dramatic moment. Produced with carefully cut stencils and flat, silkscreen color, this poster combines elements of German expressionism with American illustrational conventions. The utter powerlessness of this individual to intervene in the conflagration turns domestic disaster into a romantic image of a figure isolated and overwhelmed by flames. His desperate condition, more than the structural requirements of the basement, becomes the central focus. The implication is that a person who fails to use fire retardant in a cellar risks bringing about devastation of near-apocalyptic proportions.

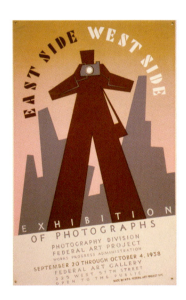

11.5 Anthony Velonis, WPA photography exhibition poster, 1938. In a manner typical of WPA designs, this poster translates the formal values of fine art, especially abstraction, into graphic communication. Unlike ads of the era that quoted fine art to signal elitism and attract consumers for high-end products, these posters aimed at a general audience. This elegant and schematic rendering is reminiscent of the hard-edged, reductive geometry of two well-known American painters of the era, Charles Sheeler and Charles Demuth. The flat forms of the city strike an intriguing contrast with the tonal transition of the glowing sky. The use of the dark central figure to isolate the bright lens of the camera is extremely effective. The treatment features conspicuously modern elements: the distortion and simplification of the figure and landscape, the diagonal division of image and text areas, and the use of evenly weighted sans serif type. But it remains sufficiently grounded in figuration to appeal to a broad public.

country. The economic aim of the WPA was to provide employment, but the program was also premised on the conviction that art should enter the daily lives of all Americans. In the early years, many posters were produced by hand, individually lettered and painted. Soon, **silkscreen** printing was adopted. Themes for posters ranged from public safety to upcoming events and opportunities. The style of these works was eclectic, incorporating popular and **American Regionalist** motifs as well as modern European influences. WPA posters acquainted varied audiences with contemporary art, introducing them to abstraction, **surrealism,** and stylized approaches to form. Figurative, realist, and photographic compositions could also be found in these posters, but, by and large, production requirements reinforced a trend toward flat color and formal simplification: Silkscreen stenciling techniques were far cheaper than the film and chemicals needed to reproduce photographs (Figs. **11.4** and **11.5**).

An illustrational style invited identification with the worker.

11.6a *Russia Did It*, **leaflet, 1919** *(above)*, **and 11.6b** *The Pageant of the Paterson Strike* **poster, 1913** *(right)*. American labor graphics contained heroic figures ready to take charge of their own destiny. The individual worker is idealized in a muscular figure of youth and energy, seemingly invincible as he strides toward his audience. By contrast, the bulky giant in the leaflet addressed to shipyard workers appears older and more worn, although no less determined in his confrontational gesture. Together, the image and title communicate the leaflet's message. They remind us of a moment in American labor history when the Russian experiment appeared to hold a utopian promise. The man in work clothes with sleeves rolled up is clearly recognizable as a symbol of virility but also carries the associations of the style in which he is rendered. A popular, illustrational approach is adopted to invite the average person—who responds to this style—to identify with the worker.

Several thousand American artists, designers, photographers, and writers earned a weekly salary of twenty-five to thirty-five dollars working for the WPA. When the United States entered the war at the end of 1941, some continued to receive a government paycheck, working on defense-related campaigns for the Office of Information. Although such employment was unusual in the United States, in the Soviet Union artists had been state workers since the revolution in 1917. When conflicts arose in the struggle of organized labor for workers' rights throughout the United States and Europe during the Depression, Soviet Russia was often cited as a triumph of humanism over capitalist oppression and exploitation. Yet while graphics for Western labor rallies and union newspapers frequently featured images of the worker as a heroic individual, Soviet graphics were more likely to draw workers' attention to the importance of their place in the larger social system of production (Figs. **11.6a** and **11.6b**).

In the 1920s and 1930s, Soviet designers developed a modern, **montage**-based informational poster style. Such graphics promoted an image of the Soviet state as a functional machine in which each person's contribution was essential to the well-being of the collective. Education and literacy were

11.7 Elena Semenova, poster, 1920s.
Soviet information graphics combine naive, literal imagery with a sophisticated organizational structure. They are instructive as historical documents of the early Soviet state's attitudes and of the invention of a new graphic vocabulary. Collectivity was an important concept in Soviet political and social life. Giving it graphic form required the development of an innovative visual language. Crowds and masses shaped into a single image or icon were one element of this vocabulary. Another consisted of figures that repeated each other's movements through a single action or as units in a larger process. Such images lent themselves to totalitarian ideology as readily as to socialism, and the course of events in the Soviet Union reinforced this ambiguity. Here, Stalin exhorts the workers to improve their productivity by contrasting the poor, adequate, and high output of three groups. The **diagrammatic** scheme, which interlinks all parts of the production system as if they were wheels in a machine, creates an image of work as integral to larger social processes. These images present labor and productivity in visual terms so that they can be understood by everyone.

important to the cultivation of a trained labor force, and newly formed workers' clubs encouraged participation in reading rooms and discussions. Meanwhile, the government's long-term goals and economic plans were presented in schematic graphics that eliminated concrete details in favor of flowcharts and diagrams. In relating individual effort to goals of national prosperity, information graphics had the advantage of abstracting economic processes from human conditions or experience (Fig. **11.7**).

As the totalitarianism of Joseph Stalin's regime took repressive form in the 1930s, the iconography of Soviet graphics changed. Instead of each person making a distinct and vital contribution to the collective, masses of individuals were absorbed into the social body, often through repetitive motifs of militaristic exhibitions. Strong shapes and recognizable silhouettes effectively imposed an organizing image on a mass of workers, soldiers, students, and other citizens. These posters were echoed by those galvanizing support for the Nazi party in Germany, Mussolini in Italy, and Franco's military regime in Spain. The capacity of such images to represent power derives from a contrast of scale between a leader, or a single symbol, and a multitude (Figs. **11.8a** and **11.8b**).

Iconography in the 1930s often propagated stereotypes. The naturalism of many illustrational styles fostered national cultural ideals through depiction of individuals enhanced by certain traits. The muscled, hard-bodied figures in German posters presented an image of invulnerability

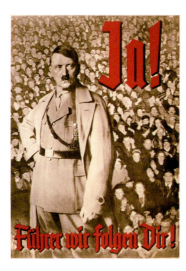

11.8a Gustav Klutsis, *Realize the Great Plan for Great Works!*, 1930 *(right),* **and 11.8b Hitler *Ja!*, 1938** *(above).* By 1930, a shift in the political climate had become apparent in the Soviet Union. Extreme contrast of scale and absorption of a crowd into a single image is echoed in these posters. The Soviet hand and the figure of Hitler impose the power of a unifying image on the anonymous populace. As fascist regimes emerged in the Soviet Union, Germany, and Italy in the 1930s, such posters helped bring about the situation they depicted. By communicating the allegiance of individuals to a single leader or symbol, they produced an affecting image of submission to power. The posters provide a symbolic affirmation of this subordination and suggest the impotence of common individuals against the unified will of the masses. They are terrifying for what they foreclose: the possibility of intervention or reflection. Political processes such as elections or parliamentary procedures are completely erased when a nation is depicted as a leader and a crowd of followers.

while promoting blond beauty as the highest aesthetic ideal. American folksy imagery, such as that chosen by Lester Beall in his posters for the Rural Electrification Administration, reinforced the notion of homespun hardiness and a pioneer spirit capable of triumphing over adversity. The work of Norman Rockwell and his imitators romanticized a particular version of Americana based in agrarian values and small-town traditionalism. National stereotypes emerged, in part, from designers' efforts to create imagery that reached its target audience through details of style and form as well as content. Some in the Nazi party promoted the use of blackletter, which they saw as carrying a strong association with ethnic roots and a connection with a mythic past. Folk imagery was invoked in national identity campaigns. Italian designers used updates of Trajan capitals to claim a modern incarnation of ancient glory, while in the United States, stenciled block letters seemed in keeping with the can-do attitude of the Depression era. This graphic rhetoric was as persuasive as any text and often served to reinforce the way individuals were judged along gender,

11.9a German worker poster, 1930s *(above left),* **11.9b Ludwig Hohlwein,** *Arbeit Brot,* **1933** *(above right),* **11.9c Norman Rockwell,** *Four Freedoms,* **1943** *(below left),* **and 11.9d Lester Beall, Rural Electrification Administration poster, 1939** *(below right).* A German worker, with a Nazi flag, is putting the building blocks of a new society into place. His muscled body and striking good looks embody the fiction of a master race and offer a ready stereotype to be planted in the public mind. A concealing shadow is cast over the eyes of Ludwig Hohlwein's hard-featured masculine soldier. The backdrop may be "work" *(arbeit)* and "bread" *(brot),* but the dark figure's call for enlistment is made with a terrifying absence of humanity. Norman Rockwell's *Four Freedoms* prints were issued as part of the effort to generate funds for the war, and their imagery delivers American ideology as clearly as Hohlwein's embodies Nazi myths. Rockwell's illustrations helped define an American idiom and sensibility. Lester Beall's posters were commissioned to inform Americans about the REA's program to bring electrical power to rural areas. The individuals he pictured were meant to represent a demographic group, part of the fabric of America. The poster's design integrates stripes and fence, flag and landscape, individual personality and generic image in such a way that they become inextricable. The deceptively simple message is that rural life and American values are indistinguishable.

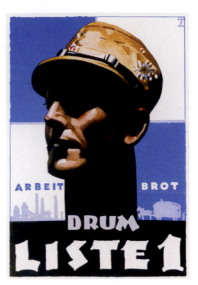

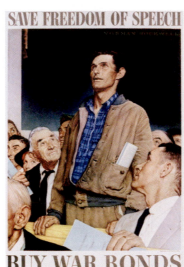

race, and class lines. Moral assumptions were implicitly encoded in such graphic images. In many cases, similar persuasive methods were applied to promote strikingly different political values (Figs. **11.9a–d**).

Photojournalism and documentary

Documentary photography became a powerful instrument of political and social commentary in the 1930s. Public attitudes toward photographic codes were conditioned by graphic designers' framing of images as documentary evidence. The New Deal, the economic recovery program that created the WPA, established the Farm Security Administration, which commissioned journalists and photographers to document the lives of America's rural poor. Published and exhibited, the photographs of Dorothea Lange, Walker Evans, and Margaret Bourke-White promoted images of American grit in the face of Depression-era difficulties. The documentary approach took the objectivity

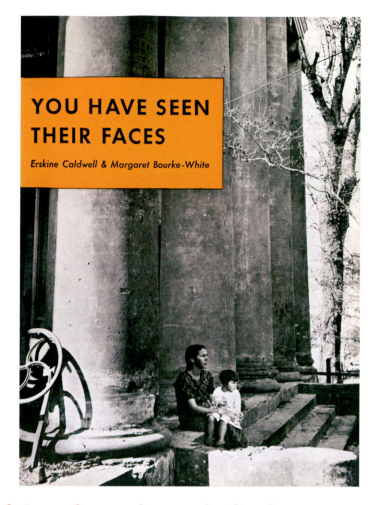

YOU HAVE SEEN THEIR FACES

Erskine Caldwell & Margaret Bourke-White

11.10 Erskine Caldwell and Margaret Bourke-White, *You Have Seen Their Faces*, 1937. Stark, striking, unadorned, the design for the cover of this publication announces the aesthetic of the photographs and text within. Documentary photography and film of this period assumed a descriptive objectivity. Narratives struck a tone of overwhelming naturalism. While some of these images capture encountered situations, some were staged, enhanced, or strategically cropped. Many were used and reused in contexts that distorted the information they carried, and all contributed to a public relations campaign meant to shift attention away from responsibility for economic misery to a demonstration of hard work and individual spirit triumphing over adversity.

Designers were quick to embrace the aesthetic of reportage.

of photographs for granted and touted the camera as a tool for empirical observation. Photojournalism became a profession. Designers were quick to embrace the ethos and aesthetics of reportage. Use of photographic images had characterized modern design, but documentary approaches established a tone of direct engagement, minimizing fine art associations in favor of an imagery of fact (Fig. **11.10**).

Print technology for photographic reproduction improved and became more affordable. Offset printing made use of a rubber blanket to optimize the transfer of halftone screen patterns from a metal plate to paper. Exposing a flat photosensitive plate was cheaper and faster than making relief engravings, and offset blankets allowed for a much higher level of resolution than relief printing. The result was a boom in reproduced photographic images. The integration of documentary imagery into mainstream magazines popularized the work of major modern photographers. In the 1940s, the British publication *Picture Post*, like the American periodical *Life*, built its reputation and audience on photojournalistic reportage. Many photographers with established reputations as fine artists or journalists also worked for fashion magazines.

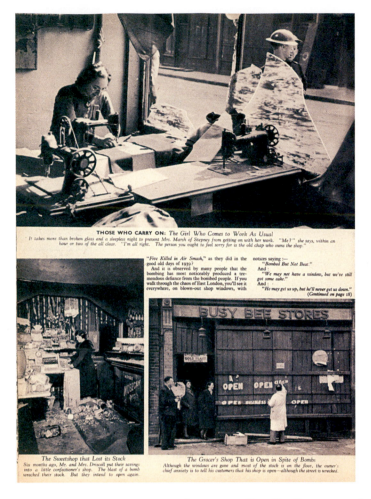

THOSE WHO CARRY ON: *The Girl Who Comes to Work As Usual*
It takes more than broken glass and a sleepless night to prevent Mrs. Marsh of Stepney from getting on with her work. "Me?" she says, within an hour or two of the all clear. "I'm all right. The person you ought to feel sorry for is the old chap who owns the shop."

The Sweetshop that Lost its Stock
Six months ago, Mr. and Mrs. Driscoll put their savings into a little confectioner's shop. The blast of a bomb wrecked their stock. But they intend to open again.

The Grocer's Shop That is Open in Spite of Bombs
Although the windows are gone and most of the stock is on the floor, the owner's chief anxiety is to tell his customers that his shop is open—although the street is wrecked.

11.11 *Picture Post*, **1940.** The framing and captions of these images are deliberately unglamorous, so that the representation of reality appears candid. Every message is the same: The British citizen will persevere in the face of German bombings. To succeed in boosting morale, such imagery had to provoke sympathy without overwhelming the viewer with despair. The texts emphasize continuity, whereas the images show destruction. Familiar references such as the "sweetshop" or the "grocer's," ground the documentary images in rituals of everyday life. The editorial tone blends the social task of reporting with the political strategy of patriotism, turning the documentation of distress into an opportunity to build support for the war. This example demonstrates the ease with which the apparently objective "truth" of photographic documents is used in the service of persuasion.

The concept of a document as a neutral record of observed

Entertainment industries thrived on photographic imagery. Celebrity magazines and black-and-white glossies were the popular currency of the age. Cameras became more portable and film stock more varied. The graphic designer's repertoire was expanded by an industry whose product range appealed to amateur, professional, and technically specialized markets (Fig. **11.11**).

The social movements that brought documentary photography to the fore stemmed from some of the same progressive and reform sensibilities that gave rise to public information campaigns and shared with them a belief in the possibility of objective representation. However, some noteworthy exceptions were produced. *Let Us Now Praise Famous Men*, a collaboration between photographer Walker Evans and author James Agee, was an experimental work. First published in 1941, it gained acclaim for its compassionate and detailed portrayal of extreme poverty in the rural South of the United States. The book did not conform to strict journalistic practices. In place of cool objectivity, its poetic voice registered self-conscious reflection on the effect of the presence of the author and photographer in their subjects' lives and vice versa. But, in general, the

11.12 Kodak ad, 1944. Technological advances in the photographic industry produced a range of new products and services for designers. The dramatic use of color in this ad calls attention to the codes of the signal corps man. His vivid costume and accessories are essential to the messages he sends and receives. Kodak is promoting the perfect registration of halftone dots, suggesting that their methods of image reproduction are as accurate as those used by the Navy to relay information. Using military images was one strategy for combining private industry interests and public war efforts.

reality informed both the use and reception of photographs.

concept of a document as a neutral record of observed reality informed the use and reception of black-and-white photographs in the 1930s and 1940s. Publication designers knew how to play the graphic codes of such imagery to full effect. Although illustration remained a feature of literary publishing well into the 1950s, photography entirely replaced drawings for journalistic purposes because the camera seemed to escape the bias of an individual eye. The great paradox of photography was that, while fine art and high fashion photographers' success depended on their ability to cultivate a recognizable style of expression, the general perception of news photography was that it presented a direct and unaltered record of the truth. Yet photographers themselves often blurred disciplinary boundaries between fine art, commercial, editorial, and personal work (Fig. **11.12**).

Wartime propaganda As World War II broke out in Europe, posters were used to mobilize sentiment and action on all sides of the political conflict. Government agencies and programs in every country resorted to graphic strategies to drum up war support. This was true even in England, where conscription had replaced recruitment among the male population.

11.13a *Jenny on the Job* poster, **1943.** Creating positive images for defense work required a new iconography for women in industrial circumstances. Physical mobility, balance, strength, and capability were valued over grace, daintiness, or cosmetic appeal. But to permit the transmission of these values, women's "other" selves as "real women" were invoked as a constant counter-theme. High heels and dresses were put aside momentarily, while women played their part without losing their "essential" femininity. Getting women back into domestic environments after the war caused conflicts that were uneasily contained by a renewed iconography of feminine styles.

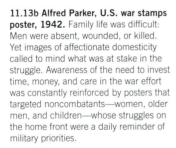

11.13b Alfred Parker, U.S. war stamps poster, 1942. Family life was difficult: Men were absent, wounded, or killed. Yet images of affectionate domesticity called to mind what was at stake in the struggle. Awareness of the need to invest time, money, and care in the war effort was constantly reinforced by posters that targeted noncombatants—women, older men, and children—whose struggles on the home front were a daily reminder of military priorities.

Women were also aggressively encouraged to volunteer for military service and war work. The female defense industry worker was idealized in such tough but feminine images as those of Rosie the Riveter and Jenny on the Job. Visually striking designs warned citizens against the dangers of spreading sensitive information. Security issues were continually stressed, provoking patriotic responses by reinforcing distinctions between ally and enemy. Scarcity of food, rubber, gasoline, and metal made every choice to limit consumption into a patriotic act. Recycling efforts became a way for noncombatants of all ages to feel that they were contributing to the war effort. Rejection of an undermining black market was linked to good citizenship. The messages were unequivocal. The iconography through which enemies were depicted was deliberately reductive and powerful enough to leave indelible impressions. The disturbing effects of deeply racist stereotypes persisted long after World War II. Graphic approaches to propaganda were often pictorial, relying on familiar conventions of realistic illusion. But flat and bold imagery could just as forcefully function symbolically. Simple visuals accompanied by trenchant slogans were designed to communicate with immediacy and clarity. A sense of urgency was embodied in the designs themselves. By their directness they suggested that action was essential and could not be delayed (Figs. **11.13a–d**).

11.13c Jean Carlu, *Give 'Em Both Barrels* poster, 1941. Jean Carlu's repetitive alignment of a defense industry worker and a combat soldier makes a strong visual connection between the realms they represent. The "barrels" of a pneumatic drill or riveting device and an automatic weapon are barely distinguishable at first glance, although the lighter tones and background placement of the worker lend the silhouette of the soldier solidity and force by contrast. Their alignment implies that the efforts of all are aimed in the same direction, essential to the same goals.

11.13d Herbert Morton Stoops, *Careless Talk* poster, 1944. Security issues demanded constant attention, and warnings against inadvertent disclosure of troop movements were frequent. The graphic impact of this design derives from its central figure, hanging with the draped hands and crossed feet of a deposed Christ. The message of martyrdom is succinct in its caution against "careless talk."

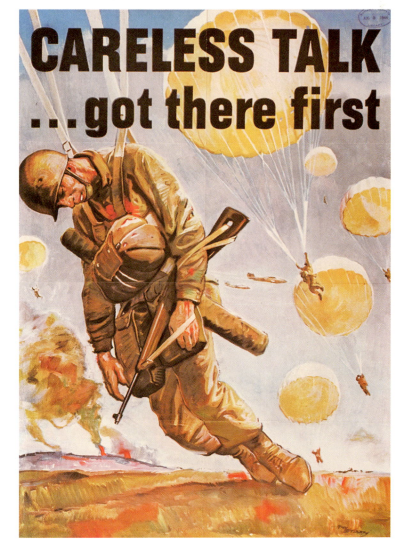

11.14a Insignia poster, Government Printing Office, 1943. The need to distinguish aircraft, insignia, and ships led to public information campaigns based on visual communication. The thoroughness of this chart's systematic organization, devised to make each item distinguishable by size and shape, provides a sense of control. Similar charts depicted enemy insignia and silhouettes of aircraft and ships. These bold graphics sensitized the public to differences between allied and enemy vehicles so that they could be recognized at a glance. But in real encounters, signs and shapes were often distorted by speed of movement or partial obscuring of sight lines.

11.14b Air raid warning system poster, Government Printing Office, 1943 *(below right).* This representation of warning sirens in graphic terms might seem obvious, but the use of color, waves, and breaks to show intermittency and continuity is a convention, not a given. The designer has attempted to make a forceful narrative link between hearing a signal and responding appropriately. No other options are to be entertained. Circumstances and limiting factors that could affect response (incapacitating illness, age, family situation, weather, etc.) are not considered. The poster addresses all citizens as if they were alike.

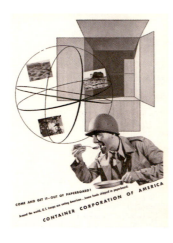

11.14c Herbert Matter, Container Corporation of America ad, 1943 *(above).* Private industry contributed to the war effort by placing defense and combat needs above other production demands. Suppliers to the armed forces turned a profit, but they promoted their engagement as cooperation. Using images of this virile, brave GI to sell its packaging materials enhanced the company's public image. The atomic model, symbolizing scientific progress, unites photographs, drawings, and type in a complicated montage. But the iconography of its basic elements clearly emphasizes private industry's aid to the war effort.

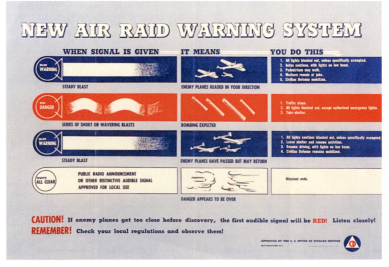

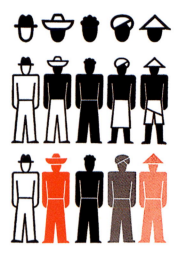

11.15a Otto Neurath and Gerd Arntz, Isotype, 1936. These figures, with symbols indicating "the five groups of men," are rendered by Gerd Arntz in Isotype. This fully developed system of icons was termed *pictorial statistics* by its inventor Otto Neurath. Other visual languages had been created for philosophical or practical purposes, but Neurath's system was firmly based in modern logic. He sought to design a set of symbols that could be easily read and remembered. His forms were legible, simple, and as unambiguous as possible. But they could not escape embodying cultural biases both in their individual shapes and in the system that governed them. ISOTYPE stood for the International System of Typographic Picture Education, and it inspired numerous symbol sets for presenting information in maps and signage. Neurath's desire for Isotype to function as a universal language, a visual Esperanto, was utopian. Such goals were poignant expressions of the period between the world wars, when Europeans sought to eliminate the possibility of future conflicts such as the one that had devastated an entire generation. Nonetheless, Neurath's iconographic principles were adapted for wartime use.

11.15b Rudolf Modley, information graphic, 1937. Rudolf Modley collaborated with Otto Neurath to develop pictographic language schemes. The idea of treating information as units, breaking complex human systems into modular elements, is essential to the function of this approach. The diagrammatic representation of an armored tank division uses flowchart graphics to map a strategy of attack. The use of pictographic symbols abstracts combat implications into an informational space, minimizing the portrayal of real conflict.

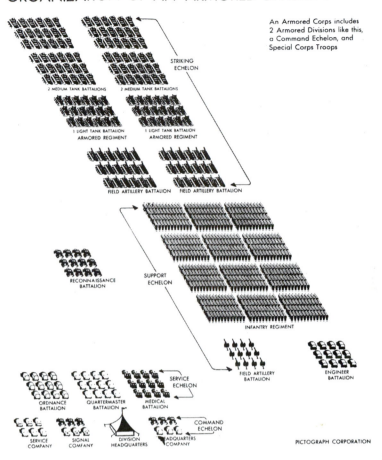

ORGANIZATION OF AN ARMORED DIVISION

Wartime information

During the war, official diagrams and charts delivered crucial information. The British Ministry of Information and the United States Office of War Information engaged designers of stature and skill, such as Herbert Matter and Leo Lionni, to develop signage and educational posters. The task of presenting dense amounts of information in an economical and well-organized form challenged such designers to adapt aesthetic means to highly pragmatic purposes: identifying insignia, warplanes, and bombs, and preparing for emergencies by familiarizing viewers with scenarios to be followed in response to circumstances or signals. Rapid visual recognition was critical to insignia design, whereas camouflage schemes sought to deceive and conceal (Figs. **11.14a–c**).

Meanwhile, another form of graphic information was on the rise, as wartime engineers raced to develop machines capable of processing massive amounts of data for such purposes as high-level cryptography. The work of code analysis laid one of the foundations for modern computing, and a continuing fascination with codes, ciphers, and symbols that could be recognized without reference to specific languages led to the development of pictographic systems. Utopian dreams of a universal (or at least international) language of pictograms underlay these projects (Figs. **11.15a** and **11.15b**).

11.16 Anton Stankowski, mechanical stresses, 1952. Stankowski's representations of visible and invisible processes crossed into the realm of abstraction to devise a graphic language that was specific enough to communicate meaningful relationships among largely nonfigurative elements. Context and captions shoulder some of the communication burden in these designs, but Stankowski's **meta-design** strategies broke new ground. His set of generalized elements was effective for narrating process rather than depicting things. His great skill lay in creating legible images to communicate activities that were not inherently visual.

The wartime intelligence community came under increasing pressure to glean military information from statistical computation. Weapons that could adjust their targets to precise measurements required unprecedented, real-time calculation capabilities. Radar, sonar, and other imaging technologies were used to gather data in defense and combat operations. These data had to be translated rapidly and accurately into graphical display. Designing such displays to communicate effectively was not easy. Electronic technology depended on monitors with limited color range and text capabilities. Although primitive, display design—and the translation of statistical data into visual forms—anticipated the challenges of **digital** interface and information design. New *information* technologies were on the horizon in the 1950s, linking military and industrial sectors in ways that would give rise to the field of **informatics**. Electronics were still in their infancy, but **cybernetics** was born during the war and advanced alongside automatic calculators. These developments were essential to ballistics and intelligence operations. Their *systems* vocabulary offered novel approaches to the graphic presentation of information. Terms and metaphors were borrowed and adapted to introduce concepts like *flow, metrics,* and *parameterization* to the graphic design field.

Commercial and technical uses of information design

In the late 1940s and early 1950s, the development of the first electronic computers changed the relationship between graphics and statistics. Grids, tabular forms, bar graphs, pie charts, and maps that served specialized

Graphic designers took on the intangible and lent it visual form.

interests were familiar ways of presenting statistical information. When computers were made commercially available in the postwar era, they were used to process huge amounts of data with unprecedented speed. Visible forms of presentation proved effective for making this information legible and comprehensible. Public and private sectors, from education to industry, from the media to the lab, sought graphic means to make information make visual sense. At the same time, they began to conceive of abstract constructs and phenomena as "information": Not only were concrete facts such as quantities, rates, or locations of people, goods, services, funds, and salaries turned into graphs, but also invisible processes (like heat transfer or money flows) were displayed as information. Graphic designers took on the intangible and lent it visible form (Fig. **11.16**).

Systems theory, cybernetics, and computer science influenced the graphic forms through which *data*—or statistical information—were expressed. Schematic graphics presented modular units of information within well-organized overarching structures. Carefully formulated rules became the basis of an information aesthetic. The legacy of Bauhaus functionality and efficient form combined with the emerging Swiss/International style

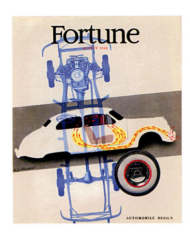

11.17a Hans J. Barschel, *Fortune* cover, 1948. Major clients for information design included journals like *Fortune* that catered to a corporate audience. In the years following WWII, manufacturing was expanding to include whole new sectors, such as the chemical and pharmaceutical industries. Specialists in administration or management needed to see large amounts of human data processed. But they often wanted individual employees and consumers clinically expunged from representation. The result was an aesthetic that emulated hygienic cleanliness and laboratory conditions and reinforced a tendency to abstract situations into processes devoid of human agency. This image presents an automobile that functions as pure drive shaft, tire, driver's seat, and auto body. The car's interlocking parts are portrayed in relation to each other without reference to a human user.

11.17b Will Burtin, *Scope* cover, 1941. Will Burtin's work for the pharmaceutical company publication *Scope* often combined technology and human figures. Bodies were compared with machines, brains with computers. Technological intervention at a micro scale placed test-tube babies and miracle cures in the same world as polymers. All had properties unheard of before synthetic processing. Technological production of new, multipurpose materials laid the foundation for links across diverse industries of manufacturing, mining, petroleum, chemistry, medicine, and food production. Visualizing scientific processes was critical in the context of research where the ability to conceptualize a problem was often directly related to the model according to which it could be represented. The impact on popular imagination was equally significant, and Burtin's capacity to design scientific findings for broad public consumption accounted for the wide circulation of his imagery.

to establish this foundation. The imagery of science and technology—laboratory equipment, mathematical formulas, electronic diagrams, and circuitry—became standard iconography. Models of atomic structure, cutaway views at micro and macro scale revealed the operation of an organism, a machine, or a production process as an abstract system. A deliberate exclusion of feeling, experience, and context became another hallmark of the information designer's universe (Figs. **11.17a** and **11.17b**).

Information analysis and design process
The influence of informational analysis affected the way graphic design saw itself. Instead of being an approach to the display of objects and communication of messages, it was conceived as a *system* in which all elements operated as integral parts of a network of flows and exchanges. Metaphors of traffic and distribution became templates on which design approaches were shaped. For example, the analysis of information into content types, according to classifications that sorted and structured images, text, and their relationship within a publication, added a level of schematization to graphic presentation. Meta-design—ways of thinking about the design process

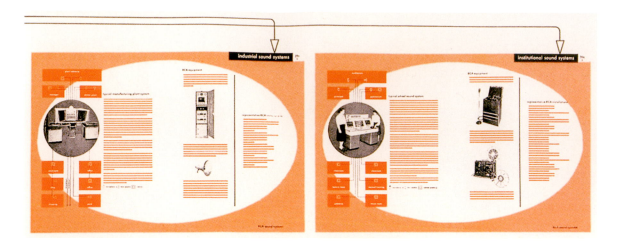

11.18 Ladislav Sutnar and Knud Lönberg-Holm, *Catalog Design Progress*, 1950. The Czech émigré Ladislav Sutnar made an outstanding contribution to twentieth-century graphic thought in the two publications that he designed with Lönberg-Holm in 1944 and 1950. In *Catalog Design* and *Catalog Design Progress,* he proposed methods for managing and presenting information that reflected systems approaches. These principles defined hierarchies for different categories of information. They created a conceptual grid that became a graphic guide for composition. Because he conceived of the catalog as a system, his work has been regarded as a guiding precedent to navigational questions raised by digital interface design.

and articulating its principles—extended earlier modern discussions of the language of form (Fig. **11.18**).

In popular imagination and in concrete application, *systems approaches* to the presentation of data became pervasive metaphors. Rather than thinking in traditional terms about static display, graphic designers began to develop a schematic visual language suitable to depicting dynamic elements and activities in flux. Imagery of paths, movements, and transitions came from the burgeoning industry of electronic circuitry. Data processing became a part of daily business, as digital computers began to be adopted by government agencies, corporations, and financial institutions. The idea of data gained credibility, in part, because of the graphic forms through which it was represented. Human knowledge, translated into a mathematical system of binary code (the basis of digital computing), had its own claim

Systems approaches became pervasive metaphors for design.

on popular imagination. The cultural authority of statistics was boosted by the visual rhetoric of information graphics. The mathematical basis of data informed both the principles (ways of conceiving) of graphic design and its iconography (specific images and motifs) in the 1950s. Graphic designers drew heavily on this highly rational approach to ordering the visual presentation of information. But graphic order has its own effects on content. Complex issues become simplified as heterogeneity and anomalies disappear. Modular elements suggest a working whole in which each unit fits in a predetermined place. A unit of information, a module of humanity, or a bit of data is a notion whose graphic form reinforces the expectation that a well-functioning system can accommodate such elements gracefully and successfully (Fig. **11.19**).

As computers became an object of popular imagination in the 1950s, graphic depictions of them and uses of their imagery ranged from literal to fantastical. Conceptions of the brain as a giant computer, and of humans as elaborate machines whose feedback loops could be used to improve their skill and capability, were intensified by graphics that appropriated electronic circuit analogies. But even as they provided metaphors that downplayed

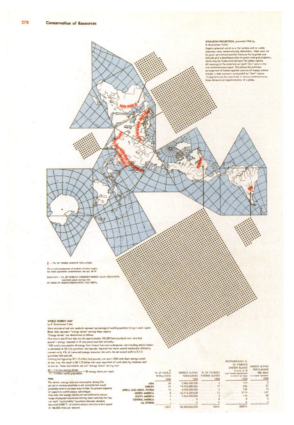

11.19 Herbert Bayer, *World Geo-Graphic Atlas*, 1953. Herbert Bayer's *World Geo-Graphic Atlas*, privately printed for the Container Corporation of America, was a remarkable realization of the new cartographic possibilities offered by pictographic logic, statistical analysis, and such novel techniques as R. Buckminster Fuller's **dymaxion** projection. Exquisitely designed to compress enormous amounts of information into graphically elegant pages, Bayer's work communicates with maximum efficiency. The visual allure of his design complements the intellectual organization of its layouts and sequences. Bringing the world into a unified graphic space may have been an expression of political optimism, but the comprehensiveness of this publication also suggests a postwar interest in a global view of economic opportunities. Real living conditions do not enter the logic of such graphics. Local contexts, political and social realities, and cultural meanings are not computable as quantitative information, so they are not represented.

human agency, computational capabilities posed new challenges to graphic designers. The scale and complexity of data processing they presented pushed designers to make tremendous leaps in the visualization of elaborate abstractions. Cartography benefited from this dynamic, as did imaging for scientific and economic modeling. Statistical information seemed to have an absolute claim to truth. Mathematical processing seemed less fallible than human decision-making. But this attitude concealed the error-prone aspects of programmed machinery. It also tended to minimize faculties such as compassion and qualitative judgment, as if these were less important than logic. Individual preference, emotional response, and cultural or gender differences had no place in these systematic processes—or in the graphic design of their operation—even when what was being depicted was fraught with such factors.

Conclusion Public interest posters, documentary photography, wartime propaganda, and information design appear to be different orders of design practice, each concerned with distinct problems in communication. But they share a common thread. All produce an argument and attempt to persuade by graphic means. All assume that certain kinds of information are self-evident and that graphic design is merely a means for presenting such information as clearly as possible. But the design methods used by these media and formats demonstrate that meaning is *made* in presentation. Ideas about what constitutes information are as much effects of presentation

as they are neutral foundations. The overt rhetorical force of *public interest* messages lies in their assumption of the voice of state authority. They seek to achieve results through social engineering, urging individuals' actions and attitudes to conform to assumed norms. Documentary photography, by claiming to be a direct record of objective observation, aligns itself with the practices of scientific method. But the coercive thrust of social reform is equally present in public interest campaigns and documentary impulses. Both use images to establish the terms of the status quo, to suggest a range of normalcy, and to position individuals within a social structure whose rules of decorum are inscribed in depictions of behavior and appearance. Wartime propaganda makes graphic arguments, and its images contain representations of identity and conduct that are more than incidental. The idea of the heroic, patriotic, loyal, thrifty, hard-working, noble, or treacherous individual is established through visual codes that quickly give rise to stereotypes. Through the rhetoric of presentation, graphic designs promote specific values (Fig. **11.20**).

The shift from overt propaganda to the subtler devices of information design marked an important turning point in twentieth-century culture. The rhetoric of grids, tables, bar graphs, maps, pie charts, and other highly formalized presentations carried an assured authority that seemed to defy challenge. How can anyone argue with facts? Part of the persuasive power of information graphics resides in their ability to make their message appear to be self-evident—as if the function of the design were merely to show something that already existed. But information design is based in a series of transformations. Information is often an abstraction by quantitative methods. Processing information into visual, graphic form re-embodies data, structuring relations and values according to a visual logic. Complex processes and situations have to be analyzed and classified before they can be incorporated in a single design. The formal logic of computational methods is translated and applied to this task, entering graphic practice in the form of metaphors and icons, but also as design principles. Yet subjective viewpoints, historical perspective,

11.22 George Giusti, Davison Chemical Corporation ad, 1944. "Progress through Chemistry" combines the diagrammatic language of information graphics with an iconography of recognizable objects. The beaker shape and the man in the white coat are the defining visual forms; the others—map, liquid, lump of raw material—are linked by a dynamic arc of energy flow. Progress, invisible in its actuality, has achieved a recognizable graphic form in a set of codes and icons. The universe of hygienic production has made its imprint on the world. Applied science was touted as the unquestioned way to a better future. The critique of progress and realization of the costs of scientific experimentation still lay in the future, even though the explosion of the atom bomb—the most advanced human capability to date—had sobered some scientists. From an industry standpoint, however, the surge of innovative technology fueled by the war and driven by its needs could now be turned to peacetime applications and profits.

and cultural biases are always part of information design, even if they go unacknowledged. The history of information design is also a history of its rhetorical uses of visual form (Fig. **11.21**).

Systematic approaches characterized another cultural change at mid-century: the extension of corporate identities into multinational organizations. Considerable overlap exists between rational approaches to information design and systematic **identity** campaigns in the corporate and public sectors. The rhetorical force of graphic design became increasingly invisible, as the logotypes and smoothly integrated style of expanding conglomerates created an ever more seamless and homogenized image under which contradictions and complexities seemed to disappear. The Depression and war had defined a role for design in the service of states. In the context of reconstruction, state-sponsored design continued to coordinate social and stylistic programs through information campaigns and industrial initiatives in Japan, Europe, and the United States. Designers' experience as participants in these novel syntheses of engineering and communication would serve them in their dealings with the new corporate and technical configurations of the postwar era (Fig. **11.22**).

Public Interest Campaigns and Information Design 1930s–1950s

1932 Reichstag election in Germany brings Nazis to power

Japanese occupy Shanghai

Stalin disbands Constructivist movement, deeming it subversive

1933 Hitler elected German chancellor

Josef Goebbels appointed Reich minister for propaganda and popular enlightenment

Henry Beck redesigns London Underground map

1934 Leni Riefenstahl directs *Triumph of the Will*

1936 John Heartfield produces anti-Nazi issues of *AIZ*

Rutherford Photo-lettering Machine, commercially viable phototypesetting, introduced

Spanish Civil War begins

35,000 designs produced for WPA posters

1937 Picasso's *Guernica* exhibited at Paris International Exposition

Nazis organize exhibition of "degenerate art"

Institute for Propaganda Analysis founded in U.S.

1938 *Kristallnacht*, an attack on Jews and Jewish property in Germany and Austria

Bradbury Thompson begins designs for Westvaco *Inspirations*

1939 Germany invades Poland

End of Spanish Civil War

Charles Coiner designs Civilian Defense symbol system

Russia and Germany sign non-aggression pact

Britain and France go to war with Germany

1940 F. H. K. Henrion designs posters for Britain's Ministry of Information

Leon Trotsky assassinated in Mexico City

Winston Churchill becomes prime minister of Britain

1941 Pearl Harbor attacked by Japanese

U.S. Office of War Information begins commissioning posters to promote war effort

1942 Herbert Bayer designs *Road to Victory* exhibit at MoMA

Gyorgy Kepes designs *Paperboard Goes to War* book for CCA

Atomic reactions research by Enrico Fermi

Food rationing begins in U.S.

Scrap drives—of rubber, metal, paper, etc.—promoted in U.S.

Japanese-Americans interned

CCA publishes Egbert Jacobson's *Color Harmony Manual*

1943 Penicillin mass-produced

Herbert Bayer designs *Airways to Peace* exhibit at MoMA

Willem Sandberg works on his *Experimenta Typographica*

1944 *Graphis* magazine launched

Smokey Bear, longest-running public service campaign in U.S., commissioned

Look at the World, designed by Richard Edes Harrison, prefigures photos of Earth taken from space

Allied troops invade Normandy

Mark I, first digital computer, created at Harvard

Gyorgy Kepes writes *Language of Vision*

1945 Germans surrender, war in Europe ends

Atomic bombs dropped by U.S. on Hiroshima and Nagasaki

Japan surrenders; WWII ends

United Nations founded

Vannevar Bush introduces concept of hypertext

Nuremberg war crimes trials begin

Tupperware developed amid increasing consumer plastic production

1946 Self-sticking bumper stickers developed by Forest P. Gill

Pacifica Radio founded for a "pacific world in our time"

HUAC (House Un-American Activities Committee) becomes permanent

Winston Churchill uses the term *iron curtain* in a speech

Dr. Spock's *The Common Sense Book of Baby and Child Care* published

1947 Polaroid camera developed by Edwin Land

Transistor invented by William Shockley, John Bardeen, and Walter Brattain at Bell Labs

Stalin refuses Marshall Plan; Cold War begins

Partition of India and Pakistan, independence from Britain

Levittown founded

Holography invented

Dead Sea Scrolls found

Laszlo Moholy-Nagy writes *Vision in Motion*

Intertype's Fotosetter photocomposition machine introduced

Silas Rhodes founds School of Visual Art in New York

Bing Crosby pioneers use of magnetic tape to pre-record his radio show

1948 Smith-Mundt Act forbids domestic use of foreign-aimed government propaganda

Apartheid established in South Africa

State of Israel proclaimed

First Arab-Israeli war begins

Mahatma Ghandi assassinated by Hindu radical

Frisbee and jukebox introduced

1949 Buckminster Fuller's first geodesic dome

NATO (North Atlantic Trade Organization) established

People's Republic of China founded

1950 Alvin Lustig designs signage system for Northland mall in Detroit, Michigan

North Korea invades South Korea

Alliance Graphique Internationale founded

Good Design Award established by Eameses, Saarinen, and Kaufmann

1951 Oil industry in Iran nationalized

Atomic generator of electricity first used in U.S.

Duck and Cover cartoons designed to prepare American children for atomic attack

1952 First pacemaker

Samuel Beckett's *Waiting for Godot* written

Marcel Bich successfully markets Bic ballpoint pens

1953 DNA structure revealed by Watson and Crick

U.S. Information Agency (USIA) established to orchestrate propaganda abroad

Sir Edmund Hillary and Tenzig Norgay climb Mount Everest

Death of Joseph Stalin

1954 First kidney transplant

Four American Graphic Designers exhibit at MoMA

"Under God" added to Pledge of Allegiance after petitions by Knights of Columbus

First book typeset using Photon's Lumitype photocomposition machine

1956 Design Center opens in London

1957 Eameses make *The Information Machine* for IBM pavilion at Brussels World's Fair

1958 European Common Market established by Treaty of Rome

1959 Guggenheim Museum, designed by Frank Lloyd Wright, opens in New York

1961 Eameses design *Mathematica* exhibit at California Museum of Science and Industry

Tools of the Trade

Acrylic paints

Process white

India ink

Paste

Ballpoint pens

Colored pencils

Electric pencil sharpener

China palette

Plastic nib holders

Paintbrushes with synthetic hair

Set square (triangle)

Cardboard

Varigraph lettering device

Typewriter with proportional spacing

Stock art books

Type copy-fitting chart

IBM

IBM

IBM

IBM

12. Corporate Identities and International Style 1950s–1970s

- The work of the graphic designer expanded from composing and stylizing messages to coordinating an "image" across products and communications. This coordination was facilitated by a logical approach and new production technologies.

- The aesthetics of corporate systematization drew on the "universal language" of visual communication developed at the Bauhaus, championed by the New Typography, and redefined by postwar proponents as an international style based on the values of clarity, rational organization, and functional efficiency.

- **Phototypesetting** and photographic manipulation in graphic design and print production supported the synthetic imagery of logotypes, house styles, and other integrated sign systems.

- Devising homogenous campaigns that communicated organizational coherence, graphic designers became insiders in a corporate culture characterized as **one-dimensional** because it integrated individuals into a single unified identity.

- With the arrival of television, graphic designers faced new challenges in the conception of corporate and brand identities that could function across a variety of media.

- The graphic design profession further advanced recognition of its own achievements; new organizations and publications set standards of excellence that established hierarchies among professionals.

12.1 Paul Rand, IBM logo, 1956–1972. Paul Rand's work embodied the aesthetic and ethos of an emerging international corporate culture. Rand distilled the principles of modernism into the very picture of formal efficiency and functionality. His designs for IBM exemplified an approach to identity programs that featured flawless logotypes that projected a unified image. The typeface he chose as a point of departure (City Medium) was designed by Georg Trump in 1930. Rand's use of outlines, striped fragmentation, and tonal manipulations transformed the dated modernity of Trump's face into letterforms that suggested information processing, automated office work, or the scan lines of a monitor. IBM, the logo suggests, is a smoothly functioning system in which all information and activity stream with seamless coordination. Rand's uncompromising attitude toward stylization was well suited to the demands of a company committed to uniformity across its many operations and offices. In the course of his career, Rand's own identity became a brand. His name became synonymous with a certain approach to graphic design.

The United States came out of World War II a more prosperous and conservative nation. Europe faced reconstruction and reform. In both contexts, graphic design played a critical role in shaping societal norms and representing new political and economic orders. Adapting their professional practices and drawing on stylistic innovations from earlier in the century, graphic designers aligned themselves with an emerging corporate culture. Modern approaches to graphic design were distilled into a rationalist, **functionalist** method. What came to be known as the **International Typographic Style** developed in Switzerland out of the legacy of Constructivism, De Stijl, and other once-experimental movements. The last gasp of modern utopianism was channeled into the neutral-seeming surfaces of a **universal style** system that served private interests with seamless efficiency. Global capitalism was on the rise in the decades following WWII. National boundaries no longer contained productive and commercial development. Money and goods flowed through interconnected systems of production, distribution, and consumption. The older model of privately held companies that concentrated on a particular product or service gave way to board-run corporations with greatly diversified assets. These complex, multinational corporations spurred the development of visual **identity** programs that went far beyond branding products and

12.2 James K. Fogleman, CIBA packaging, 1956–1960. One of the first corporations to create a uniform style was CIBA (Company for Chemical Industry Basel). Graphic design director James K. Fogleman pioneered a model that defined identity through color, typeface, and a few basic visual elements, such as the solid rectangular background from which the company's initials are dropped out. CIBA's products clearly belong to a single line and stem from the same seriousness of purpose. Authority and reliability are expressed by the packaging's consistency. Graphic design disappears into functionalism here, as it is supposed to do. The packaging makes it seem as though these products simply existed, as though their contents were as straightforward as their graphic identity.

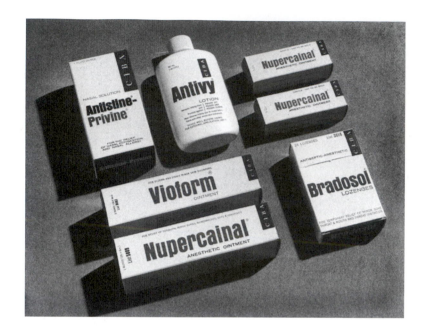

services. They became a means of making complex organizations seem like a single entity. Not incidentally, the **logotypes** and other identifying features of these campaigns did not rely on any particular language but drew on the **universal language** of graphic design meant to be legible throughout an international network of communications. Uniformity (conformity) and abstraction were the hallmarks of corporate style. Not all graphic designers were absorbed into this programmatic approach, but it defined the prevailing **ethos** and aesthetic of the postwar decades in both the private and the public sectors (Fig. **12.1**).

Beyond branding products, identity systems became a means

Image and identity systems In the 1950s, the field of graphic design entered a new stage when it was called upon to respond to a change in the character, not just the scale, of businesses. As companies became corporations, graphic designers were hired to provide identifiable images for complex entities comprised of multiple divisions and activities. Vertical integration (the incorporation of all facets of an industrial process from raw materials to final product marketing, distribution, and service) meant that many corporations had employees and offices worldwide. Horizontal integration (ownership of several subsidiaries that sell similar products to different markets) required that corporations achieve brand recognition across wider ranges of products and contexts. International corporations struggled to coordinate their practices and customs throughout diverse cultures and locations. Defining and holding market share required careful construction and management of corporate identity (Fig. **12.2**).

The unified image afforded by a distinctive logo and corporate identity system might well conceal a host of inequities or abuses, even as it functioned with clear, rational effectiveness in strategic communications. A consistent style conferred authority and reliability. But the apparent unity

Corporate Identities and International Style

12.3 Lester Beall, International Paper, 1960. Lester Beall's identity program for International Paper preserves the source image of a tree, abstracting its form to be read simultaneously as an *I* and a *P*. The surrounding circle encloses the letters in a stable overall design that is enlivened by the diagonal thrust of the tree shape. International Paper had become one of the largest paper companies in the world by 1960, and its logo had to be recognizable in a variety of media, including labels, cartons, trucks, and other internationally distributed materials. The robust simplicity of Beall's design made it adaptable for many scales, surfaces, and circumstances.

provided by a single logotype also hid the diversity of practices and people involved in the production of goods and services. A company like CIBA had a wide variety of geographically dispersed chemical plants, factories, and mining concerns. Chase Manhattan Bank had many branches and subdivisions with holdings in real estate, currency markets, and other financial enterprises. The image of a single entity concealed this complexity, as well as the risks to investors and workers, or costs in natural resources that might be involved. Meanwhile, the movement of large amounts of

of making complex organizations seem like a single entity.

capital into a global economy began to undermine some of the traditional powers of national governments. The impact of this shift on fiscal and environmental regulations, safety, quality standards, and a host of other social responsibilities is still being felt and evaluated today (Fig. **12.3**).

A generation earlier, graphic designers' roles had been limited to layout, composition, and style choices for print design. Now their work involved large-scale, coordinated communication campaigns that not only maintained the identity of a corporation but also added value to its products through symbolic investments in this identity. Slogans, catchphrases, logotypes, and other compact messages made the corporation seem like an individual entity with a voice and personality. Highly professional firms such as Chermayeff & Geismar and Unimark established their own brand identities while purveying them to others. The visual landscape was transformed, as corporate identity systems for Alcoa, Ford, J.C. Penney, the National Park Service, Memorex, Westinghouse, UPS, Xerox, Steelcase, Panasonic, British Petroleum, Chase Manhattan, the International Paper Company, and other giants accustomed the public to a coded language of sovereign logos, signature typography, and proprietary color schemes. The

12.4 Chermayeff & Geismar, Chase Manhattan, 1960. The Chase Manhattan symbol, designed by the firm Chermayeff & Geismar, has no obvious meaning. It may have been based on the Chinese coins collected by the Rockefeller family, but this reference is lost in the logo's abstraction. The symbol is made up of shapes whose systematic repetition forges an association of solidity. The interlocked form is heavy, bold, and confident. But the symbol communicates "logo-ness" rather than any specific characteristics of the bank or its services. The vogue for logos was at its peak in the 1960s and early 1970s, and corporations were under pressure to have striking symbols on which to hang their public image. The use of such a symbol by a bank provided the same reassuring uniformity that stamped franchises in the rapidly growing fast-food industry. Brands and logos provided a quick visual cue to customers who responded to familiar and reliable products in an increasingly dense commercial landscape.

corporate report, an annual description of financial achievements sent to shareholders, became a major opportunity to showcase graphic design. Good visual communication constructed an image of smooth operations that could gloss over uncertainties in business activity or irregularities in accounting practices. The graphic designer's art sometimes raised ethical questions of accountability (Fig. **12.4**).

Ultimately, "universal" signs succeed by becoming familiar.

12.5a Unimark, signage system, 1967–1970. In the 1960s, Bob Noorda and Massimo Vignelli of Unimark International designed public signage systems. The Unimark approach promoted recognizability and legibility and produced an overall image of order. Unimark developed programs for New York and other urban transit systems, airports, and public environments. Graphic uniformity carried over from station to station, providing passengers with an identifiable visual code made up of numbers, arrows, consistent colors, and very few words. The system relied on recognition as much as reading. What was to be "read" in its distilled forms was functionality throughout the transit network.

In addition to private corporations, public entities such as railways and postal systems assumed visual identities. The role of the graphic designer was to convey the essence of an organization's identity. In-house personnel who handled communications both within and outside the company maintained style conformity. This conformity often governed the dress and decorum of individual employees, as well as the consistency of product and image design. Keeping all elements of a corporation's graphic identity unified was a challenge, especially when companies had multiple, scattered offices, each with its own design staff and production capabilities. Graphic designers developed stylistic guidelines for large corporations. These had to be specific enough to control consistency while allowing staff the necessary flexibility to work in various contexts. Requirements for layout, images, typefaces, text settings, and even punctuation were often specified down to the last detail. Printed manuals disseminated these specifications in an age before electronic communications (Figs. **12.5a** and **12.5b**).

Graphic identity extended from letterheads and logos to packaging, trucks and shipping containers, point-of-purchase displays, and architectural signage. Immediate recognition relied on clear and distinctive

12.5b Massimo Vignelli, National Park System, 1977. Emphasis on systematicity not only created new visual vocabularies but also shifted approaches to the designer's task. A systems approach established general principles, separate from specific uses. These principles could be applied across a range of needs within an organization. Massimo Vignelli's designs for the National Park Service proposed a "unigrid" that could be used in any number of graphic situations. As a set of instructions and specifications, it functioned as a meta-design. Vignelli's method is directly related to that of the 1950s Swiss style *neue grafik*. His approach depends on standardized formats, overlapping grids, consistent alignments, and predetermined sizes of two specified typefaces.

12.6 Roger Cook and Don Shanosky, signage system, 1974. In the early 1970s, the AIGA (American Institute of Graphic Arts), in collaboration with the Department of Transportation, assembled a committee to make recommendations for a public signage system. The firm of Cook and Shanosky Associates was charged with the design of pictographic signs to locate amenities and services, such as food, drink, baggage and no smoking areas, first aid, telephones, taxis, bus services, and so on. The challenge of communicating to an international audience through a set of visual symbols was not new. Indeed, the committee's recommendations to Cook and Shanosky were based on an initial survey of existing systems. The resulting "symbol signs" had a built-in familiarity that made unknown environments less threatening. However, these signs often incorporated biases and assumptions. The sign for women shows a figure in a skirt ending at the knees, for instance, an image that is problematic for different reasons in different cultural contexts.

symbols rather than substantive texts or images. Symbol systems had already attracted considerable military attention. As international patterns of trade and shipping intensified, so did the search for visual signs that would read across cultures. Ultimately, these "universal" signs succeed by becoming familiar conventions, rather than by any inherent, immediate legibility (Fig. **12.6**).

International style The spread of the International Typographic Style paralleled the growth of corporate culture. The Swiss style sprang from its own aesthetic sources, but its clean, neutral forms were so well suited to the image needs of the new business patterns that the entire movement could have been invented to serve those interests. Visually, the International style was characterized by underlying grid structures, asymmetrical layouts, and sans serif type. It also favored straightforward, "objective" photography, geometric forms, and an almost total absence of decoration or illustration. Journals, corporate communications, and serial advertisements were designed as stylistic wholes that affirmed consistency as much as clarity. Clean, unfussy directness was the primary aim of this approach. But the

12.7 Josef Müller-Brockmann, *Schützt das Kind! (Mind the Child!)*, Swiss Automobile Club, 1955. Dramatic use of photography and simple typographic treatment of a text reduced to its essentials make this a classic of Swiss graphic design. But claims that its design is entirely rational are contradicted by its emotional impact. The scale distortion between wheel and child, the lines of motion coming from the brakes, and even the elevation of the exclamation point to the status of a separate word by the introduction of a space after "Kind" are all expressive elements. The poster is emotionally manipulative, and no grid or logical structure organizes its composition. Instead, the design makes use of a reduced and carefully managed set of elements for maximum effect.

Swiss style claimed a neutral basis for rational communication.

pretense of a neutral, universal basis for rational communication also served to erase ethnic, cultural, economic, and political differences. By definition applicable to anything, the International style's systematic design dominated the field in the 1950s and 1960s. Critics found the method formulaic: The insistence on sans serif type and geometric compositions marked these graphics with a predictable aesthetic. But the programmatic approach of the International style has endured and proved useful in many contexts, including that of Web-based information design (Fig. **12.7**).

In their teaching and their practice, key graphic designers such as Max Bill, Josef Müller-Brockmann, Emil Ruder, and Armin Hofmann stressed a highly logical, grid-based system of layout. Proportion and harmony had been elements of classical book design since the Renaissance. But the new method took its cue from concepts of efficiency and rational organization and approached all formats, including posters and promotional materials, as forms of information design. The prevailing practice often made use of the impassive presence of underlying structures to provide a reassuring visual effect of control and functionality. Every element seemed to have a place within a hierarchical and categorical system that gave it stability and

12.8 Josef Müller-Brockmann, *Konzerte Tonhalle-Gesellschaft* poster, 1969.
The abstract structure that organizes this poster alludes to the temporal patterns of a musical performance. Color separates the text from the background and establishes a hierarchy of information. The composition immediately locates separate events and their programs, musicians and their instruments, featured artists and works—all within an orderly stair-stepped arrangement. The dynamism of the descending vertical and the back-and-forth movement across the page is stabilized by the regularity of the text's spacing and leading. The poster could serve to advertise any festival, series, or set of coordinated events. The nonspecificity of its design is fundamental to its neutral tone.

12.9 Carlo Vivarelli, *Neue Grafik*, 1959.
Carlo Vivarelli's 1959 cover for *Neue Grafik* embodies the principles of Swiss style through its ordered grid and tightly set sans serif type (here, as often elsewhere, Akzidenz Grotesk). The use of three languages in graphic design publications emphasized the internationalism of their audience and suggested that translation was a simple, almost mechanical matter. The austerity of Vivarelli's design relies on the shapes generated by lines of text while maximizing the interaction between negative space and the definition offered by baselines, margins, and aligned edges. The layout seems to celebrate logical principles. The implication that an architectonic form underlies the page provides absolute authority and balance—as if no individual preference or emotion could disturb its order. Müller-Brockmann, Richard Lohse, and Hans Neuburg were members of the Zurich-based *Neue Grafik* editorial team who approached the magazine as a means of demonstrating the tenets they espoused.

meaning. But the emotional impact that could be achieved by minimal-seeming means was an equally successful use of the International style (Fig. **12.8**).

The International Typographic Style traced its roots to the Bauhaus and De Stijl and drew selectively on principles of the ***neue typographie*** advocated before the war by Jan Tschichold. One of the most powerful forces for dissemination of the approach came through its institutionalization in design schools. A foundation program in design, established by Ernst Keller in the 1910s at the School of Applied Arts (*Kunstgewerbeschule*) in Zurich, pioneered the spirit of professionalism that later characterized Swiss style. This approach found support among former Bauhaus students and faculty such as Max Bill, who developed an influential curriculum at the Institute of Design in Ulm, Germany, in the 1950s. Official links between the graduate program in design at Yale and that of the School of Applied Arts (*Kunstgewerbeschule*) in Basel facilitated faculty and student exchanges and contributed to the internationalization of the Swiss approach (Fig. **12.9**).

Educational programs institutionalized graphic design doctrines to an unprecedented degree in the 1960s. But another major force for the dissemination of the International style in the 1950s and early 1960s came in the form of publications that embodied the aesthetic they promoted. The Zurich-based publication, *Neue Grafik*, was a primary organ for

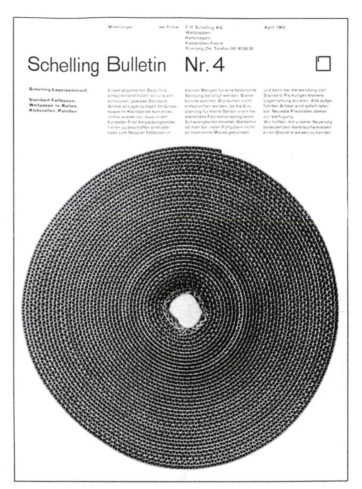

Schelling Bulletin Nr. 4

12.10 Siegfried Odermatt, Schelling Bulletin, 1963. Odermatt's design for a packaging firm's catalog is a quintessential embodiment of Swiss principles: clean, gridded, rational, and without any apparent excess. These principles were very teachable because they could be organized into a set of operations and procedures. The decision-making process by which titles, content lists, publication information, and other elements became distinguished echoed the automated tasks of data sorting and processing that were increasingly restructuring corporate life. Design of this kind both emulated and enabled such automated processes. The extent to which the grid was a generalizable and repurposable structure becomes evident when this design is compared with that of *Neue Grafik* (Fig. 12.9). Publications played an enormous role in internationalizing graphic design styles in the 1950s.

12.11 Masaru Katsumi, symbol designs for the Tokyo Olympics, 1964. An enthusiast of European design, Masaru Katsumi laid the groundwork for a modern graphic design profession in Japan in the 1950s. He prompted the establishment of graphic design schools and founded the Society for the Science of Design. His translation of Herbert Read's *Art and Industry* in 1954 brought the concerns of modern graphics to a Japanese public, as did the journal *Graphic Design,* which he launched and edited. In 1964, he was named design director of the Tokyo Olympics and oversaw the creation of its symbol system. This system would, in turn, serve as the basis for Otl Aicher's pictographic program used at the 1972 Munich Games.

demonstrating and proselytizing. Books like Josef Müller-Brockmann's *Grid Systems in Graphic Design* and Emil Ruder's *Typography* were widely translated (Fig. **12.10**).

Through this international network of creative and critical exchange, the principles of a grid-based, rational approach became common practice. European graphic designers worked for American companies and vice versa. The flow of graphic ideas followed patterns of trade. Advocates for Swiss design included the American, Rudolph de Harak, as well as those, like Siegfried Odermatt and Rosmarie Tissi, who never left Switzerland but whose work circulated influentially. Along with many others, they practiced and taught in the spirit of Swiss graphics or developed their own variants. In Japan, *Graphic Design*, a magazine established by Masaru Katsumi in 1959, promoted the International Typographic Style. In turn, Japanese graphic design caught the editorial eye of Western magazines like *Graphis*. Yet, although the term *international* suggested a global nexus, in fact, the influence of internationalism mainly moved in one direction from Europe and North America to countries elsewhere. And while indigenous motifs and visual sensibilities could be incorporated within the International style, alternative principles of composition were overwhelmed by a uniformity that left little room for cultural differences in approach (Fig. **12.11**).

12.12a Alvin Lustig, *A Season in Hell*, 1945. Alvin Lustig's cover design for the nineteenth-century French Symbolist poet Arthur Rimbaud's *A Season in Hell* makes a stylish, lively pattern of biomorphic and hand-lettered forms. Lustig's design communicates the relevance of Rimbaud's revolutionary and imaginative work to a new generation. Lustig's sense of style was light, nimble, and uniquely animated. His design interests—like those of the famous California husband-and-wife team, Charles and Ray Eames—crossed into many media and disciplines. Whether for exhibitions, advertisements, books, fabrics, or furniture, his designs were grounded in a profound understanding of abstract form. Perhaps more than any of his contemporaries, Lustig had an eye for the applicability of lessons learned from the cutting edge of visual arts. His compositions play on the work of modern painters such as Piet Mondrian, Bradley Walker Tomlin, Stuart Davis, and Hans Arp, all of whom were considered definitive artists in the 1950s. The levity and wit of Lustig's approach distinguished him from many of his peers.

Style, systems, and graphic design concepts

Graphic designers of the 1950s and 1960s had an unprecedented variety of source materials and production methods to draw on, and, although the International style predominated, particularly in civic and corporate environments, it did not entirely foreclose other aesthetic possibilities. Some graphic designers did not fit the universal model and developed their own equally contemporary styles. A tremendous sensitivity to the visual character of old illustrations, wood type, script and decorative faces, and photographically manipulated letterforms is displayed by some of their work. Biomorphic forms distilled from surrealism and the bold, broad brushwork of abstract painting became chic motifs in the graphic repertoire. In the United States, Lester Beall, Bradbury Thompson, Alvin Lustig, and others developed individual styles that absorbed European approaches while preserving an American idiom and including vernacular imagery. Imaginative eclecticism and creative use of technology often went together in their projects (Figs. **12.12a** and **12.12b**).

12.12b Charles and Ray Eames in their studio, 1974. The well-organized but very full bulletin board in this photograph by Arnold Newman gives an idea of the creative energy and rational organization of Charles and Ray Eames' approach to design. The husband-and-wife team became known in the 1950s and 1960s for their innovative practice in many areas of industrial, exhibition, and graphic design. They drew on the richness of pattern and structure in the natural and cultural world for their inspiration. The message of their work is that design can be observed in a wide variety of forms that provide an inexhaustible source of inspiration. The Eameses' furnishing designs set style trends. They incorporated geometric motifs and abstract organic shapes into objects for daily use and brought ideas about modern design to a broad public. The notion that "design" was equivalent to a set of systematic principles relating form, function, materials, and production methods came out of earlier twentieth-century dialogues between art and industry. But through the prolific efforts of the Eames Office, this perspective became accessible and popular. The Eameses' legacy remains visible in graphics and objects of their design that are still produced and in designs inspired by their energetic example.

12.13 Bradbury Thompson, Westvaco, 1958. The multitalented designer Bradbury Thompson worked for Westvaco (West Virginia Pulp and Paper Company) for more than twenty years, from the late 1930s until the early 1960s. During that period he produced designs that exploded the graphic vocabulary of his times. Because he worked under severe budget constraints, he made inventive use of existing elements in his designs. He used letterpress display type and other found materials with a keen sense of the specific aesthetic properties of different print technologies. In this instance, he exploited the nature of **offset** printing, exposing the magenta, yellow, cyan, and black plates used in the **four-color process**. His graphic designs transposed images from earlier eras, such as printers' cuts, decorative elements, and novelty type into contemporary compositions. His recycling of these vernacular elements kept them circulating in an era when abstraction, rather than figurative references, predominated. Thompson's humanism lay in a revelation that all visual forms carry history. His sensibility stood out in a period when many graphic designers seemed to embrace the ahistorical universalism claimed for abstract forms.

In the corporate environment, programmatic approaches to graphic design subsumed most individual voices. Indeed, conversion of the very notion of *identity* from a subjective experience to a floating form of signage that presented a nonhuman entity—the corporation—was the goal in this context. Nonetheless, a few corporate visionaries realized that they could gain prestige in the marketplace by commissioning artistic and humanistic graphic campaigns rather than promoting goods or services. The resulting elevation of a company's status in public perception, the investment in its sign value, was sometimes worth the separation of its identity from specific products (Fig. **12.13**).

12.14 Herbert Matter, Knoll Associates ad, 1956. Herbert Matter's chic campaigns for Knoll Associates in the mid-1950s equated the furniture company's signature *K* with the ultimate in style awareness. The sense of play in these ads attributes a fashionable smartness to the furnishings themselves. Matter was working as something of a conceptual artist in sequences such as these successive pages. By creating a series of communication events rather than composing a single design, Matter was playing with the temporality of the print environment and trusting to the sophistication of his readers. Eero Saarinen's space-age, streamlined designs for Knoll furnishings, produced by adventurous new industrial processes, also became icons of 1950s style. These ads and products anticipate the cleverness of 1960s campaigns.

12.15 Armin Hofmann, Herman Miller Collection ad, 1962. Armin Hofmann's poster for Herman Miller furniture emphasizes the coordination of the furniture-maker's designs and contrasts tellingly with Matter's approach to Knoll (Fig. 12.14). An appearance of unity is created by fitting the profiles of various mold-made forms into a series. These abstract shapes combine geometry and **biomorphism**, while the use of red, white, and black recalls the Constructivist aesthetic that helped define modernism. The act of abstraction removes the furniture from any context. These are industrial products, made with repeated templates and modular processes. Formally echoing the logo above them, the pieces pictured function as expressions of a brand identity and a unified system, rather than as objects for human use. In 1965, Hofmann published a manual outlining the principles of his approach to graphic design.

Systematic branding went beyond graphics. Design as a mode of distinctive form-giving took hold in the style-driven world of consumer goods as well. Graphic designers played a key role in the public image of these products, creating campaigns that embodied an aesthetic of mass style production. Consumption had always been fueled by trends and fashions, but, in the 1950s, the term *design* came to signify a high-end, sophisticated sensibility in furniture, housewares, office equipment, and other product lines. The notion that style could be branded and that consistency was not just a matter of quality control but also of identity was not new, but the scale of stylized production and consumption increased dramatically. Mass-produced objects were promoted as much on the grounds that they embodied design concepts as for the quality of their materials or workmanship. Big ideas became as essential to industrial and graphic designers as any tool or skill (Figs. **12.14** and **12.15**).

Technology Systematic approaches to graphic style were supported by changes in the technological means at a designer's disposal. Photographic production methods became the standard platform for static and animated graphics in the 1960s and 1970s. Although many designers were trained to hand-letter type and make thumbnails and sketches with pencil or ink, the sleek surfaces and functional look of International style formalism depended on mechanical means of production. Handwork became a sign of eccentricity, unwelcome in the corporate world of conformity and efficiency. Marks of individualism vanished in the photographic production of type, images, and layouts. The notion of professionalism in graphic design was associated with a capacity to command technological means of production, rather than with skills at the drawing board (Fig. **12.16**).

American television boomed in the 1950s and 1960s. Attracting advertisers became a high-stakes enterprise, and networks vying for audience share needed a successfully branded identity as much as other corporate identities. Other new markets for graphic design opened in the film industry and in commercials involving animation. Graphics entered

Lemon.

This Volkswagen missed the boat.

The chrome strip on the glove compartment is blemished and must be replaced. Chances are you wouldn't have noticed it; Inspector Kurt Kroner did.

There are 3,389 men at our Wolfsburg factory with only one job: to inspect Volkswagens at each stage of production. (3000 Volkswagens are produced daily; there are more inspectors than cars.)

Every shock absorber is tested (spot checking won't do), every windshield is scanned. VWs have been rejected for surface scratches barely visible to the eye.

Final inspection is really something! VW inspectors run each car off the line onto the Funktionsprüfstand (car test stand), tote up 189 check points, gun ahead to the automatic brake stand, and say "no" to one VW out of fifty.

This preoccupation with detail means the VW lasts longer and requires less maintenance, by and large, than other cars. (It also means a used VW depreciates less than any other car.)

We pluck the lemons; you get the plums.

60

13. Pop and Protest 1960s–1970s

- Pop culture sparked a dynamic dialogue between the graphic language of commerce and those of counterculture and protest.

- Slick photography and self-conscious humor introduced elements of sophistication and complicity into the graphic design of mainstream advertising.

- Graphic designers began to develop signature styles and aspired to the celebrity status of rock musicians and other media stars.

- Counterculture designers used ever more readily available means of graphic production to create messages that registered effectively within the media landscape.

- While graphic designers participated in an increasingly mediated culture, critical approaches to the study of mass communication developed a new vocabulary for "understanding media."

- Pop designers produced images that circulated as signs in media systems, without necessarily bearing any connection to a reference base in lived reality.

13.1 Doyle Dane Bernbach, Volkswagen ad, 1960. Still famous, this series of ads for Volkswagen marked a major shift in graphic design. A prime example of the "big idea" approach at the heart of advertising's Creative Revolution, the campaign assumed that readers were hip enough to "get" its jokes and grasp the larger point. Seriousness was gone. Cleverness was in. Smart campaigns that appealed to the savvy consumer trumped older convictions about product information or brand loyalty. Flippant copy and polished, ironic photography set a new tone in the industry. Consumers wanted to identify themselves as in-the-know sophisticates, and the facetious image of the VW appealed. The product was sold by association with the "coolness" of ads that inverted the logic of earlier promotional strategies. These advertisements demonstrate how smoothly the establishment (in this case, a major manufacturer) could appropriate countercultural style for its own purposes.

Graphic design permeated American and European visual culture in the decades following World War II. The prolific presence of graphic images became a *given*. But in the 1960s, **pop** art and style introduced a new appreciation of graphic media. "Pop" drew heavily on mass-media productions shaped by commercial interests, advertising, and the entertainment industry. Film and television celebrities led the way, but artists, politicians, newscasters, business leaders, and athletes—indeed, people in every walk of life—grasped the importance of their "image." Mass-media logic became central to contemporary life. This mediated condition of existence was the subtext of pop culture. Self-consciousness about graphic design was one symptom of this emerging awareness of media. Graphic designers forged an idiom from and for the sign systems established in television, magazines, and slick advertisements. Comics, **op art**, media imagery, and **psychedelic** patterns burst into view along with long hair, short skirts, and a highly graphic in-your-face attitude. Pop design linked commercial graphic art with fast-paced, super-cool, and ultra-hot styles. Witty and playful, the pop impulse defined itself as free-spirited in calculated opposition to the straight corporate world with which it was contemporary. The antiauthoritarian, nonconformist stance of the **counterculture** was identified with rock and roll, fashion, drugs, sex, and radical politics by contrast to the button-down, pin-stripe values of the **establishment**. Revolutionary rhetoric connected youth culture to real and imagined political engagement. The entertainment industry harvested talent and recycled outsider individualism into marketing ploys. In design terms,

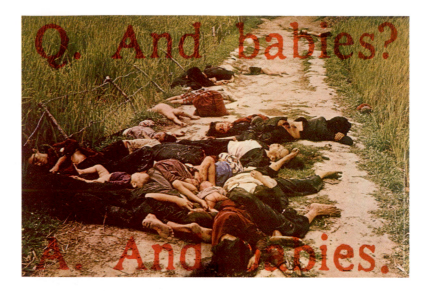

13.12 Ron Haeberle and Peter Brandt, *And Babies?* poster, 1970. Produced by the Art Workers' Coalition, this poster was one of the most controversial and effective of the antiwar movement. Sponsored by a group of artists whose own crises included disaffection with established art institutions (such as the Museum of Modern Art in New York), the poster used photographs of the infamous My Lai massacre in Vietnam. The shock of the image is not softened at all. The poster's close-up cropping, direct *Q* and *A* statement, and hard-edged reference to journalism via typewriting succeeded in cutting through layers of national denial. *And Babies?* generated considerable debate, but it succeeded in calling public attention to the events of My Lai.

silkscreened, photocopied, offset, and otherwise printed images. Designers, convinced of the power of their skills, saw opportunity and responsibility intertwined (Fig. **13.12**).

Use of the streets as a zone of public discourse peaked with enormous rallies and marches. Although guerilla artists would continue to use posters and stickers as strategic means of communication for decades to come, belief in the power of visible graphic art to sway public opinion and galvanize individuals to political action has perhaps never run as high as it did in the 1960s and early 1970s. The Civil Rights and Women's Liberation movements were struggles for self-determination in the symbolic as

Designers saw opportunity and responsibility intertwined.

13.13 Elena Serrano, *Day of the Heroic Guerilla*, Cuba, 1968. The Cuban Revolution of the 1950s—the outgrowth of a long struggle for national self-determination—produced its own graphic forms. After his murder in Bolivia in 1967, Argentine revolutionary Che Guevara became a martyr and a cult figure. His idealized features were made into a media icon that came to symbolize the spirit of revolution and armed struggle. Here, Che's outline transforms through a series of radiating steps to take the shape of South America, suggesting that the revolutionary spirit will expand.

well as the political realm. Shaping new images of blackness, feminist empowerment, and homosexuality had a powerful impact on popular culture and public imagination. But no movement used graphic imagery as effectively to advocate mass action as the antiwar movement (Fig. **13.13**).

In 1968, student strikers, joined by labor unions, brought major capitals to a standstill in France and other European countries. Calling for radical social transformation, these strikers managed to bring about changes in the educational system and, occasionally, engineered local social experiments (such as the **Provo** movement in Holland). Although the events of 1968 failed in their goal of a socialist revolution or anarchist overthrow of existing governments, they left their mark on a generation by providing a common frame of reference for political struggle. The media spectacle of strikes and protests was an important part of the cultural moment. For a brief period, it seemed possible that the tide of self-interested capitalism served by the legal systems of nation-states might actually turn. Posters expressed cultural upheaval with raw directness. The graphic design of revolutionary protest also left a legacy. The posters of that era have a savage poignancy that expresses both the optimism of their creators and,

13.14a Berkeley strike poster, 1970.
University campuses around the United States were the sites of organized protests against the Vietnam War. Student strikes in Berkeley in 1969, like those at other colleges, brought life as usual to a standstill. Students printed posters, staged sit-ins, conducted consciousness-raising sessions, and worked in coalition with community allies and in national organizations to bring the war to an end. Increased military aggression in Southeast Asia inflamed opposition as the decade ended, and antiwar efforts became increasingly visible in the streets. The rough quality of this design lends its message urgency, but crudeness was not the only strength that antiwar graphics wielded.

13.14b Grapus, "Public Debate" poster, 1972. Founded in 1970, the Paris-based Grapus group was an outgrowth of acquaintances and collaborations struck up in the revolutionary context of 1968. Drawing on the theoretical writings of Guy Debord and other members of the influential **Situationist International**, the student movement had found expression in a flood of posters and flyers. A community graphics studio, the Atelier Populaire, produced placards for strikes and protests. Grapus took its name from a contraction of the word *graphic* and the phrase *crapules staliniennes*—a term of derision applied by conservatives to left-wing intellectuals. These designers worked as a collective, eschewing professional hierarchy and signature styles. They had an eclectic whatever-does-the-job approach rather than a consistent method or look. In addition to design for progressive cultural organizations and political causes, they took on major public projects. Through their commitment to collective work—a living demonstration of their 1968 beliefs—they supported themselves as designers without compromising their convictions.

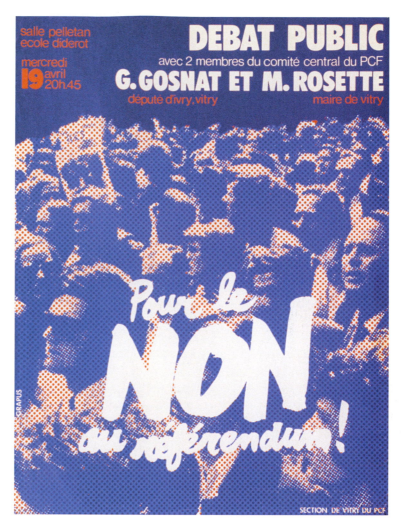

retrospectively, the defeat of an entire generation's youthful idealism (Figs. **13.4a** and **13.4b**).

Changes in the profession
Photocomposition of lettering moved from experimentation to full-blown production and adoption by the end of the 1960s. Type cast in hot lead became an outmoded technology. The capabilities of photographic typesetting seemed to have every advantage. Letters could be drawn using almost any graphic approach or technique. Outlined, fragmented, figurative, textured, and imaginative faces of all kinds could be readily transformed into photographic strips for composition. The set and fit of letters in photo-fonts could be manipulated. Overlapping letters, physically impossible in metal type, became one of the hallmarks of photocomposition, an indulgence that demonstrated the distinctive capabilities of the new technology. This shift in technology was reflected in the establishment of new photo-based "foundries," such as ITC (International Typeface Corporation), and the rise of existing ones. The firm known affectionately as PLINC (PhotoLettering Inc.) had been a leader in phototypesetting since it introduced phototype technology

13.15 Herb Lubalin, *U&lc*, 1973. In 1970, Herb Lubalin and Aaron Burns cofounded ITC, the International Typeface Corporation, to design and license typefaces. In 1973, they launched the publication *U&lc* to publicize ITC's wares. *U&lc* showcased individual designers and the company's typefaces, but it also promoted awareness of issues relevant to the profession. The journal featured spacing, scaling, and kerning capabilities afforded by phototype, as well as the challenges that the new technology posed. The first issue of *U&lc* addressed typeface piracy and other intellectual property concerns that were escalating because of the ease of copying that photographic methods made possible. The publication's exclusive use of ITC faces did not prevent its art direction from inspiring imitation or generating excitement about changes in the field.

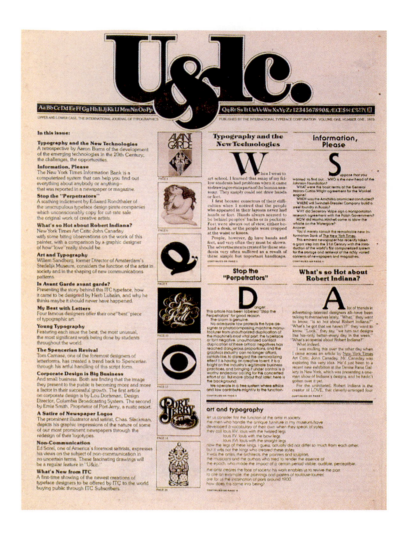

ABCDEFGHIJKLMNOPQRSTUVWXYZ
abcdefghijklmnopqrstuvwxyz

13.16 Hermann Zapf, Optima, 1958. One of the most significant twentieth-century type designers, Hermann Zapf drew on his training in traditional metal type design and his skill as a calligrapher to ground his conception of phototype faces and, later, digital fonts. Optima combines features of a serif and sans serif face. Its wide-ended strokes catch the eye and provide definition, while signaling a newly synthetic sensibility. Optima was extremely useful in phototypesetting because its robust characters could be adequately reproduced even when production conditions were not ideal. Its synthetic character made it typical of its era, when polymers and other industrially processed materials were being introduced in a wide range of products.

in 1936. Industry leaders in the 1960s, their prominence spanned a half century before they were eclipsed by digital media and disappeared from view (Fig. **13.15**).

Photographic composition required careful attention to the effects of light and projection. Letters designed without consideration for the swelling in counters or serifs lost definition, while underexposure could turn a delicate face into a spindly one. But these were temporary setbacks, and designers soon learned to compensate for the optical distortions of photo-rendering. The technical loosening allowed by photographic methods led to an outpouring of designs that echoed the enthusiasm of late nineteenth-century display-type designers freed by the pantograph. Photographic production of typography became the norm in the 1970s, and typographic piracy increased considerably because making negatives from display samples was far easier than copying type had been when metal punch cutting was involved (Figs. **13.16** and **13.17**).

The range of typographic designs that photographic production made possible was enormous. Graphic designers delighted in the available number of clever, figurative, and decorative display faces meant to be used sparingly for highly specialized purposes. The Letraset revolution offered individual designers independence from the high costs of phototypesetting. For one-off or camera-ready layouts, Letraset was a boon. The difficulties of managing letter spacing and alignment required care, and keeping the letters from cracking took skill, but, by the same token, Letraset letters could be scraped, distressed, placed in any arrangement, and treated with an unusual degree of compositional abandon.

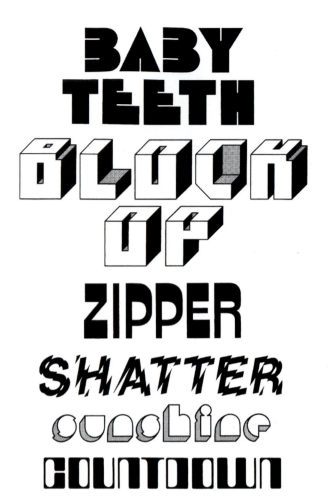

Photographic type production became the norm in the 1970s.

13.18a Herb Lubalin, *Mother and Child*, 1967, and 13.18b Herb Lubalin, *Ice Capades*, 1967. Herb Lubalin's penchant for turning type into icons is evident in these two designs in which words form images that mirror their meaning. Lubalin's cleverness is matched by his graphic skill. (Such attempts by lesser talents tend to be awkward.) The naturalness of these icons gives them an "of course" recognizability that also makes their message seem obvious rather than constructed. But this mother-and-child image conflates maternity with the biological condition of gestation. Motherhood can be understood in many other ways. The *Ice Capades* image quickly becomes a logotype, revealing a branding sensibility that is also fundamental to Lubalin's approach.

Dry transfer lettering (such as Letraset) further freed designers from the constraints of metal. **PMT** (photomechanical transfer) became a studio tool for designers by the late 1960s. It allowed highly flexible manipulation of images and texts and a broad range of scale and montage effects at an affordable price. The production methods of industrial photography—halftone screens, process colors, solarization and polarization, silkscreen, and offset printing—provided the elements of a rich graphic vocabulary. Offset printing improved in quality. Printed photographs took on a saturated, hyperreal character that made certain images seem more vibrant than direct experiences of reality. Media images became the standard of intensity to which to aspire, rather than a pale imitation of life (Figs. **13.18a** and **13.18b**).

Critical vocabulary French theorist Guy Debord published *Society of the Spectacle* in 1967. He argued that **spectacle** was an advanced condition of cultural alienation. Lived experience had been replaced by the symbolic expression of ideas, and contemporary life was profoundly integrated with representations. We consume images, he said, as signs and symbols

13.19 Tadanori Yokoo, John Silver, theater poster, 1967. The combination of traditional Japanese treatments and bright pop contemporary style in Yokoo's designs exemplifies a generation whose work synthesized Western commercialism and Japanese graphic art. The deliberate use of culturally specific iconography claimed a place for Japanese design in the graphic marketplace, a place comparable to that being assumed by Japanese goods in other sectors. The only other major national presence to take a place in the global arena alongside Western European and North American design was Poland. Other countries had graphic industries, but an international context for exchange of their productions did not really exist in the 1960s.

13.20 Peter Max, zodiac sign, 1968. Peter Max's signature cartoons were readily adaptable to any and all commercial forms from advertising to shower curtains. The overexposure of Max's work led to imitation, and derivative styles abounded. The consumability of his work sometimes made it hard to read it for a message because it always overwhelmingly announced its authorship. In this sense, Max, like other artists of the period, participated in the celebrity culture that 1960s media brought into being. Every poster or campaign by the designer was first a "Peter Max" before serving its client's purpose.

informed by the discourses of popular culture, as well as those of high culture, education, religion, and politics. Debord and Canadian media theorists Marshall McLuhan and Harold Innis provided crucial insights into the way the iconography of mass culture shaped behavior and imagination. The emphasis placed by these and other theorists on the symbolic value of images mirrored the change the era witnessed in approaches to visual design. While early twentieth-century graphic designers and educators had focused on formal values, approaches to composition, or design as a system, pop graphics emphasized the social and cultural associations of images and styles. The striking imagery of Japanese design, with its blend of historical traditions and contemporary cultural references, had a huge impact in the 1960s. Polish poster design had a recognizable profile and a particular power in Western European and North American contexts at a time when Soviet and Chinese graphics were kept from international circulation by government controls. Pop style was global, although every culture expressed it in a different idiom (Fig. **13.19**).

Trade publications for graphic designers continued to expand, as *Print, AD,* and other industry magazines sought a readership beyond that of practitioners. The selling of visual style was an important aspect

13.21 Muriel Cooper, *Learning from Las Vegas*, 1972. *Learning from Las Vegas* helped usher in an era of postmodern aesthetics. In a major critical move, Denise Scott Brown and Robert Venturi exposed modernism as a style, debunking its claim of being a universal language of form. Designed by Muriel Cooper, the book's content and format insisted on paying attention to vernacular architecture and signs in a way that moved beyond pop art's interest in mass media. Focusing on Las Vegas, the work charged the term *vernacular* with an unprecedented historical and theoretical value, and, although their chosen site was filled with commercialism, it was seen to have virtues that modernism had repressed. Imitation, artifice, **kitsch**, and all sorts of other representational features of the material world that would have been anathema to modern architects were suddenly praised. **Simulation** became a catchword. All pretenses of authenticity or originality were suspect. Postmodernism had been launched. Although it would be wrong to imagine that this book alone brought about an entire movement, its didactic juxtapositions of text and imagery provided a powerful reference for criticizing modern aesthetics. By reflecting and commenting on its subject matter, the book itself seemed to shift historical discussion to a new awareness of the cultural meaning of designed forms.

of pop culture, and graphic designers were eager for their moment in the spotlight—not only for the extra attention and higher professional profile it offered, but also because success was defined as fame, and fame could only be generated in the media. The works of signature designers like Milton Glaser, Seymour Chwast, and Peter Max were reproduced as posters that were consumed in a global market. Graphic designers' and fine artists' work became the basis of home and clothing textiles at a time when op, pop, and commercial art blurred many boundaries (Fig. **13.20**).

Conclusion By the early 1970s, the pop era was passing. In 1972, Denise Scott Brown and Robert Venturi published *Learning from Las Vegas*. Designed by Muriel Cooper, the book marked a turning point from pop and modern sensibilities to postmodern historical reflection. Youth culture's earlier hopeful visions were sobered by economic downturns at the end of the Vietnam War. The graphic design industry was particularly hard hit, as corporate communications were trimmed, in-house services downsized, and advertising budgets cut. The era of radical politics was succeeded by one of complacency and conservatism, and the exuberance and experimentation that had characterized pop and protest graphics were eclipsed. The 1970s had an air of dejected entrepreneurialism, as if a party had ended in an anticlimax and defeated expectations. But graphic designers took some of the best impulses of pop invention, strategic activism, and historical awareness into a new phase of exploratory work under the rubric of **postmodernism** (Fig. **13.21**).

Pop and Protest 1960s–1970s

1951 Marshall McLuhan's *The Mechanical Bride: Folklore of Industrial Man* published

1952 First commercial jet planes in service

1957 Situationist International forms

Brown v. Board of Education results in desegregation of schools

Allen Ginsberg's *Howl* seized by customs officials as obscene

1958 Little Rock, Arkansas, schools closed in desegregation dispute

1959 *Twen* magazine launched in Germany, aimed at youth culture

Barbie doll first sold

First photos of far side of the moon

Doyle Dane Bernbach's VW ads epitomize New Advertising

1960 Sunset Strip youth confront police for right to cruise (El Cajon Blvd. Riot)

Birth control pills go on sale in U.S.

Kennedy/Nixon debates televised: Kennedy looks better and wins election

1961 Roy Lichtenstein's first comic-inspired paintings

1962 George Maciunas founds Fluxus movement

1962 *Eros* magazine begins short-lived publication

John Glenn orbits earth

Death of Marilyn Monroe

Andy Warhol paints his first *Campbell's Soup Can*

Beatles' first hit record

Cuban Missile Crisis; nuclear war narrowly averted

Rachel Carson's *Silent Spring* published

Algeria gains independence from France

Ramparts magazine launched

1963 Guggenheim Museum mounts pop art exhibit, *Six Painters and the Object*

Oz magazine launched

Timothy Leary fired from Harvard for giving LSD to students

Betty Friedan's *The Feminine Mystique* published

John F. Kennedy assassinated

CORE and NAACP pressure entertainment industry to hire African American actors

Civil Rights March on Washington, D.C.; Martin Luther King, Jr.'s *I Have a Dream* speech

1964 American Surgeon General's report on risks of smoking tobacco

Herbert Marcuse's *One Dimensional Man* published

Civil Rights Act signed into law

Nelson Mandela sentenced to life in prison in South Africa

First poster museum opens in Warsaw, Poland

Beatles cause fan chaos on *Ed Sullivan Show*

Ken Garland's *First Things First* manifesto calls for social responsibility of graphic design

Student Nonviolent Coordinating Committee sends volunteers to Mississippi to register African American voters

Free Speech movement begins at UC Berkeley; Jack Weinberg says, "Don't trust anyone over thirty."

Marshall McLuhan's *Understanding Media: The Extensions of Man* published

1965 U.S. officially sends combat troops to Vietnam

Malcolm X assassinated

March for voting rights from Selma to Montgomery, Alabama

MoMA mounts op art exhibit, *The Responsive Eye*

1966 Michelangelo Antonioni's *Blowup* captures swinging London fashion photography scene

Fillmore Auditorium in San Francisco begins its concert poster series

Cultural revolution in China begins

National Organization of Women founded by Betty Friedan and twenty-seven other women and men

Black Panther Party founded in Oakland by Bobby Seale and Huey Newton

1967 First successful heart transplant by Christiaan Barnard

De Pas, D'Urbino, Scolari, and Lomazzi design inflatable chair

Six million copies of Milton Glaser's Bob Dylan poster sell

Herb Lubalin designs "No More War" poster

Timothy Leary says, "Tune in, turn on, drop out."

R. Buckminster Fuller's geodesic dome featured at U.S. pavilion of Expo '67 in Montreal

Che Guevara murdered in Bolivia

Summer of Love: 100,000 people converge in Haight-Ashbury district of San Francisco

Marshall McLuhan and Quentin Fiore's *The Medium Is the Massage* published

March on Pentagon to protest war in Vietnam

1968 Tet Offensive in Vietnam

First *Whole Earth Catalog* published

Advanced Course in Graphic Design instituted at Basel School of Design

Compugraphic produces Model 2961 phototypesetting machine

MIT establishes Center for Advanced Visual Studies

Martin Luther King, Jr., assassinated: African American uprisings in 125 American cities

Robert Kennedy assassinated

My Lai massacre in Vietnam

Student strikes in France, Germany, Italy, Spain, Czechoslovakia, U.S.

Third World Liberation Front organized by Black Student Union at SF State University

Herb Lubalin begins designing *Avant-Garde* magazine

1969 Stonewall Rebellion in New York City begins Gay Liberation movement

Woodstock festival and concert

Sacco bean bag chair designed by Gatti, Paolini, and Teodora

Friends of the Earth founded by David Brower

Hundreds of thousands participate in National Moratorium antiwar protests in U.S.

First moon landing; pictures of earthrise sent from the moon

1970 International Typographic Corporation (ITC) formed

Kent State protest, four killed

Grapus design studio forms in Paris

First Earth Day held

Rubella vaccine

Death of Jimi Hendrix at 27

Death of Janis Joplin at 27

747s first used by commercial airlines

Metal type begins to be phased out from commercial printing

1971 Greenpeace founded in Vancouver, BC

1972 *Ms.* magazine launched

1973 *Our Bodies, Ourselves* published

U.S. Supreme Court *Roe v. Wade* decision legalizes abortion

Tools of the Trade

Pantone felt markers

Letraset dry transfer lettering

Letratone screens

Cello-tak shading and flat color film

Fototype compositor

Clip art

Instamatic camera

Kodachrome slide and movie film

Spray paint

Mylar

PMT (photomechanical transfer)

Color key proofs

Phone answering machine

Halogen lamps

14. Postmodernism in Design 1970s–1980s and Beyond

- Postmodernism was a deliberate, self-conscious reaction to the "universal" formal language of modernism that sparked an eclectic interest in historicist, **retro**, **techno**, and vernacular styles.

- Postmodernism sought to discredit the idea of originality yet spawned a cult of celebrity designers whose idiosyncratic styles broke rules and new ground.

- Postmodern emphasis on *products* often concealed *conditions of production* within global capitalism, ignoring increasingly complicated economic systems and political contexts.

- In the language of simulation, images and signs were treated as if history, culture, gender, and ethnic identity existed *only* in systems of representation; conversely, the power of **sign systems** came under intense study.

- Activist designers produced powerful campaigns to raise public awareness about AIDS, feminist issues, and other political concerns; and many participated in a backlash against the cultural effects of brand supremacy.

- A commitment to foster historical and critical understanding of graphic design fueled new directions in publishing, conferences, and curricula, while theoretical discourse introduced its own cultural divide within the design community.

14.1 April Greiman, Vertigo business cards, 1979. April Greiman was well trained in modern methods of graphic design. But she drew on her education by Basel-based instructors both at the Kansas City Art Institute and in Switzerland to make a major contribution to the emergence of postmodern graphic design. Her decorative eclecticism became an almost instantly recognizable characteristic of the new trend. Distinct from pop art's media hipness and modernism's clean rational order, her modular approach to the **appropriation** and mixing of styles was immediately notable. A new freedom and innovative method underlay her segmentation of elements into formal units without regard for their original context or function. Form followed style, not function, in postmodernism's break with the orthodoxies of modern design.

In the 1970s, a new wave of design defined itself in reaction to modernism. The prefix in *post*modernism signaled at least a momentary eclipse of the International style and its assumptions of neutrality, universality, and rationality. The term also announced a stage beyond the exuberance of pop. Postmodern style was immediately recognizable by its lively pastiche sensibility, its absorption of retro and techno motifs, its disregard for the grid and rational rules, and its keenness to absorb funky, fresh, and decorative elements. **Punk**, beach culture, heavy metal, and **grunge** groups launched their own **zines** and ephemeral graphics. But the critical claims for postmodernism went beyond a change in style, raising profound questions about knowledge, history, and power. Modernism had claimed that a design aesthetic grounded in universal principles could be put to any purpose without regard for historical conditions. Postmodernism played on historical associations as stylistic references, reconfiguring political meaning in the process. Authenticity and originality were discounted. Images were discussed as **simulacra**—figures without connection to a source or context that function as free-floating signs. At the same time, the late 1970s and 1980s witnessed an upsurge of interest in links between identity politics and social sign systems. Ethnicity, sexual orientation, otherness, and *difference* commanded attention. World music, thrift-store fashions, and fusion cooking had a counterpart in the eclectic and **hybrid** aesthetic of an apparently anything-goes approach to design. Some

14.2 William Longhauser, *The Language of Michael Graves*, **exhibition poster, 1983.** The idea of a "language" of design was revived with enthusiasm in postmodern theory. Theoretical writings promoted the study of semiotics (sign systems) and created an interest in developing a critical approach to graphic design. Longhauser's design uses a set of graphic elements in a self-consciously modular-looking system. This strategy mimics Graves's architectural style and suggests that his **combinatorial** approach to form is governed by principles similar to those of a grammar. The design appears whimsical but is governed by a single stylistic decision: Letterforms must be composed of circles, triangles, squares, or rectangles. By the mid-1980s, this geometric approach became recognizable, even formulaic. Its decorative elegance suited the upscale markets of 1980s entrepreneurial affluence. Everything from housewares to furnishings and interiors took on motifs of flat screens punctuated by geometric forms in varying combinations. These patterns were meant to signify the trendy sophistication of their owners.

14.3a April Greiman, Cal Arts viewbook, 1979. Not only did the example of April Greiman—and others—open the still male-dominated graphic design field to women, but also the playfulness of her design seemed to open International style to a world of possibilities. Bright colors, pastels, letters, and shapes floated without any grid to anchor them. No underlying structure restricted the activity of patterns and forms; they were combined as if no rules applied. The apparent easiness of Greiman's imagery becomes soberingly complicated when its production is taken into account. Photomechanically rather than digitally produced, this piece was composed without monitors, previews, or automation of technical tasks. Making camera-ready art required a thorough understanding of the printing process, including color separations and screens in the late 1970s.

graphic designers expressed a renegade irreverence, even in work for conventional clients. Corporate executives sought a competitive advantage in global markets through innovative advertising that often promoted brands over products. These marketing campaigns mirrored the rise of *sign* over substance. Consumption was promoted in expensively produced campaigns that hid traces of the human or environmental costs of production. The "no-logo" movement gained popularity as a backlash and a platform for progressive reform. Activist designers applied their professional sophistication to successful public service projects (Figs. **14.1**, **14.2**, **14.3a**, and **14.3b**).

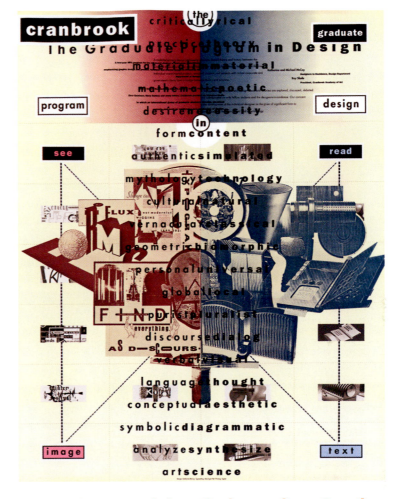

14.3b Katherine McCoy, poster for Cranbrook's graduate program in design, 1989. Katherine McCoy's impact on the design field derived, in part, from her compelling belief in theory as a basis for practice. Her teaching, design, and critical writings exemplify this conviction, and her work often introduces theoretical issues both textually and visually. Both modes are certainly operative in McCoy's poster for the graduate program at Cranbrook where her pedagogy helped direct the course of American design in the 1980s. The school became a center for design innovation, and the graphics that promoted its programs were important vehicles for disseminating postmodern aesthetics. This poster is organized diagrammatically: The four basic nouns and verbs at each corner of the lower field are related by dotted lines. Juxtaposed terms are stacked in the center of the poster over a collage of designed objects and surfaces, creating a nearly illegible field. But the texts are anchored by their intersection in the central image of a human brain. Overload and density prevail, and a theoretical vocabulary hovers tantalizingly, as if promising to unlock the complexity of a design to which it is integral.

Young designers seemed to be parodying their modern teachers.

Postmodern styles The first signs of postmodern graphic design appeared in the late 1970s and early 1980s. The 1981 exhibition of the **Memphis** group in Milan sent a ripple through the design world. Decorative eclecticism proliferated. Postmodernism entered the built environment, and a dialogue developed in which architecture and graphic design were mutually influenced. Environmental graphics and a visual vocabulary borrowed from architecture exposed a common interest in shifting away from the monolith of modernism and a shared reference base in theories about historical meaning and cultural sign systems. A generation of young designers seemed to be parodying their modern teachers and running amok in flagrant disregard for the rules that had prevailed in the International style. Even the playful works of pop looked internally coherent by contrast to the hodgepodge that burst forth in this new wave of design. Not only did postmodern designers dispense with any rigid adherence to formal organization and rational order, but also they seemed to throw out legibility itself (Figs. **14.4a** and **14.4b**).

The roster of designers who defined postmodern style included many who had been students of modernists. Paula Scher, April Greiman,

14.4a Deborah Sussman and Paul Prejza, Los Angeles Olympics, 1984.
Deborah Sussman and Paul Prejza's design of an environmental identity system for the 1984 Olympics in Los Angeles marked a watershed moment in postmodern graphic design. Sussman's background included exposure to conceptual, visual, and performance art as well as work in the office of Charles and Ray Eames. In their project for the Olympics, Sussman and Prejza demonstrated the viability of extending postmodern graphic design into a continuous environment of large-scale graphics, signage, and built form. The idea of total design had been part of modernism from its earliest formations, but this approach to design as eclectic and playful style was emphatically different. Supergraphics and vivid iconography were assembled into what Sussman and Prejza called "a kit of parts" that could be adapted throughout the Olympics Games environment while presenting a unified brand.

14.4b Studio Dumbar, performance poster, 1987. Gert Dumbar was among the leading figures of Dutch New Wave design. Founded in 1977, Studio Dumbar combined elements of older, De Stijl formalism (here apparent in the use of diagonals and geometric motifs) with visual effects produced photographically and later digitally. The complicated spatial and visual manipulations that make up the word *festival* follow no particular logic except the principle of graphic surprise. The pairing of chaotic and orderly elements provides enough traction for a viewer intent on getting information from the poster while suggesting something of the event's innovative aesthetic.

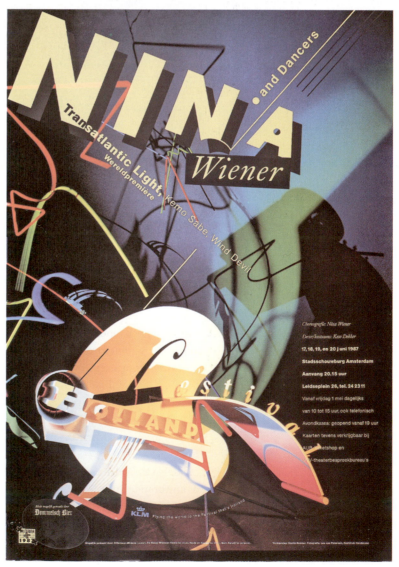

14.5a Wolfgang Weingart, *The Swiss Poster*, exhibition poster, 1983. The transition from modern to postmodern graphics was a process in which continuity and change both played a part. Weingart's training and early career in Basel had instilled in him the basic precepts of modernism. As a result, he was well positioned to rebel against its constraints. Even in the early 1970s, he had begun to produce designs that deliberately defied the rules by jamming margins, violating grids, and mixing typefaces. The commission to design publicity for this 1983 exhibit of twentieth-century Swiss posters was a high-profile opportunity to introduce an alternative aesthetic. The almost arbitrary use of the margins as a framing device, the crude granularity and messy moiré of the halftone screens, and the juxtaposition of a cute red crescent moon and an ugly, muddy sun in a field that says "graphic mountain" all contribute to a distinctly un-modern effect. The text is set in a serif face, and the words are pushed into not-quite-columns on a maybe-grid. Rules have definitely been broken here, although in a manner far less polemic than some of Weingart's later designs and critical writings.

14.5b Terry Jones, *i-D*, 1985. Jones's designs for *i-D* used torn edges, collage, scribbling, and scratching to create an overall effect of aggression and distress. This cover's heightened color and brash composition destroy the human face, disregarding its contours and individuality to achieve a striking design. **Antihumanism** was one of the lynchpins of postmodern theory that trashed precious assumptions about the value of the individual. As an expression of a culture of excess, such attitudes read with anthropological clarity. As a political mood, they suggest disenfranchisement, disaffection, and disillusionment with collective action. These designs were not digitally produced, and the ripped materiality of their photographic elements contributes to their aesthetic effect.

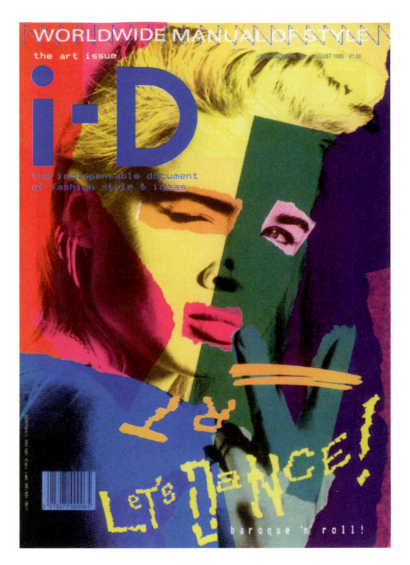

Wolfgang Weingart, Rosmarie Tissi, and Neville Brody, to name just a handful, had been trained in the International style. Yet they turned its operative premise, "form follows function," upside down. Postmodern formal manipulation was often antifunctional, deliberately chaotic, and averse to message-driven, information-delivery approaches to communication. Weingart, one of the pioneers of postmodernism, had studied with Emil Ruder in Basel. In the 1970s, he began to question basic conventions of typography, layout, and design: use of negative space, standards for typesetting and capitalization, consistency of size and weight within words and phrases, and so on. Articulate and graphically expressive, Weingart and others turned to critical publications like *Visible Language* to stir up their colleagues. Once the question "why" was raised with regard to any graphic convention, every assumption was up for interrogation (Figs. **14.5a** and **14.5b**).

Postmodernism did not comprise a single, unified graphic style. In fact, one of its characteristics was that retro, techno, punk, grunge, beach, **parody**, and **pastiche** were all conspicuous trends. Each had its own

1970s–1980s and Beyond

14.6 Art Chantry, *The Night Gallery*, **performance poster, 1991.** Art Chantry's poster presents a vivid example of *détournement*, an early form of **culture-jamming**. This approach to remaking meaning in a mass-cultural artifact was invented by the French Situationists in the 1960s. The Situationists saw their interventions as political acts, subversive attempts to restructure cultural meaning. Chantry's appropriation produces an effect of integration and identification, rather than alienation or distance, even as it exploits the quizzical surprise produced in his viewers by seeing graphic forms designed to sell tools used to promote a performance art event. The systematic and repetitive imagery of an advertisement for a wrench kit is put to a whole new purpose with which it seems ironically at odds. But the concept of standardized products and interchangeable parts seeps very easily from one register (machined tools) into the other (creative work), whether or not the effect was intentional.

Lifting and copying old styles was no longer seen as nostalgic

sites and venues, detractors and advocates. Retro style, for instance, was superficial in its relation to historical sources, not respectful or considered. This lack of consideration could be read as freedom from literal imitation of specific historical styles or designers, as an invocation, a general look that suggested a period or epoch. Pop had been nostalgic, borrowing from Art Nouveau's organicism and other nineteenth-century motifs. But retro was ironic, merely a production of surface effects. Lifting and copying features of old styles was no longer seen to serve a nostalgic purpose because the past was also considered to be an invention. History itself seemed to be constituted by style motifs, a set of forms to be appropriated, rather than studied seriously as a record of production conditions, political systems, or material circumstances. If you could redraw, imitate, or simulate a past style, then you could use it (Fig. **14.6**).

Techno style had a streamlined, New Age, metallic quality, hard-edged and robotic, verging on electronic. By contrast to modernism's utopian vision of the future, techno was often pessimistic. In the late 1980s, the term **post-human** entered the lexicon as part of a growing cyber-culture. The line between organic life and machines seemed to blur. Like many

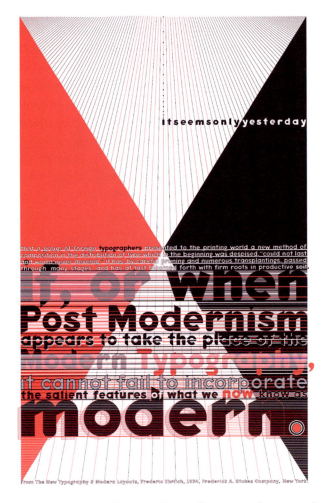

14.7 Jeffery Keedy, Emigre type foundry specimen series booklet no. 4, 2002.
By 2002, when this statement by Keedy appeared in an Emigre specimen series booklet, the blush of postmodernism was long past. Keedy's design borrows the geometric language and primary red, black, and white palette of early modern avant-garde design. Its knocked-out and outlined type is shot through with pseudo-**raster** lines. The look of a rapid refresh mode is conspicuously contemporary in its references to digital design. The piece asserts that modernity and postmodernity have more commonalities than differences. Critical controversies and partisan attitudes intensified in the design world of the 1990s. As the profile of graphic design and individual designers was raised, communities of discourse within the field dug in their heels, and philosophical lines were drawn in the shifting sands of style. Keedy's polemic exemplifies a contrarian attitude meant, in part, to curb exaggerated claims for postmodern novelty.

because the past itself was considered to be an invention.

postmodern themes, the post-human had a corollary in music into which synthesizers and drum machines had introduced an automated beat and artificial sound. Techno style in design favored elaborately produced, photomechanically—and later digitally—layered and manipulated imagery. Conspicuous exploitation of new technological capabilities was symptomatic of an approach that called attention to innovation while concealing actual production factors (such as labor costs or ecological effects) under an exceedingly complex surface (Fig. **14.7**).

Punk style took pop nonconformism and pushed it to extremes, generating a subculture of aggressive display with piercings, vividly shaved and dyed hair, leather clothes, and a dropout, drugged attitude. By contrast to pop's bright, psychedelic, flower-power tone, punk was dark and slightly ghoulish. An unhealthy look with heroin undertones found its way into style magazines. Punk design played on ransom-note, do-it-yourself collage style with a calculated anti-design attitude. A revival of interest in Dada aesthetics stemmed from a sensibility that combined **nihilistic** anarchism and the idea that anyone could be a cultural producer. Zines and underground publications continued to flourish as

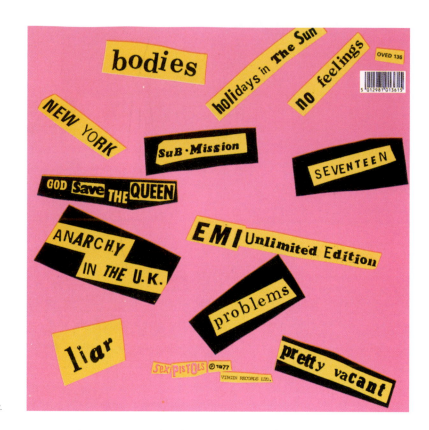

14.8 Jamie Reid, Sex Pistols album cover, *Never Mind the Bollocks*, 1977. Punk's embrace of the void is not immediately visible in this vivid album cover, designed while the British band was at its height. The ransom-note style became a generic punk motif, used in alternative publications and the branding of albums, books, and fashion accessories. The text and its themes are as telling as their design, reinforcing a nihilism that was culturally based in the social difficulties of the time. Unemployment rates were high among young people in Britain, and the 1970s drug culture featured heroin and cocaine rather than the psychedelics and marijuana of the optimistic 1960s. For the most part, Punk dealt in anger and despair rather than organized political action. Quickly commodified, it was nevertheless an expression of resistant subculture and outsider identity. Taken together, album covers, buttons, and posters of bands constituted a major field of cultural production and style generation. Although this trend had begun in the 1960s, by the 1970s it had become an enormous and diverse industry.

counterculture venues, and style variations served as a set of codes for identification. Punk's anger was an expression of frustration in response to the perception that the mass-media and political language were increasingly divorced from reality. Subcultures formed as alternatives to the repressive

Punk style took apart the workings of clean, seamless design.

social rhetoric of a new conservatism. Passions ran high. The politics of economic constraint introduced in the 1970s led to battles over social programs and safety nets. Culture wars raged. Graphic design provided a platform for nuanced definition of groups and subgroups within broader movements, and music industry graphics were an important site of cultural exchange. A destructive impulse drove much of punk culture, and its self-consciously **deconstructive** attitude took apart the workings of clean, seamless design. Chewed up, slashed, cut, crumpled, and battered, punk style was also distinctive and calculated in process and effect (Fig. **14.8**).

By contrast to the severe elegance and conformist character of the International style, postmodernism was eclectic and playful. Pop design had generated an enthusiasm for mass-cultural forms, but postmodernism had none of pop's purity of pleasure. Vernacular imagery regained authority in postmodern design. Hand-painted signage and kitsch iconography provided source materials, even as hybrid and **hyperreal** graphics asserted their own vivid power. Typographers who used new and traditional modes of composition were presented with an almost infinite range of possibilities. Computers made typeface design more accessible as specialized software

14.9a Edward Fella, exhibition poster, 1988. Fella's work combined skills developed in corporate communications work with a deep appreciation of vernacular forms. Interested in hand-painted signs and the common language of public spaces, Fella collected a photographic inventory of lettering to inspire his own work. He made letterforms that incorporated drawing with Letraset and other low-tech media. The results are unique, and his style is unmistakable. His lettering and doodled ornaments recall W. A. Dwiggins set in a new key. Some were scanned and rendered as digital fonts, but he himself eschewed digital tools. Uneven spacing and inconsistent letter shapes were characteristics that Fella cultivated, making his process distinctly unsystematizable.

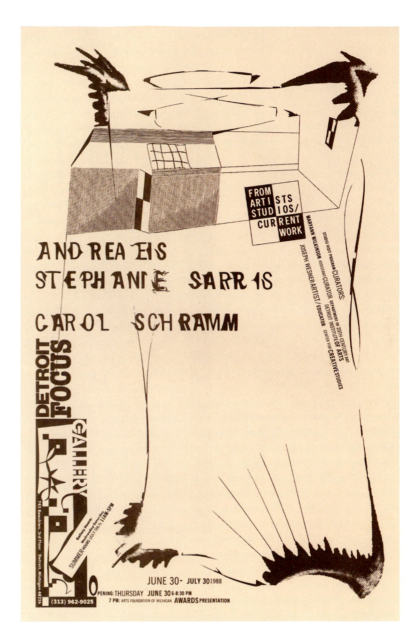

ABCDEFGHIJ
KLMNOPQRST
UVWXYZabcd
efghijklmnop
qrstuvwxyz12
34567890 ampers-AND et

14.9b Barry Deck, Template Gothic, 1990. This notoriously "imperfect" font, with its peculiarities of weight and shape, became an emblematic face of the 1990s. Along with other faces that Emigre promoted, it practically defined the first wave of digital typography. Template Gothic's hi/lo-tech quality found a sympathetic reception in the design community and seemed to appear instantly everywhere. The font's machined look made it seem manufactured rather than designed, reinforcing the popular notion that type simply exists, an anonymous, mass-produced industrial product. The idea that a typeface is an authored artifact barely registers in public imagination: Type seems simply to appear in the visual landscape.

became widely available, although many designers were sobered by the difficulty of resolving issues of fit, shape, consistency, scale, and weight. Appropriation escalated when scanners became affordable, but the interest in found images and common iconography was as much a response against the modernist banishment of handmade and context-specific imagery as it was an effect of technological change (Figs. **14.9a** and **14.9b**).

Postmodern consumption and conservatism
The 1970s and 1980s were a time of contraction and contradiction. State-sponsored violence went underground. The lessons of Vietnam War era protests had been learned by mainstream media and the status quo interests they served. The military activities of North American forces in Guatemala, Nicaragua, and El Salvador had little media visibility in the United States.

14.10a and 14.10b David Carson, *Ray Gun*, 1993. David Carson's designs for *Beach Culture* and *Ray Gun* shook up established ideas about what editorial graphics could be. Creating a different, radically inventive design for each issue, Carson made a virtue of the intense, attention-deficit-producing illegibility of his method. His interventions at every level of normative, conventional communication were defiant in their disregard for functionality. If design was going to matter, it had to mess things up, make them not work, call attention to expectations of smooth delivery and self-effacing communication structures. One aspect of postmodern deconstruction was systematic, but Carson's theory-as-practice was unpredictably disruptive.

Guerrilla training and warfare never made it to domestic television screens. Repression was well served by the postmodern idea that simulation (the primacy of images over reality) was inevitable, contemporary, and chic. A period of economic depression followed the end of the Vietnam War in the early 1970s. Smaller, more conservative governments shrank benefits and programs that had been considered central to the social contract in earlier decades. The 1980s were fraught with economic boom-and-bust cycles, oil shortages, global tensions, credit-based consumerism, and major changes in the regulation of labor, capital, and resources. A turn toward political conservatism in the mainstream formed the backdrop against which graphic design responded to the rhetoric of downsizing and a pervasive complacency. Tax cuts decreased support for education, social services, and infrastructure in the administrations of Ronald Reagan and Margaret Thatcher. At the same time, their economic policies were credited with a rise in stock market values in the 1980s. Outsourcing and deregulation brought the postindustrial character of **late capitalist** economies into focus. Tensions surrounded guest workers and undocumented immigrants. Organized labor, once the foundation of progressive movements, began to

14.11 Dan Friedman, *Artificial Nature*, 1992. Friedman's catalog designs for exhibitions curated by Jeffrey Deitch combined apparent simplicity with an enigmatic effect. Suggestive theoretical terminology and the hyperreal, manipulated images produced designs that were highly consumable. The composition has a **reifying** effect, making each image its own product, yet its insistence on hybridity makes the whole much more than the sum of its parts. The glib superficiality of effects gives rise to an air of sinister ease. The inventory of somatic transformations implies a consumerist body of replaceable, reprogrammable parts. That sense of availability, produced, in part, by high-end commercial photography and printing, creates a soulless atmosphere of consumption that seems to eclipse ethical, psychological, political, and economic considerations.

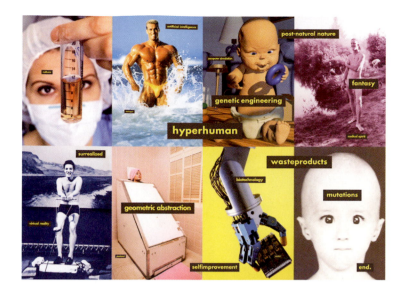

erode in the United States, even as the Solidarity movement gained power in Poland. Consumerism continued to thrive, however, and designers' disregard for rules and embrace of a culture of superficial abundance were an all-too-apt trend for the times. The language of simulation suited an era in which global capital flows were often masked by consumable signs freed from context or accountability (Figs. **14.10a** and **14.10b**).

The fall of the Berlin Wall in 1989 marked a crucial moment in the history of the West: the end of the Cold War. Political alliances, whose rigid forms had embodied dogmatic, highly polarized oppositions between the so-called Free World and the Soviet bloc behind the "Iron Curtain," began to dissolve. This structural change was reflected in larger patterns

Transnational capitalism's aesthetic counterpart was hybridity.

of economic expansion that left colonial models of First and Third World relations far behind. The impact and memory of the two world wars began to recede. The flow of capital, rather than the identity of nation-states, shaped global politics. State regulation in the name of the common good still functioned to some extent within national borders. But the networks of power that governed exchanges of cultural and natural resources (labor and raw materials, including oil, coal, gas, diamonds, gold, uranium, and other crucial ingredients) transcended these boundaries. Transnational capitalism found its aesthetic counterpart in hybridity and border-crossing styles that had little to do with the search for authenticity that had been important a decade earlier (Fig. **14.11**).

Spending by major manufacturers shifted increasingly away from production toward brand promotion. For multinational companies like Kraft, McDonald's, and Nike, creating brand awareness came first. Products-of-the-moment came second. The sign value of the Nike swoosh was what made a pair of sneakers worth its price. Graphic designers were among those responsible for the campaigns that invested these brands not only with general associations of goodness, but also with specific cultural

14.12 Michael Jordan and Air Jordan logo, 2007. Twenty years before this picture was taken, Michael Jordan leapt straight into the air for another camera and struck the Jumpman pose that would brand his line of Nike shoes. In the silhouette lifted from that photograph, Jordan appears poised for one of his signature dunks. The magic of this silhouette lies in its suspension of a moment and its invocation of Jordan's gravity-defying virtuosity on the court. By capturing this magic, the logo makes Jordan's athletic achievement into a value that is transferable to anything it touches. Once contained in such a detachable form, Jordan's triumph could be combined with any number of other signs, such as city streets and scrappy type, to weave specifically targeted groups into its associations.

meanings via visual and stylistic references to recognizable contexts. The Nike versus Reebok brand war was emblematic of the inversion of marketing and manufacturing that occurred in the 1980s and 1990s. What began with fairly direct investments in the sign value of the brands by endorsement deals with star athletes quickly moved on to more complex subcultural identifications. **Appellation**—the constructive strategy by which a message or image positions a viewer as its addressee—was achieved by a game of mirrors in which urban backdrops, **hip hop** associations, and a graphic language that seemed to emanate from these sources situated Reebok and Nike products in a context that related them to a specific group of buyers. Hip hop would prove to be an endlessly powerful source of cultural references. Yet perhaps because it, too, was based in complex strategies of appropriation and reconstruction, hip hop was not to be quickly exhausted by commercial vultures. Its endurance and vitality mark it as one of the richest expressions of postmodernism (Fig. **14.12**).

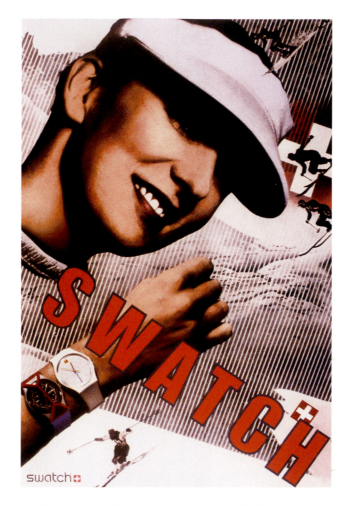

14.13a Herbert Matter, Swiss tourism poster, 1936 *(opposite)*, **and 14.13b Paula Scher, Swatch poster, 1985** *(right)*. Scher's design for the popular watch brand Swatch took Herbert Matter's well-known 1936 Swiss travel poster as its source. Swapping the historical model for a contemporary substitute and throwing in a wrist of watches barely changed the composition, but the statement made by self-conscious quotation had an enormous impact among graphic designers. Within a postmodern critical frame, the notion that nothing original could be done and that originality was itself a suspect concept justified this kind of imitation.

Utopianism was gone, along with unwavering faith in progress.

Critical theory and postmodern sensibility
Postmodernism was, in part, an attitude toward origins and change: in the beginning was the quotation, and in the end, more of the same. Utopianism was gone along with the unwavering faith in progress that had been characteristic of modernity since the beginning of the Industrial Revolution. That myth of progress and the search for universal forms had been central to modern design. But theoretical discussions of the "end of history" and the "death of the author" raised questions about the possibility of originality in design and the arts. In practical terms, such theses suggested that the history of art and design constituted a vast archive to be quoted, appropriated, reused in a newly critical, reflective way. First, the photocopier, then clip-art inventories and image banks made the idea of original or authentic expression seem naive and outmoded. The suspicion that everything had already been said, drawn, photographed, written, recorded, or thought stood in contrast to the modern enthusiasm for innovation that had dominated the early part of the century. Postmodern artifice seemed to spring in part from ennui and disenchantment, even as it embraced a fresh set of graphic possibilities (Fig. **14.13a** and **14.13b**).

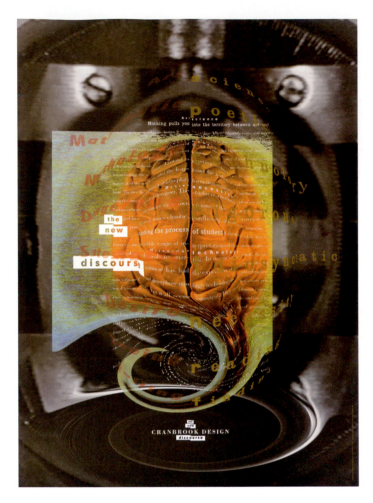

14.14 P. Scott Makela, *Cranbrook Design: The New Discourse*, exhibition poster, 1990. Photoshop filters created effects most designers had only dreamed of prior to the advent of the Apple Macintosh computer. Although digital work was not a practical necessity for theoretical postmodernism, the ability to manipulate images in all sorts of new ways was irresistible to graphic artists who wanted to denaturalize visual conventions. Makela's twisting, turning, disappearing vortex of text and image and fish-eye distortions are simply the work of software tools and options. The binarism in this image betrays the **structuralist** basis of Cranbrook's deconstructive approach, its roots in fundamental oppositions. Makela's work pairs the systematic rigor of theoretical investigation with playful digital effects, as if to suggest that the seriousness of critical insight might vanish in a twist of design, if allowed.

History as a narrative of causal forces and culminating events

Debates about postmodernism made a distinction between an aesthetic movement characterized by shifts in style and a cultural change described as the end of the Enlightenment project. A belief in reason and science had prevailed in Western culture since the eighteenth century. Now it was shaken. On the surface, postmodern design seemed largely a matter of style. But, in fact, postmodern designers questioned assumptions about representation and communication that had been the basis of graphic design since its origins. Printing, after all, had been a part of the early modern sensibility: The standardization of information enacted by print media had embodied rational principles. Throughout the modern era, design was as much an instrument of cultural administration as it was an expression or means of enlightenment. But belief in progress still underlay its practice and reception, and the loss of this belief amounted to a general crisis (Fig. **14.14**).

Attitudes shifted. The notion of history as a narrative of causal forces and culminating events was criticized by **post-structuralists** as storytelling in the interests of the powerful. The act of interpretation as an associative **play** of meaning-production took precedence over concepts like inherent

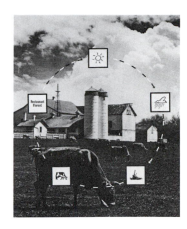

14.15a Tibor Kalman, Florent, 1988. Kalman's design firm, M & Co., produced a number of groundbreaking and high-profile projects in which elements of the American vernacular figured prominently. For the Manhattan restaurant Florent, Kalman designed an identity that extended to menus, matchbooks, and other collateral materials, using images clipped from the Yellow Pages. He also worked with the restaurant's owner Florent Morellet to create hard-hitting political ads. These campaigns combined promotion for the restaurant and engagement with issues and organizations, including the Society for the Right to Die. Characterized by bold partisanship and confrontational political messages, these ads stand out as examples of a client-designer partnership that advanced both a business and a social agenda.

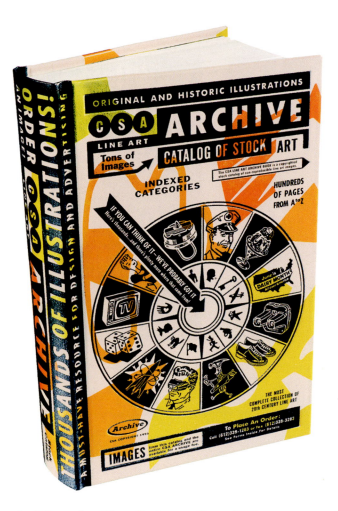

was criticized as storytelling in the interests of the powerful.

14.15b Charles S. Anderson, stock art catalog, 1995. Anderson has a knack for manipulating colors and images to generate a nostalgic look. Rather than quoting a specific historical moment, his work references history as a general field of past styles. The resulting nostalgia does not really express a longing for a particular time but suggests that a past of the imagination offers a reprieve, an ideal for which the present yearns. Anderson's palette and kitsch iconography do much of the work to render a 1940s and 1950s tone. Here, Anderson promotes the stock art of CSA Images—an affiliate of his design firm—by demonstration. The vogue for recycled images was reinforced by the digital environment in which sampling, copying, and remixing are all easy to do.

truth and transcendent meaning. No wonder designers saw historical styles and materials as an inventory of signifiers, each potentially relevant to any present purpose. The critical sensibility that uncoupled "truth" and "meaning" from signs also created a climate in which designers felt they could disconnect the texts and images they used from any relation to a real reference base. Meaning was understood as a product of signs combined according to the laws of a semiotic system, and designers were skilled in the manipulation of such systems with all of their multivalent possibilities; they always had been. Postmodernism had simply caught up with, made explicit, and accelerated the complex **codes** that had been refined by design since the beginning of mass markets (Figs. **14.15a** and **14.15b**).

Postmodernism and activism
A flexible sense of history and a free association of styles made postmodern design feel like it had no rules or restraints. This liberation often involved disillusionment with the utopianism of earlier generations. But such skepticism did not preclude activism. Postmodernism included strikingly successful political advocacy campaigns by well-organized groups of artists and designers in the

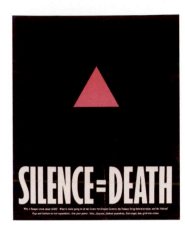

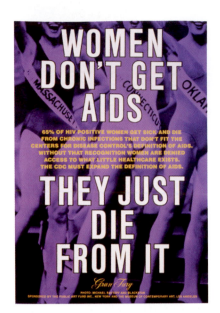

14.16a ACT UP, *Silence = Death*, **1987.** The pink triangle, an inversion of the sign used by the Nazis to mark homosexuals, was adopted by ACT UP (the AIDS Coalition to Unleash Power) in 1987. The group developed a highly visible campaign to combat prejudice against AIDS as well as the disease itself. They embraced the high production values of the design profession, turning its tools and skills to advocacy for a cause. Unlike an earlier generation of activist artists whose fast and dirty graphics were of and for the street, ACT UP produced commercial-grade work.

14.16b Gran Fury, *Women Don't Get AIDS*, **1991.** Gran Fury was another activist collective organized around the agenda of combating the spread of AIDS. The public information campaigns they orchestrated brought a great deal of attention to the disease and contributed to its being brought under control in certain sectors, particularly the sexually active gay community. Gran Fury also worked aggressively to change public perception of homosexuality and AIDS by confronting the public with stereotypes about HIV-positive individuals. Although the battle against AIDS is a medical, political, and economic one, the symbolic order of images and language, in which the terms of these struggles are defined, is crucial to the way the disease is understood and treated. The contributions of Gran Fury demonstrate the vital capacity of activist graphics to work as socially transformative forces.

14.17 Bill Texas, *Adbusters*, **Jonathan Barnbrook, guest art director, 2001.** Launched in 1989 as a forum for criticizing corporate and commercial culture, the Canadian publication *Adbusters* is also a highly consumable, professionally designed product. This contradiction is well recognized by the designers who participate in the journal. *Adbusters* registers the unease of a generation of designers whose day jobs often make them uncomfortably complicit with mainstream culture. The difficulty of working within and against corporate and commodity culture is a dilemma for many designers. The sharp edge of *Adbusters'* humor expresses anger and frustration. Whether this expression has any political efficacy is another question.

struggle against AIDS and the public ignorance that surrounded it. These information campaigns became models of activist work. Critical analysis of social conditions and the rise of **cultural studies** also had an impact on graphic design, offering tools for thinking about intervention and change. Activist design groups took professional experience into broad-based communications campaigns meant to alter public awareness and opinions. On particular issues, such as the education of at-risk communities and the broader public about AIDS, safe sex, and homophobia, these groups were enormously successful. Awareness of sweatshop labor, the "no logo" movement, the influence of *Adbusters*, and "buy nothing day" were all the results of successful publicity. "Green" approaches to consumption brought ecological issues to the fore, and notions of sustainable design gained a

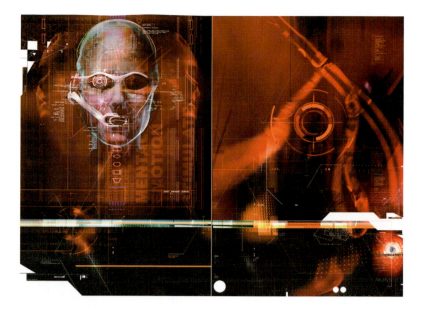

14.18 Attik, *Noise 3.5: Analytical Experiments in Graphic Science*, book, 1999. Techno's **dystopic** impulse embodied a fascination with machines as destructive and seductive agents. Robotics and cybernetics, cyborgs, simulants, and virtual worlds were central to this cultural zone. A sense of strange science, of hybridizing capabilities brought on by cloning, genome mapping, and the dehumanization of information manipulation, permeates these dark patterns of rearranged parts that exist in a fully designed but completely uncharted universe of transformations. At the same time, a tinkerer's pleasure in making is revealed by the sheer complexity of these designs, and, for all of their alienated thematics, their aesthetic richness demonstrates engagement.

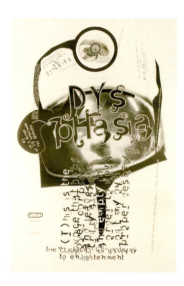

14.19 Elliott Earls, Dysphasia, 1995. In this announcement for his typeface, Dysphasia, Earls makes a point of corrupting the letterforms and their communicative functionality. The effect is obvious, and the dark statement of individual nihilism in the text suits the destructive aesthetic of the face. Such expressions of artistic voice indicated a rarefied design, a chic, custom line of just-for-me elitism meant to cultivate celebrity status. The phenomenon of a star system, prevalent in most cultural fields in the latter part of the twentieth century, reached design in the 1980s and 1990s, often forcing designers into extreme parodies of self-differentiation. "I am not like anyone else," this design proclaims. But such claims were not uncommon. A flurry of publications focused on individual designers, celebrating their achievements with unqualified praise and unabashed promotion. Lecture circuits and exhibitions offered opportunities for designers to circulate as artists or cultural heroes, and the high-stakes rewards of celebrity culture became a part of the graphic design universe.

foothold in the profession through exemplary projects. Graphic designers drew on a progressive base and sophisticated skills to mount campaigns that had an impact on public consciousness (Figs. **14.16a**, **14.16b**, and **14.17**).

Changes in the profession

Technological changes were on the horizon in the late 1970s, but early postmodern design was a photomechanical production, not an electronic one. The use of photographic negatives to layer and manipulate content in self-canceling sandwiches of images and text preceded desktop computers by a decade. By the time computers were adopted, the work of 1970s practitioners had already sensitized designers to many of the possibilities they offered. Pastiche and collage served the purposes of disunity and fragmentation. Parody was an act of appropriation and deformation. A highly mannered, decorative, even baroque excess weighted the graphic arts, as if to negate the possibility of order or simplicity. An edge of dark irony, skepticism, even cynicism often came into view—as if the task of communication had been abandoned in favor of critical reflection and a deliberate dismantling of the rules of the game (Fig. **14.18**).

The curious, often perverse complicity of designers with societal forces with which they felt at odds became a topic of conversation and debate, even as the industries that absorbed students from design programs expanded in variety and scale. Designers seemed increasingly sensitive to the role they played in promoting consumer culture. Anxiety about the implication of the profession in larger cultural forces registered in various ways. But, if the culture of graphic design was changing, so were the tasks and challenges it faced. By the end of the 1980s, graphic design was no longer the predominantly static composition of advertising, packaging, and editorial design but was moving into special effects, animation, film, television, and music video graphics, and disappearing into global corporate identity systems, branding, and so on. Collectively, this work produced a significant share of mass visual culture (Fig. **14.19**).

14.20a Bruce Mau, *Zone*, 1986. In his work for MIT Press and other editorial clients, Bruce Mau perfected a distinctive, technologized atmosphere. His synthetic style was far less jarring than that of many of his contemporaries. Mysterious and alluring, it seemed to make veiled surfaces and deep spaces on the page without resorting to standard means of illusion. The tension Mau created between specificity and ambiguity suited the book covers and pages he designed. The abstract complexity of theoretical language and the claims for critical insight into culture—from an academic remove—were well served by designs that were suggestive. Exactly *what* they suggested did not seem to matter.

14.20b Allen Hori, *Typography as Discourse*, Katherine McCoy lecture poster, 1989. Hori's poster is a classic of postmodern design. Abstract and apparently unstructured, the design is a well-organized deconstruction of information hierarchies and readers' expectations. It also functions exquisitely by virtue of its clean and rather distilled aesthetic. The appearance of scattering that is produced by disassembling standard categories of information-presentation is countered by a clear respect for vertical and horizontal stability. The colors are gentle and harmonious and unify the design in a single field of activity. The design's balance of solidity and dynamics, action and inertia, order and disorder artfully demonstrates that deconstruction is not a chaotic free-for-all but a rethinking of the ways in which order is achieved. **Discourse** became a popular theoretical term emphasizing the use, rather than the content, of **language** and the conditions of a statement's construction to be revealed by analysis.

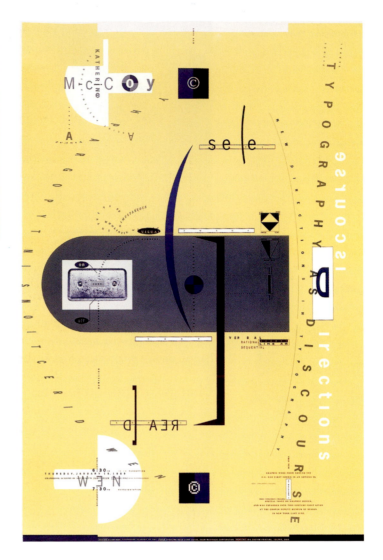

Many designers combined their practice with roles as teachers, lecturers, and critics. While their design work shed the last vestiges of modern decorum, their teaching and writing took on critical issues. A thoughtful new vocabulary arose to support the efforts of design practitioners with a theoretical framework. The influence of French critical theory brought attention to concepts of simulation, pastiche, and hyperreality (a media-permeated condition in which nothing and everything is real). Guy Debord's work on spectacle (in which experience is replaced by, or lived entirely through, images), Jean Baudrillard's theories of hyperreality and simulation (representation without a model, a copy without an original), and Jean-François Lyotard's critique of grand narratives (the definitive stories we tell ourselves to support our belief systems) offered new understandings of sign and image systems. Designers often expressed these ideas graphically without a full appreciation of their theoretical implications. High-profile, critically engaged designers contributed to the visual culture that became the object of theoretical investigation, often in a tight feedback loop (Figs. **14.20a** and **14.20b**).

14.21a Tibor Kalman and Oliviero Toscani, *Colors* magazine, 1990s. Edited by Kalman and cofounded by Benetton's creative director, Oliviero Toscani, *Colors* took its name from a prevailing interest in **multiculturalism**. Toscani's photography and Kalman's graphic sensibility produced a unique publication that pushed the limits of convention. *Colors* was funded by Benetton, and yet its creators were allowed to operate without editorial intervention from the company. This arrangement echoes earlier twentieth-century projects such as the "Great Ideas of Western Man" campaign supported by the Container Corporation of America, which showcased artists, literary figures, and cultural leaders without any overt connection to the company's products. But in *Colors* the earlier earnestness and lofty rhetoric had been replaced by a complex, even sardonic, point of view. Controversial topics like race and AIDS were treated in ways that shocked some viewers and provoked others. But Kalman's reputation as a man of integrity and generosity gave the projects credibility, as did Toscani's perceptive and revealing photography.

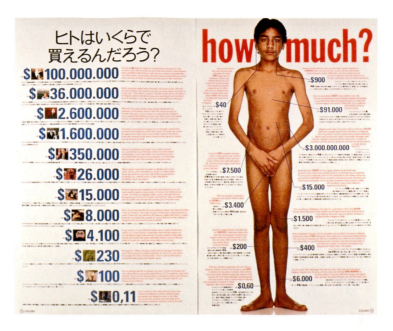

14.21b Oliviero Toscani, Benetton ad, 1992. Benetton's provocative billboard campaigns were the work of photographer, art director, and author Oliviero Toscani. Toscani shocked viewers by displaying images of a newborn baby, the stained clothes of a young soldier killed in the Yugoslavian conflict, and a man with AIDS on his deathbed *(above)*. The question of whether this imagery was appropriate in a commercial space challenged the way propriety is understood and regulated by the media and design industries. "Appropriateness" was exposed as a convention for policing sense and sentiment, as if keeping an image in its place would keep its uncomfortable message from leaking into the business of daily life or the daily life of business. Whether this approach was exploitative or engaged remains a matter of discussion and debate.

Conclusion

As major theorists of postmodernism questioned the way basic categories like knowledge, power, authority, sexuality, discipline, and disease had been defined in symbolic discourses, designers continued to push conventional limits of legibility in visual expression. New questions arose about whose interests were served by these discourses and whose were not, and how values taken as "natural" were fixed within cultural activities. The role of designers as cultural critics, sociologists, and provocative agents intensified. The capacity to manipulate symbolic systems was no longer seen as a matter of deception versus truth, or simple persuasion. Elaborate ideological machinery was seen to engineer contemporary life, successfully integrating graphic design into many aspects of its operations. In the postmodern condition, design had clearly become one of the forces of culture. Earlier modern awareness of the effects of communication had been based on ideas of mechanistic impact. The postmodern critical sensibility wrestled with the complexities of complicity, as the scale of mass visual culture escalated. The design profession rose to new heights of hype and influence. Designers were in the complicated position of producing mass ideology and, at the same time, knowing that they were being produced by it. The paradox and dilemmas of this situation remain intertwined and seemingly inescapable. Neomodernist trends have proposed a path around these complexities—as if a return to the universal approach to graphic design could bracket cultural conflicts and contexts from view (Figs. **14.21a** and **14.21b**).

Postmodernism in Design 1970s–1980s and Beyond

1968 Wolfgang Weingart joins faculty of Basel School of Design

1970 Dan Friedman teaches at Yale

First handheld electronic calculators on the market

Kraftwerk starts making electronic pop music, inspires techno

1971 Food processors marketed

1972 Venturi, Izenour, and Scott Brown's *Learning from Las Vegas* published

HBO starts cable pay-TV service

President Nixon visits China

Pong, early mass-produced video game, invented by Nolan Bushnell

1973 DJ Kool Herc originates hip hop in the Bronx, raps over extended breaks

The Exorcist opens

Harsh Rockefeller Drug Laws lead to massive imprisonment of African Americans and Latinos

CBGB, underground/punk venue, opens in New York

Watergate hearings begin

1974 Philip Meggs begins teaching history of visual communication and working on his book

President Nixon resigns

Liposuction introduced

1976 Death of Mao Tse-tung

Sony's Betamax and JVC's VHS battle for dominance of videotape market

The Sex Pistols' *Anarchy in the UK* debuts

1977 MRI imaging introduced

Douglas Crimp organizes *Pictures* exhibition at Artists Space in New York

Star Wars opens

1978 Philip Johnson's postmodern AT&T building in New York commissioned

First test-tube baby born

VisiCalc spreadsheet software introduced

First cases of what will come to be called AIDS

1979 Tibor and Maira Kalman found M&Co

Jean-François Lyotard's *Postmodern Condition* published

Margaret Thatcher becomes Prime Minister of Britain

Sony Walkman introduced

First cell phones marketed

Three Mile Island nuclear disaster

Bantam books launches *Choose Your Own Adventure* series

1980 Iranian hostage crisis constantly covered on television; thus begins *Nightline*

Sussman/Prejza and Company founded

Solidarnosc (Solidarity) logo designed by Jerzy Janiszewski

Post-it notes introduced by 3M

Programmable drum machines, keyboards, and samplers used by techno and hip hop musicians

Ronald Reagan elected U.S. President

Terry Jones founds *i-D* magazine

The Face magazine launched

Nintendo introduces Game and Watch handheld video game

Midway Games introduces Pac-Man in U.S.

CNN begins 24-hour news

Calvin Klein's controversial ad featuring Brooke Shields highlights designer jean craze

1981 Frank Olinsky and Manhattan Design design MTV logo with changeable colors

Sherrie Levine introduces re-photography with *After Walker Evans*

Jean Baudrillard's *Simulacres et Simulations* published

First Memphis exhibition in Milan

Neville Brody becomes art director of *The Face*

France Telecom introduces dedicated Minitel videotex terminals into French homes

John Lennon assassinated

Space shuttle launched

1982 Los Bros Hernandez' serial graphic narrative, *Love and Rockets*, launched

U.K. and Argentina fight Falklands War

Blade Runner opens

Israel invades Lebanon

USA Today typeset regionally from satellite transmission

1983 U.S. invades Grenada

Reagan proposes Strategic Defense Initiative, dubbed *Star Wars* after the popular movie

Cell phone networks established

1984 University of Illinois at Chicago launches *Design Issues*

Cybotron release *Techno City*, legendary African American techno recording

Michael Jackson's first plastic surgery

Madonna puts out *Like A Virgin*, starts pattern of changing persona with every album

Brian Wallis edits *Art After Modernism: Rethinking Representation*

Negativland coins phrase *culture jamming*, referring to media sabotage

Nancy Reagan's *Just Say No* campaign launched

Crack cocaine epidemic; imprisoned population continues to rise

1985 Art Spiegelman's Garbage Pail Kids trading cards parody Cabbage Patch Kids

Donna Haraway's *The Cyborg Manifesto* published

MDMA (Ecstasy) made illegal, becomes major club drug

MIT Media Lab opens

Gorbachev becomes General Secretary of the Communist Party in the Soviet Union

USDA approves of genetic engineering

Guerilla Girls founded

Brazil opens, satirizes technological society

Color photocopiers introduced

Bruce Mau designs *Zone 1*

1986 Chernobyl nuclear catastrophe

Congress passes anti-apartheid bill after years of campaigning by students

Run-DMC's cover of Aerosmith's *Walk This Way* hits top ten on pop charts

Challenger disaster

1987 ACT UP (AIDS Coalition to Unleash Power) forms in New York

Iran/Contra hearings

Prozac receives FDA approval

Glasnost and Perestroika advocated by Gorbachev

1989 Time/Warner Communications merger

Berlin Wall comes down

AdBusters launched

U.S. invades Panama; Manuel Antonio Noriega captured and tried

Tiananmen Square demonstrations in Beijing

Graphic Design in America, first major historical exhibition, at Walker Art Center

1990 German reunification

Nelson Mandela released from prison after twenty-seven years

1991 Oliviero Toscani and Tibor Kalman co-found Benetton's *Colors* magazine

Three out of four U.S. homes own a VCR

Soviet Union dissolves

1992 David Carson designs *Ray Gun*

Wayne's World brings postmodernism to youth culture

NAFTA treaty signed by U.S.

1994 Elections held in South Africa without race restrictions

1996 Dolly the Sheep cloned

Tools of the Trade

Fine-line markers

Gel pens

Plotter pen

Glue stick

Post-it notes

Macintosh computer

Early graphics software

Click art

Word processing

Color photocopier

Electronic typesetting

Dot matrix printer

Daisy wheel printer

LaserWriter desktop printer

ThinkJet inkjet printer

Fax machine

#8 Fall 1983 $3.00 U.S.

SEND

Video & Communications Arts

COMPUTER ARTS ISSUE

NEW DRAWING TOOLS

15. Digital Design 1970s–2000s

- Digital technology posed new conceptual and graphic challenges for design. Images, texts, and other forms of information became variable expressions of data files. Distinctions grounded in older technologies and media disappeared or became more fluid.

- Powerful production capabilities became available within a single **desktop** environment. Once-specialized tasks, such as prepress processing and animation, initially fell to designers not formally trained in these areas. But tools, training, and professional roles evolved to close gaps in competency.

- Global networking allowed for easy movement of information and capital, giving rise to new labor conditions and new ways around existing regulations through outsourcing and distributed production.

- Graphic design integrated display and functionality in electronic environments that modeled behaviors and real-time interaction. Many functions were codified in the visual metaphors of menus, windows, and icons before design for the Web introduced a generation of dynamic interface features that incorporated users' input.

- A new critical awareness of the rhetorical force of graphic forms and the challenges of cross-cultural translation was brought to the study of information design.

- Evidence of designers' labor tended to disappear in high-end digital productions. This invisibility reinforced the myth of **immateriality** that prevails in a technology that conceals the complex social systems through which networks function, as well as the environmental price of rapid obsolescence.

15.1 *SEND* cover, 1983. Before Apple sold desktop computers, digital tools were adopted by experimental artists. But the graphic capabilities offered by the new machines promoted a sense that everyone was a potential designer or artist. Scanners and point-and-click copying seemed suddenly to wipe out awareness that images were authored and made, or that artistic work should be valued and remunerated. Flyers made by overworked clerks or secretarial staff who used clip-art inventories and MacPaint patterns cluttered bulletin boards and mailboxes. Personal computers were marketed as empowering a broad public, putting graphic tools into their hands, along with automatic calculators and **spreadsheets**. When the World Wide Web arrived in the 1990s, communications and entertainment offerings, rather than production capacity, would speed consumption of electronics. Dot-com marketers revived the rhetoric of progress at a moment that also marked the peak of postmodern reflection on the myth of modernity and the benefits of innovation.

Postmodern attitudes toward style and graphic meaning anticipated issues raised by **digital** design. But electronic technology brought its own practical and conceptual changes to the field. On a practical level, desktop computers offered individual designers unprecedented involvement with every aspect of production. For a brief period, it seemed that graphic designers would assume the tasks of photographers, art directors, prepress technicians, and animators. But specialization reestablished itself, as the complexity of digital skills became clear, and as the number of practitioners expanded to meet the demands of the dot-com boom in the 1990s. Digital infrastructure supported distributed production. Any phase of a complex production process—whether it involved coding, scanning, text input, prepress output, printing, binding, or packaging—could be handled in a separate location. Global electronic networks made information and capital highly mobile. These changes shifted the social structures in which graphic design and production operated. At the same time, digital technology brought conceptual changes to graphic design. Electronic media introduced a basic distinction between traditional **analog** documents and digital files. Analog documents possess the properties of their material production (continuous

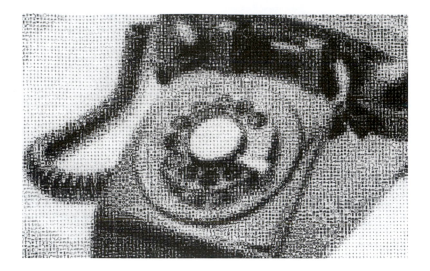

15.2 Leon Harmon and Kenneth Knowlton, computer-generated image, 1960s. Working at Bell Labs in the 1960s, engineer-designers Leon Harmon and Kenneth Knowlton experimented with image generation, using the input, output, and processing capabilities available at the time. Without a mouse, monitor, or printers, they designed an image-production program that used symbols to create a grayscale pattern. By dividing up an original image and assigning a value to each of its units, they were able to generate recognizable transformations of photographs. The explicitly mediated condition of these images has made them objects of acclaim and interest not envisioned by their inventors. The issue of whether such work is art, design, or engineering draws attention to the cultural tendency to redefine creativity and imagination in an attempt to understand what is meant by "human" at any given time. The imitation of an older technique—photographic halftone screens—in the new medium of computer-generated images is an example of cultural continuity in the face of technological change.

tone photography, line engravings, halftone screens, and so on). But all digital files are data, processed and stored as binary code. The implications of this abstraction are far-ranging. The reconceptualization of image and text as expressions of information involved intellectual leaps. Many designers simply engaged with new tools and their immediate capabilities. Others took up the theoretical questions these new tools raised. Most designers stopped short of learning complex programming, but Web-based work required new skills (knowledge of HTML, basic principles of file formats and style sheets). Digital technology brought more than a style shift. It wrought a fundamental change in designers' tasks and knowledge. Graphic design now involves structuring environments for use rather than simply creating effective displays. Responsibility for shaping information has profound implications for the role of design in contemporary culture and global society (Fig. **15.1**).

Digital technology: from punch cards and plotters to desktop computing

When the term *computer graphics* was coined by the Boeing Aircraft Company in the 1960s, electronic computing was still limited to mainframe computers with no graphical user interface (**GUI**). Such technology appealed to a very limited community. Only a few highly skilled or adventurous technicians were willing and able to write programs that depended on punch cards for their encoding and execution. Output was usually produced by a plotter pen, a kind of robotic arm that traced a path dictated by mathematically specified coordinates. The value of visualization for processing and analysis of complex statistical information was immediately obvious (it was efficient, legible, and condensed large amounts of information into a small graphic space). But it was not so evident that graphic designers had much to offer to the computing world. Engineers tended to downplay aesthetics, emphasize functionality, and call anything with any pictorial value at all a work of "computer art." By the mid-1960s, experiments at Bell Labs and a handful of other industrial and academic sites had created enough of this "art" for computer graphics to begin to be exhibited and appreciated, if only as curiosities (Fig. **15.2**).

Digital Design

Meanwhile, conceptual artists took an active interest in information processing. Interaction with early monitors was conducted via **command-line** interface, a system of written instructions for various computational functions. The notion that a set of instructions could generate an image, or that an image might be the outcome of statistical processing, caught the imagination of artists and curators. The emerging forms of **telematic** art, robotics, and electronic music and images all had their passionate advocates. Artist Sol Lewitt had proclaimed that "the idea is the machine that makes art," so it was not a huge leap to the idea of a real machine actually producing aesthetic objects (Fig. **15.3**).

Graphic designers played a role in visually interpreting and packaging new technologies. They helped sell the products of IBM, Apple, Microsoft,

All digital files are data, processed and stored as binary code.

and other entities that drove the microchip and dot-com booms of the 1980s and 1990s. Conversely, and more significantly, these technologies—in the form of affordable desktop capabilities—had a profound impact on the practice of graphic design. The development of an intuitive graphical user interface was a crucial turning point. Introduced in the mid-1980s, Apple computers succeeded in their campaign to capture the graphics market. Their operating systems were designed for graphical processing, and their icons and applications, including MacPaint and MacDraw, quickly established a direction for the industry. By 1985, the LaserWriter offered 300-dpi print resolution for desktop printing. Postscript software enabled smooth rendering of fonts and increased the quality of home and office output. The development of affordable printers and the establishment of industry standards for outputting film from data files closed the loop between desktop and print production. Glitches and compatibility problems plagued many early adopters. But, by the mid-1980s a designer could, in principle, design a font, set up a layout, input and manipulate an image or text, and produce a file that, more or less, conformed to the **WYSIWYG** (what-you-see-is-what-you-get) expectation. On the other hand, the

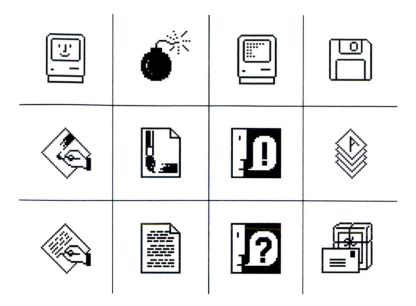

15.4 Susan Kare, Apple Macintosh icons, 1984. Kare's 1984 designs for Apple had to be constructed for the low-resolution display of early monitors. Within that constraint, her task was to create icons that would communicate effectively and unambiguously, to make the pictograms and palettes in MacDraw or MacPaint function as writing, drawing, painting, or layout tools. Convention plays a large part in legibility. These images are now so universal (familiar) that it is hard to recall their first appearance in the visual landscape. The functionality of Kare's designs should get some credit for the longevity of their basic shapes. These icons define a worldview in which a hierarchy of folders and files, palettes and tools organizes information and behavior. The extent to which we have accustomed ourselves to their use makes the values on which they are premised difficult to see. Wands, lassos, and marquees all offer ways to isolate parts of an image, but no tool exists for tearing out a scrap, for instance.

availability of design technology on virtually any desktop meant that clerical staff were often charged with basic design tasks that had once required the skills of professionals. The accessibility of production tools undercut the design profession since "anyone" could make a flyer or a brochure. The tools of design were momentarily confused with the skills of designers. Instantly accessible stock photography banks, click art, and a seemingly infinite variety of decorative elements removed some of the specialized aura from image production. Once digital design had become the professional standard, commercial designers who worked electronically had to contend with the constant overhead costs of rapid software and hardware

The tools of design were confused with the skills of designers.

obsolescence. Graphic designers were at the mercy of the industries they helped promote, and their own skills were constantly under upgrade pressure as well (Fig. **15.4**).

Many designers picked up new tools as useful extensions of what they already knew and did. But others embraced the specific aesthetic capabilities of new media. Electronically manipulated files had their own look, reflecting their processed, data-driven character. Jaggy type and **pixelated** images were both a fact of life and a formal opportunity for designers with first-generation equipment. But the most profound changes were not stylistic. The real shift was conceptual and involved understanding that images and texts were actually *information* stored as code. Digital files separate input from output. A sound file can be used to generate an image, and a typewriter keyboard can produce music. Code does not carry any constraints on its expression. The passage from design production to reproduction, whether from a sketch to camera-ready art or from a manuscript page to a typeset text block, had always entailed gaps and interpretation. But storing information in an abstract (digital) rather than material (analog) form introduced greater possibilities for manipulation.

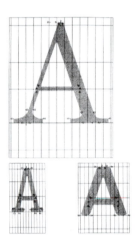

15.6 Donald Knuth, TeX and Metafont, 1979. Knuth's designs for TeX and Metafont were early experiments in generating type by mathematically formulating a description of each letter. Knuth was trying to solve the pragmatic problem of typesetting mathematical textbooks. Much to his surprise, he found that letters did not have simple, essential forms. They could not be described generally but could vary radically, depending on the face to which they belonged. In mathematical terms, letters belong to "open-ended" rather than finite sets because the design of the twenty-six letters can be varied almost infinitely. Style rather than logic establishes the relationships upon which typefaces rely for their functionality. Knuth also realized that details of fit, shape, form, and scale were not mechanical. Many decisions had to be made intuitively to achieve designs that were legible and pleasing to the eye—a fact well known to designers since antiquity. Knuth's experiments established useful foundations for digital type design.

Because all data files were, at base, machine code, they could be subjected to infinite processing. A photograph could be easily restructured to present a visual fiction indistinguishable from material fact. A new level of disbelief and distrust accompanied digital image composition, and ethical questions arose alongside fascination with the new capabilities (Fig. **15.5**).

Media transitions: type design and publications

Digital typeface design introduced philosophical questions as well as aesthetic challenges. What is a letter? Mathematician Donald Knuth asked this question with a distinct purpose in mind when he set out to design his typesetting and font creation programs TeX and Metafont in the 1970s. He was convinced that each letter must have a unique algorithmic identity. An **algorithm** is a set of specific instructions that describes a form fundamentally and completely. Knuth tried to discover algorithms for the alphabet, but he came to the realization that letters functioned primarily by being distinguished from each other within a stylistic system. This observation may seem obvious, but it made clear that letters were not independent "forms" that could be described by a single set of computational instructions. For the mathematician, as well as the designer, this was a revelation. Knuth's endeavor was related to earlier modern attempts at simplification in the design of a single, modular alphabet. Although initially guided by reason and logic, Knuth, like his predecessors, ultimately had to contend with the role played by aesthetics (Fig. **15.6**).

Such heady insights may not have been grasped by every practitioner. But progress in designing usable fonts for electronic environments did require grappling with the fundamentals of information processing and storage. Limits on output, questions of scalability, and the differing demands of screen display versus print quality had to be considered. The first system fonts for the Mac were designed by Susan Kare, based on a 72-dpi screen resolution. The search for multiple master fonts that could be modified to generate a range of weights, serif variations, and degrees of

15.7a Zuzana Licko, Oakland, 1985 *(right)*. Licko's typeface designs began to appear in the mid-1980s. Oakland, among the earliest, made a virtue of necessity by letting the jaggies define the look of an explicitly digital font. Technical restrictions of output devices, screen displays, postscript descriptions, type management programs, and other software were reflected in her designs for Emperor and Matrix. Licko's early fonts gave digital design a style that was distinctive, recognizable, and immediately popular. Her designs have become ubiquitous. Licko's contributions to the development of a wide range of approaches to the aesthetics of digital design found a forum in *Emigre*, a print publication that, from its start, showcased digital fonts.

We Read Best What We Read Most (Oakland 8)

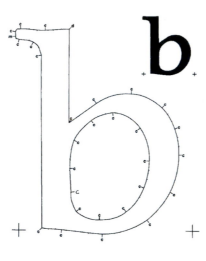

123 456

15.7c Matthew Carter, Bell Centennial, 1978 *(above)*. When Carter drew the original designs for Bell Centennial, he was adapting a metal face for use with Mergenthaler's phototypesetting equipment. The detailed adjustments he made involved calculating stair-stepped edges to minimize optical distortion. These drawings were hand-inked enlargements that delineated every tiny step of the curves he constructed. The insight Carter gained into problems of legibility and his rethinking of forms in the transition from one medium to another gave him a foundation on which to draw when designing digital fonts. Carter's screen fonts, Verdana and Georgia, helped define the style and functionality of digital type across a wide range of contexts and uses.

15.7d Matthew Carter, Bitstream Charter, 1987 *(above right)*. Like Bell Centennial, Bitstream Charter was conceived computationally as well as graphically. Its forms were designed using a computer's capabilities. Its various weights and sizes were interpolated by calculation rather than redrawn. Programming letterforms and providing rules for the relationships that constrain a style make explicit many assumptions about the way design functions. The procedural analysis of this approach requires that elements of drawing or design that might be left ambiguous in an analog medium be completely distinguished and explicitly described for digital processing.

15.7b Sumner Stone, Bézier points, 1985 *(left)*. Like many of the first digital type designers, Sumner Stone was able to transfer skills from earlier technologies and reconceptualize their foundation in digital media. Stone's working designs for letterforms show the pattern of **Bézier** points needed to define a shape effectively. The concept of a Bézier point might be applied to the design of metal or photographic type, but only in theory or at a drawing board. In digital design, however, manipulation of these points to create shapes at the intersection of a series of discrete arcs (sections of differently defined curves) is a fundamental means of design. These differences in the links between production and conception are profound, even if many designers work with them on an intuitive rather than an analytic level.

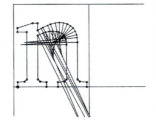 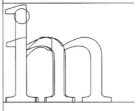 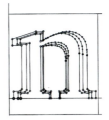

slant or italicization became a grail-like quest for some who, like Knuth, saw the value of mathematics for digital design of type. Meanwhile, the capacity of electronic images to support the illusion of three-dimensional space and motion led to typographic experiments with rendering perspective, shading, and spatial distortion (Figs. **15.7a** and **15.7b**).

Many traditionally skilled type designers shifted into electronic font design. Sumner Stone, Lance Hidy, Muriel Cooper, and Matthew Carter were established designers who embraced the computer's capabilities. Other professionals began their careers just as computers arrived on the scene. Bitstream, Font Bureau, Hoefler, Adobe, and other digital "foundries" designed fonts in two versions: one for print and one for the screen (Figs. **15.7c** and **15.7d**).

Print publications remained important venues for the promotion of digital design and provided a platform for serious conversation among practitioners. Along with *Emigre* and long-running journals like *Visible Language* and *Print*, *Wired* magazine galvanized public attention to "digital" graphics, as did industry publications like *Macworld*. But the presentation of digital graphics in static media also limited perception of the difference between stylistic features and the design of functionality. For most

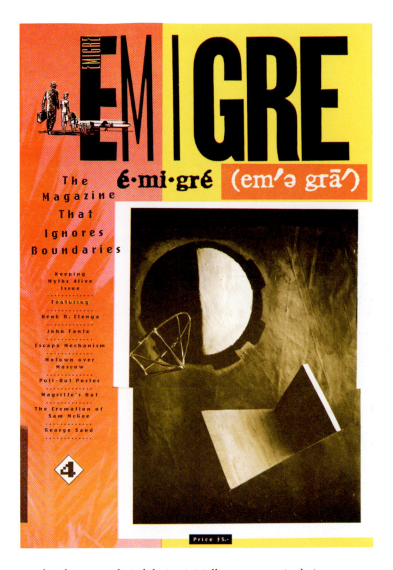

15.8 Rudy VanderLans, *Emigre*, 1986. First published in 1984, *Emigre* magazine became a premier site for design discussion. A collaboration between Rudy VanderLans and Zuzana Licko, *Emigre* also served to launch their new font designs. Each issue was different, and each change in mood and attitude was expressed graphically. Clearly intent on staying ahead of any particular curve, *Emigre* succeeded in creating a niche not occupied by older trade journals or academic reviews. It combined theoretical and practical approaches and promoted artists and designers working in traditional as well as digital media. Iconoclastic, heterodox, and seemingly insatiable, *Emigre* established a forum for frequently heated exchanges in the design community.

graphic designers, digital design initially meant manipulating type, vector graphics, and **pixel-based** images in the display space of an application. But interactivity itself soon became a focus of design, a focus that required attention to user scenarios and behaviors. Online sites like *Electronic Book Review* provided a forum for critical discussion that pushed practical issues of navigation, time-based structures, and multiple-state forms to the fore. The cultural dimensions of new media assumed increasing importance as a topic of concern and debate (Fig. **15.8**).

The practice of design for print changed. What had been specialized prepress tasks, entailing detailed knowledge of screen percentages, dot angles, and ink colors became the responsibility of individual designers. The specific attributes and limitations of output devices (printers, presses, and screens) also had to be understood and taken into account. Many designers who created fabulous imagery on screen were disappointed to find that the electronic aesthetic was not always matched in print. Learning to translate effectively from screen to paper was a skill to be acquired with experience (Fig. **15.9**).

15.9 Fred Davis, *Wired*, 1993. *Wired* magazine became the organ of digital culture for a generation that identified with its title. For mainstream readers, accustomed to the ordered environments bequeathed by modern editorial design, *Wired*'s format presented a challenge. Texts and images overlapped and intersected, disrespecting traditional boundaries and rules. This spread may not have been as radical as Carson's work for *Ray Gun*, but *Wired*'s visibility made its design particularly influential. Its pages demonstrated the effects that screen conventions (icons, menus, headers, navigation bars, and devices) were having on print culture. Formal influences move across media, and not just in one direction: While "pages" were linked on a Web site, newspapers borrowed sidebars and other features from networked environments.

15.10a Neville Brody font designs, 1991. Questioning communication and challenging legibility became a fetish of sorts in the 1980s and early 1990s. This trend coincided with digital typeface design, which spread so widely and quickly that new faces seemed to appear daily. Beginning in 1991, the experiments staged by Neville Brody and Jon Wozencroft as the Fuse project were one reaction to the proliferation of faces. Although not meant for actual use, these designs were part of a broader pattern of nonfunctional, almost anticommunicative practices. Superfluity and excess were motifs of early 1990s economics and culture. Against this backdrop, a disregard for normative rules produced a high-pressure, synthetic approach to typography and design. This attitude and its tactics contributed greatly to Brody's status as a celebrity designer.

15.10b Luc(as) de Groot, Jesus Loves You, 1995. Mutant design and extreme typography took full advantage of electronic capabilities. The shapes of letters spiraled out of all recognizable form, sporting spikes and haloes, trailing ribbons and fragments. These outrageous letterforms, with their crown-of-thorns neo-gothicism, owe their expressivity to the programmable medium that inspired them. The violence done to the letters intensifies from one iteration to the next, and the "thorns" spike to varying degrees. This design feature would be impossible in an analog format.

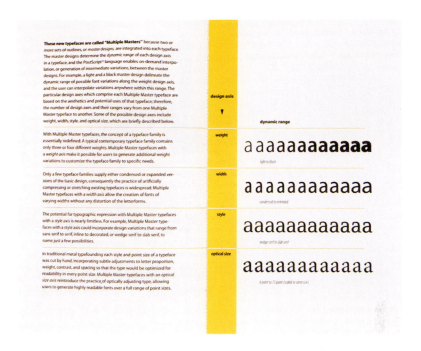

These new typefaces are called "Multiple Masters" because two or more sets of outlines, or master designs, are integrated into each typeface. The master designs determine the dynamic range of each design axis in a typeface, and the PostScript® language enables on-demand interpolation, or generation of intermediate variations, between the master designs. For example, a light and a black master design delineate the dynamic range of possible font variations along the weight design axis, and the user can interpolate variations anywhere within this range. The particular design axes which comprise each Multiple Master typeface are based on the aesthetics and potential uses of that typeface; therefore, the number of design axes and their ranges vary from one Multiple Master typeface to another. Some of the possible design axes include weight, width, style, and optical size, which are briefly described below.

design axis ▼

dynamic range

With Multiple Master typefaces, the concept of a typeface family is essentially redefined. A typical contemporary typeface family contains only three or four different weights. Multiple Master typefaces with a weight axis make it possible for users to generate additional weight variations to customize the typeface family to specific needs.

weight

aaaaaaaaaaa
light to black

Only a few typeface families supply either condensed or expanded versions of the basic design, consequently the practice of artificially compressing or stretching existing typefaces is widespread. Multiple Master typefaces with a width axis allow the creation of fonts of varying widths without any distortion of the letterforms.

width

aaaaaaaaaaaa
condensed to extended

The potential for typographic expression with Multiple Master typefaces with a style axis is nearly limitless. For example, Multiple Master typefaces with a style axis could incorporate design variations that range from sans serif to serif, inline to decorated, or wedge serif to slab serif, to name just a few possibilities.

style

aaaaaaaaaaa
wedge serif to slab serif

In traditional metal typefounding each style and point size of a typeface was cut by hand, incorporating subtle adjustments to letter proportion, weight, contrast, and spacing so that the type would be optimized for readability in every point size. Multiple Master typefaces with an optical size axis reintroduce the practice of optically adjusting type, allowing users to generate highly readable fonts over a full range of point sizes.

optical size

aaaaaaaaaaa
6 point to 72 point (scaled to same size)

15.10c Büro Destruct fonts, 1995–2001. The sheer variety of typefaces designed in the 1990s was dazzling. Their forms and names were imaginative, playful, and diabolically insightful as an index of the times. As poetic as the sample sheets of nineteenth-century display faces, these type specimens capture the fast-paced promotional entrepreneurship of their moment. Brands and logos, once signs of stability and global reach, became start-up shingles for fly-by-night companies to hang on a Web site. A look, a style, an identity were just a click or two away. The shortened feedback loop between design and production resembled other abbreviated life cycles in consumer culture—of businesses, profits, markets, and trends. These typefaces embody a trend-tracking marketing sensibility, an easy-come and too-easily-gone disposability. Few have any substantive presence or lasting power, and all are rendered more seductive by appearing in a vast menu of options, as if each one carried with it the whole field of possibilities. Once selected, however, they lose much of their allure, as the superficiality of their individual design becomes apparent.

15.10d Multiple master fonts, 1991. Multiple master fonts took advantage of the conceptual and computational capabilities of digital design. Their **parameters** could be manipulated to produce a range of weights, serif styles, and widths in sizes from 6 to 72 points. The construction of these faces depends entirely on processing. They are forms abstracted into a set of instructions that define a font's identity. Minion and the aptly named Myriad were two multiple master fonts launched by Adobe in the early 1990s. Adobe would eventually abandon the format, which always made more sense to typographers than to average users. In their conception, these fonts may be seen as an extension of Donald Knuth's earlier experiments in mathematical type design.

Fluidity and functionality

The basic characteristic of the digital environment—that all information is stored in binary code—made boundaries among formats fluid, overturning material distinctions that had been rigidly enforced by earlier print technologies. Letterpress printing, which had held graphic forms in its conceptual as well as technical grip since the 1450s, had separated texts and images according to their respective production requirements. Images had to be carved in relief on a block of wood or metal. Type was also printed relief but was cast and either set by hand or by machines that did not handle images. The concept of the page seemed to divide among discrete areas: text blocks and image blocks. The introduction of lithographic techniques to poster and handbill production in the nineteenth century made it easier to integrate image and text on a single drawn surface. But no efficient technology for setting text replaced letterpress until photocomposition arrived in the 1950s and 1960s. Even then, text and image production methods remained distinct. Only at the stage of **mechanicals** was a composite of text and image artwork assembled for platemaking purposes. Digital media changed this relationship dramatically, bringing text and image files together in radically innovative ways (Figs. **15.10a–d**).

Early digital design programs were clumsy, hampered by limited memory and processor speeds. But as they developed, Photoshop, Pagemaker, and QuarkXPress proved well suited to the sophisticated layering and collaging of images and texts that had been characteristic of design in the 1970s and 1980s. Freedom from the constraints of traditional darkroom and copy-camera production was palpable in the enthusiasm with which digital manipulation was explored. Every visual form was treatable as either a **bitmap,** pixel-based image, or a **scalable** vector graphic. Whether the original was a letter, a text, a hand-drawn picture, a photograph, or a film

15.11 Warren Corbitt, one9ine, modular type, 2002. These type-design projects take advantage of high-resolution screen display to render letterforms as if they were three-dimensional objects. The shadows and illusions of overlapping depth in one9ine's NEXT design for ESPN make the letters seem to belong to a hyperreal universe. The spinning *X* is from Corbitt's Quicktime typeface, WhyX. These simulations are made from pixels and inhabit a world of imitation light where complex polygons can be programmed and manipulated. In a computational environment, these shapes and transformations can be executed with speed and variation unimaginable in traditional design. Stylistically, they embody a mutant sensibility, lending their trendiness to the idea of cloning. They do not appear aberrant but novel, and their fully synthetic look makes them seem almost hygienically safe, as if to reassure us that they live only in the digital world.

still did not matter. As a digital file, it could be mixed and cut, copied and pasted, merged and flattened, selected, reversed, and filtered through any operation available in a program. While conspicuous manipulation of images and text marked a first phase of digital design, later practitioners found subtler ways to use electronic media. Initial public reactions to the alteration of photographic images subsided, as synthetic imagery that was "born digital" became more familiar (Fig. **15.11**).

If image and text were no longer distinguished by their production, did that erase the difference between seeing and reading? Questions about word and image relations became charged, as long-held attitudes were challenged. The concept of **fungibility** gained new meaning. Taken from economics, the term describes the way assets can be moved from one form to another

Questions about word and image relations became charged.

15.12 Pixar, *Tin Toy*, 1988. © 1988 Pixar. Fantasy images generated by graphics programs morphed rapidly, but even early imaging capabilities produced some striking effects. Since simulated surfaces were rendered with very little texture or variation, the result was sometimes an odd blend of unreality and realism. An enthusiasm for sheer technical possibility gave rise to a rhetoric of the "virtual" that reached hyperbolic levels in marketing contexts. Promoters saw potential benefits to the entertainment industry in heightened special effects that suggested a **fantasmatic** universe in which all forms of imaginative desire might be satisfied. The programmatic character and repleteness of these worlds, however, risked shutting down the very impulses that give rise to desire for engagement with less finished effects.

(stock to cash to bonds or gold). Unlike real estate, fungible assets are fluid. The notion of graphic fungibility suggested that a file could migrate easily from one form to another. The collapse of information and capital into a single concept was more than incidental. The discourses of design tellingly engaged other vocabularies as well. Digital hybridity and mutation affirmed metaphors of genetics, cloning, and **recombinant** production of organic material that postmodern design had explored. The cultural implications of this disposition became apparent. The idea of abstracting information from context and repurposing it electronically produced a chilling effect when issues of privacy, property, and identity came into play. The hyperbolic rhetoric of progress served market interests, but cultural critics raised questions about the unqualified and celebratory claims for a recombinant world (Fig. **15.12**).

Page layout programs, beginning with very simple tools for blocking text, choosing type style, size, and color, and integrating graphics were not merely ways of making documents. They gave designers the means to specify layout instructions. This "meta" aspect of design was perhaps clearest to those who ventured into the definition of style sheets. These

15.13a Interface metaphors: Windows 95. Windows and desktops are the two basic metaphors that emerged from the competing models of PC and Mac environments. The contrast is a telling one. "Windows" suggest frames through which to see and move. Although technically "windows" kept applications distinct, the ease of shifting from one document to another, or one program to the next, reinforced the sense that information had no specific properties and could be manipulated without loss. The use of windows in Web environments produced a seamless set of portals through which the illusion of "surfing" brought the sensation of constant movement and access to a single workstation. But the isolated and sedentary circumstances of Web viewing contradict this illusion. Tensions between the metaphors of travel and easy access and the realities of user experiences have been the subject of critical study and debate, exposing the ways in which graphic design shapes expectations and hides assumptions.

15.13b Interface metaphors: Apple IIgs desktop, 1988. Whereas the windows environment proposes a portal into interconnected space, the "desktop" interface presents an environment in which to work. The studio and study approach to the desktop is organized by icons that are actually object-oriented elements of programming. These mimic the attributes of the "real" objects they represent, translating familiar habits of work into electronically mediated activities. The constraints imposed by software design and programming often disappear in the process (a file folder cannot be emptied onto the desktop by shaking, for instance, and the strict hierarchies of information structures impose many value judgments on files). Windows and desktop metaphors are fictions through which our relation to the activities of daily computer use is organized. The two have merged and so have their axes—of networked exchange, on the one hand, and intensely absorbing, highly structured, and powerful workspaces, on the other. The computer is a site of intersection, a point of complex intersubjective mediation and personal production, although we rarely pause to think of it in these terms. Denaturalizing the computer and analyzing the bases of calculation, classification systems, symbolic logic, and electronic communication on which it gains its authority are important for understanding its effects.

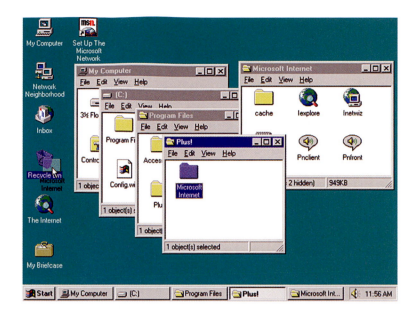

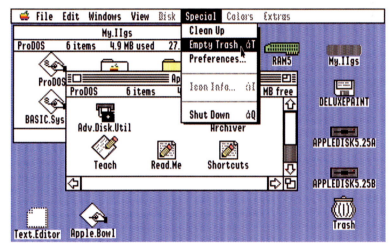

linked particular choices of type style, size, color, or weight to an identified type of information (such as header, subhead, or paragraph). Graphically formatting data types became routine. The conceptual complexity of this task was soon hidden by its familiarity. Style sheets made all graphic designers into information designers. Here again, the fundamentally abstract condition of information stored as data came into play, as designers realized they could call forth multiple graphic expressions from a single file.

Software created opportunities but also structured and restricted options. Designers had to work within the choices offered by a menu or palette. These translated analog functions, such as painting with a brush, drawing with a pencil, or using an airbrush, into step-by-step actions. All production was mediated by an electronic interface. The **transparency** of the windows interface and desktop metaphors came to be assumed as givens. Digital icons like trash cans or file folders mimicked the attributes of their analog counterparts. A file put into the "trash" was effectively "thrown away." A digital pencil *appeared* to have the properties of a graphite one (although

15.14 Microsoft's Bob, 1995.
Early interface designs often produced environments that were too literal in their attempts to render the features of a physical experience in digital form. Such interfaces tended to be clunky, taking up more screen space and work time than was necessary. A computer environment is not literal but abstract. The schematic organization of monitor space supports many activities because its components are not task-specific (a file folder is as useful for recipes as it is for video clips or sound recordings). Literal analogies, like cartoon furniture or architecture, have limited usability. Microsoft's infamous Bob was an interface meant to be user-friendly, and its cartoon design included animals and objects that talked. These "agents" were supposed to assist new users with applications, but the design missed its mark. Users found that the mediation of activity by complicated agents and devices took up too much time, and the novelty of the cute factor wore off quickly. A lesson well-learned, Bob was an industry failure that was not repeated outside the gaming sector.

one handled it very differently in an electronic environment). The interface produced the expectation that a digital tool was a familiar object with known behavior. Creating this illusion required sophisticated programming that disappeared behind the iconographic display. Users did not need to see or know the code. But these simulations also had unintended effects, naturalizing certain presentations and uses of information and marginalizing others (Figs. **15.13a** and **15.13b**).

Windows and desktop imagery merged in the 1990s under market pressures for low-cost graphical operating systems and cross-platform compatibility. Each program was accessed separately through its own discrete pane in the windows environment. But, increasingly, these applications were functionally integrated: Text, image, spreadsheet, and communications software shared tools and files. The windows metaphor was apt for an environment that was premised on transparency and ease of operation. But how did it relate to the metaphors of menus and desktop icons? These visual and functional analogies differed not only in their technical bases, but also in the associations they carried. The struggle to determine exactly how much metaphoric value was enough and how much was too much led to some curious experiments in interface design. Over-cluttered interfaces were quickly rejected by users. They preferred the schematic suggestion of a desktop to a literal rendering of a physical environment (Fig. **15.14**).

Soon multimedia, CD-ROM, and game designers were confronting the challenges of interface design on a daily basis, inventing the features of dynamic electronic environments. The graphic task was no longer limited to communication but extended to the functional structuring of information and scenarios for its access and use. The human factor was paramount. User-driven design required rapid transformations of display that integrated many different kinds of data. The development of the World Wide Web made such design demands common in the field. First-generation sites

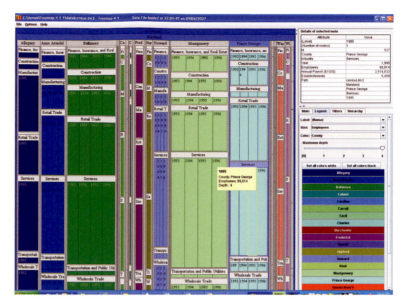

15.15 Starlight Information Visualization interface, 2007. Information interfaces place a high demand on screen real estate. Visual conventions borrowed from print media are often too restricting to support real-time integration of multiple feeds rendered against a series of variables. Various forms of projection and dimensional rendering allow an experimental interface like Starlight, developed at Pacific Northwest Labs, to generate a complex information space. Learning to use and navigate these spaces can be a challenge; their graphic design is often constrained by computational issues.

15.16a Ben Shneiderman, treemap interface, 1992. One of the leading figures in information display and interface design, Shneiderman has contributed pedagogical and practical principles to the field. Graphic features have to function within the constraints of basic cognitive capabilities (short-term memory, for example) and anticipate user satisfaction to arrive at a logical breakdown of tasks into manageable units. Graphic designers work with technical and conceptual teams on these large-scale projects to coordinate visual information and functionality. The way a site works becomes part of its basic information, while choices about what is left behind the scenes and what is visualized go beyond issues of display to an integration of input and output that combines content, service, and use. These tree maps allow massive amounts of information to be displayed in real time, but this efficiency conceals the cultural conditions from which these patterns arise. Many essential features of human behavior cannot be "parameterized" into metrics suitable for display.

offered limited kinds of access to the information they displayed. Second-generation sites responded in real time to a much broader range of input by users. Paying bills, making travel reservations, selecting and purchasing just about anything, participating in online auctions and polls, and, of course, communicating for business, education, and social purposes depended on designers and programmers breaking complex scenarios into step-by-step interactions. Third-generation sites were designed to be adaptive and mutable in relation to an emerging user profile. The conception of interactivity in both immediate and evolutionary senses involved **HCI** (human computer interaction) studies and cognitive science in addition to programming logic and networking structures. A new vocabulary of dynamic systems, flow and exchange, sequence and cuts, and links and connections, was essential to understanding information architecture. The economic pressure and financial incentive of the highly competitive dot-com boom in the 1990s (fueled by stock market speculation as to the potential of digital technologies) pushed the demand for skills that had not been part of a traditional design education. Needless to say, the challenge for educators and practitioners was considerable (Fig. **15.15**).

The myth of immateriality and challenges of digital design

Designers who were making the transition from print to the Web were faced with substantive challenges that reconfigured their profession. They were increasingly called on to give visual form to complex problems that involved massive databases and interactive systems. This meant grappling anew with the understanding that design was not just *delivering* information—it *was* information. Graphic designers had always been aware that display was part of content, but new media demanded new critical terms to account for the ways in which information design shaped knowledge. Relations among elements and narratives of use were not inherently visible on the screen. They had to be understood behaviorally and translated into graphic form (Fig. **15.16a**).

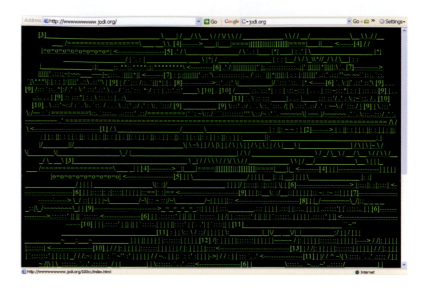

15.16b www.jodi.org, 2007. The jodi.org site has been an energetic source of critical commentary on the established graphic vocabulary of digital design. Their mission is to undercut the predictability and logic according to which computers function and on which people depend. By creating site-works that defy expectations, jodi.org playfully discharges its critical force, placing viewers in situations that conflict with interface norms and conventions. The resulting frustration creates distance, as intended. The self-reflexiveness of jodi's work extends a postmodern impulse into deconstruction of the electronic environment's otherwise smooth operations. This work also demonstrates the continuing importance of designers' involvement with unpaid experimentation. The potential of new media depends on such explorations. Finding out what interactive design could do required that groups like jodi.org, firms like Post Tool Design, and projects like Ben Benjamin's superbad.com push it to its limits. The humor and playfulness of this work offered a welcome island of alternative thought in the increasingly commercialized world of the Internet.

Although many companies retained in-house design staffs, much design activity—like labor in other sectors—was outsourced. Manufacturing was removed to locations where regulations of working conditions, wages, or environmental impact were different. Unseen costs had no way of registering in the promotion campaigns that touted each new generation of consumer electronics. Unions and benefits shrank in the 1990s, and designers found themselves sharing the plight of other independent contractors, absorbing responsibility for their own overhead and for the upkeep of studio equipment and software. Individuals assumed business,

Significantly, the hours of effort that went into electronic design

tax, and insurance liabilities that had traditionally been borne by employers. Their work promoted the same companies whose labor policies affected them on a daily basis (Fig. **15.16b**).

The independent designer had to maintain a steady rate of consumption just to keep pace with the "upgrade addiction" fostered by computer software and hardware industries. Each generation of computer technology introduced new platforms, devices, and ports that rendered older models and software obsolete within a very short time. Such planned obsolescence also had environmental costs, as hardware parts piled up in landfills or were shipped off to be unsafely disassembled. Issues of licensing, particularly where fonts were concerned, had troubling implications when file-sharing and copying were easy to do and hard to monitor. Perhaps most significantly, the hours of effort that went into electronic design tended to disappear in the seamlessness of the final product. Few images or compositions have ever seemed so "natural," so completely and simply *there* as those that come out of a high-end inkjet or laser printer or appear on the screen. Digital photography and production capabilities, online archives of graphic materials, all make the designer's art seem trivial to many who

15.17 www.mcdonalds.co.jp. The global reach of Web designs requires a grasp of basic cultural translation techniques. Attitudes toward communication differ, as do notions of individuality, power relations, social decorum, and other basic concepts that govern acceptable behavior. Aimed at communicating across language barriers, the welcoming screen for McDonald's in Japan uses only images. The graciously bowing woman is not a neutral icon, and her gesture could be interpreted in a variety of ways by different users according to their locations and backgrounds. Colors, compositional structures, shapes, forms, gestures, and stylistic elements carry connotations that are culturally specific.

imagine that "the machine does it all." By the same token, virtual spaces of electronic communication often conceal the complex human networks necessary to most production processes. The change in vocabulary—from international, to multinational, to global—reveals changes in thinking. The term *global* absorbs all forms of cultural difference and national or local identities into a single entity. The erasure of differences creates an illusion under which political and social struggles are masked (Fig. **15.17**).

tended to disappear in the seamlessness of the final product.

Conclusion The role and identity of the graphic designer are seriously challenged in the twenty-first century. Many designers no longer work with stable, flat compositions but instead conceive of graphic systems that coordinate multiple behind-the-scenes tasks in constantly changing systems. These systems depend on display and infrastructure to aggregate emerging conditions. The once innovative concept of a "language of form" is now being reconfigured through cognitive studies and advanced systems theory, aided by new strains of psychology, cultural theory, and social analysis. The graphics of "situated," "emergent," and "adaptive" design have built-in responsive properties. Everything from games to government documents, medical records to traffic and weather reports, requires a dynamic online interface. Even design for print has been affected, often shifted into complementary roles, by the rise of online and on-screen forms of promotion, communication, and management. Patterns of labor outsourcing by European- and North American-owned companies to workforces in remote locations mean that graphic designers who are seeking to define their role in service economies need to have something to contribute besides basic production skills. Environmental considerations

in the high-tech sector press increasingly on every aspect of the industry, as awareness of the contradictions of promoting consumption at the cost of sustainability rises. Graphic design is now information design in the broadest sense, and a high demand for technical sophistication is built into the profession. Online games, multiplayer virtual worlds, and their attendant economies and social dynamics promote a do-it-yourself approach to customized experience through interactive narrative, avatars, and fantasy scenarios. Graphic designers envision and establish conditions for production in these environments, rather than designing products themselves. This difference marks a critical shift in the nature of graphic design. Whether serving commercial, entertainment, public, or private sector interests, graphic designers will increasingly be called on to design conditions of use, not just effective or aesthetic displays of useful information. The graphic designer is continually summoned and tested in such a world, as the definition of the profession becomes a moving target (Fig. **15.18a**).

In the twenty-first century, graphic designers work with increased awareness of the critical stakes of their contributions. The celebrity culture of late capitalist economies promotes a mythic image of individual talent identified as aesthetic branding. But this ideology is underwritten by a global corporate culture driven by strategies geared to maximize returns on investments and minimize regulations or restrictions that would make it accountable to local populations. The image of the graphic designer as a commercial artist who sets style trends is largely illusory, even if a handful of individuals rise to that level of professional influence and recognition. Daily design practice is inseparable from issues of labor, consumption, ecology, and exploitation in a global context. Information designs integrate dynamic, real-time processing, and user-driven Web content creates cross-cultural communities in a networked world. The rhetorical force of interface design—its emphasis on information over conditions of knowledge—quickly disappears under its familiarity. The logical foundations of computational media force certain methods of work and discourage others. The image and experience of control through the manipulation of metaphors in the form of screen icons are often out of synch with realities of political and social agency. The mediating aspect of graphic design carries enormous weight, but it also creates a safe distance, reifying reality. The more the screen disappears through habits of use, the more it becomes a means of structuring expectations about

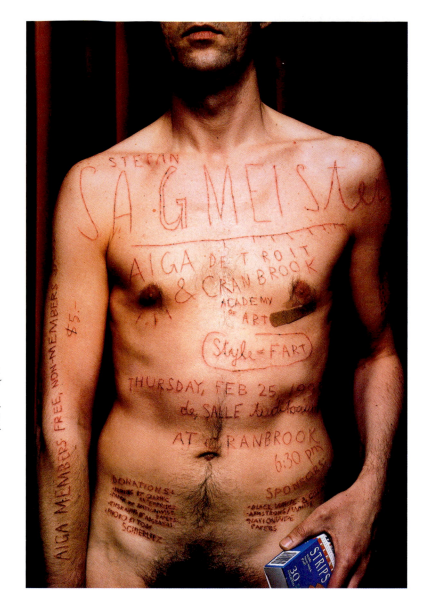

15.18b Stefan Sagmeister, AIGA Detroit poster, 1999. This self-promotional poster makes a graphic point by reinserting the designer's body into the process of design. The disappearance of work into product is part of a larger set of economic conditions. This tendency toward effacement of labor is one reason why the cultural values of design are not always reflected in the economic benefits that accrue to designers. The rhetoric of "immateriality" that accompanied the development of electronic tools tended to gloss over a material basis of production that involved real people doing real work in lived conditions. Here, Sagmeister makes a striking argument against reducing the flows of information, capital, and labor to abstractions, even as he creates a fetishistic image of the designer himself.

what is feasible, possible, even imaginable in graphic and cultural terms. Design in the virtual environment can take on an insidious authority that translates into ideas about the workings of the world. Designers often feel caught in an ethical bind, working for industries whose values they may not support, or whose policies seem destructive to local cultures, opposed to individual belief systems, or simply unsustainable. Devising viable approaches to information design and keeping pace with changing professional demands diminish the time for reflection on a profession that contributes so powerfully to the signs and symbols that shape our world. The basic questions of whose interests are served by any and every instance of graphic work, how design is complicit with agendas of coercion or education, and what effects are produced by the way information is profiled and accessed, stored and used, will continue to be crucial to graphic designers (Fig. **15.18b**).

Digital Design 1970s–2000s

1959 Microchip invented

1960 Ted Nelson conceives of "hypertext"

1963 Douglas Engelbart's experimental mouse

1964 BASIC (Beginner's All-Purpose System Instruction Code) programming language introduced

1969 Compu-Serv Network, Inc. launches dial-up computer time-sharing service

1970 Daisy wheel printers introduced

First affordable dot matrix printers

1971 Intel microprocessor invented

1975 Microsoft founded by Bill Gates and Paul Allen

Laser printers introduced

1976 Inkjet printers introduced

Apple computer, designed by Steve Jobs and Steve Wozniak, introduced

Richard Saul Wurman coins phrase *information architecture*

1977 Apple II, featuring color display and floppy disk storage, released

1978 Donald Knuth develops first versions of his typesetting and font creation programs, TeX and Metafont

1981 First commercially available CDs

First IBM PC with Microsoft MS-DOS software

Mouse commercially available

Bitstream, first digital type design company, founded

TCP/IP protocol adopted as standard for Internet communication

1982 CompuServe sells connectivity to its nationwide network

Disney film *Tron* uses computer graphics

Two hundred computers connected to Internet

Charles Geschke and John Warnock found Adobe, invent Interpress page description language

1983 Apple Lisa released

1984 William Gibson coins term *cyberspace*

Apple Macintosh computers with Graphical User Interface introduced

Emigre magazine launched

1985 Voyager company founded for CD-ROM publishing

The WELL (Whole Earth 'Lectronic Link), prototypical online community, started by Stewart Brand and Larry Brilliant

First 300 dpi laser printer (for the Macintosh)

Adobe introduces PostScript; combined with Apple hardware, makes "desktop publishing" possible

Adobe develops Illustrator for the Macintosh, using its PostScript file format

Aldus introduces Pagemaker, first page layout program

1986 Microsoft Windows launched

1987 QuarkXPress released

1988 Prozac marketed

Legal battle between Microsoft and Apple over use of GUI elements begins

1989 Font Bureau founded by David Berlow et al.

Tim Berners Lee develops a hypertext browser that he calls World Wide Web

1990 Adobe launches Photoshop 1.0

Dial-up access widely available

Electronic Frontier Foundation founded

1991 Tomahawk cruise missiles used in Operation Desert Storm

Nintendo introduces Gameboy to U.S. market

1992 V-chip prototype introduced by Tim Collings

1993 Mosaic, first Internet browser with a GUI, leads to exponential growth of Internet traffic

Six hundred Web sites online

1993 Myst, a lushly illustrated CD-ROM adventure, originates immersive narrative games

Wired magazine launched

1994 First digital cameras for consumers

Yahoo! launched

South by Southwest (SXSW) festival adds multimedia conference
W3C World Wide Web Consortium founded
Netscape browser launched
Amazon.com founded
First banner ads; first shopping sites
1995 One-hundred thousand Web sites online
Java software released
DVDs introduced
Craig Newmark starts Craigslist
eBay founded
Real Audio begins streaming on Web
Microsoft releases Internet Explorer, starts browser wars
1996 John Perry Barlow posts his *Declaration of the Independence of Cyberspace*
Human genome halfway mapped
Macromedia releases Flash 1.0
1997 Communications Decency Act declared unconstitutional
For the first time, more e-mails sent than letters
One million Web sites online
Fair Trade Labelling Organizations International (FLO) founded
1998 Digital Millennium Copyright Act
Viagra launched by Pfizer
Google founded
1999 Napster file-sharing software introduced
Second Life founded by Philip Rosedale
Y2K scare; demand for reprogramming begins wave of outsourcing to India
2000 AOL merges with Time Warner
Dot-com stock market crash
2001 September 11 attacks
U.S. invades Afghanistan
Apple introduces iPod
Toyota introduces Prius hybrid worldwide
2002 Nano-tex, wearable nanotechnology fabrics developed
Queen Elizabeth II celebrates fifty years of rule
Venezuelan Hugo Chavez ousted and reinstated as president
Boston Archbishop Law resigns amid growing sex abuse scandals
2003 U.S. invades Iraq
Space shuttle *Columbia* explosion kills all seven astronauts
Saddam Hussein captured by U.S. troops
MySpace launched
2004 Abu Ghraib prison images made public
2005 Iraqi elections held
Hurricane Katrina
2006 Donald Rumsfeld resigns as U.S. Secretary of State
Bill Gates steps aside as Microsoft chairman to concentrate on philanthropy

Tools of the Trade

Macintosh computer
Graphical user interface (GUI)
Mouse
Wacom tablet
Digital fonts
Digital stock photography
Drawing software
Image manipulation software
Page layout software
Font design software
Motion graphics software
Rendering software
Animation software
Multimedia software
Scanner
Digital camera
Inkjet printer
Inkjet cartridges
Broadband Internet access
Wireless network
Digital offset
SGML
HTML
XML
XHTML

16. Graphic Design and Globalization

- Graphic designers give visual form to the abstractions of **globalization** and make legible the vast scale of its dynamic networks of influence and exchange.

- Graphic design practices exemplify the complex conditions of globalization, building cultural bridges among stakeholders whose agendas and values may be at odds.

- A wide array of cultural traditions inform approaches to graphic communication that challenge the legacy of Western modernism, as graphic designers synthesize local and global styles.

- Graphic designers promote social entrepreneurship and responsible consumerism by modeling the interconnectedness of all activities in a global context.

- Graphic design education incorporates the basic technological fluency necessary to participate in the digital dissemination of global communications.

16.1a Earth from space, NASA, 1968.
Breathtaking images of the earth were transmitted from space during the United States' Apollo 8 mission in 1968. In searching for the moon, human beings discovered their earth, and the impact on collective consciousness was enormous. A recognition of the beauty and fragility of the planet gave new impetus to ecological and political movements based on the idea of a shared world. Since then, the impacts of human activity on the environment, which do not tend to be contained within national boundaries, have become a challenge to global relations. In the process, both the disproportionate responsibilities and the common lot of the world's inhabitants have been exposed. In this sense, the need to address the causes of climate change, for example, encapsulates many of the issues that characterize a globalized condition.

The concept of globalization invokes an interconnected world of networked information and mobile assets, labor, goods, and services. The impact of globalization on graphic design has been profound, affecting approaches to style, visual organization, and the training and tasks of the designer. The skills of graphic designers are needed to make the virtual and complex conditions of globalization graspable. As national identity and state sovereignty are challenged by global trends, many corporate, non-governmental, and activist organizations operate across traditional boundaries. Thus graphic designers often play the role of bridge-builders among cultures and communities. While the internationalist style of the mid-twentieth century aspired to universality in the design of identity systems that unified diverse aspects of production, designers in a global context may choose to apply their abilities to visualizing the costs and complications of consumption, whether environmental, political, or economic. New technological and cultural constraints shape the work of designers, who wrestle with the agendas of multiple stakeholders and value systems in projects that serve global commerce and communication. Designers also have to cope with seeing their work migrate across technological platforms that may strip away the visual and stylistic integrity that have traditionally been the hallmark of carefully crafted design. Formally and conceptually, graphic designers are involved in a cross-cultural fertilization that is more absorptive and synthetic than the hybrid graphics of late twentieth-century postmodern eclecticism and appropriation. Global encounters place the work of graphic designers in productive dialogue with a range of design cultures that exceeds the bases of Western training and tests the assumptions of modernism and

16.1b Craig Roth and Wordle, word cloud, 2009. A word cloud imposed on an image of the earth seen from space creates a graphic synthesis so familiar that it hardly needs to be seen to be recognized. The once striking planetary image here serves as a mere surface for an automated typographic rendering. Warped text obliterates the features of the earth, evoking the extent to which concepts of globalization gloss over specific features of the cultural landscape.

postmodernism. The notion of globalism brings the recognition that all of our actions and decisions are interdependent. As agents of global communication systems, designers contribute to networked conditions that affect lived local realities (Fig. **16.1a**).

Designers put into play a powerful set of metaphors that shape

Globalization and design
Globalization points to the interdependency and integration that underpin many aspects of contemporary life. It also marks significant shifts—from the political foundations that shaped the modern era to the current primacy of economic forces, and from production to a focus on consumption. Design is called upon to provide images of a situation in which policy planning, resource management, human rights, and other crucial dealings occur at a global scale. Designers give visual form to the interconnections of money, power, and cultural ideas. By creating images of a consolidated world, designers put into play a powerful set of metaphors that shape common understandings of our complex global environment. Devising graphic forms that communicate multiplicity but avoid clichés, trendy effects, and bland generalizations can be difficult (Fig. **16.1b**).

The rise of non-governmental organizations and other transnational entities parallels the emergence of globalism. Working for organizations that operate outside the boundaries of nations or states, designers create graphic identities that circulate in many cultural contexts and networks of exchange. Whether representing a non-governmental organization or

16.2a Donal McLaughlin, United Nations emblem, 1945. A quintessential symbol of international cooperation, the United Nations came into being in 1945, in the immediate aftermath of World War II. Its mission was to promote world peace by advocating principles of justice, human rights, and dignity in a forum that would allow small and more powerful countries to balance interdependence and self-interest. Olive branches embrace the globe of its emblem in a sign of optimism whose Western roots are traceable to classical antiquity. The continents are arranged around the north pole—a view that may reinforce the dominance of the northern hemisphere but has the virtue of not placing any particular nation at its center. The UN continued work begun by the League of Nations after WWI, but with the formation of its Economic and Social Council and agencies such as the World Bank and International Monetary Fund, the UN also announced a new era in which economic development would be seen as key to the maintenance of international security.

16.2b World Bank logo, undated, *(above).* Conceived in 1944 at Bretton Woods, New Hampshire, the World Bank initially helped rebuild Europe after World War II. As an independent specialized agency of the UN, the World Bank continues to provide financial assistance to developing nations. The World Bank's logo replaces separate land masses with longitude and latitude lines that unite an abstract globe. In contrast to this simplified image, the Bank's business often involves negotiations among private and public entities with potentially diverging interests.

promoting global business interests, identity campaigns tend to center on a unified image. Such images can conceal as much as they reveal about the organizations for which they stand, wherever these organizations may fall on the political spectrum. Global branding operates as a graphic ideology, reifying values into images. The question raised by such images is whether the design of any global graphic identity, or indeed information campaign, can communicate the complexity of the relations it represents. The most

common understandings of our complex global environment.

widely circulated graphic currency, logos signal the persistence of modernist approaches to universal legibility (Figs. **16.2a** and **16.2b**).

Graphic designers have helped clarify the distinction between internationalism and globalism. These notions share a realization that all parts of the world are connected, but they construe major forces and patterns of behavior differently. Internationalism posits a world in which people and things move from one place to another along physical routes. Internationalism was premised on a desire for cooperation orchestrated by treaties negotiated among sovereign nations whose local regulations governed political and economic activities. Globalization is focused on processes and exchanges themselves, rather than the territories they cross. In a global world, networks are conceived as independent of nation-states and often operate beyond their control or regulation. The shift from international to global conditions cannot be pinpointed in any single moment or event. But the impact of digital communication has played a significant role in abstracting value from context, as if information circulated freely, independent of the conditions of its production. The sense that ideas, assets, power, ownership, or cultural

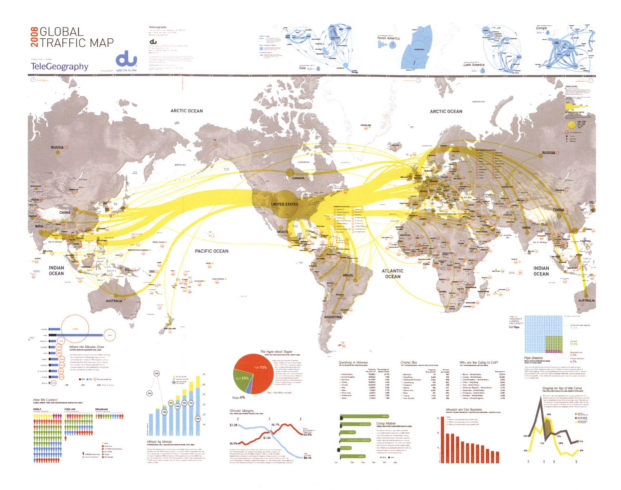

16.3a *Global Traffic Map*, TeleGeography, **2008** *(above)*, and 16.3b *World Internet Traffic Flow*, **1998** *(right)*. Transforming enormous amounts of data into a legible graphic produces an image of the world united by traffic on the Internet. Although the graphic language of information design has developed over centuries, the scale and refreshing of data to be expressed test the designer's skills in new ways. Oversimplification is one of the prices paid for legibility. In looking at such graphics, one might ask what is not, or cannot be, shown within their parameters, even as one notes the expertise that shapes what is presented. A shift in perspective between these maps changes the basic sense of the information they configure. There are clear rhetorical trade-offs between emphasizing the overall volume of traffic or the quantity of its points of origin and destination.

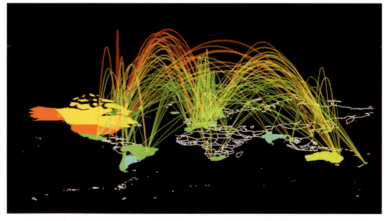

materials can be manipulated or managed digitally contributes to the conception of a global world constituted by networked systems. Such notions can mask inequities in human and environmental costs or conceal the grounds for political struggle under a design banner that creates an illusion of commonality (Figs. **16.3a** and **16.3b**).

Design firms have to balance local style and global reach. As a result, the concept of cultural translation has gained purchase. Whether working with large entities that command substantial resources or with groups

16.4 Alan Jacobson, Jody Graff, and their students, identity and collateral designs for a sunflower oil cooperative in the Rugerero Survivors Village, Rwanda, 2009. Designed by a class at Drexel University that worked in dialogue with members of a cooperative in Rwanda, these coordinated materials include a logo, a banner, tags, labels, and other collateral. Students began the project in their freshman year and visited the cooperative several times over four years. As a final phase of the project, the group returned to Rwanda with an inventory of ready materials. Rather than impose their sensibility on the community they hoped to help build, students worked to incorporate lessons learned on-site and to design a project of maximal benefit within the context of its use.

16.5a New Leaf Paper logo, 1999, and 16.5b Kiva logo, 2005. Design in the service of green consumption and social entrepreneurship has increased with global awareness. Whereas modern identity design concealed the life cycle of products, designers working in a global context tend to be more sensitive to the relations between labor conditions, environmental factors, and profits that underpin a commodity's identity. Like the leaf that sprouts on Kiva's logo, symbolizing the generative effect of microloans to developing countries, organic imagery is chosen for the paper company's logo to signify a sustainable practice. A manufacturer's reputation is tied to the public image constructed by such designs. Changes in ownership or shifts in the policies of parent companies are not registered in the designs of established brands. Such designs may promote identity recognition using the techniques of modernism, even as they seek to define and serve a new agenda.

that see design as a means of self-determination and empowerment, designers often serve as cultural bridge-builders among disparate communities. Some designers find it advantageous to immerse their work in local customs. Successful design firms from Europe and North America maintain branches in Japan, China, India, and other major markets, realizing that genuine relevance requires firsthand cultural knowledge. By the same token, manufacturers have been prompted to open offices outside of Europe and North America as bases for aggressive campaigns suited to new markets for their products. These moves are part of a growing trend. As graphic designers work outside their own cultures, they learn about traditions that extend their understanding of communication in diverse communities (Fig. **16.4**).

Global perspectives have also brought the values of social entrepreneurship and green design into focus. Environmental impacts and the need for responsible consumption have become considerations for designers in their own practices as well as in the choices made by clients for whom they work. Many designers are sensitive to the ways in which globalization can make benefits to local communities dependent on profits to corporations. Designers concerned about the effects of promoting consumable brands rather than sustainable products have worked to expose and reconfigure links between class position, marketing, and consumption. Meanwhile, demand for imagery that identifies responsible businesses offers designers opportunities to communicate the progressive values of companies whose brands they help build. Yet in a rapidly changing world, these businesses' practices are apt to evolve, while the images and styles by which they are identified may not. Visual conventions can be quickly naturalized in the global sign system: organic forms become associated with the environment, flow diagrams with communication and finances, and mapping techniques with the repercussions of epidemics and disasters. Like all graphic reductions, these can easily take the place of communication rather than serve its needs (Figs. **16.5a** and **16.5b**).

16.6a Farhad Fozouni, exhibition poster, 2007, and 16.6b Iraj Mirza Alikhani, Yogu logo, 2010. These Iranian designs exemplify a synthesis of tradition and contemporary style and show how graphic forms may or may not reference their places of origin. No area of the globe has an exclusive hold on graphic approaches that speak to a broad audience without reference to a particular tradition. Likewise, each use of indigenous motifs is different. Some seek to achieve a sense of authenticity, while others spin traditional devices into a contemporary look.

Global encounters in design The values of modernism and the International Typographic Style were challenged in the late twentieth century by multiculturalism and postmodernism, which introduced eclectic iconography, vernacular styles, and imaginative production methods, ranging from material and hand making processes to the smooth artifices of digital techniques. Narrowly defined, modernism had aspired to a universal language of design that would transcend historical and cultural circumstances through a graphic system of signs based on rational principles. The International style remains influential in many parts of the world to which designers returned after studying at schools in Europe and North America whose design programs were founded on modernist principles. Modernism colonized design practices in Asia, Africa, the Middle East, and other parts of the globe, where the very concept of local traditions may be challenged by curricula that have institutionalized this influence. At the same time, a synthetic graphic language is emerging that draws on diverse traditions and produces imagery that cannot be pinned to any particular set of conventions or principles. The rate at which the symbolic value of such imagery comes to be commonly understood shows the powerful part played by graphic design in establishing the terms and viability of a global communication system (Figs. **16.6a** and **16.6b**).

16.7a Han Meilin, Beijing Olympics mascots, 2005. Each occurrence of the Olympic Games has been a preeminent occasion for identity and information design. These designs, in turn, have been the object of intense scrutiny by design communities. In addition to a logo and icons for events, the Beijing Olympics presented a set of five mascots, each bearing a message of peace and harmony through Chinese symbols that have particular cultural resonance. The playful characters represent the fish, the panda, the Tibetan antelope, the swallow and the Olympic flame. Graphically, they speak volumes about the potential of a popular art idiom to become a consumable global style.

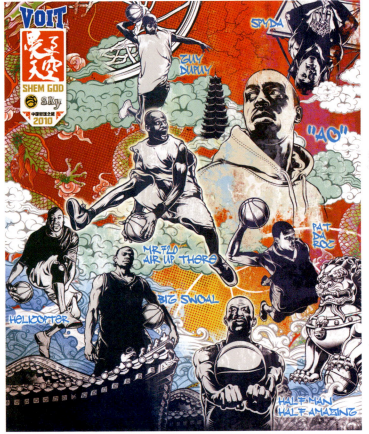

16.7b S.K.Y. Streetball Syndicate event announcement, 2010. In this announcement, images of athletes who are members of a basketball team recruited from the world's best street players are combined with traditional Chinese graphic motifs—waves, dragons, ships, and temple architecture—to advertise a tour bringing blacktop basketball to Chinese fans. The tour is co-sponsored by Voit, a Chinese sports clothing brand, and Shemgod Streetball Company. According to biblical legend, Chinese people claim their descent from Shem, one of the three sons of Noah. A blend of Asian and Western cultural traditions is embodied in the mix of styles, colors, and printmaking effects applied to photographically derived imagery.

Because globalism is not a design style but a set of conditions for design activity, the range of graphic sensibilities it includes runs the gamut from elegance to playfulness, invoking many historical and contemporary associations. The graphic repertoires of different cultures often encode political and economic histories whose events have left their traces in styles and forms. Contrasts between monoculture and multiculturalism are evident in designs that attempt to preserve indigenous or authentic motifs and yet communicate globally. Even when imagery springs from a culturally specific source, it can be made readily consumable by popular style choices (Figs. **16.7a** and **16.7b**).

Design archaeology is practiced in projects and educational settings as a way of bringing graphic elements from local archives and historical collections back into use. Few national or ethnic communities have a design culture that has remained intact and immune to influence from modern

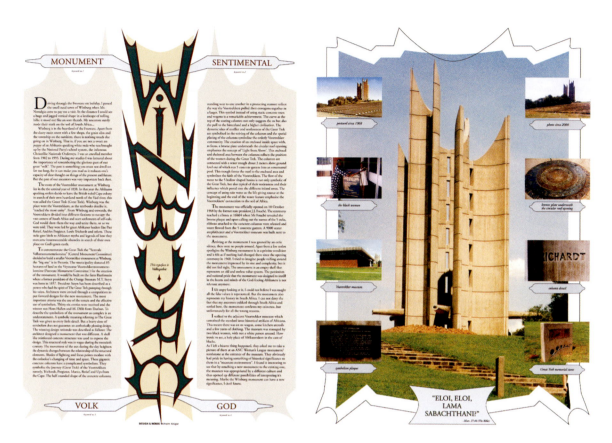

Actively engaging global influences, a hybrid approach has

16.8a Garth Walker, *i-jusi* magazine, 2002. This South African publication is a showcase for African graphic design. In this issue, design archaeology revisits an apartheid era monument that inspires a lettering style. Productive tensions fuel an interchange between images from a repressive past and the creative possibilities of the present. Each issue of *i-jusi* has a different theme and a different direction for its exploration of a "new visual language"—a phrase that is almost nostalgic in its invocation of the modern era's search for a universal language of form. Yet the adventurous graphic imagination in *i-jusi*'s pages is fresh and forward-looking.

and postmodern styles in mass media or consumer culture. Actively engaging global influences or pressures, a hybrid approach has developed that incorporates culturally specific decorative elements and iconography. Yet hybrids are not always possible. Print designers decide whether to tap local traditions or avoid them, while Web designers may be caught between wanting to appeal to the medium's broad user base and trying to preserve some trace of their design's origins. Some use historical research to critique the politics of past and present regimes by pointedly linking graphic and cultural associations (Fig. **16.8a**).

Diverse traditions register in hand-painted and expertly drawn lettering, official and unofficial signage, and other graphic media. Through popular art, activist graphics, and underground publications, as well as highly produced and art directed campaigns, these references are being embedded in global communications. The integration of digital tools, analog sources, and simulacral techniques has pumped up the visual intensity of color and forms that express an imaginative energy in contemporary graphic design. Forging connections with music, entertainment, and the infinite cultural productivity of consumerism, graphic designers create images that defy

developed that incorporates culturally specific iconography.

16.8b Ricardo Juarez, EvokeOne online exhibition entry, 2010. The exuberance of this design is expressed in an aesthetic that seems independent of any particular tradition or culture. Its synthetic quality presents itself as the product of a world without borders or boundaries, an illusion that is as consummate as its plastic organicism and infinite tangle. Juarez's vivid image can be read as a sign of a global monoculture or as a multicultural manifestation of popular and commercial art.

characterization within historical or stylistic categories. A truly global graphic culture, without allegiance to locale or tradition, has come into being. Analog modes of production, such as spray painting or airbrushing, might be associated with specific cultural circumstances, but digital tools remediate these processes, importing the contexts they represent into a common kit of stylistic effects (Fig. **16.8b**).

Global networks and technology Contemporary graphic designers are subject to the constraints and advantages of global technological conditions. The tools of the Web are largely composed in First World languages, and international standards have resisted the incorporation of non-alphabetic characters on the Web. At the level of file formats and protocols, the design of the Web was driven by principles of efficient exchange. The rapid and fluid migration of content in the current media environment poses conceptual and technical challenges for the preservation of expressive attributes in the design of forms and formats that cross platforms. The contingencies of device-independent design can eliminate the features on which communication depends.

16.9 Chinese keyboard, 2007.
The ubiquitous QWERTY keyboard and touchpad are vivid reminders that human-computer interaction is embodied in tactile forms, no matter how abstract our concepts of information flow and communication become. The accommodation of Chinese characters on this keyboard points to the dominance of English language protocols on the Web, beginning at the level of keystrokes and ASCII code. Language differences introduce their own barriers to globalization, since software programs and technical standards for many features of Web-based interaction are developed in Western languages.

Cueva de las Manos, Río Pinturas

16.10 Cave of the Hands, Argentina, World Heritage List interactive map, 2011. This design is built on a TerraMetrics/Google Earth map that allows users to access information about cultural heritage sites through a zoomable geographic interface. Each site has its own documentation to which user-generated content is contributed locally as well as globally. The design of such ambitious initiatives involves contributions from different sources and teams, whose work must be successfully integrated. The visual designer's task is multiplied by the need to understand information structures and technical requirements.

The long-standing practice of designing for a particular medium—print, signage, film, television—is complicated by the delivery of digital content on mobile devices and distributed platforms. Designers may be called upon to coordinate many aspects of a project's production—from its look and resonance to its functionality within the affordances of Web 2.0 interactivity. Like the art directors of an earlier era, who were familiar with the demands and possibilities of layout, typesetting, and photographic reproduction, graphic design professionals require knowledge of several fields, even if they do not have expertise in all of the areas that their work involves. While they may not need to know the ins and outs of a programming language or coding method, designers who can speak effectively to Web developers and take responsibility for the ways in which different parts of a digital project fit together are valued collaborators (Fig. **16.9**).

Web-based projects can have enormous scope. Unlike designs for print, Web-based projects incorporate social media and dynamic interfaces. Content can change frequently, sometimes supplied by a live feed that must be integrated into a site's design. Information structure and navigation design may serve users scattered across many countries, cultures, and language groups. In such large-scale projects, designers bring many types of information into legible and navigable form, often coordinating user-generated content within a coherent vision of an organization, consortium, or community (Fig. **16.10**).

16.11 Shai Carmi et al. using Ignacio Alvarez-Hamelin et al.'s vizualization program, LaNet-iv, *Hierarchical Structure of the Internet*, 2007. Not only is the scale of global communication rapidly exploding, but the complexity of personal interactions and social networks exceeds the formal vocabulary of an earlier era. Designers provide images of a world that cannot be grasped in its particulars, only as an overall pattern that suggests that our place in the global world is nodal and dynamic, not bounded or static. The aesthetics of such images have great rhetorical force. They present ways of imagining globalization in graphic form. Although it purports to reveal the structure of its subject, an image at this scale more readily conveys the concept than the nature of the complexity of global communication.

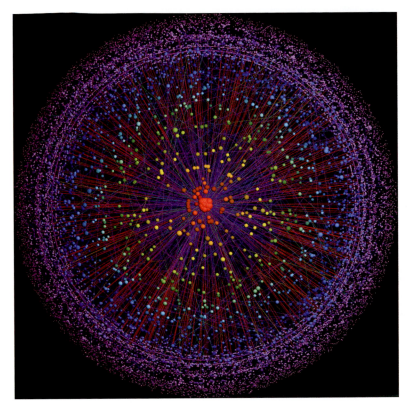

Conclusion Globalization introduces challenges of scale and diversity into the work of graphic designers. When designers tailor campaigns that address messages to local communities in global systems, they participate in the establishment of a cross-cultural network of economic, political, and social exchange. Design can be used to promote global business activity but also to conceal differences among the zones of this activity by creating an illusion of common benefits and beliefs. Questions regarding the interests served by globalization and by the images that represent it can only be answered by gauging systematic effects in relation to local impacts. The homogenizing influence of an emerging monoculture can be seen to be in conflict with local styles and modes, or to be a means of overcoming boundaries. Design can be a force for co-optation and commodification, or a medium of authentic extension. True diversity often means incommensurable differences that cannot be unified, only recognized and respected. Graphic designers face the challenge of defining principles for responsible design that recognize interconnectivity, engage diversity, and address the need for practices that sustain the limited resources of a fragile ecology, while making global complexities meaningful in multiple contexts (Fig. **16.11**).

Graphic Design and Globalization

1945 International Monetary Fund (IMF) established

CARE founded to provide international relief to survivors of WWII

1963 International Council of Graphic Design Associations (Icograda) founded in London

1964 First International Biennial of Graphic Design in Brno, Czechoslovakia

1971 Médecins Sans Frontières (Doctors Without Borders) founded in France

1979 Second "oil crisis" calls attention to energy and technology policies

1981 AIDS epidemic recognized

Icograda, Icsid, and IFI hold first joint World Design Congress in Helsinki

1985 Live Aid, billed as the world's largest pop concert, raises money for famine relief

1986 Chernobyl nuclear disaster in Ukraine

1988 Intergovernmental Panel on Climate Change established

1989 Berlin Wall removed; reunification of East and West Germany begins

1990 *Eye* magazine founded by Rick Poynor

Nelson Mandela released from prison, leads negotiations to end apartheid in South Africa

1991 Global climate temporarily affected by eruption of Mount Pinatubo in the Philippines

U.S. fights Gulf War against Iraq; "smart bomb" videos televised

Soviet Union ceases to exist; many former Soviet states gain independence

1992 Scientists for Global Responsibility formed in the United Kingdom

First Golden Bee, Moscow International Biennale of Graphic Design

1994 NAFTA creates a trilateral trade block among Mexico, U.S., and Canada

Genocide in Rwanda

First blog by Justin Hall

1995 World Trade Organization (WTO) established

Oxfam International affiliates national organizations to combat famine

Communication Arts launches Web site

1996 First cell phone with Internet connectivity launched by Nokia in Finland

1997 Economic crisis in Asia causes fears of worldwide financial contagion

Control of Hong Kong transferred from Britain to People's Republic of China

Kyoto Protocol adopted to address climate change; U.S. does not sign

1998 El Niño weather pattern warms ocean, causes disasters

Society of Typographic Aficionados (SOTA) holds first TypeCon in Massachusetts

1999 Claes Källarsson conceives of Font Aid to benefit international relief organizations

1999 Protests at WTO meetings in Seattle

BlackBerry wireless email device launched in Canada

2000 Rockport publishes *Global Graphics: Designing with Symbols for an International Market*

Vladimir Putin sworn in as Russian president

Naomi Klein's *No Logo* published by Knopf Canada

March 10, NASDAQ peaks before dot-com bubble bursts

ILOVEYOU computer virus infects millions of computers worldwide

International AIDS Conference in Durban, South Africa

President Bush denies link between human activity and climate change

2001 World Social Forum (WSF) meets to "reinvent democracy" in Porto Alegre, Brazil

China joins the World Trade Organization

President Bush asks for "continued participation" in American economy after 911 attacks

Bonn Agreement on climate change signed by 178 nations; not the U. S.

USA PATRIOT Act reduces rights to privacy, expands definition of terrorism

U.S. National Research Council concludes that human factors contribute to global warming

Enron collapses amid scandal over systematic fraud

Wikipedia launched

2002 World Association of Non-Governmental Organizations (WANGO) issues ethics code

Euro adopted as European currency

SARS (Severe Acute Respiratory Syndrome) causes worldwide scare

American Idol debuts on Fox

2003 IMF and World Bank take stock of progress toward Millennium Development Goals

Networks and viewers look to Al Jazeera for unembedded coverage of Iraq War

DesignObserver.com launched

Deadly heat wave in Europe

Mad cow disease scare

Human Genome Project completed

Dolly, the cloned sheep, dies

2004 World donates over $14 billion to victims of Indian Ocean earthquake and tsunami

Same-sex marriage legalized in Massachusetts

European Union membership rises to twenty-seven nations

"Thefacebook" launched by Mark Zuckerberg

Flickr image and video hosting Web site launched

2005 YouTube launched by Steve Chen, Chad Hurley, and Jawed Karim

First human face transplant in France

Emigre magazine ceases publication

IMF approves 100 percent debt relief for nineteen countries

Kyoto Protocol in force

2006 Pluto demoted to "dwarf planet" status

Twitter launched

2007 Gary Hustwit's feature-length film about a typeface, *Helvetica*, premieres

Benazir Bhutto assassinated at an election rally in Rawalpindi

Avian flu scare

Global Water Initiative started by seven cooperating NGOs

Kindle launched by Amazon

World food price crisis, due in part to biofuel demand and commodities speculation

2008 Beijing Olympics

Japanese scientists create artificial DNA

World economic crisis, brought on by burst of housing bubble in U.S.

Barack Obama elected first president of African-American descent

Bernard Madoff arrested for massive investment fraud

2009 H1N1 swine flu outbreak declared a pandemic by World Health Organization (WHO)

UN issues warnings about hunger in East Asia

AIGA presents *The Living Principles for Design*, a framework for sustainability

Aspen Design Summit invites designers and NGOs to tackle social problems

SixthSense "wearable gestural interface" prototype presented

China moves into third place among world's largest economies

Mean global temperature highest on record

Michael Jackson dies

Indian Space Research Organization finds evidence of water on the moon

Microelectronic retinal implants for the blind developed

Sixty-seven percent of the world's population uses cell phones

Twenty-eight percent of the world's population uses Internet

2010 Same-sex marriage legal in eleven nations

Icograda launches online journal of design research, *Iridescent*

WikiLeaks release secret government and military documents

iPad launched

First live Internet link to a spacecraft in low orbit

Thirty-nine percent of the world's population lives with inadequate sanitation

2011 Inaugural International Design Alliance (IDA) Congress

WHO publishes preparedness guidelines for global pandemics

Twitter and Facebook play key roles in Middle Eastern revolutions

Tools of the Trade

Kindle, iPad, and other tablets

Google image search

SourceForge (open source software site)

Many Eyes visualization platform

Computer generated image (CGI) programs

Processing, visual programming language

Geographic information systems (GIS)

WOFF (Web Open Font Format) standards

Print-on-demand services

USB flash drive

3D printer

(See also Chapter 15)

Glossary

abstraction of visual forms, reduction or simplification, usually of a representational or realistic image to one that has less visual information; partial or total elimination of referential or representational aspects in favor of elemental forms.

acrophonic from the Greek *acro* (initial or top) and *phonic* (sound), the principle of naming a letter with a word that begins with that letter: for example, calling A *aleph* (ox), or B *beth* (house); through association, such words came to seem like the pictorial origins of these letters, but this link is not supported by archaeological evidence.

advertising campaign a coordinated series of promotions for a particular entity, product, or event; a crafted message, often to be carried by a variety of media.

aesthetic having to do with questions of value, knowledge, or judgment of perceptions.

aestheticism a late nineteenth-century art movement associated with the concept of art-for-art's sake.

aesthetics a branch of philosophy concerned with perception and questions of taste, knowledge, and judgment in sensory phenomena; associated with concepts of beauty, although other categories of value may be equally relevant.

agency a professional group formed to advance an issue or serve a client's interest; as a concept, *agency* implies the capacity to act and the power to cause an effect or achieve an end.

algorithm from the name of ninth-century Arab mathematician al-Kwarizmi, a set of step-by-step instructions for calculating or problem-solving; the basis for accomplishing any task in a computational environment.

allegorical of or pertaining to the use of an image or literary figure to represent something other, and often larger, than itself (an idea, a principle, or a quality); for example, a painting of a young woman decorated with flowers might be an allegory of spring.

alphabetic of or pertaining to the alphabet, a set of letters that derive from a single source in the second millennium BCE.

alphabetic script a writing system that uses letters; any of several scripts derived from a common root that developed in the second millennium BCE in the region between Mesopotamia and Egypt, under the influence of cuneiform and hieroglyphic systems.

American Regionalism an artistic movement that focused on rural or local imagery and often expressed agrarian cultural values as an answer to the modern world of industrial and urban development.

analog of or pertaining to forms (information, expressions, or representations) stored in, or rendered by, media that have continuously variable values, such as photographic film or magnetic tape—as opposed to values coded in discrete or digital units.

anthropological of or pertaining to the study of human beings and their cultures (physical evolution, language, kinship structures, values, and rituals).

antihumanism a philosophical stance that challenges the belief that universal values or inherent moral principles are shared by human beings and replaces it with a conviction that all such values are historically and culturally determined.

appellation a rhetorical strategy that uses cultural codes and references to position a viewer as the intended recipient of a message; the stylistic equivalent of statement in the second person *(you).*

appropriation the act of taking existing images or texts as the basis for a new work; distinguished from imitation by the fact that the materials borrowed or cited are often absorbed directly into the new work without significant alteration.

archaeological of or pertaining to the study of ancient history, usually through the excavation and analysis of physical remains.

architectonic of or pertaining to design that has a systematic or logical form, usually associated with architectural structure; in graphic design, of or pertaining to a composition that appears to have the structural integrity of built form.

art directors people responsible for the visual conception and style of an advertising campaign, publication, film or theater set, or any other project or product that involves a team of professionals.

artifacts things made by human work or effort; objects whose value and identity are linked to their material existence and properties.

artists' books original works of art made in the book format, usually made entirely by an artist, either in unique or multiple forms.

ascenders strokes that rise above the x-height of a typeface, such as the upper part of an *h.*

attributes features that distinguish or add value to a thing, sign, figure, or entity; often, defining characteristics that identify a person or an object, as in the attributes of a saint.

aura an air that surrounds a work of art, object, or person that cannot be attributed to any material quality but adds value that may be mysterious or magical in its strength.

auratic of or pertaining to properties that are not strictly part of the physical, factual existence of a material thing but that give it some of its meaning, power, or value.

autonomy the condition of being free-standing and self-sufficient; of artwork, the quality of being created for its own sake rather than commission, or of not depending on any referent or context for its aesthetic value.

avant-garde in military terms, those in advance; of artists and movements, those that are innovative and, often, interested in shocking demonstrations of originality.

baroque in graphic arts and architecture, of or pertaining to an ornate design style, popular in the seventeenth and eighteenth centuries, that favored dramatic compositions of complex curved forms.

bastarda a mixture of blackletter and cursive writing, the result of cross-cultural influences in the Middle Ages.

bestiaries texts that concentrate on depictions and descriptions of animals.

Bézier a method of drawing curves, devised by French mathematician Pierre Bézier in the 1960s, which defines a curve using as few as three points: a beginning, an end, and one or more "handles" by which its shape may be altered; Bézier points are these dynamic nodes.

billhead a graphic element at the top of a bill or receipt that visually identifies a business and/or its owner.

bills of fare menus or lists of dishes available for consumption in dining establishments.

bill-sticker a person who pasted handbills or posters on walls or other available surfaces; a familiar figure in nineteenth-century urban environments.

biomorphism the use of organic forms in art and design.

bitmap a means of describing the position and value of pixels in a display; a bitmapped image has a tapestry structure that contains information for each pixel in a display (as opposed to a vector graphic that simply plots coordinates and lines between them); GIF and JPEG are bitmap formats.

blackletter a heavy and angular manuscript hand that developed in the twelfth and thirteenth centuries; a model for early printing types and a style that came to be associated with Germany, where the use of blackletter faces continued after other countries had shifted to roman type.

bohemianism the unconventional sensibility of late nineteenth-century artists who eschewed bourgeois values and engaged in imaginative behaviors and expressions; the term links a stereotype of gypsies from Bohemia (in Eastern Europe) with an unruly artistic attitude in a way that has racist overtones; bohemianism was often associated with posturing and playing at the artistic lifestyle rather than serious commitment to artistic practice.

book of hours a prayer book that contains observances for appointed times of the day, often highly decorated, with illustrations of seasonal cycles and so on.

bourgeoisie a social class between the aristocracy and the proletariat that enjoys a certain amount of material wealth and status and benefits from the status quo (things being the way they are).

boustrophedon from the Greek *bous* (ox) and *strophos* (turning), literally, as the ox turns in plowing; writing that continues from right to left and left to right in alternate lines.

bracketed serifs fine lines attached to the ends of letter strokes with transitional curves where they meet.

brand originally, a metal rod with a figure or device at the end that was heated and applied to cattle or property to identify its owner; both the graphic device through which the identity of a company or product may be recognized and the concept of fostering such an identity as an idea or image in the mind of the public.

broadsheets single sheets used for printing one-sided notices or announcements to be posted or circulated.

broadsides single sheets used for one-sided printing. (See **broadsheets.**)

calendared of paper, processed by a machine (called a calendar) with two cylinders that polish the surface to a smooth finish.

calligraphy from the Greek *kalos* (beautiful) and *graphia* (writing), literally, beautiful writing; lettering drawn by hand with a brush or pen.

caricature a depiction that comments critically or humorously on a person's character by exaggerating aspects of his or her appearance.

cartography the art and science of making charts and maps.

celebrity culture a condition in which star status is granted to a few people whose stature then defines the rest of the population as ordinary by contrast; usually characterized by a large publicity industry and mass-media networks that construct and circulate identities of exaggerated importance.

chancery handwriting associated with the courts or with a *chancellor* who kept records; a particular style of writing used exclusively for legal documents.

characters letters, glyphs, or other signs in a writing system; elements of hieroglyphics, cuneiform, the alphabet, or other forms of writing.

chinoiserie decorative art or graphics in a Chinese style; in Western art, any images, techniques, decorative approaches, or stylistic motifs influenced by objects and images imported from China.

chromolithography color lithographic printing from stone or plate, popularized in the second half of the nineteenth century.

code a set of signs with agreed-upon values that are used to convey information or messages within a communication system; signs in a code can be visually arbitrary in relation to what they represent.

codex a book format in which sheets or signatures are bound at one edge; originally, a code of laws.

codify to organize thought, language, signs, or ideas into a system that can be represented by a code; to turn an analytic system into a formal code.

collage from the French *colle* (glue), fragments of images or materials glued together to form a whole composition.

colophon the final text in a book, which often provides information about the book's production and edition.

combinatorial able to be used in variable arrangements or combinations.

comix a variation of the standard spelling of *comics* used to indicate an underground sensibility; usually reserved for graphic works with adult content (explicit sex, violence, or drug-related imagery).

command-line a text-based interface to a computer's operating system; the actual line through which a command is typed and entered.

commercial art any visual work done for money or to serve a client's interests, usually in contrast to fine art or work done on the initiative of an artist.

communication the effective exchange of ideas through a common language or system of signs, gestures, sounds, marks, or other means; communication assumes some degree of mutual understanding of the system in which ideas are exchanged, even if differences of outlook exist among the persons involved; communication does not have to be face-to-face but can occur across space and time through the use of sign systems such as writing.

communication systems technological or human networks for the transmission and dissemination of information or ideas.

communities of belief social networks formed around a shared value or understanding of an idea or issue, often brought about through mediated communication or bonds formed for a common purpose.

composition the organization of graphic elements within an image or design; this organization may be analyzed and discussed, independent of its informational or representational content, in terms of dynamism, stasis, hierarchy, complexity, legibility, and other formal qualities.

compositor a person who sets type, whether by hand or by mechanical or digital means.

consonantal script a writing system for languages in which vowels can be readily supplied by a reader.

constructed forms letters made up of drawn parts, often with the aid of a mechanical device, such as a compass or straightedge, often according to mathematically calculated ideals of proportion and distinguished from letterforms that bear the trace of a (continuous) hand gesture.

Constructivism a branch of Russian and Soviet experimental art concerned with understanding the properties of materials and exploring techniques for their combination and use; Constructivism saw art as production and sought the integration of art into everyday life.

consumer capitalism an economic system based on assumptions about the widespread development of markets, rather than on earlier models of production.

conventions rules or approaches that have come to be accepted through use but for which explicit guidelines or manuals may not exist; shared habits of thought or understanding with regard to a practice.

copperplate engraving an intaglio printing technique in which lines are carved into the surface of a copper plate. (See **intaglio**.)

copy camera a large camera used to photograph finished artwork and create film for offset printing plates, capable of producing large-format negative or positive images for production or reproduction; formerly, an essential piece of equipment in a print shop.

counterculture any movement or group, whether formally organized or not, that promotes values opposed to those of the mainstream; in the 1960s, associated with alternative lifestyles, drugs, rock-and-roll music, radical politics, sexual freedom, and early ecological activism.

counters spaces or openings that are enclosed by strokes in a letterform, such as the center of an *o*.

courantos manuscripts or printed forms of information circulated in a timely manner; the term was adopted as a popular element in newspaper titles, along with others, like *journal, clarion,* and *times*.

craft the skilled practice of an art or technique, often associated with the trades as distinct from the arts.

Cro-Magnon from the name of the Cro-Magnon cave in France where remains were first discovered, the oldest modern humans in Europe; indicates a stage of cultural rather than physiological development.

cultural literacy knowledge of basic references (factual or conceptual) that are common to a culture; a shared frame of reference created through acknowledged or unacknowledged consensus.

cultural studies a field of cultural criticism concerned with interpreting a broad range of representations, texts, or experiences as expressions of, or reactions to, the ideological values specific to a historical moment and its particular arrangements of power relations.

cultural value a qualitative assessment of the worth of an image, sign, object, or material that is shared by a group or culture.

culture-jamming any activity or process that disrupts mainstream cultural practice by altering the message of an image or text to expose its underlying assumptions or interests.

cuneiform writing composed of wedge-shaped signs made in wet clay with a stylus by ancient Sumerians, Akkadians, Assyrians, and others.

cursive from the Latin currere, 'to run,' a script written quickly, often with looped forms and joined letters.

cybernetics from the Greek *kubernan* (to steer), the study of feedback and control; the science of systems that give direction to themselves, associated with artificial intelligence and other higher-level computational functions.

Dada a nonsense word invented around 1916 to identify an international group of artists in Zurich, Switzerland, whose sometimes whimsical, sometimes nihilistic, work was deliberately conceived in an irrational mode.

daguerreotypes photographs produced by a technique named for French inventor Louis Daguerre that involved exposing a light-sensitive solution on a metal plate to create a one-off image; daguerreotypes required long exposures and faded if left in bright light, but their mirrorlike surface held tremendous detail.

deconstructive of or pertaining to a philosophical method of interpretation premised on the idea that texts and images do not reveal truths but create fields of signification and that reading their signs through a play of difference produces meaning that is always shifting.

demotic from the Greek *demos* (the people), of or pertaining to a highly simplified form of Egyptian writing.

descenders strokes that drop below the baseline of a typeface, such as the tail of a *y*.

design community a group of individuals, organizations, or institutions that shares and communicates beliefs about the nature and value of design.

desktop a computer environment, modeled on the physical analog, in which icons act like the objects they represent, so that folders contain files, and a trash can is a place to throw away (delete) files.

De Stijl in Dutch, The Style; an artistic movement founded by Theo van Doesburg in 1917 that distilled formal elements of the avant-garde into a unique graphic mode that favored primary colors and geometric forms and produced bold, elemental compositions.

determinatives signs used to attribute a linguistic or conceptual category to a group of letters or glyphs to guide their interpretation.

détournement a technique developed by the Situationists for deforming or transforming an image or text as a way of reformulating cultural values; an intervention in the cultural meaning of a text or image that calls attention to the system of beliefs within which it functions.

diagrammatic of or pertaining to diagrams and schematic designs that show the structure or arrangement of elements or forms rather than details; usually line-based.

difference nonidenticality; the substantive character of incommensurability; the fact that no two things, moments, events, or entities are the same as each other; the significance or substantive value of the distinction between things.

digital of or pertaining to anything composed of a code of discrete units; now usually with reference to the binary code underlying computational calculations or the representation of information in such a binary code.

discourse in linguistic terms, an extended or complex statement; also, writing or speech marked by its subjective source, enunciation, narration; in social sciences, knowledge and thought institutionalized in certain forms and implicitly bounded by existing power relations.

display site, method, or instance of showing something for the express purpose of drawing attention.

display types large or decorative letterforms used to call attention to themselves and their texts for the purpose of publicity or informational hierarchy.

ductal of or pertaining to a letter stroke or form that follows the course of the movement by which it is made; gestural.

duplicating machines mechanical devices that produce more than one copy of an image or text.

dymaxion word coined by the twentieth-century visionary inventor Buckminster Fuller to mean "doing more with less"; an approach or object that maximizes the potential of any situation or system.

dystopic of or pertaining to a dark vision of the fate of human culture; the opposite of utopic.

effigies representations of people or animals, usually in three-dimensional form, often specific and recognizable.

Egyptian (type) faces with square or slab serifs.

electrotyping an application of electroplating technology to printing in which a thin shell of copper was made from wax molds and used to produce multiple copies of a single form (text or image block).

emblem an image, usually accompanied by a verse or motto, often depicting an allegory with a moral or religious message; in Renaissance culture, emblem books had three parts—an allegorical image, a text, and a motto—all of which were to be contemplated and synthesized for the advancement of one's spiritual education.

empirical, empiricism (an approach to knowledge) grounded in direct observation and the testing of experience, rather than in abstract reason or theory.

endgrain of or pertaining to woodblocks cut across the grain and polished to produce a smooth and hard surface that does not splinter and holds a much finer line than blocks cut with the grain; used for white line wood engraving.

ephemera literally, lasting only a day; printed matter for short-term use such as handbills, tickets, announcements, and menus; any items of brief utility or fleeting value.

establishment the mainstream bulwark of power; institutions and individuals aligned with traditional values and maintenance of the status quo.

etching a process in which acid is used to bite lines or patterns into a plate for intaglio printing; metal plates are treated with an acid-resistant coating from which lines or dots are removed before the plate is put into an acid bath that bites exposed areas. (See **intaglio**.)

ethos from the Greek *ethos* (habit or character), the prevailing values of a particular group or culture.

fantasmatic of or pertaining to a mental image that appears to be real, an illusion; of or pertaining to immersive belief in such an image.

fat face type that exaggerates the contrast between stroke weights which is characteristic of modern faces by adding extra heft to the thick strokes.

figure an image that comes into focus as a legible, individuated sign or form, often representing a person, animal, or thing; also, as a verb, to give something a definite shape.

fine press any printing or publishing venture established with the goal of producing work distinguished by its quality of materials, design, and production.

fit the spatial relation of letters to each other in a particular face; the spaces created between letters by their respective positions on the metal blocks of letterpress type.

fleurons flower designs, often made of smaller ornaments in variable combinations, known as printers' flowers.

folk of the people—particularly common people or peasants—rather than of industrial or commercial origin; also, with reference to an ethnic identity or tradition.

font originally, a complete set of characters for a particular typeface in a certain size, cast in metal; by extension and in digital terms, a typeface.

Fordism a production method derived from Henry Ford's automobile assembly line that required workers to know just one part of a complex process rather than being skilled in all aspects of production.

foundry a shop in which fonts of type are designed and cast in metal or digitally generated.

four-color process a printing technique that superimposes halftones to make all colors from just four inks: cyan, magenta, yellow, and black (CMYK); also called *process color;* the industry standard for color printing.

frontispiece an image at the front of a book, usually facing the title page.

functionalism an attitude according to which the effective operation of an object, space, or communication is of paramount value in its design; a principle of early twentieth-century movements that applied art to design problems and ran counter to art-for-art's-sake's embrace of purposelessness.

functionalist of or pertaining to functionalism. (See **functionalism**.)

fungibility interchangeability; of assets that can be moved from one financial form to another without change in value; with reference to information in electronic environments that is stored as data and can thus be shifted easily from one form (e.g., binary code) to another (e.g., musical sound or notation).

furniture in letterpress printing, pieces of wood and metal in standard sizes used on the bed of a press to position and hold a form in the lock-up process.

Futurism an artistic movement of the early twentieth century that called for a radical break with the past and all traditions in the name of creating an art for the future; associated with F. T. Marinetti, author of the first manifesto to bear the name *Futurist* in its title (1909).

galleys metal trays used to hold lead type that has been set for proofing in advance of printing; by extension, the pages proofed from such type.

geometric generated by the branch of mathematics concerned with forms that can be measured on a surface or in space; in graphic design, pertaining to hard-edged abstract forms.

Gestalt psychology from the German word for "shape," a branch of psychology that studies how people perceive arranged elements as a parts of a whole rather than as a number of individual forms.

gestural pertaining to movements of a hand, limb, or other part of the human body; here, most often, related to writing that bears a trace of the body's movement within its forms.

globalization the interconnected condition of the world brought about through networks of trade, communication, and cultural exchange.

gloss a commentary explaining or commenting upon a text.

glyphs carved signs, often more complex, detailed, or pictorial than letter forms; if undecipherable, surrounded by an aura of mystery.

gothic (type) sans serif faces, often heavy; an American equivalent of the European term *grotesque*.

graphic of or pertaining to the arrangement of visual elements with regard to their composition as forms on a surface or in a visual field; graphic forms need not be pictures or signs but can be abstract shapes or patterns.

graphic art any visual work produced in a two-dimensional format.

graphic journalism any visual work that is used to report events in print, film, or other media.

graphic metric a unit or standard of measure in visual form.

graphic principles guidelines for the production or analysis of visual works; basic tenets as to the ways in which elements of composition and layout produce meaning within formal and cultural systems.

grotesque (type) sans serif faces, often heavy; a European equivalent of the American term *gothic*.

ground part of an image that serves as the field of undifferentiated information on which a figure comes into focus; often, a material substrate or support is integrated with the ground (as in the case of a wall, clay tablet, paper, or canvas), but the support is a physical feature, whereas the ground is part of the representational field.

grunge a word meaning dirt achieved through neglect, appropriated to describe a style of music identified with a nihilistic or self-consciously apathetic attitude that originated in the Pacific Northwest of the United States; sometimes associated with beach and skateboarding cultures.

GUI (graphical user interface) the visual means by which data in a computational environment are accessed and manipulated by a user; the development of the GUI (pronounced "goo-ey") was a major breakthrough in computer design because it allowed nontechnical users to work in a digital environment.

halftone a photographic process that uses a screen to translate an image of continuous tone into the patterned dots of a reproducible image; the result of this process.

half-uncials rounded letterforms with ascenders and descenders that extend beyond the x-height and baseline; the first minuscules.

hand a particular style of writing, often associated with a specific monastery or geographical region.

handbills single printed sheets used to advertise goods or services or to promote an event or entertainment, circulated by a person who passed them out in public places.

hand press any printing press that is operated manually.

HCI (human computer interface) any aspect of a computer that mediates between its functionality and a user; most frequently, the screen and its graphical interface; also, a mouse, a joystick, and other extensions.

hierarchy graphic distinctions of weight, color, placement, and so on that produce relative value among elements within a structure, system, or composition.

hieratic generally, of things associated with the priestly caste; specifically, a simplified cursive form of Egyptian hieroglyphics developed by priests.

hieroglyphics literally, sacred carvings; generally, Egyptian written signs; these came to be associated with mysterious and sacred practices after encounters with Greek culture in the eighth and seventh centuries BCE but had been used for secular and political inscriptions as well for several millennia; also, other writing systems, such as those of the Mayan or Aztec cultures.

hip hop an urban style and musical movement that began with house parties, DJs, MCs, and turntable arts and became a highly developed and influential cultural form and identity.

historiated of letters, decorated with figures or vignettes.

horror vacui the notion of a space that did not include the presence of God as a source of religious terror and theological conundrum; in graphic terms, an aversion to leaving open spaces in a composition.

humanistic grounded in a human-centered view of the world, as distinct from a God-centered or religious orientation; pertaining to Renaissance scholars of classical antiquity who promoted this outlook; with reference to type, any face that emulates the writing style associated with this tradition.

hybrid an organism produced by mixing genetic material; a thing composed of heterogeneous elements; in design, a mixed style or form.

hyperreal of or pertaining to appearances in which it is impossible to distinguish reality from illusion, either because a representation is so believable or because conditions of perception or cognition do not allow for distinctions between real and imagined phenomena or experience.

iconographic of or pertaining to the symbolic meaning of images and its study or interpretation.

iconography the meaning of images and its interpretation, especially the study of symbolic forms in religious and mythological imagery.

identity (visual, graphic) a unique profile for a group or enterprise, designed to be established in the public mind or marketplace through formal devices, such as logos and slogans.

ideology a set of beliefs that express the values of a culture at a particular moment, often so familiar that they pass as natural.

illumination lighting up a text with visual information; the decoration of a manuscript, often with elaborate designs and images in gold or silver and color.

"image" an intangible or virtual concept that has specific visual properties that are perceived as concrete but are not grounded in any single or specific material expression or form.

immateriality the quality of something that does not consist of matter, thus abstraction or spirituality.

imposition the organization of page forms in preparation for printing.

incunabula the infancy period of printing, from its invention in the 1450s through 1500.

indices plural of *index;* a sign that points directly to its referent; one of several important textual elements developed for navigation in the codex form; a list of names, ideas, or themes with page numbers for locating them.

informatics the study of data or knowledge represented in a form that can be stored or manipulated by digital or computational means.

information any bit of knowledge communicated about something; according to the philosopher Gregory Bateson, "any difference that makes a difference."

information design the use of graphic means to organize and communicate data or knowledge, often emphasizing quantitative rather than qualitative knowledge and seeking formal clarity and legibility.

information graphics visual designs that frame and present facts, usually with as little decorative or nonessential material and in as legible and compact a form as possible.

inline of or pertaining to typefaces designed with a white line running through the downstrokes.

inscription a written form that leaves a mark or trace in a material support; such a mark need not be part of a sign system but may be a gestural or decorative expression.

intaglio from the Italian *intagliare*, literally, incised or engraved; of or pertaining to any printing process—including engraving and etching—that involves removing material from a surface, pressing ink into the incised areas, and wiping the rest of the surface clean before transferring the ink onto paper (as opposed to relief printing, such as woodblock or letterpress, or planographic processes, such as lithography).

intellectual property any product of human creativity that has value by virtue of originality of conception or expression, rather than through inherent material properties or industrial utility.

International Typographic Style an approach to design premised on the conviction that formal choices and effects could be governed by rational principles that transcended historical and cultural frameworks.

interval a perceptible, significant space that separates elements or signs in a sequence, composition, or system.

journeyman a tradesperson who has completed an apprenticeship and is qualified to be hired for work.

kiosk from a Persian word meaning "pavilion," any small, freestanding structure, often used as a booth for sales; a newsstand.

kitsch works of art meant to appeal to a broad public, often characterized by superficial or sentimental qualities; works considered to be of bad faith or mind-dulling character on account of being produced for easy consumption rather than to express serious or lofty ideas; a term of disdain for works considered to be inauthentic by contrast to genuine works of art.

knowledge production information and its framing or codification into a field or discipline.

language a stable system of human communication that depends on consensual sign values for the exchange of information, ideas, and feelings.

late capitalist of or pertaining to a phase of economic (and cultural) development based on consumption and spectacle rather than production; in contrast to earlier phases of industrial or consumer capitalism; implying a decadent condition of culture.

layout the arrangement or composition of graphic elements within a design, usually in print media; the organization of type and/or images from a basic structure or scheme through finished artwork for reproduction.

leading metal strips in thicknesses of regular point sizes set between lines of type; by extension, the measure of space produced by these strips.

letterform the shape or style of a letter.

letterhead the element at the top of stationery that identifies its sender, often designed to give a business or individual a distinctive graphic identity.

letterpress relief printing technology that inks the raised surfaces of metal type or image blocks and impresses them on paper.

letters written characters that are part of the alphabet; although letters may be considered a means of transcribing speech, letters and speech sounds in any given language do not have a one-to-one relationship.

lexicons dictionaries or word lists that define vocabulary, often for a specialized field.

lifestyle a way of living that implies choices made according to certain values or tastes; generally, an approach that gives priority to the material plane of existence over the spiritual and political planes but need not exclude these; more narrowly, an approach to existence based on patterns of consumption and display as primary criteria.

likeness an image, object, or sign that resembles an original source or referent, whether it be a person, animal, place, or thing; the quality of resemblance.

linear arranged in a line or row; of things ranged one after another so that their formal order determines the consecutive order of their being read, viewed, or heard.

Linotype a mechanized process of setting type with the aid of a keyboard and casting it in lines of text.

literacy in a narrow sense, the ability to read; in a broader use, participation in a knowledge-base by means of a common communication system, consensual values, and shared references.

literate able to use letters; hence, capable of reading; usually, characteristic of a person for whom, or a culture in which, written language is an integral part of daily life.

lithography a printing process that treats limestones or metal plates with chemicals to create ink-receptive areas on the printing surface.

logographic (logogram) of or pertaining to writing that represents words with visual signs (an element of such a system).

logotype two or more letters cast as a single graphic on the same block; a logo.

mail art an artistic movement that used the postal system, both as a means of distribution and as an element of the work itself (in the form of cancellation stamps and other official notations).

majuscules uppercase letters; capitals.

manifesto a succinct statement of beliefs; a document used to proclaim the tenets of an artistic movement, particularly common among early twentieth-century avant-garde artists inspired by Karl Marx and Friedrich Engels's 1848 *The Communist Manifesto*. By stating their beliefs in this form, artists deliberately associated their agendas with political aims of social transformation.

marginalia any notes or commentary appended to a text in the space left at the top, bottom, or edges of a page.

marks any inscription that registers as the trace of a deliberate gesture or intentional act, whether or not it belongs to a stable language system; a mark is of a lower order than a sign; signs, images, patterns, and designs are made of marks.

mass of things, produced in large quantity or bulk, usually by mechanical means; of people, a large, undifferentiated segment of the population; a group thought to act as an entity rather than as individuals; also, the working classes or lower socioeconomic strata of a culture.

mass culture aspects of social life, such as products, entertainment, printed matter, or spectacles, that are thought to appeal to, and be consumed by, many people in more or less the same way.

mass media any form of communication that reaches a broad audience through reproduction, broadcast, or distribution; dissemination of the same information or representation to a large segment of the population.

masthead the section of a newspaper or printed journal that identifies the publication and its publisher by name, usually carries the date and other timely information, and is generally placed at the top of the first page.

matrices in printing technology, molds (usually brass) made from the imprint of a punch and used to cast type; matrices are used over and over again in the production of a font of lead letters. (See **punch**.)

mechanicals finished artwork (including text, images, layouts, and so on) that has been prepared to be photographed for reproduction; short for "mechanical art," so called because it represents a stage in the process of reproduction, rather than original or creative work.

media plural of *medium,* from the Latin *medius* (middle); any means or method of inscription and transmission of information in a material support or format (stone, clay, wood, paint, paper, film, electrical impulse, radio wave, light wave, digital code, and so on) that stands between a producer and a receiver in communication.

Memphis an Italian design group founded in 1981 in response to the bland conservatism that dominated modernism; characterized by a vivid, colorful, playful style that came to be associated with postmodernism.

meta-design the establishment of principles and guidelines for design as a practice, as distinct from the application of such principles to the design of specific objects, spaces, or graphics; the design of design.

meta-technology a technology that enables other technical processes, such as photography in the service of print reproduction.

minuscules letters with ascenders and descenders; the calligraphic predecessor of lower case type.

model a scheme or template from which any number of realizations can be made; a model allows knowledge or thought to be represented in a generalized form for the purposes of analysis, design, or production; a model often presents an ideal that undergoes variation when the model is applied.

modern movement any one of several artistic groups that aimed to define styles, forms, or values for contemporary life; more generally, the sum of these groups in the late nineteenth and early twentieth centuries (although the term is not exclusively reserved for this historical moment).

moderne a French term for a style that became popular after the 1925 *Exposition des Arts Décoratifs et Industriels Modernes* in Paris; associated with the cool, streamlined look of the 1920s in which the elaborate motifs of an earlier era were banished in favor of more industrial forms; Art Deco.

modernism the attitude or approach of artistic and design movements that distinguish themselves from classical, historical, or traditional styles and stake their validity on claims of currency and participation in formal and/or social progress.

modernity the historical period of cultural change associated with the effects of the industrial revolution; the qualities or conditions of this period.

modular made in standard forms or measures that allow for interchangeability or variable combinations of parts; in the case of printing, produced in the standardized units that made movable type possible.

monocular from the Latin *mono* (single) and *oculus* (eye), of or pertaining to a single eye; seen by one eye, as in drawing systems that organize the visual field from a single point of view, without parallax effect (the difference in vision of an object caused by the space between two eyes) or movement.

monoline type or writing in which ascenders and descenders are the same height as the body of the letters.

Monotype in printing technology, a mechanized process of setting type with the aid of a keyboard and casting it one letter or character at a time; in printmaking, a one-off impression taken from a plate or block.

montage from the French *monter* (to mount), combining various pieces of images, music, or film to construct a new whole.

monumental large in scale and importance; in the case of inscriptions, usually formal, authoritative, and conspicuously placed in a public space.

morphology the analysis of forms; the study of any class of things or species of animal or plant through attention to shape.

movable type type cut and cast in standard sizes of individual letters so that it can be set multiple times in variable combinations.

movement any group of artists or activists who align themselves behind an aesthetic program, a social or political cause, or some other common goal.

multiculturalism an attention to, or allowance for, traditions and practices from a variety of ethnic or social sources; an awareness of the cultural relativity of value judgments and their location within specific historical contexts.

multiples art made in many copies so that there is no single original; intended to be democratic and inexpensive and to circulate more widely than unique works of art.

neoclassicism a revival of Greek and Roman styles and motifs accompanied by an embrace of theories of proportion and harmony that sought universal forms and ideal compositions through the application of rational principles, rather than emotion or sensation; popular in the early nineteenth century in association with Napoleon's empire and its utopian view of the Classical age.

networks technical, physical, or social systems of links and circuits for the circulation of tangible or intangible goods or information.

neue grafik in German, new graphics; a movement to found an international style in the late 1950s that was promoted by a Swiss publication of the same name.

neue sachlichkeit in German, the new objectivity; an approach to the arts in the 1920s that rejected the mystical, pseudo-primitive, and emotional aspects of Expressionism in favor of a stark grasp of everyday reality; in photography, an embrace of the rationalism afforded by technology and a rejection of pictorialism.

neue typographie in German, new typography; a name coined in the 1920s for a functionalist approach to typography that rejected ornament, embraced standardization, and promoted asymmetrical dynamism and the use of sans serif type; associated with designer Jan Tschichold whose writings outlined its principles.

new objectivity See ***neue sachlichkeit***.

New World the Western hemisphere, including all of the Americas, described from a European perspective; the term carries the cultural bias of its historical origin when it implied that the Old World had a long history of civilization, whereas the New World was a place of primitive peoples living in a natural state.

news ballads publications that recorded and communicated the particulars of a recent or current event in verse.

newsbooks printed accounts of recent or current events that were folded into pamphlets or signatures (as opposed to news sheets that were single sheets).

news sheets an early form of newspaper that consisted of a single sheet, flat or folded; news sheets were produced regularly, had an identifiable masthead or title, and presented timely information or commentary.

nihilistic of or pertaining to an attitude governed by the conviction that there are no grounds on which to establish truth, values, or bases for moral or other judgment.

notation a written system in which signs have a specific and fixed value; a method of recording language, mathematical calculations, scientific information, musical scores, or any other stable code.

notice a sign meant to make something known, usually posted in public view.

objectify to turn an idea, person, or event into an object of thought; to make something appear to be distinct from the perceiver or subject; to treat as an object; the distinction between subject and object is a basic tenet of

Western philosophy that comes to be reconsidered through the influence of phenomenology, psychoanalysis, cognitive studies, and Eastern philosophies.

octavo a book size resulting from the gathering of sheets folded three times so that each page is one eighth the size of the original sheet.

offset short for offset lithography, a printing process that involves the transfer of an image or text from the printing plate to a rubber blanket and then onto paper; allows for fine resolution of images because of rubber's capacity to receive and transfer visual information.

Old Style of or pertaining to type designs that moved away from strict imitation of humanistic handwriting and took advantage of the specific physical properties and formal possibilities of metal to improve legibility; the first Old Style faces appeared at the end of the fifteenth century, soon after the invention of movable type.

one-dimensional having only a single quality or characteristic as an idea or representation; in a mathematical system, a single dimension has neither extension nor duration and consists only of points.

op art an artistic movement of the late 1950s and 1960s that explored and manipulated optical effects, especially of geometric patterns.

optical of or pertaining to optics, the science of vision or sight; of or pertaining to seeing in the physiological or technical sense (as distinct from *visual,* which describes things available to sight).

oral of or pertaining to the mouth; of communication, vocal forms, such as speech, chants, grunting, cries, screams, or song.

ordinator a person responsible for laying out a design to be inscribed by a carver or rendered by a calligrapher; the person who directs a design.

organic of or pertaining to living organisms; of or pertaining to forms that resemble those of the natural world, in contrast to mechanical or geometric constructions; characterized by an integration of all parts in one whole.

orthography correct spelling.

ostraca plural of the Greek *ostracon* (shard), fragments of pottery or stone used as writing surfaces.

palimpsest a document that records a series of texts, one written over another that has been erased but that may show through.

pamphlet a printed form that consists of relatively small folded sheets collected in a signature or otherwise fastened together; a popular format for political essays, religious tracts, and other short but often provocative texts meant to be circulated quickly and widely.

papyrus a writing material made from the stems of a reedy plant, cut into strips, overlaid, and pressed together.

parameterized literally, defined by limits; of information to which constant measures have been applied for the purpose of evaluation.

parameters limits that define values in a system; used in the assessment of data.

parchment a writing surface made of animal skin that has been scraped free of hair or fur and treated.

parody a work that imitates another in exaggerated form for the sake of ridicule or critique.

pastiche a composition made of parts taken from various sources, or in the style of a particular artist or moment; in a postmodern context, the appropriation of historical or canonical materials to make a new work that assumes that all ideas have already been expressed and that originality is a mythic concept.

patents legal documents that grant exclusive rights to an invention and its use for profit.

performative of or pertaining to a speech act that, in itself, has consequence or effect, such as a vow, a promise, or a command.

perspective a drawing system devised to represent objects accurately with regard to distance or depth; a method of mapping three-dimensional space onto a two-dimensional surface from a single, stationary viewpoint.

phonogram a visual sign that represents a sound (in a phonographic writing system).

photocomposition type composed by projecting characters through negative film onto photo-sensitive paper and using lenses to adjust sizes; phototypesetting.

photography any technology that produces an image by recording traces of light; any process that enables the production or reproduction of images through the exposure and fixing of light-sensitive materials (plates, paper, film) or the recording of light as numerical values (and their storage as pixels).

photogravure an etching process renowned for rich tonal values that involves coating a plate with photosensitive gelatin and powdered resin, exposing it, and etching it in an acid bath.

photomontage fragments of photographs combined to form a single composition. (See **montage**.)

photo-offset printing technology combining the photographic production of plates and a printing process that uses a rubber blanket to transfer ink from plate to paper. (See **offset**.)

photostat a process used to make camera-ready (scaled, black and white) artwork for platemaking purposes; a copy made in this way. (See **PMT**.)

phototype(setting) type produced or set using film. (See **photocomposition**.)

pictographic (pictogram) of or pertaining to writing that represents words or ideas with pictorial signs (an element of such a system).

pictorial the quality of an image that has recognizable elements of a scene, figures, or objects.

pigments materials used to create color, derived from minerals, plants, animals, or chemically synthetic sources; generally ground and mixed with a medium to produce ink, paint, or glazes.

pixelated of or pertaining to an image or graphic that shows the basic units of its digital display (pixels), usually because the resolution of the file or screen is not high enough to render a smooth line or image but also, sometimes, as a deliberate aesthetic effect.

pixel-based made up of, or making use of, the smallest units of screen display in a digital system.

plakatstil in German, poster style; a design trend in the early 1900s that emphasized its subjects by setting them off against flat areas of color in simple compositions featuring bold lettering.

planned obsolescence a strategy for increasing sales by designing products that will quickly need to be replaced, either because they wear out or because they are surpassed by more effective or stylish models.

platen plate in a letterpress that exerts pressure to transfer ink from the surface of metal type or image blocks to paper.

play the movement or space between elements of a device or apparatus; the allowance for difference in a system; the interactivity of signs that produces their meaning within a system.

PMT (photomechanical transfer) the process by which a photosensitive paper transfers an image to another piece of paper without use of a negative; the print resulting from this process; used to make camera-ready mechanicals. (See **photostat**.)

point size the measure of type in terms of a standard system. (See **point system**.)

point system a standardized system for measuring the height of type, the thickness of leading, and so on; there are 72 points to the inch.

pop an artistic movement of the late 1950s and 1960s that took the objects and icons of commercial and media culture as its subject matter and whose practitioners often adopted the techniques of industrial production and commercial art to produce fine art; art or graphics that echo popular or consumer culture.

popular of the people; of products, common or readily available, as opposed to rarified or scarce; finding favor among a wide segment of the population; originally, issuing from the grass roots as a direct expression of the sentiments of a broad base of the population, in contrast to ideas or values imposed from outside or above.

post-human with reference to the idea that humans are no longer simply or independently an organic, biological species but that we exist in hybrid forms with machines, industrial parts, or digital technology.

postmodernism a cultural moment at which modernism's claims for universal, formal, and autonomous qualities in works of art or design were replaced by notions of relativism, contingency, and *play* within sign systems.

post-structuralist of or pertaining to a twentieth-century philosophical movement in which the logical premises of structuralism were superseded by an analysis of the cultural and historical conditions within which such formal structures come into being and serve particular interests; of or pertaining to this critical stance, according to which meaning is relative and contingent rather than formal or transcendent.

Pre-Raphaelite of or pertaining to the art and writings of a group formed around English painter Dante Gabriel Rossetti, who believed that the best work in Western culture had been done before that of the Italian Renaissance painter Raphael and who deliberately created a style that they believed reflected the qualities of Medieval art; of or pertaining to work in the style of these artists, with its decorative trappings and Medieval literary themes.

printers' flowers metal ornaments and elements designed to be combined in different patterns or forms for borders or other decorative devices in letterpress composition.

private press a publishing house that is owned and operated by a small group or an individual who directs all editorial, design, and production decisions, often without the influence of commercial considerations.

proofs first stages of the printing process in which type, blocks, or plates are printed and checked for errors.

propaganda language or images used to persuade a group to adopt a particular set of ideas; systematic indoctrination by means of verbal or visual messages.

prototype the first model of a design, made in advance of full-scale production to test functionality.

proto-writing signs, glyphs, marks, and other forms of inscription that anticipate more systematic writing systems but do not have a stable representational relation to language.

Provo a radical political movement in Holland in the 1960s based on a playful, anarchist sensibility that used nonviolent methods to provoke authorities and institute alternative policies.

psychedelic mind-altering; of or pertaining to a certain class of drugs and their effects on perception; also, of or pertaining to a graphic style that imitated the hallucinatory effects of these drugs.

public relations a field that specializes in constructing communications campaigns to manage the interests or identity of a firm, party, or individual.

public sphere a virtual space of discourse and understanding created through media and networks of communication, considered crucial to the workings of participatory government.

pulp a material that has been finely shredded or ground and mixed with liquid to become the basis of paper production (beginning in the early nineteenth century); also, cheaply printed matter meant to appeal to a lower socioeconomic class on account of its affordability and tendency to sensational imagery.

punch a letter or design cut on the end of a stick of hard metal used to produce a matrix, or mold, for casting lead type; a punch had to be cut for every letter of every typeface in each size, style, and weight. (See **matrices**.)

punch cutter a person who cuts type designs in hard metal punches. (See **punch**.)

Punk a rebellious counterculture movement that began in Britain and the United States, whose harsh sound and abrasive lyrics attacked the pretenses of middle-class culture and conservative politics; a street fashion characterized by shaved heads, starkly artificial hair dyes, piercings, and leather.

quadrivium the four *higher* arts among the seven inherited from antiquity that structured Medieval learning: arithmetic, geometry, music, and astronomy. (See **trivium**.)

raster lines used to generate the display on a cathode-ray tube; thus, of or pertaining to images or texts that are drawn by lines on such a display.

rationalization of space a logical and formal approach to the representation of space; the imposition of a grid or other regular metric onto space; the use by perspectival drawing systems of grids and vanishing points to create an illusion of three-dimensional space through projection onto a two-dimensional plane.

recombinant of or pertaining to elements that can be put together in a variety of ways to produce new outcomes, products, or systems; of or pertaining to information or programming that can be repurposed for new uses; in genetics, of or pertaining to DNA, cells, or organisms formed by recombination.

reifying (reification) the conceptual conversion of an idea, a state, or a value into a thing; in Marxist theory, the transfer of human or social qualities to material things and, conversely, the understanding, treatment, or representation of a historical situation or social relation as a solid thing.

relief print a print made by a process that involves removing areas from the surface of a block or plate, inking the raised surface that remains, and transferring the image to paper.

Renaissance a cultural period beginning in the fourteenth century that witnessed a rebirth of knowledge outside the confines of church teachings and control; generally associated with revived knowledge of classical texts, arts, and architecture, as well as the rise of scientific methods based on observation.

rendering drawing, often finished to a point of high polish, usually in a naturalistic style that imitates the visual experience of reality (through shading, perspective, and so on); the generation of realistic effects, such as highlights, textures, and shadows, by a digital display.

representation a sign or image that stands for something else; abstract or arbitrary signs may function as representations, but representational art always contains recognizable elements of that which it depicts.

retro of or pertaining to a nostalgic style that appropriates past motifs or forms, often without regard for historical accuracy.

rhetorical of or pertaining to rhetoric, the art of persuasion or effective presentation; of techniques and devices designed to frame information in such a way as to elicit a particular interpretation.

rococo literally, rocklike; of or pertaining to a decorative style that featured elaborate, even excessive, organic and protruding forms, popular in the early eighteenth century and associated with the decadence of aristocratic lifestyles and attitudes.

romanticism an artistic movement that arose in the late eighteenth century in response to cultural changes brought about by industrialization; a sensibility that celebrated emotions and sensations over reason and was associated with a passion for nature as an image of uncontrollable force and constant change.

rotogravure a printing process in which photogravure plates were wrapped around the cylinder of a high-speed rotary press. (See **photogravure**.)

rotunda any of many Medieval and Renaissance book hands, associated with religious texts, used as models for type designs.

rule in letterpress composition, metal cast to print straight lines.

run a single pass of a sheet through a press; short for print or press run.

rustic of or pertaining to rural life; having an authenticity rooted in tradition or, in negative senses, a crude lack of sophistication; of early lettering, displaying a handmade quality rather than constructed regularity.

sans serif type that is designed without finishing lines at the ends of strokes.

sarcophagus a stone coffin or tomb.

scalable in digital media, of or pertaining to an object or image whose size or proportions can be automatically (computationally) changed.

schematic of or related to a scheme; a diagrammatic or abstract outline that communicates information in a reduced or generalized manner, often lacking in realism or pictorial detail.

scholasticism a Medieval approach to knowledge and method of speculation based on a formal logic derived from Aristotle (as distinct from approaches grounded in religious doctrine or empirical observation).

screen patterns halftone dots in various weights and designs used to translate continuous tone into values that can be printed by photo-offset technology.

scribe person who writes, usually a professional; also, to act as a scribe, to write.

script a writing system in any visual form, whether carved, inscribed, painted, drawn, or printed.

scrolls rolled parchment or paper; an ancient text format.

secular worldly or pertaining to those realms of activity that are distinct from spiritual or theological influences or concerns.

Semitic of or pertaining to Semitic peoples of the ancient Near East, Semites;

their cultures or languages, including Arabic, Aramaic, and Hebrew.

serifs small finishing lines at the end of the strokes of a letter; any variation thereof.

signs any sound, object, mark, or other token that can be used to represent something else in a systematic way.

sign systems finite networks within which symbols circulate and gain their value; language and other systems of communication and representation.

silkscreen a printing technique that uses stencils in combination with stretched fabric through which ink is pressed.

simulacra illusions that pass for reality.

simulation an image or representation that may be taken for reality; in the critical writing of twentieth-century theorist Jean Baudrillard, a simulation has no referent in lived experience but is an image that produces belief.

Situationist International a movement with roots in the early twentieth-century avant-garde and Marxist theory, founded by European artists and writers who believed that radical art could bring about social change and who emphasized awareness of circumstances, events, and forces, rather than the making of objects.

slab serif type with squared serifs, such as Stymie; also known as Egyptian faces because angular, geometric motifs were associated with hieroglyphic carvings and other stylistic elements of Egyptian art.

social contract the idea that a government rules by consent of the people: Individuals give up a certain amount of freedom in exchange for protections and benefits from the state.

specimen sheets printed examples of available typefaces and designs, used by printers to show clients what they had to offer and by foundries to sell type to printers.

spectacle something meant to be seen; in contemporary theory, associated with the work of French theorist Guy Debord, a condition of culture in which experience has been replaced by images; an organization of everyday life under capitalism within which social relations and the relationship of individuals to their own lives are mediated by representations; the ubiquity of such mediation.

spread an opening in a book, journal, or newspaper across the gutter or fold.

spreadsheet a display of information in columns for the purpose of comparison of values across a number of variables or fields; electronic spreadsheets that could automatically recalculate and display changing information for financial analysis were considered the "killer application" that converted businesses to the use of digital computers in the early 1980s.

standardization making a process or product uniform by setting a basis for comparison, or minimum level of quality, to which operations or production must conform.

stereotypes plates made from molds in an industrial print technology that produced multiple copies of a single form (text or image block) from a papier mâché or rubber casting; ideas or figures replicated in a similar form.

stoichedon a written form in which letters are aligned both horizontally and vertically, as if marshaled into files for a military drill.

structuralist of or pertaining to a formal approach to the study of a society, system, or cultural form according to which the value of any instance derives from its place within an overarching structure rather than from any intrinsic quality. For example, in structuralist linguistics, the meaning of a word derives from its relation to other words, rather than from its roots, just as the value of a coin is fixed by its place within a monetary system.

Suprematism a name coined in 1915 by Kasimir Malevich to describe experimental art that aimed to transcend the limits of all past art and create works that were concerned almost entirely with geometric forms.

surrealism an artistic movement developed in the 1920s and 1930s by André Breton and others who were intent on infiltrating ordinary life with elements of the marvelous and who drew on dreams, the unconscious, and methods of automatism to escape the confines of rationality in art-making.

swash a long, decorative stroke at the beginning or end of a letter, usually imitating calligraphic forms.

syllabaries writing systems whose signs represent syllables or complex sounds; usually composed of considerably more signs than the alphabet but fewer signs than logographic systems, which represent words.

symbolic forms signs or objects whose value derives from their meaning as representations rather than from their material properties or literal form; in psychoanalytic terms, the *symbolic* designates the realm of language and representation systems as the site of meaning production and identity formation.

symbolic value meaning that exceeds the literal, physical, or material value of a thing, word, or gesture; the value generated by sign systems, such as language, mathematical notation, or ritual performance; a culturally specific expression of the value systems of a society.

Symbolism a late nineteenth-century movement in art and literature concerned with values not contained in realistic or literal representation but metaphysical or transcendent and only evocable through signs and symbols.

symbols any mark, glyph, sign, object, or image that stands for something else; a symbol does not have to share any visual properties with what it represents but can be completely arbitrary; an *X* on a map may be a symbol for a place, a piece of military equipment, a building, or the site of buried treasure.

synesthesia a transposition of the properties of one sense perception into the form of another, as in tasting or hearing a color.

systems theory the understanding of any entity as part of a set of relations in a closed circuit; the idea that an organization or framework defines the roles and identities of elements in a codependent relationship of parts to the whole.

taxonomic of or pertaining to a classification system or to the laws and principles that govern such a system; of or pertaining to the science of classification or ordering.

Taylorism a rational method of analyzing production to achieve maximum efficiency; the method was applied to all kinds of labor, including office and management work, and was often extremely detailed in its study of body movements in terms of their expenditure of time and energy.

technicolor an elaborate industrial process that used filters, multiple film strips, and dyes to produce a very dense, vivid, but unnatural photographic color image.

techno of or pertaining to a style that uses the imagery and motifs of contemporary technology not as functional forms but as elements of an aesthetic.

technological from the Greek *tekhne* (art or craft), of or pertaining to the application of knowledge.

telematic of or pertaining to the processing of information at a distance, often using wireless technology.

templates patterns that can be repurposed, often used to establish uniformity across the production of multiple versions or copies of a design.

textual apparatus any marginal notes, footnotes, headers, footers, appendices, indices, front matter, back matter, or other added elements that scaffold a text to assist in its navigation or provide commentary.

textura a tightly written manuscript hand or typeface with narrowly spaced strokes, suggestive of a woven pattern; condensed blackletter hands.

titling face type in a size and/or style meant to be used for titles, usually larger than text faces and sometimes, but not always, more decorative in appearance.

touch-up work removal of spots or flaws from a photograph or other graphic artwork; cleaning of paste-up or other final artwork in preparation for photographic reproduction.

trade card a small printed item used to identify and promote a business or service.

trademarks any marks or devices used by a manufacturer or tradesperson to identify goods or products; registered and protected by law in the modern era.

transfer type lettering designed to be removed from a backing sheet and adhered to a layout by pressure; beginning in the 1960s, it allowed designers to set display type and headlines at their drawing tables without recourse to cumbersome phototypesetting methods.

transitional faces type designs that combine characteristics of Old Style and modern faces, generally, with more contrast between thick and thin strokes than Old Style but without the strict geometric regularity of modern faces; first appeared in the eighteenth century.

transparency the quality of a text or image whose meaning seems to be perceptible without being mediated by the material or format of its representation or delivery.

trivium the three *lower* arts among the seven inherited from antiquity that structured Medieval learning: logic, rhetoric, and grammar. (See **quadrivium**.)

Tuscan (type) display faces that often feature mid-stem decorations and split serifs.

tympan from the Latin *tympanum* (drum), in printing, the taut covering on a cylinder or platen that brings paper into contact with an inked form. (See **platen**.)

typecasting the repeated use of a mold to produce multiple copies of a letter in metal.

typeface a full set of letters and punctuation marks designed to work together in a single style.

typesetter a person who composes type either by hand or by mechanical, photographic, or digital methods.

typography the science and art of using type to convey ideas, information, or style.

unbracketed serifs fine lines attached to the ends of letter strokes without transitional curves where they meet; square, linear, or geometric in style.

uncials from the Latin *uncia* (inch), rounded letterforms in which ascenders and descenders extend slightly beyond the x-height and baseline (beyond the lines used as guides for the height of the body). (See **x-height**.)

underground the site of production of alternative culture; of or pertaining to films, comic books, journals, and other art and media produced in quasi-clandestine or low-profile environments outside of the parameters of mainstream or straight commercial enterprise.

universal applicable to all; used to invoke values or beliefs that are ascribed to humanity in general, as if they did not have a historical context or cultural connection.

universal language the idea of a form of expression that could be understood by all people regardless of their native tongue and that would accurately encode knowledge in a systematic way.

universal style an approach to design based on the presumption that the truth (meaning or effect) of certain formal principles do not depend on history or culture but is shared by all human societies and could be articulated as a logical ideal.

vector graphics visual objects whose identity is described in terms of directional lines that connect coordinate points; these objects have the advantage of small file size and automatic scalability.

vernacular from the Greek *verna* (home-born slave), a native language; also, the specialized languages of trades or professions.

versals capitals used at the beginning of a verse or paragraph in a manuscript, often decorated with filials or other line work or color.

visual able to be perceived by the eye and optic system, available to vision; also, any properties of things that are only perceptible through the sense of vision.

visual code a stable sign system in a graphic form.

visual culture the realm of images and information in graphic form; more than a collection of images, visual culture constitutes and communicates a system of values and beliefs.

wire services agencies that once disseminated information or images by means of telegraph or telephone and now mainly operate electronically.

woodblock a relief printing surface made of wood; negative spaces are carved away from the block, and the remaining area is inked and printed.

woodcut a relief print made from a woodblock. (See **woodblock**.)

wood type letters carved or cut from wood, usually in display sizes.

writing any act of inscription or notation that involves making marks to present language in visual form.

writing systems stable codes of graphic signs used to represent language in a visual form; Chinese characters and alphabetic letters are the writing systems currently in use; vanished systems include Sumerian and Hittite cuneiform, Egyptian hieroglyphics, Mayan glyphs, runes, and Indus Valley and Easter Island scripts.

WYSIWYG (what you see is what you get) the representation of text and images on a screen, exactly as they will appear on a page.

x-height the height of the lowercase *x* in any typeface; the height of the body of letters in any typeface; a standard way of gauging the size of a face, as well as the proportions of the body to ascenders and descenders; type with a large x-height is often considered more legible.

zine an independent, underground, or alternative publication, often associated with artists and counter-culture sensibilities; an abbreviation of the word *magazine*.

Bibliography

*Titles of works used in more than one chapter are not repeated after the first listing. Titles in **bold** are recommended as further reading or resources.*

1. From Prehistory to Early Writing

Christin, Anne Marie, ed. *The History of Writing*. Paris: Flammarion, 2001.

Edey, Maitland, and the editors of Time-Life Books. *The Missing Link*. New York: Time-Life Books, 1972.

Fischer, Steven Roger. *A History of Language*. London: Reaktion Books, 1999.

Gaur, Albertine. *A History of Writing*. London: British Museum Books, 1984.

Gelb, Ignace. *A Study of Writing*. Chicago: University of Chicago Press, 1952.

Healey, John F. *The Early Alphabet*. London: British Museum Publications, 1990.

Howell, F. Clark and the editors of Time-Life Books. *Early Man*. New York: Time-Life Books, 1965.

Moore, Oliver. *Reading the Past: Chinese*. Berkeley, CA: University of California Press, 2000.

Naveh, Joseph. *Early History of the Alphabet*. Leiden, The Netherlands: E. J. Brill, 1982.

Sampson, Geoffrey. *Writing Systems*. Stanford, CA: Stanford University Press, 1985.

Schmandt-Besserat, Denise. *How Writing Came About*. Austin, TX: University of Texas, 1996.

Senner, Wayne M. *The Origins of Writing*. Lincoln, NE: The University of Nebraska Press, 1989.

Stokstad, Marilyn. *Art History*. Englewood Cliffs, NJ: Prentice Hall, 1995.

2. Classical Literacy

Avrin, Leila. *Scribes, Script, and Books*. Chicago: American Library Association and London: The British Library, 1991.

Bischoff, Bernard. *Latin Paleography: Antiquity and the Middle Ages*. Cambridge: Cambridge University Press, 1990.

Briquel, Dominique. "The Script of Ancient Italy." In Anne-Marie Christin, ed. *A History of Writing*. Paris: Flammarion, 2001.

Dobias-Lalou, Catherine. "The Greek Alphabets." In Anne-Marie Christin, ed. *A History of Writing*. Paris: Flammarion, 2001.

Gray, Nicolete. *A History of Lettering*. Boston: David R. Godine, 1986.

Knight, Stan. *Historical Scripts: From Classical Times to the Renaissance*. New Castle, DE: Oak Knoll Press, 1998.

Mason, William. *A History of the Art of Writing*. New York: The Macmillan Company, 1928.

Petrucci, Armando. *Public Lettering*. Chicago: University of Chicago Press, 1990.

3. Medieval Letterforms and Book Formats

Alexander, Jonathan, J. *Medieval Illuminators and their Methods of Work*. New Haven, CT: Yale, 1992.

Alexander, Jonathan, J. *The Decorated Letter*. New York: George Braziller, 1978.

Daniels, Peter, and William Bright. *The World's Writing Systems*. Oxford: Oxford University Press, 1996.

De Hamel, Christopher. *A History of Illuminated Manuscript*. Boston: David R. Godine, 1986.

Drogin, Marc. *Medieval Calligraphy*. Montclair, NJ: Allanheld and Schram, 1980.

Hamilton, Frederick. *Books Before Typography*. Chicago: United Typothetae of America, 1918.

Harthan, John. *The History of the Illustrated Book*. London: Thames and Hudson, 1981.

Hutchinson, James. *Letters*. New York: Van Nostrand Reinhold Co., 1983.

Jean, George. *Writing: The Story of Alphabets and Scripts*. New York: Harry N. Abrams, 1987.

Kapr, Albert. *The Art of Lettering*. Munich: K. G. Saur, 1983.

Lawson, Alexander. *Anatomy of a Typeface*. Jaffrey, NH: David Godine, 1990.

Mason, William. *A History of the Art of Writing*. New York: The Macmillan Company, 1928.

McMurtrie, Douglas. *The Book: The Story of Printing and Bookmaking*. New York: Dorset, 1943.

Morison, Stanley. *Politics and Script*. Oxford: The Clarendon Press, 1972.

Myers, Robin, and Michael Harris, eds. *A Millennium of the Book*. Winchester, DE: Oak Knoll Press, 1994.

Steinberg, S. H. *Five Hundred Years of Printing*. New Castle, DE: Oak Knoll Press and London: The British Library, 1996.

4. Renaissance Design: Standardization and Modularization in Print

Ivins, William. *Prints and Visual Communication*. Cambridge, MA: Harvard University Press, 1953.

Jensen, Kristian, ed. *Incunabula and their Readers*. London: The British Library, 2003.

Johnson, Henry Lewis. *Decorative Ornaments and Alphabets of the Renaissance*. New York: Dover, 1991. Reprint of *Historic Design in Printing*. Boston: Graphic Arts Company, 1923.

Levarie, Norma. *The Art and History of Books*. New Castle, DE: Oak Knoll Press and London: The British Library, 1995.

Needham, Paul. *Early Printed Books*. New York: The Pierpont Morgan Library, 1974.

Nesbitt, Alexander. *200 Decorative Title Pages*. New York: Dover, 1964.

Smith, Margaret. *The Title Page*. London: The British Library and New Castle, DE: Oak Knoll Press, 2000.

Tory, Geofroy. *Champfleury*. New York: Grolier, 1927. Reprint, New York: Dover, 1967.

Tyson, Gerald, and Sylvia S. Wagonheim. *Print and Culture in the Renaissance*. Newark, DE: University of Delaware Press, 1986.

Whitfield, Peter. *The Image of the World*. San Francisco: Pomegranate Art Books, 1997.

5. Modern Typography and the Creation of the Public Sphere

Barnhurst, Kevin G., and John Nerone. *The Form of News: A History*. New York: The Guilford Press, 2001.

Benton, Josiah Henry. *John Baskerville: Type-Founder and Printer 1706–1775*. New York: Burt Franklin, 1968.

Carter, John, and Percy Muir, eds. *Printing and the Mind of Man*. Munich: Karl Pressler, 1983.

Clarke, Bob. *From Grub Street to Fleet Street*. Aldershot, UK: Ashgate, 2004.

Darnton, Robert, and Daniel Roche. *Revolution in Print*. Berkeley, CA: University of California Press, 1989.

Diderot, Denis, and Jean le Rond D'Alembert. *L'Encyclopédie*. Paris: Bibliothèque de l'Image, 2001.

Eisenstein, Elizabeth. *The Printing Press as an Agent of Change.* Cambridge: Cambridge University Press, 1979.

Lewis, John. *Anatomy of Printing.* London: Faber and Faber, 1970.

Morison, Stanley. *The English Newspaper.* Cambridge: Cambridge University Press, 1932.

Mosley, James, ed. *Le Romain du Roi, La Typographie au Service de l'État 1702–2002.* Lyon, France: Musée de l'Imprimerie, 2002.

Moxon, Joseph. *Moxon's Mechanick Exercises,* edited by Theodore de Vinne. New York: Typothetae, 1896.

Nelson, C., and M. Secombe. *Occasional Papers of the Bibliographic Society: Periodical Publications 1641–1700, A Survey with Illustrations.* London: The Bibliographical Society, 1986.

Pardoe, F. E. *John Baskerville of Birmingham: Letter-Founder and Printer.* London: Frederick Muller Ltd., 1975.

Shaaber, Matthias. *Some Forerunners of the Newspaper in England 1476–1622.* Philadelphia, PA: University of Pennsylvania Press, 1929.

Stephens, Mitchell. *A History of the News.* New York: Viking, 1988.

Straus, Ralph, and Robert K. Dent. *John Baskerville, A Memoir.* Cambridge University Press for Chatto and Windus, London, 1907.

Wainer, Howard, and Ian Spence, eds. *The Commercial and Political Atlas and Statistical Breviary of William Playfair.* Cambridge: Cambridge University Press, 2005.

Williams, Keith. *The English Newspaper: An Illustrated History to 1900.* London: Springwood Books, 1977.

6. The Graphic Effects of Industrial Production

Anderson, Patricia. *The Printed Image and the Transformation of Popular Culture.* Oxford: Oxford University Press, 1991.

Berry, W. Turner, and A. F. Johnson. *Encyclopedia of Type Faces.* London: Blanford Press, 1953.

Conboy, Martin. *The Press and Popular Culture.* London: Sage Publications, 2002.

Hornung, Clarence. *Handbook of Early Advertising Art.* New York: Dover Publications, 1947.

Jobling, Paul, and David Crowley. *Graphic Design: Reproduction and Representation.* Manchester, UK: Manchester University Press, 1996.

Livois, René de. *Histoire de la Presse Française.* Vol., 1, *Des Origines à 1881.* Lausanne, Switzerland: Editions Spes, 1965.

Myers, Robin, and Michael Harris, eds. *Serials and Their Readers: 1620–1914.* New Castle, DE: Oak Knoll Press, 1993.

Peach, Annette. "Portraits of Byron." *Publications of the Walpole Society,* Vol. 62, 2000.

Robin, Harry. *The Scientific Image.* New York: Harry N. Abrams, 1992.

Scharf, Aaron. *Art and Photography.* London: Penguin, 1974.

Twyman, Michael. *Lithography 1800–1850.* London: Oxford University Press, 1970.

7. Mass Mediation

Bain, Iain. *A Memoir of Thomas Bewick: Written by Himself.* London: Oxford University Press, 1975.

Beevers, Robert. *The Byronic Image: The Poet Portrayed.* Abingdon, UK: Olivia Press, 2005.

Chick, Arthur. *Towards Today's Book.* London: Farrand Press, 1997.

Cleary, David Powers. *Great American Brands.* New York: Fairchild Publications, 1981.

De Vries, Leonard. *Victorian Advertisements.* Philadelphia: J. B. Lippincott Co., 1968.

Fox, Celina. *Graphic Journalism in England During the 1830s and 1840s.* New York: Garland Publishing Co, 1988.

Gelman, Barbara. *The Wood Engravings of Winslow Homer.* New York: Bounty Books, 1969.

Gitelman, Lisa. *Scripts, Grooves, and Writing Machines.* Stanford, CA: Stanford University Press, 1999.

Gress, Edmund. *Fashions in American Typography 1780–1930.* New York: Harper and Brothers, Publishers, 1937.

Hornung, Clarence P. *Handbook of Early Advertising Art, Mainly from American Sources.* New York: Dover Publications, 1947.

Kelly, Rob Roy. *American Wood Type, 1828–1900.* New York: DaCapo, 1969.

Lewis, John. *Printed Ephemera.* Woodbridge, Suffolk: Antique Collector's Club, 1962.

Thomson, Ellen Mazur. *The Origins of Graphic Design in America.* New Haven, CT: Yale University Press, 1997.

Ward, Gerald, ed. *The American Illustrated Book in the Nineteenth Century.* Winterthur, DE: Winterthur Museum, 1987.

8. Formations of the Modern Movement

Banham, Reyner. *Theory and Design in the First Machine Age.* London: Architectural Press, 1960.

Baroni, Daniele, and Antonio D'Auria. *Kolo Moser.* New York: Rizzoli, 1984.

Bruckner, D. J. R. *Fredric Goudy.* New York: Harry N. Abrams, 1990.

Buck-Morss, Susan. *The Dialectics of Seeing.* Cambridge, MA: MIT Press, 1989.

Crane, Walter. *Line and Form.* London: G. Bell and Sons, Ltd. 1925.

Goudy, Fredric. *Goudy's Type Designs [Complete].* New Rochelle, NY: Myriade, 1946.

Jones, Owen. *The Grammar of Ornament,* originally published in 1856. New York: Dover Publications, 1987.

Louis, Eleonora, ed. *Secession: The Vienna Secession from Temple of Art to Exhibition Hall.* Stuttgart: Verlag Gerd Hatje, 1997.

Massey, Anne. *Interior Design of the 20th Century.* London: Thames and Hudson, 1990.

Müller-Brockmann, Josef. *History of the Poster.* Zurich: ABC Verlag, 1971.

Peterson, William S. *The Kelmscott Press.* Berkeley, CA: University of California Press, 1991.

Pevsner, Nicolas. *Pioneers of the Modern Movement.* New York: Museum of Modern Art, 1949.

Taylor, John Russell. *The Art Nouveau Book in Britain.* Cambridge, MA: MIT Press, 1966.

Weisberg, Gabriel P., Edwin Becker, and Évelyne Possémé. *The Origins of L'Art Nouveau: The Bing Empire.* Amsterdam: Van Gogh Museum, 2005.

Weisser, Michael. *Im Stil der "Jugend."* Frankfurt: Verlag Fricke, 1979.

Wilhide, Elizabeth. *The Mackintosh Style.* San Francisco: Chronicle Books, 1995.

Windsor, Alan. *Peter Behrens, Architect and Designer.* New York: Whitney Library of Design, 1981.

9. Innovation and Persuasion

Blotkamp, Carl, et al. *De Stijl: The Formative Years.* Translated by Charlotte and Arthur Loeb. Cambridge, MA: MIT Press, 1982.

Dickerson, Leah. *Building the Collective.* New York: Princeton Architectural Press, 1996.

Drucker, Johanna. *The Visible Word: Modern Art and Experimental Typography 1909–1923.* Chicago: University of Chicago Press, 1994.

Guggenheim Museum. *The Great Utopia.* New York: Guggenheim Museum, 1992.

Kandinsky, Wassily. *Point and Line to Plane.* New York: Dover, 1979. Reprint of 1947 edition published by the Solomon Guggenheim Museum.

Lavin, Maud. *Cut with a Kitchen Knife.* New Haven, CT: Yale University Press, 1993.

Margolin, Victor. *The Struggle for Utopia.* Chicago: University of Chicago Press, 1997.

McLean, Ruari. *Jan Tschichold, Typographer.* Boston: David R. Godine, 1975.

Meggs, Philip, and Rob Carter. *Typographic Specimens: The Great Typefaces.* New York: Van Nostrand Reinhold, 1993.

Museum of Modern Art. *Aleksandr Rodchenko.* New York: Musuem of Modern Art, 1998.

Museum of Modern Art. *Bauhaus: 1919–1928.* New York: Museum of Modern Art, 1993.

Rothenstein, Julian, and Mel Gooding. *ABZ More Alphabets and Other Signs.* San Francisco: Chronicle Books, 2003.

Spencer, Herbert. *The Liberated Page.* San Francisco: Bedford Press, 1987.

Spencer, Herbert. *Pioneers of Modern Typography.* London: Lund Humphries, 1969.

10. The Culture of Consumption

Bogart, Michele. *Artists, Advertising, and the Borders of Art.* Chicago: University of Chicago Press, 1995.

Dreier, Thomas. *The Power of Print and Men.* New York: The Merganthaler Linotype Company, 1936.

Dwiggins, W.A. *Layout in Advertising.* New York: Harper and Brothers, Publishing, 1928.

Ewen, Stuart. *Captains of Consciousness, Advertising and the Social Roots of the Consumer Culture.* New York: McGraw-Hill, 1976.

Holme, Bryan. *The Art of Advertising.* London: Peerage Books, 1982.

Jones, Edgar R. *Those Were the Good Old Days: A Happy Look at American Advertising 1880–1930.* New York: Simon and Schuster, 1959.

Marchand, Roland. *Advertising the American Dream.* Berkeley, CA: University of California Press, 1985.

Watkins, Julian Lewis. *The 100 Great Advertisements: Who Wrote Them and What They Did.* New York: Moore Publishing Company, 1949.

11. Public Interest Campaigns and Information Design

Brinton, Willard C. *Graphic Methods for Presenting Facts.* New York: McGraw-Hill, 1914.

Dondis, Donis A. *A Primer of Visual Literacy.* Cambridge, MA: MIT Press, 1973.

Hacker, Louis M. Rudolf Modley, and George R. Taylor. *The United States and Graphic History.* New York: Modern Age Books, 1936.

Harrison, Richard Edes. *Look at the World.* New York: Alfred A. Knopf, 1942.

Horn, Robert E. *Visual Language.* Bainbridge Island, WA: MacroVU Inc, 1998.

Kepes, Gyorgy. *Language of Vision.* New York: Paul Theobold and Co., 1944.

Lönberg-Holm, Knud, and Ladislav Sutnar. *Catalog Design Progress.* New York: Sweet's Catalog Service, 1950.

Mijksenaar, Paul. *Visual Function.* New York: Princeton Architectural Press, 1997.

Modley, Rudolf. *How to Use Pictorial Statistics.* New York: Harper and Brothers, 1938.

Modley, Rudolf, and Dyno Lowenstein. *Pictographs and Graphs.* New York: Harper and Brothers, Publishers, 1937.

Moholy-Nagy, Laszlo. *Vision in Motion.* New York: Paul Theobold and Co., 1961.

Neurath, Otto. *International Picture Language,* facsimile reprint of 1936 edition. Reading, UK: University of Reading, 1980.

Riggleman, John. *Graphic Methods for Presenting Business Statistics.* New York: McGraw-Hill, 1936.

Rogers, Anna. *Graphic Charts Handbook.* Washington, DC: Public Affairs Press, 1961.

Stankowski, Anton. *Visual Representation of Invisible Process.* Teufen, Switzerland: Arthur Niggli, 1956.

Wurman, Richard Saul. *Information Architects.* New York: Graphis Publications, 1992.

12. Corporate Identities and International Style

Gerstner, Karl, and Markus Kutter. *Die Neue Graphik.* Teufen, Switzerland: Arthur Niggli, 1959.

Hofmann, Armin. *Graphic Design Manual.* New York: Van Nostrand Reinhold, 1965.

Kröplien, Manfred, ed. *Karl Gerstner.* Basel, Switzerland: Hatje Cantz Verlag, 2001.

Morrison, Philip, Phylis Morrison, and the Office of Charles and Ray Eames. *Powers of Ten.* New York: Scientific American Books, 1982.

Müller-Brockmann, Josef. *History of Visual Communication.* Teufen, Switzerland: Arthur Niggli, 1971.

Remington, R. Roger. *American Modernism: Graphic Design 1920–1960.* New Haven, CT: Yale University Press, 2003.

Thompson, Bradbury. *The Art of Graphic Design.* New York and New Haven, CT: Yale University Press, 1988.

13. Pop and Protest

Clay, Steven, and Rodney Phillips. *A Secret Location on the Lower East Side.* New York: New York Public Library and Granary Books, 1998.

Heller, Steven. *Merz to Emigre and Beyond: Avant-Garde Magazine Design of the Twentieth Century.* London and New York: Phaidon, 2003.

McLuhan, Marshall. *The Mechanical Bride: Folklore of Industrial Man.* New York: Vanguard Press, 1951.

McLuhan, Marshall. *Understanding Media: The Extensions of Man.* Originally published in 1964. Cambridge, MA: MIT Press, 2001.

14. Postmodernism in Design

Lupton, Ellen. *Mixing Messages: Graphic Design in Contemporary Culture.* New York: Cooper Hewitt and Princeton Architectural Press, 1996.

Poynor, Rick. *No More Rules.* New Haven, CT: Yale University Press, 2003.

15. Digital Design

Greene, Rachel. *Internet Art.* London and New York: Thames and Hudson, 2004.

Poggenpohl, Sharon. *Graphic Design: Computer Graphics,* special issue of *Visible Language,* Volume IX, Number 2, Spring 1985.

Reichardt, Jasia. *The Computer in Art.* London: Studio Vista, 1971.

Richin, Fred. *In Our Own Image.* New York: Aperture, 1990.

Siegel, David. *Creating Killer Web Sites.* Indianapolis: Hayden Books, 1996.

Würtz, Elizabeth. *A Cross-Cultural Analysis of Websites from High-Context and Low-Context Cultures, Journal of Computer-Mediated Communication, 11*(1), article 1, http://jcmc.indiana.edu/vol11/issue1/wuertz.html (accessed September 15, 2011).

16. Graphic Design and Globalization

Appadurai, Arjun, ed. *Globalization (Public Culture Book).* Durham, NC: Duke University Press, 2001.

Barnard, Malcolm. *Graphic Design as Communication.* New York and London: Routledge Press, 2005.

Barnbrook Design, eds. *The Little Book of Shocking Global Facts.* London: Fiell Publishing, 2010.

Caban, Geoffrey. *World Graphic Design.* London: Merrell Publishers, 2004.

Brown, Bruce, with Richard Buchanan, Dennis P. Doordan, and Victor Margolin, eds. *Design Issues: Design in a Global Context*, Volume 25, Issue 3. Cambridge, MA: MIT Press, 2009.

Fiell, Charlotte, and Peter Fiell. *Graphic Design for the 21st Century*. Köln: Taschen, 2003.

Friedman, Thomas L. *The World is Flat: The Globalized World in the Twenty-First Century.* New York: Farrar, Straus, and Giroux, 2005.

Giddens, Anthony. *Runaway World: How Globalization is Reshaping our Lives.* New York and London: Routledge, 2002.

Klein, Naomi. *No Logo: Taking Aim at the Brand Bullies*. Toronto: Knopf, 2000.

Worldstudio Foundation. http://www.worldstudioinc.com/ (accessed August 2, 2011).

Yunker, John. *The Art of the Global Gateway.* Ashland, OR: Byte Level Books, 2010.

General References

Audin, Maurice. *Histoire de L'Imprimerie.* Paris: A. and J. Picard, 1972.

Bierut, Michael, with William Drenttel, Steven Heller, and DK Holland, eds. *Looking Closer: Critical Writings on Graphic Design.* New York: Allworth Press, 1994.

Bierut, Michael, with William Drenttel, Steven Heller, and DK Holland, eds. *Looking Closer 2: Critical Writings on Graphic Design.* New York: Allworth Press, 1997.

Bierut, Michael, with Jessica Helfand, Steven Heller, and Rick Poynor, eds. *Looking Closer 3: Classic Writings on Graphic Design.* New York: Allworth Press, 1999.

Bierut, Michael, with William Drenttel and Steven Heller, eds. *Looking Closer 4: Critical Writings on Graphic Design.* New York: Allworth Press, 2002.

Bigelow, Charles, with Paul Hayden Duensing and Linnea Gentry, eds. *Fine Print on Type.* San Francisco: Bedford Arts, 1989.

Blackwell, Lewis. *20th-Century Type*. New Haven, CT: Yale University Press, 2004.

Booth-Clibborn, Edward, and Daniele Baroni. *The Language of Graphics.* New York: Harry N. Abrams, 1979.

Calhoun, Craig. *Habermas and the Public Sphere.* Cambridge, MA: MIT Press, 1992.

Carter, Sebastien. *20th Century Type Designs*. London: Lund Humphries, 1987.

Craig, James, and Bruce Barton. *Thirty Centuries of Graphic Design.* New York: Watson Guptill Publications, 1987.

Curwen, Harold. *Processes of Graphic Reproduction in Printing.* London: Faber and Faber, 1934.

Daniels, Peter T., and William Bright. *The World's Writing Systems.* Oxford: Oxford University Press, 1996.

Febvre, Lucien, and Henri-Jean Martin. *The Coming of the Book*. London: Verso, 1976.

Friedman, Mildred. G*raphic Design in America.* Minneapolis, MN: Walker Art Center and New York: Harry N. Abrams, 1989.

Gallo, Max. *The Poster in History*. New York: W.W. Norton & Co., 1972.

Gascoigne, Bamber. *How to Identify Prints.* London: Thames and Hudson, 1986.

Hamilton, Frederick. *Books Before Typography.* Chicago: United Typothetae of America, 1918.

Harris, Neil. *Cultural Excursions.* Chicago: University of Chicago Press, 1990.

Heller, Steven, with Karrie Jacobs, Mary Siskin, and Anne Fink. *Angry Graphics: Protest Posters of the Reagan/Bush Era.* Salt Lake City, UT: Peregrine Smith Books, 1992.

Heller, Steven, and Karen Pomeroy, eds. *Design Literacy: Understanding Graphic Design.* New York: Allworth Press, 1997.

Heller, Steven, and Anne Fink. *Faces on the Edge: Type in the Digital Age.* New York: Van Nostrand Reinhold, 1997.

Heller, Steven, and Seymour Chwast. *Graphic Style*. New York: Harry N. Abrams, 1988.

Hollis, Richard. *Graphic Design: A Concise History*. London: Thames and Hudson, 1994.

Hornung, Clarence, and Fridolf Johnson. *200 Years of American Graphic Arts.* New York: Braziller, 1976.

Hutchinson, James. *Letters.* New York: Van Nostrand Reinhold, 1983.

Jean, Georges. *Writing: The Story of Alphabets and Scripts.* New York: Harry N. Abrams, 1987.

Jussim, Estelle. *Visual Communication and the Graphic Arts*. New York: R.R. Bowker, 1983.

Kinross, Robin. *Modern Typography*. London: Hyphen Press, 2004.

Lawson, Alexander. *Anatomy of a Typeface.* Jaffrey, NH: David Godine, 1990.

Lupton, Ellen, and J. Abbott Miller. *Design Writing Research*. New York: Princeton Architectural Press, 1996.

Margolin, Victor, ed. *Design Discourse: History/Theory/Criticism.* Chicago: University of Chicago Press, 1989.

Meggs, Philip B. *A History of Graphic Design*, 2nd edition. New York: Van Nostrand Reinhold, 1992.

Myers, Robin, and Michael Harris. *A Millennium of the Book.* New Castle, DE: Oak Knoll Press and Winchester, UK: St. Paul's Bibliographies, 1994.

Perfect, Christopher, and Jeremy Austen. *The Complete Typographer*. Englewood Cliffs, NJ: Prentice Hall, 1992.

Pope, Daniel. *The Making of Modern Advertising.* New York: Basic Books, Inc., 1983.

Poynor, Rick, and Edward Booth-Clibborn. *Typography Now.* London: Internos Books, 1991.

Presbrey, Frank. *The History and Development of Advertising.* New York: Doubleday, Doran and Company, 1929.

Steinberg, S.H. *Five Hundred Years of Printing*. New Castle, DE: Oak Knoll Press and London: The British Library, 1996.

Thomas, Isaiah. *The History of Printing in America.* New York: Weathervane Books, 1970.

Updike, Daniel Berkeley. *Printing Types: Their History, Forms, and Use*. Cambridge, MA: Harvard University Press, 1937.

Image Credits

Chapter 1

1.1 Jean Vertut/Yvonne Vertut; 1.3 © RMN/Loïc Hamon. Musée des Antiquités Nationales, Saint-Germain-en-Laye, France; 1.4 Giraudon/The Bridgeman Art Library; 1.5 © RMN/Franck Raux. Louvre, Paris, France; 1.6a Simon & Schuster; 1.6b Bibliothèque Nationale, Paris, France/The Bridgeman Art Library; 1.7 © The Trustees of The British Museum; 1.9 © RMN/Daniel Arnaudet/Gérard Blot. Louvre, Paris, France; 1.10 Fig. 35 from G. Moller, in "Zeitschrift des Deustchen Vereins für Buchwessen und Schrifttum," ii (1919), 78. Published in A Study of Writing, by I.J. Gelb (Chicago, Illinois: The University of Chicago Press, 1952); 1.11 Simon & Schuster; 1.12a From A Study of Writing by Ignace Gelb, Chicago: University of Chicago Press, 1952, end sheets. ASIN: B0007DXWY6; 1.12b © RMN/Hervé Lewandowski. Louvre, Paris, France; 1.13 akg-images/Erich Lessing; 1.14 © Dorling Kindersley.

Chapter 2

2.1 Simon & Schuster; 2.2a From A History of the Art of Writing by William A. Mason. © 1920. Reprinted by permission of Macmillan Publishers; 2.2b © Gail Mooney/CORBIS. All Rights Reserved; 2.3 © The Trustees of the British Museum; 2.4a Simon & Schuster; 2.4b Getty Images; 2.5 Courtesy of University of Pennsylvania Museum of Archaeology and Anthropology. Object MS4842, image 163526; 2.6 Simon & Schuster; 2.7 akg-images/Erich Lessing; 2.8 Bibliothèque Nationale de France; 2.9 Forum, Rome, Italy/The Bridgeman Art Library; 2.10 Photograph courtesy of Bill Jennings; 2.11 © The Trustees of the British Museum; 2.12 Museo Archeologico Nazionale, Naples, Italy/Art Resource, NY; 2.13 © The Trustees of the British Museum; 2.14 Simon & Schuster; 2.15 By permission of The British Library; 2.16a Courtesy of the Library of Congress; 2.16b Courtesy Woodfin Camp & Associates; 2.17 Photo © Vatican Museums; 2.18 Photo © Vatican Museums; 2.19 Photo: Theodore Liasi.

Chapter 3

3.1a Courtesy of the Library of Congress; 3.1b Staatsbibliothek Bamberg. Photo: Gerald Raab; 3.2 Simon & Schuster; 3.3 "The Roman Collapse and the Shaping of Europe" (p.281) from The Pelican History of the World by J. M. Roberts, 1976 © J. M. Roberts, 1976, 1980, 1983, 1987. Diagrams © Hutchinson Publishing Ltd., 1976. Maps © Penguin Books 1980; 3.4 © British Library Board; 3.5a Musée de la Tapisserie, Bayeux, France/The Bridgeman Art Library; 3.5b By permission of The British Library. © Dorling Kindersley;

3.6a Bibliothèque Nationale de France; 3.6b Photograph reproduced by permission of The Master and Fellows of University College, Oxford. MS.67, fol.52v; 3.6c Bodleian Library, University of Oxford; 3.6d Bodleian Library, University of Oxford; 3.7a bpk/SBB; 3.7b Simon & Schuster; 3.7c © The Board of Trinity College, Dublin, Ireland/The Bridgeman Art Library; 3.7d Musée de L'Histoire de France, Paris, France/Archives Charmet/The Bridgeman Art Library; 3.7e From figures 63, 64 & 65 of The Art of Lettering: The History, Anatomy, and Aesthetics of the Roman Letter Forms by Albert Kapr. Published by K.G. Saur, Munich, Germany, 1983; 3.7f From figures 89, 90, 91, 92 & 93 of The Art of Lettering: The History, Anatomy, and Aesthetics of the Roman Letter Forms by Albert Kapr. Published by K.G. Saur, Munich, Germany, 1983; 3.7g By permission of The British Library; 3.7h From figure 159 of The Art of Lettering: The History, Anatomy, and Aesthetics of the Roman Letter Forms by Albert Kapr. Published by K.G. Saur, Munich, Germany, 1983; 3.7i Bayerische Staatsbibliothek; 3.7j By permission of The British Library; 3.7k © British Library Board. All Rights Reserved (Picture number 1022251.621); 3.8a The Pepys Library, Magdalene College, Cambridge; 3.8b The Granger Collection, New York; 3.8c Bibliothèque Royale de Belgique; 3.8d Fitzwilliam Museum, University of Cambridge, UK/The Bridgeman Art Library; 3.9a By Permission of the President and Fellows of Corpus Christi College, Oxford (Oxford, CCC MS 283 fol. 165 r); 3.9b Bodleian Library, University of Oxford; 3.9c By permission of The British Library; 3.10a ÖBN/Wien; 3.10b Photo Pierpont Morgan Library/Art Resource/Scala, Florence; 3.12 Bibliothèque Nationale de France; 3.13 Reproduced by courtesy of the University Librarian and Director, The John Rylands University Library, The University of Manchester.

Chapter 4

4.1 The Granger Collection, New York; 4.2 INTERFOTO/Alamy; 4.3a The Granger Collection, New York; 4.3b Figure on page 25 of The Practice of Typography, A Treatise on Title-Pages by Theodore Low DeVinne (The Century Company, 1902); 4.3c Private Collection/The Bridgeman Art Library; 4.4 bpk/Kupferstichkabinett, SMB/Jörg P. Anders; 4.5a–b Octavo Corp. and the Rosenwald Collection at the Library of Congress; 4.6 The New York Public Library/Art Resource, NY; 4.7 © S. Blair Hedges; 4.8 Courtesy of the Library of Congress; 4.9 Harry Ransom Humanities Research Center, The University of Texas at Austin; 4.10 Courtesy the Cary Collection, RIT Libraries, Rochester Institute of Technology; 4.11a The Newberry Library;

4.11b Courtesy the Cary Collection, RIT Libraries, Rochester Institute of Technology; 4.11c The Newberry Library; 4.11d By permission of The British Library; 4.11e From figures 181 & 182 of The Art of Lettering: The History, Anatomy, and Aesthetics of the Roman Letter Forms by Albert Kapr. Published by K.G. Saur, Munich, Germany, 1983; 4.11f Courtesy of the Library of Congress; 4.12a Courtesy of the Library of Congress, Rosenwald Collection, Rare Book and Special Collections Division; 4.12b Stadtbibliothek Nurnberg, Cent. II, 98, f. 53v and 54r; 4.12c Courtesy of the Library of Congress. Rare Book and Special Collections, Rosenwald Collection; 4.13 Wellcome Library, London; 4.14 Courtesy of the Library of Congress; 4.15a German National Museum, Nuremberg, Germany; 4.15b From page 69 (Figure 74) of A History of Visual Communication by Josef Muller-Brockman. Courtesy of Verlag Niggli AG; 4.15c University of Glasgow Library, Dept. of Special Collections; 4.16a National Archives and Records Administration; 4.16b © National Maritime Museum Picture Library, Greenwich London; 4.17 Getty Images; 4.18 University of Glasgow Library, Dept. of Special Collections; 4.19 Simon & Schuster; 4.20a Octavo Corp. and the Rosenwald Collection at the Library of Congress; 4.20b Photo: Theodore Liasi; 4.21a Wellcome Library, London; 4.21b Musée de l'imprimerie de Lyon; 4.21c Museum Plantin-Moretus/Prentenkabinet, Antwerpen-UNESCO World Heritage.

Chapter 5

5.1 Beinecke Rare Book and Manuscript Library, Yale University; 5.2a left © American Antiquarian Society; 5.2a right © Massachusetts Historical Society, Boston, MA, USA/The Bridgeman Art Library; 5.2b Courtesy of the Library of Congress (Rosenwald Collection, Rare Book and Special Collections Division); 5.3 Courtesy of the Library of Congress; 5.4 Beinecke Rare Book and Manuscript Library, Yale University; 5.5 Harvard University, Houghton Library; 5.6 Columbia University Butler Library; 5.7 Beinecke Rare Book and Manuscript Library, Yale University; 5.8 The National Archives of the UK, ref. C05/855 (121); 5.9a The Pepys Library, Magdalene College, Cambridge; 5.9b © National Maritime Museum Picture Library, Greenwich London; 5.10 © American Antiquarian Society; 5.11a Snark/Art Resource, N.Y.; 5.11b © Roger-Viollet/The Image Works; 5.12a–b Courtesy of the Library of Congress; 5.13a Taken from William Playfair, Introduction by Howard Wainer, Ian Spence, Playfair's Commercial and Political Atlas and Statistical Breviary, (2005), published by Cambridge University Press. By permission of Cambridge University Press; 5.13b Printed Ephemera by John Lewis (Dover 1962)/Courtesy of the

Library of Congress; **5.13c** The Pepys Library, Magdalene College, Cambridge; **5.14a** © The British Library Board; **5.14b** From figures 271 & 272 of *The Art of Lettering: The History, Anatomy, and Aesthetics of the Roman Letter Forms* by Albert Kapr. Published by K.G. Saur, Munich, Germany, 1983; **5.15a** © Imprimerie nationale. Atelier du Livre d'Art et de l'Estampe; **5.15b** Musée de l'imprimerie de Lyon; **5.16** From *The Art of Lettering* by Albert Kapr. Reproduced by permission of K.G. Saur Verlag; **5.17** The Newberry Library; **5.18** Columbia University Butler Library; **5.19a** Reproduced by permission of Birmingham Library & Information Services; **5.19b** Courtesy of the Library of Congress; **5.20a** From *Printing Types: Their History, Forms and Use, A Study in Survivals*, by Daniel Berkeley Updike. Copyright 1922 and 1937 Harvard University Press. Courtesy of Harvard University Press, Cambridge, MA; **5.20b** From figure 306 of *The Art of Lettering: The History, Anatomy, and Aesthetics of the Roman Letter Forms* by Albert Kapr. Published by K.G. Saur, Munich, Germany, 1983; **5.21a** © Tate, London 2011; **5.21b** © The Trustees of the British Museum; **5.22** Åbo Akademi Picture Collection.

Chapter 6

6.1 Bibliothèque Nationale de France; **6.2a** © National Portrait Gallery, London; **6.2b** Mary Evans Picture Library /Alamy; **6.3a** *Printed Ephemera* by John Lewis (Dover 1962)/Courtesy of the Library of Congress; **6.3b** The Granger Collection, New York; **6.3c** *Printed Ephemera* by John Lewis (Dover 1962)/Courtesy of the Library of Congress; **6.4** From page 81 of *The Press and Popular Culture* by Martin Conboy, 2002/Courtesy of Sage Publications; **6.5** Columbia University Butler Library; **6.6** Illustrated London News Ltd/Mary Evans Picture Library; **6.7** By permission of The British Library; **6.8a** David M. Rubenstein Rare Book and Manuscript Library, Duke University; **6.8b** Rare Book Division, The New York Public Library, Astor, Lenox and Tilden Foundations; **6.9** The New York Public Library, Astor, Lenox and Tilden Foundations; **6.10** University of Virginia Library, Special Collections Department; 6.11 The Granger Collection, New York; 6.12 Les Arts Décoratifs, Musée de la Publicité, Paris. Photos Laurent Sully Jaulmes. Tous droits réservés; **6.13** Tyne Bridge Publishing; **6.14a** The Granger Collection, New York; **6.14b** Musée de la Ville de Paris, Musée Carnavalet, Paris, France/The Bridgeman Art Library; **6.15** © Judith Miller/Anastacia's Antiques; **6.16a** The Granger Collection, New York; **6.16b** *Printed Ephemera* by John Lewis (Dover, 1962)/Courtesy of the Library of Congress; **6.17a** Clarence P. Hornung, *Handbook of Early Advertising Art*, page xiv. (Dover 1947);

6.17b–c *Printed Ephemera* by John Lewis (Dover 1962)/Courtesy of the Library of Congress; **6.18** Musée de la Ville de Paris, Musée Carnavalet, Paris, France/Giraudon/The Bridgeman Art Library; **6.19a–c** Plenum Publishing Corporation; **6.20** 1981.54.2 Felix Octavius Carr: Scenes from Indian Life. Lithograph, 1843, 7 x 9 inches. Amon Carter Museum, Fort Worth, Texas; **6.21** Bibliothèque des Beaux-Arts, Paris, France/Giraudon/The Bridgeman Art Library; **6.22** Yale Center for British Art, Paul Mellon Collection, USA/The Bridgeman Art Library; **6.23** CartoonStock Ltd.; **6.24** Columbia University Butler Library; **6.25a** Courtesy of the Library of Congress; **6.25b** William Hone Collection, Special Collections, Adelphi Universities Libraries.

Chapter 7

7.1a *Printed Ephemera* by John Lewis (Dover, 1962)/Courtesy of the Library of Congress; **7.1b** Mucha Trust/The Bridgeman Art Library; **7.2** Les Arts Décoratifs, Musée de la Publicité, Paris. Photos Laurent Sully Jaulmes. Tous droits réservés; **7.3a** *Printed Ephemera* by John Lewis (Dover, 1962)/Courtesy of the Library of Congress; **7.3b** Getty Images; **7.4** *Printed Ephemera* by John Lewis (Dover, 1962)/Courtesy of the Library of Congress; **7.5a** INTERFOTO/Alamy; **7.5b** Plenum Publishing Corporation; **7.5c** Plenum Publishing Corporation; **7.6** *Printed Ephemera* by John Lewis (Dover, 1962)/Courtesy of the Library of Congress; **7.7a–b** Courtesy of the Library of Congress; **7.8** David M. Rubenstein Rare Book and Manuscript Library, Duke University; **7.9a** The Picture Desk; **7.9b** © CORBIS. All Rights Reserved; **7.10** *Printed Ephemera* by John Lewis (Dover, 1962)/Courtesy of the Library of Congress; **7.11** "Youth—an Illustrated Journal," from page 70 of *The English Newspaper—An Illustrated History to 1900* by Keith Williams. Courtesy of Springwood Books Limited; **7.12** National Currency Collection, Currency Museum, Bank of Canada; **7.13** su concessione del Ministero per i Beni e le Attivita Culturali "Soprintendenza P.S.A.E. per le province di Venezia, Padova, Belluno e Treviso;" **7.14** US Patent & Trademark Office; **7.15–16** National Archives and Records Administration; **7.17** deskofdavid.com; **7.18** Reproduced from *Scripts, Grooves, and Writing Machines: Representing Technology in the Edison Era*, by Lisa Gitelman. © 1999 by the Board of Trustees of the Leland Stanford Junior University. Courtesy of Stanford University Press; **7.19a** Courtesy of the Library of Congress; **7.19b** Courtesy of Sunset Magazine; **7.20a** The Advertising Archives; **7.20b** Collection Kharbine-Tapabor, Paris, France/The Bridgeman Art Library; **7.21** Courtesy of Campbell Soup Company; **7.22** Courtesy of the Library of Congress; **7.23** Warsaw Collection of Business Americana,

Archives Center, National Museum of American History, Smithsonian Institution; **7.24** © Historical Picture Archive/CORBIS. All Rights Reserved; **7.25** © Peter Harholdt/CORBIS. All Rights Reserved; **7.26** Courtesy of the Library of Congress; **7.27** Minneapolis Institute of Arts, The Modernism Collection, gift of Northwest Bank Minnesota © DACS 2011.

Chapter 8

8.1 University of Wisconsin System Board of Regents/Digital Library for the Decorative Arts and Material Culture: Image and Text Collections; **8.2** University of Glasgow Library, Dept. of Special Collections; **8.3** King's College London, Foyle Special Collections Library; **8.4** Courtesy of the Library of Congress; **8.5a** Yale Center for British Art, Paul Mellon Collection, USA/The Bridgeman Art Library; **8.5b** This item is reproduced by permission of The Huntington Library, San Marino, California; **8.7** National Archives and Records Administration; **8.8a** Courtesy of the Library of Congress; **8.8b** © The Hunterian, University of Glasgow 2011; **8.9, 8.10a** Les Arts Décoratifs. Musée de la Publicité, Paris. Photo: Laurent Sully Jaulmes. Tous droits réservés; **8.10b** Courtesy of the Library of Congress; **8.11a** General Electric Company; **8.11b** From page 123 of *Kolo Moser: Graphic Artist and Designer* by Daniele Baroni and Antonio D'Auria. Courtesy of Rizzoli International Publications, Inc.; **8.12a** IMAGNO/Austrian Archives; **8.12b** Courtesy of Klingspor-Museum, Offenbach, Germany; **8.13** akg-images/Erich Lessing; **8.14a** akg-images/Erich Lessing; **8.14b** akg-images/Erich Lessing; **8.14c** Private Collection/The Bridgeman Art Library; **8.15** IMAGNO/Austrian Archives; **8.16** akg-images; **8.17** John Hay Library, Brown University; **8.18** Courtesy of the Library of Congress; **8.19** Courtesy of the Library of Congress, Pforzheimer-Rogers Collection, Rare Book and Special Collections Division; **8.20a** Division of Rare and Manuscript Collections, Cornell University Library; **8.20b** Courtesy of the Library of Congress; **8.21** Henry van de Velde, Gebrauchsgraphik Tropon Eiweißnahrung/Karl Ernst Osthaus Museum der Stadt Hagen. Foto: Friedrich Rosenstiel, Köln/© VG Bild-Kunst, Bonn 2007; **8.22** National Archives and Records Administration **8.23** bpk/Kunstbibliothek, SMB/Knud Petersen; **8.24a** Courtesy of Klingspor-Museum, Offenbach, Germany; **8.24b** Courtesy of the Library of Congress; **8.25** Historisches Museum Der Stadt Wein.

Chapter 9

9.1 Digital image © 2011, The Museum of Modern Art, New York/Scala, Florence. © DACS 2011; **9.2** Sunset Magazine; **9.3a** Collection Stedelijk Van Abbemuseum, Eindhoven, Holland; **9.3b** V&A Images; **9.4** Reproduced from *Pioneers of Modern Typography* by Herbert Spencer. © 1969 Herbert Spencer. Courtesy of Lund Humphries Publishers Limited; **9.5a** Spencer Collection, The New York Public Library, Astor, Lenox and Tilden Foundations. © DACS 2011; **9.5b** Digital image © 2011, The Museum of Modern Art, New York/Scala, Florence. © DACS 2011. **9.5c** Merrill C. Berman Collection. Photo: Jim Frank. © DACS 2011; **9.6** Digital image © 2011, The Museum of Modern Art, New York/Scala, Florence. © ADAGP, Paris and DACS, London 2011; **9.7a** International Dada Archive, University of Iowa Libraries. © The Heartfield Community of Heirs/VG Bild-Kunst, Bonn and DACS, London 2011; **9.7b** akg-images/Erich Lessing. © DACS 2011; **9.9** Digital image © 2011, The Museum of Modern Art, New York/Scala, Florence. © Rodchenko & Stepanova Archive, DACS, RAO, 2011; **9.10** Merrill C. Berman Collection. Photo: Jim Frank. © DACS 2011; **9.11** The Bridgeman Art Library; **9.12** The Picture Desk. © DACS 2011; **9.13** The Picture Desk; **9.14** Courtesy of the Library of Congress. © DACS 2011; **9.15a–b** Courtesy of the Library of Congress; **9.16** © SSPL/The Image Works; **9.17** The New York Public Library/Art Resource, NY; **9.18** Purchased with funds from the ICP Acquisitions Committee with additional funds provided by Jack Benning and Elihu Rose, 1999. © ARS, New York and DACS, London 2011; **9.19** The Stapleton Collection/The Bridgeman Art Library. © DACS 2011; **9.20 top and middle** Rodchenko & Stepanova Archive, Courtesy Howard Schickler Fine Art LLC. © Rodchenko & Stepanova Archive, DACS, RAO, 2011; **9.20 bottom** The Print Collector/Alamy. © Rodchenko & Stepanova Archive, DACS, RAO, 2011; **9.21** Merrill C. Berman Collection. Photo: Jim Frank. © Hattula Moholy-Nagy/DACS 2011; **9.22a left** Photo: Theodore Liasi; **9.22b right** V&A Images/London Transport Museum; **9.22b** Figure 298 from *Graphic Style: From Victorian to Post-Modern* by Steven Heller & Seymour Chwast. © 1988 Steven Heller, Seymour Chwast and Pushpin Editions. Reproduced by permission of Harry N Abrams, Inc.; **9.23** Reproduced from Pioneers of Modern Typography by Herbert Spencer. © 1969 Herbert Spencer. Courtesy of Lund Humphries Publishers Limited. © Hattula Moholy-Nagy/DACS 2011; **9.24a–b** Kurt Schwitters, "Merz 11 Typoreklame. Pelikan-Nummer," Hannover 1924. Kurt und Ernst Schwitters Stiftung, Hannover. Photo: Kurt Schwitters Archive at the Sprengel Museum Hannover. Photographer: Aline Gwose/Michael Herling, Sprengel Museum Hannover. © DACS 2011; **9.24c–d** International Dada Archive, University of Iowa Libraries; **9.25a** Merrill C. Berman Collection. Photo: Jim Frank; **9.25b** Courtesy of Klingspor-Museum, Offenbach, Germany; **9.26–**

9.28b Reproduced from *Pioneers of Modern Typography* by Herbert Spencer. © 1969 Herbert Spencer. Courtesy of Lund Humphries Publishers Limited.

Chapter 10

10.1a The Advertising Archives; **10.1b** The Advertising Archives. © ADAGP, Paris and DACS, London 2011; **10.2a** The Advertising Archives; **10.2b** Museum für Gestaltung Zürich, Poster Collection. Franz Xaver Jaggy © ZHdK; **10.3a** © MOURON. CASSANDRE. Lic 2011-09-10-01 www.cassandre-france. com; **10.3b** Museum für Gestaltung Zürich, Poster Collection. Franz Xaver Jaggy © ZHdK; **10.4** Reproduced from *Pioneers of Modern Typography* by Herbert Spencer. © 1969 Herbert Spencer. Courtesy of Lund Humphries Publishers Limited. © DACS 2011; **10.5** Cover for "Begegnungen," 1933. From page 59 of *Jan Tschichold: Typographer*, by Ruari McLean. Copyright © 1975 by Rauri McClean. Courtesy of David R. Godine, Publisher, Inc.; **10.6a** Digital image © 2011, The Museum of Modern Art, New York/Scala, Florence. © DACS 2011; **10.6b** Museum für Gestaltung Zürich, Poster Collection. Franz Xaver Jaggy © ZHdK. © DACS 2011; **10.7, 10.8a–b** National Archives and Records Administration; **10.9** Private Collection/The Stapleton Collection/The Bridgeman Art Library. © DACS 2011; **10.10** Alexandra Truitt & Jerry Marshall; **10.11** The Advertising Archives; **10.12a** National Archives and Records Administration; **10.13** The Advertising Archives; **10.14a** Eduardo Garcia Benito/Vogue. © Condé Nast Publications, Inc.; **10.14b** Bruehl-Burges/Vanity Fair. © Condé Nast Publications, Inc.; **10.15a** London Transport Museum; **10.15b** © NRM/SSPL/The Image Works; **10.16** Herbert Bayer, Cover for "Bauhaus 1," 1928. Photomontage. Photo: Bauhaus-Archiv, Berlin/VG Bild-Kunst, Bonn. © DACS 2011. **10.17** © Hattula Moholy-Nagy/DACS 2011; **10.18a** From page 289 (left column) of *Those Were The Good Old Days: A Happy Look at American Advertising, 1880–1950* by Edgar R. Jones; **10.18b** The Advertising Archives; **10.19a–b** Young & Rubicam, New York; **10.20** Courtesy the Cary Collection, RIT Libraries, Rochester Institute of Technology. Art © Estate of Lester Sr. Beall. DACS, London/VAGA, New York 2011; **10.21a** Courtesy the Lester Beall Collection, RIT Libraries, Rochester Institute of Technology. Art © Estate of Lester Sr. Beall. DACS, London/VAGA, New York 2011; **10.21b** Courtesy of the Library of Congress; **10.22** © MOURON. CASSANDRE. Lic 2011-09-10-01 www.cassandre-france.com; **10.23** Type designs, 1928, from pages 124 & 125 of *Commercial Art* by E.C. Matthews. Courtesy of Illustrated Editions Company, Inc, New York, 1938; **10.24** Courtesy of the Library of Congress.

Chapter 11

11.1 National Archives and Records Administration; **11.2** Fortune Magazine; **11.3–5** Courtesy of the Library of Congress; **11.6a** University of Washington Libraries, Special Collections (UW 27275z); **11.6b** The original Paterson Pageant Program, on which this drawing appeared, is part of the collection of the American Labor Museum/Botto House National Landmark. The poster is a copy of the program cover; **11.7** Merrill C. Berman Collection. Photo: Jim Frank; **11.8a** Digital image © 2011, The Museum of Modern Art, New York/Scala, Florence. © ARS, New York and DACS, London 2011; **11.8b** bpk. © ARS, New York and DACS, London 2011; **11.9a** Courtesy of the Library of Congress; **11.9b** Mary Evans Picture Library/Alamy. © DACS 2011; **11.9c** Printed by permission for the Norman Rockwell Family Agency Copyright © 1943 the Norman Rockwell Family Entities/CORBIS; **11.9d** © Estate of Lester Sr. Beall. DACS, London/VAGA, New York 2011; **11.10** Penguin Group (USA) Inc.; **11.11** Bert Hardy/Picture Post/Getty Images, Inc.; **11.12** Fortune Magazine; **11.13a–b** Courtesy Northwestern University Library; **11.13c** Courtesy Northwestern University Library. © DACS 2011; **11.13d** Courtesy Northwestern University Library; **11.14a–b** Courtesy Northwestern University Library; **11.14c** The Advertising Archives; **11.15a** National Archives and Records Administration; **11.15b** "Organization of an Armored Division" from figure VIII-2, page 102 of *Pictographs and Graphs: How to Make and Use Them* by Rudolf Modley and Dyno Lowenstein, 1937, Harper & Brothers. Courtesy of HarperCollins Publishers; **11.16** Verlag Niggli, AG; **11.17a** Fortune Magazine; **11.17b** Courtesy the Will Burtin Collection, RIT Libraries, Rochester Institute of Technology and Used with Permission of Pfizer Inc.; **11.18** Museum of Decorative Arts in Prague; **11.19** © DACS 2011; **11.20** Imperial War Museum, London. IWM PST 3400; **11.21–22** Fortune Magazine.

Chapter 12

12.1 Courtesy of IBM Corporation; **12.2** Copyright Novartis Pharmaceuticals Corporation. Reprinted with permission; **12.3** Historical photos by permission of International Paper Company. International Paper logo is a registered trademark of International Paper Company; **12.4** Courtesy of Chermayeff & Geismar; **12.5a** Emin Kuliyev/Shutterstock.com; **12.5b** National Park Service photo; **12.6** Design Firm: Cook and Shanosky Associates Inc.; Designers: Roger Cook & Don Shanosky; **12.7** Museum für Gestaltung Zürich, Poster Collection. Franz Xaver Jaggy © ZHdK; **12.8** Museum für Gestaltung Zürich, Poster Collection. Franz Xaver Jaggy © ZHdK; **12.9**

Pearson Education/PH College; **12.10** Odermatt & Tissi; **12.11** © IOC/Olympic Museum Collections; **12.12a** Alvin Lustig's design for *A Season in Hell*, 1945. © Collection: Elaine Lustig Cohen; **12.12b** Getty Images; **12.13** From Westvaco Inspirations 210, (1958) Courtesy of MeadWestvaco; **12.14** © Knoll Inc.; **12.15** Courtesy of Herman Miller; **12.16** Center for Advanced Research in Design, United States Department of Labor; **12.17–18** CBS Photo Archive; **12.19** © Everett Collection; **12.20** Reproduced from *American Modernism: Graphic Design, 1920 to 1960* by R. Roger Remington. © 2003 Laurence King Publishing. By permission of Yale University Press; **12.21–22** Pearson Education/PH College; **12.23** From Westvaco Inspirations 180 (1950). Courtesy of MeadWestvaco; **12.24** Reprinted from *20th Century Type* by Lewis Blackwell. © 2004 Lewis Blackwell. By permission of Yale University Press; **12.25** Design: Paul Rand; **12.26** Courtesy Hearst Communications and the Cipe Pineles Collection, RIT Libraries, Rochester Institute of Technology and Courtesy of The Francesco Scavullo Foundation; **12.27** Wright's Reprints LLC; **12.28** From Steve Heller, *Merz to Emigre and Beyond: Avant-Garde Magazine Design of the Twentieth Century*. NY: Phaidon, 2003, pages 136–137; **12.29** Design: Paul Rand; **12.30** Photo: Smithsonian American Art Museum/Art Resource/Scala, Florence. © DACS 2011.

Chapter 13

13.1 Gaslight Advertising Archives, Inc. N.Y.; **13.2** Courtesy of Stewart Brand, *Whole Earth Catalog*; **13.3a** Random House Inc.; **13.3b–c** Courtesy of The Herb Lubalin Study Center of Design and Typography at The Cooper Union School of Art; **13.3d** Carl Fischer Photography, Inc. By permission of Esquire magazine. © The Hearst Corporation. Esquire is a trademark of The Hearst Corporation. All Rights Reserved; **13.4a** Milton Glaser, "Bob Dylan" poster, reprinted version. Original design published in 1967; **13.4b** Pushpin Group, Inc.; **13.5** Courtesy of the Library of Congress; **13.6** Pearson Education/PH College; **13.7** The Advertising Archives; **13.8a** State Library of Victoria (Accession number H2000.190/1). La Trobe Picture Collection; **13.8b** Ken Garland & Associates; **13.9** Lora Fountain Literary Agency; **13.10a** From page 187 of *Merz to Emigre and Beyond: Avant-Garde Magazine Design of the Twentieth Century* by Steve Heller, Phaidon, 2003; **13.10b** © Ed Ruscha. Courtesy Gagosian Gallery; **13.10c** The New York Public Library; **13.11a** © Wes Wilson; **13.11b** © 1967 Neon Rose. Artist: Victor Moscoso; **13.12** Digital image © 2011, The Museum of Modern Art, New York/Scala, Florence; **13.13** OSPAAAL; **13.14a** CED Collection, Environmental Design Archive, University of California,

Berkeley; **13.14b** © Grapus/droits réservés. Cote Archives d'Aubervilliers: 10Fi473; **13.15** Reprinted from *20th Century Type* by Lewis Blackwell. Copyright © 2004 Lewis Blackwell. Monotype Imaging, Inc.; **13.16** Reprinted from page 159 of *The Complete Typographer* by Christopher Perfect and Jeremy Austen. © 1992 Quarto Publishing plc. By permission of Pearson Education/Prentice Hall, Inc.; **13.17** © Letraset Limited; **13.18a–b** Courtesy of The Herb Lubalin Study Center of Design and Typography at The Cooper Union School of Art; **13.19** Courtesy of Tadanori Yokoo; **13.20** © Judith Miller/Dorling Kindersley/Wallis and Wallis; **13.21** Pages 4–5 from *Learning From Las Vegas* by Robert Venturi, Denise Scott Brown and Steven Izenour. © 1972 Massachusetts Institute of Technology, by permission of the MIT Press.

Chapter 14

14.1 April Greiman; **14.2** Courtesy & © William Longhauser, Los Angeles, www.longhauser.com; **14.3a** April Greiman; **14.3b** Katherine McCoy AGI IDSA; **14.4a** Sussman/Prejza & Company, Inc.; **14.4b** Nina Wiener,' Poster design for international theatre festival. Design: Studio Dumbar. Client: Holland Festival. Year: 1987. Photography: Lex van Pieterson; **14.5a** Archive-Weingart; **14.5b** i-D August 1985 no28 The Art Issue. Photography: Nick Knight. Hair and make-up: William Faulkner. Graphics: Moira Bogue. Art direction: Terry Jones; **14.6** Courtesy of Art Chantry; **14.7** Jeffrey Keedy; **14.8** Rhino Entertainment Company; **14.9a** Ed Fella; **14.9b** Barry Deck LLC; **14.10a–b** David Carson Design; **14.11** Deste Foundation for Contemporary Art, Athens; **14.12** © Steve Marcus/Reuters/CORBIS. All Rights Reserved; **14.13a** Digital Image © 2011, The Museum of Modern Art/Scala, Florence; **14.13b** Paula Scher/Pentagram; **14.14** Katherine McCoy AGI IDSA; **14.15a** M & Co; **14.15b** © CSA Images.com; **14.16a** The New York Public Library/Art Resource, NY; **14.16b** The New York Public Library; **14.17** Courtesy www.adbusters.org; **14.18** Courtesy of ATTIK, www.attik.com; **14.19** Elliot Earls; **14.20a** Bruce Mau Design; **14.20b** Design and photography: Allen Hori; **14.21a** COLORS MAGAZINE, FABRICA S.p.a.; **14.21b** Benetton USA, Corp.

Chapter 15

15.1 Johanna Drucker; **15.2** Leon Harmon and Ken Knowlton, 1968; **15.3** Jeffrey Keedy; **15.4** Susan Kare/Courtesy of Apple; **15.5** Courtesy of Dorothy Shamonsky; **15.6** From page 368 of *Computers in Typesetting Series: Computer Modern Type Faces Volume E* by Donald Knuth. © 1986 Pearson Education, Inc. Reproduced by permission of Pearson Education, Inc. All rights Reserved; **15.7a** © Zuzana

Licko, Emigre, Inc.; **15.7b** Stone Type Foundry; **15.7c–d** Courtesy of the Library of Congress; **15.8** Courtesy of Emigre, Berkeley, California; **15.9** Image by Fred Davis/Courtesy of Condé Nast Publications; **15.10a** M & Co; **15.10b** Courtesy of LucasFonts.com (Lucas Fonts GmbH); **15.10c** All fonts © Büro Destruct, Switzerland. www.typedifferent.com; **15.10d** © 2009 with express permission from Adobe Systems Incorporated; **15.11** Courtesy of Warren Corbitt. © ESPN The Magazine; **15.12** © Pixar/Buena Vista Pictures; **15.13a** Microsoft product screen shot reprinted with permission from Microsoft Corporation; **15.13b** Apple Computer, Inc.; **15.14** Microsoft product screen shot reprinted with permission from Microsoft Corporation; **15.15** Pacific Northwest National Laboratory; **15.16a** Courtesy of Ben Shneiderman, University of Maryland, Human-Computer Interaction Lab, http://www.cs.umd.edu/hcil/treemap-history; **15.17** McDonald's Corporation; **15.18a** © 2007 Linden Research, Inc. All Rights Reserved; **15.18b** SAGMEISTER, INC. Photography: Tom Schierlitz.

Chapter 16

16.1a Courtesy of NASA; **16.1b** Image by Craig Roth, text layout by Wordle; **16.2a** © United Nations. Reproduced with permission; **16.2b** Courtesy of the World Bank; **16.3a** Courtesy "TeleGeography" www.telegeography.com; **16.3b** © Stephen Eick, Bell Labs/Visual Insight; **16.4** Courtesy of Alan Jacobson; **16.5a** Elixir Design. Art Director: Jennifer Jerde. Designer: Nathan Durrant; **16.5b** Courtesy Kiva; **16.6a** Courtesy Farhad Fozouni; **16.6b** Client: YOGU Healthy Eating. Designer: Iraj Mirza Alikhani. Design firm: Ashna Advertising. © 2010 Iraj Mirza Alikhani; **16.7a** © 2011 International Olympic Committee; **16.7b** Concept and Design: Sean Chu/Windy Zhang; **16.8a** Design and Words by Wilhelm Krüger: Winburg, I-jusi #14: The A-Z issue; **16.8b** Courtesy Ricardo Juarez; **16.9** Getty Images/Photolibrary; **16.10** Courtesy UNESCO World Heritage Centre; **16.11** J.I. Alvarez-Hamelin, L. Dall'Asta, A. Barrat, A. Vespignani, M.G. Beiró. LaNet-vi: http://lanet-vi.soic.indiana.edu/.

Index

Page numbers in *italics* refer to figure captions.